A Lillian Smith READER

A Lillian Smith READER

EDITED BY Margaret Rose Gladney

AND Lisa Hodgens

Published in association with Piedmont College and the Estate of Lillian Smith

The University of Georgia Press
ATHENS

Athens, Georgia 30602
www.ugapress.org

Designed by Kaelin Chappell Broaddus
Set in 10/13 Kepler Std Regular by Kaelin Chappell Broaddus
Printed and bound by Thomson-Shore, Inc.
The paper in this book meets the guidelines for
permanence and durability of the Committee on
Production Guidelines for Book Longevity of the
Council on Library Resources.

Most University of Georgia Press titles are
available from popular e-book vendors.

Printed in the United States of America
20 19 18 17 16 P 5 4 3 2 1

Library of Congress Cataloging-in-Publication Data

Names: Smith, Lillian (Lillian Eugenia), 1897–1966 author. |
Gladney, Margaret Rose, editor. | Hodgens, Lisa, editor.
Title: A Lillian Smith reader / edited by Margaret Rose Gladney
and Lisa Hodgens.
Description: Athens : The University of Georgia Press, 2016. |
Includes bibliographical references and index.
Identifiers: LCCN 2016006361 | ISBN 9780820349985 (hard bound : alk. paper) |
ISBN 9780820349992 (pbk. : alk. paper)
Classification: LCC PS3537.M653 A6 2016 | DDC 813/.52—dc23

LC record available at https://lccn.loc.gov/2016006361

CONTENTS

ACKNOWLEDGMENTS

From its inception this work has been a collaborative effort. We gratefully acknowledge the steadfast support of Dr. James Mellichamp, president of Piedmont College; Craig Amason, director, Lillian E. Smith Center; and Smith Center board members: Dr. Nancy Smith Fichter, John Templeton, and John Siegel. For aid in research and possibilities, we thank Bob Glass, dean of libraries and Piedmont College librarian. For prompt and gracious assistance with selected materials from the Hargrett Rare Books and Manuscript Library, we thank Charles Barber. For technical assistance with manuscript preparation we thank Brittany Stancil, Katherine La Mantia, Kristen Gray, Jon Davies, and Michael Sandlin. For encouragement, creative suggestions, and unwavering faith in our project, we thank Elise Benoit.

We especially appreciate Joan Titus's generous and insightful contribution to this collection. Her prescient documentation of Lillian Smith's voice and physical presence, as well as her thorough research and meticulous preservation of Smith's life as creative writer, are immeasurably valuable to all present and future Smith scholarship.

No words of appreciation adequately express the immense gratitude we owe to Marcia Winter. By all rights she should be named our third editor. From the beginning of this project, she has read and transcribed every document and critiqued all commentary. For her insightful opinions as well as her unfailing moral support, we are immeasurably grateful.

ABBREVIATIONS

References to the following Lillian Smith works are abbreviated like so throughout this book:

From the Mountain: An Anthology of the Magazine Successively Titled *Pseudopodia*, the *North Georgia Review*, and *South Today*	*FTM*
How Am I to Be Heard? Letters of Lillian Smith	*HH*
The Journey	*J*
Killers of the Dream	*KD*
Memory of a Large Christmas	*MLC*
North Georgia Review	*NGR*
Now Is the Time	*NT*
One Hour	*OH*
Our Faces, Our Words	*OFOW*
Strange Fruit	*SF*
The Winner Names the Age: A Collection of Writings by Lillian Smith	*WNA*

CHRONOLOGY

The information used to compile this Chronology came from autobiographical materials in the Lillian Smith Collection 1283, Hargrett Rare Books & Manuscripts Library, University of Georgia.

1897 Born December 12—Jasper, Florida, Hamilton County.
Parents: Calvin Warren Smith and Anne Simpson Smith
Brothers and sisters from eldest to youngest:
Calvin Willie Smith died in infancy
Warren Austin Smith
Bertha Mae Smith
Josephus Anderson Smith
DeWitt Smith
Annie Laurie Smith
Frank Adams Smith
Lillian Eugenia Smith
Esther Cordelia Smith
Clarence Wallace Smith

1910 Eldest sister, Bertha, marries Eugene Barnett and goes to live in Hangchow [now Hangzhou], China. Beginning of Lillian Smith's world awareness; weekly letters brought China close to Jasper, Fla.

1911 Older brother DeWitt dies of typhoid fever while attending Meridian College in Mississippi. Takes first big trip away from South with Aunt Janie to Chicago, Denver, and Manitou Springs, Colorado.

1912 Father purchases property in Clayton, Ga., for a summer home.

1913 Closest friend Marjorie White moves to Gainesville, Fla.

1915 Graduates from high school in Jasper, Fla.

1915 Father's lumber and naval stores fail because of World War I shipping vagrancies; parents and four younger children (Frank,

Lillian, Esther, and Wallace) move to Clayton, Ga., and make summer home their permanent residence.

Attends Teachers Institute, gets First Class teaching certificate; teaches as principal at Dillard, Ga.; lives in log cabin with a mountain family.

1915–16 Attends and completes freshman work at Piedmont College, Demorest, Ga. Only thirty-four students in college division; professors from Wellesley, Smith, Harvard, and Yale. Two in math class, three in Latin; twenty-three in English lit from Beowulf to Twentieth Century with Wendell Brooks Phillips (MA Harvard) whose pedagogy and progressive ideas she admired. Begins learning about rural and mountain people.

1916 Helps family manage a winter hotel at Daytona Beach, Fla., and plays piano with a symphony orchestra. First serious love affair with head of the orchestra.

1917–18 Studies music at Peabody Conservatory of Music in Baltimore, Md. Brother Frank Smith pays her way there plus money for one private lesson a week. Piano teacher Emmanuel Wad gives her an extra lesson each week. Earns money for living expenses and tuition as accompanist for voice students, dance and gym classes at YWCA. Lives in women's boarding house; dates medical students at Johns Hopkins.

1918–19 Stays with parents in Clayton; volunteers for Student Nurse Corps, but World War I ends before called to serve.

Teaches for four months as principal of two-teacher school in Tiger, Ga.

1919–22 Studies music in fall and spring terms at Peabody Conservatory, Baltimore.

1920 Summer: Father opens Laurel Falls Camp, first private camp for girls in Georgia, and rents a summer hotel, The Bynum House, which Lillian and her brother Frank manage.

1921 and 1922 Summers: Music counselor at Laurel Falls Camp.

1922–25 Head of music department at Virginia School (Methodist) in Huzhow [Huzhou], Chekiang [Zhejiang] Province, China. Summers: travels to Peking [Bejing] and up Yangtze River to Kuling.

1925–48 Summers: Director of Laurel Falls Camp for Girls.

1925–26 Falls and Winters: takes care of niece Marianne, 2½ -year-old daughter of newly widowed brother Austin, city manager of Ft. Pierce, Fla.; also works as his executive secretary and plays pipe organ for the Methodist church.

1927 Fall term Columbia University Teachers College: courses in psychology, history, education, public school music; teaches music to students in Harlem.

1928 June: Buys Laurel Falls Camp for Girls.

1930 Father dies; leaves her with heavy family responsibilities.

Begins ten-year study of psychoanalysis and Gestalt psychology.

1930–35 Spends time writing in Clayton and in Macon, Ga., where she shares an apartment with Paula Snelling during fall and winter.

Completes a novel on China, titled *And the Waters Flow On*; a novel on a Southern family, titled *Tom Harris and Family*, and two novellas, titled *Every Branch in Me* and *Julia*, respectively. Only *Julia* escaped 1955 fire that burned her study.

1935 Mother suffers a severe heart attack. Lillian Smith leaves Macon, returns to Screamer Mountain, renovates her mother's cottage, Bide-A-Wee, and assumes caretaking responsibilities until her mother's death in 1938.

1936 Edits and publishes, jointly with Paula Snelling, a little magazine called *Pseudopodia*. Begins study of Southern history and literature and every available book by or about African Americans.

Begins to write novel, *Strange Fruit*.

1937 *Pseudopodia* becomes *North Georgia Review*. Continues work on novel and novella. Travels to Nova Scotia. Begins to dissent strongly against racial segregation.

1938 Mother, Anne Simpson Smith, dies.

1938–39 Smith and Snelling travel on a British freighter to Caribbean Islands and Brazil. Spend months at Belem on Amazon River; Smith works on *Strange Fruit*.

1939 Smith and Snelling receive a Julius Rosenwald Fellowship to travel in the South for *North Georgia Review*. Visit sharecroppers, plantation owners, labor unions, mental hospitals, Negro and white colleges, industrialists in effort to broaden knowledge of their homeland.

1940 Receive second Julius Rosenwald Fellowship to continue their travel-study project for *North Georgia Review*. Laurel Falls Camp has become an experimental and creative project where much is being done by her and camp staff in sculpture, painting, "growing plays," music, and dance. Smith intensely interested in modern art and dance.

1942 *North Georgia Review* becomes *South Today* and is widely known among intellectuals in North and South as the most liberal magazine published in the South. "Burning Down Georgia's Back Porch" published in *Common Ground.*

1943 Completes *Strange Fruit.*

Named to 1942 "Honor Roll of Race Relations" by Schomberg Collection of the New York Public Library. "Democracy Was Not a Candidate" and "Growing into Freedom" published in *Common Ground.*

1944 *Strange Fruit* published February 29; translated into fourteen languages, record-breaking best seller, banned in Boston and throughout Massachusetts. Makes speech, "Freedom and Shame," under sponsorship of *Herald Tribune* Forum;

"Humans in Bondage" published in *Social Action*; "Today's Children and Tomorrow's World" published in *Childhood Education*;

"Southern Defensive" published in *Common Ground*; writes letter to Blue Ridge Conference urging the integration of white and Negro YMCAs and YWCAs. Receives the Page One Award, given by the Newspaper Guild of New York.

Laurel Falls Camp enrollment largest ever. In winter, accidental fire destroys *South Today* office. *South Today* discontinued after Fall-Winter 1944–45 issue.

1945 *Strange Fruit* dramatized by Lillian and Esther Smith; José Ferrer directs the play on Broadway. The novel, *Strange Fruit,* defended in court in Massachusetts. Receives Constance Lindsay Skinner Award given by the Women's National Book Association. "Personal History of Strange Fruit" published in *Saturday Review of Literature*; "What Segregation Does to Our Children," *Child Study*; "Growing Plays: *The Girl,*" *Educational Leadership*; "How to Work for Racial Equality," *New Republic*; "Children Talking," *Progressive Education*; "Why I Wrote Strange Fruit," *Southern Literary Messenger*; "Addressed to White Liberals," *Primer for White Folks.*

1946 June trip to India as a member of the Famine Commission and guest of British government. Returns after Laurel Falls Camp opens. Lives during fall and winter in Brooklyn Heights, N.Y., and works on novel, *Julia.*

1947 Continues to direct Laurel Falls Camp in summer and work on novel in winter.

Travels through western United States with young niece.

1948 Lays *Julia* aside and begins writing *Killers of the Dream.* Closes Laurel Falls Camp after season of 1948.

1948–49 Writes weekly column, "A Southerner Talking," for the *Chicago Defender.*

1949 *Killers of the Dream* completed in July; published in October. Seen as more shocking than *Strange Fruit*; arouses tremendous anger.

1950 Receives: Honorary Doctorate of Humane Letters from Howard University

Honorary Doctorate of Letters from Oberlin

National Book Award Committee's Special Citation for Distinguished Contribution to American Letters for *Killers of the Dream*

Southern Authors' Award for *Killers of the Dream*

Teaches "The Novel," at U. of Indiana Writers Conference in July and at U. of Colorado in August. Reads art and anthropology; spends much time in art galleries.

1951 Reads European contemporary literature; studies effect of World War II and atom bomb explosions on the creative mind. Works three months on *Julia*. Continues to lecture on the dehumanizing effects of a segregated culture. Delivers speech on childhood in a biracial culture at Savannah, Ga.;

Speech "Ten Years from Today," at Kentucky State College (reprinted in *Vital Speeches*);

"Walls of Segregation are Crumbling," published in *New York Times Magazine*.

Becomes interested in the anxiety-inducing effect of the body image.

Visits several rehabilitation centers, interviews many who were blind, deaf, paralyzed, or have had limbs amputated.

Collaborates with Snelling on proposed anthology about research relating to mental, emotional, and physical disabilities.

Begins new book on the meaning of ordeal, its creative and destructive effects, called *The Journey*.

1952 Concentrates on *The Journey*. Gives speech before the NAACP in Atlanta, Ga., in protest of segregated schools: "Declaration of Faith in America" published in *New York Times Magazine*.

1953 Undergoes surgery for cancer. Completes *The Journey*. Gives up apartment at Hotel Margaret in Brooklyn Heights.

1954 *The Journey* published in April; praised as thoughtful and sensitive. Gives a Sidney Hillman Lecture at Roosevelt University on topic "Demagoguery: World-Size Danger. Have We World-Size Defenses?"

1954 Writes *Now Is the Time*, urging support for Supreme Court decision in *Brown v. Board of Education of Topeka, Kansas*.

1954–55 Dec.–May, travels with Snelling to India, interviews Prime Minister Nehru, his daughter, and other prominent political and social figures, for book to be called *Breakfast with Mr. Nehru*, never completed. Visits Rome, Paris, and London.

1955 *Now Is the Time* published in spring. On November 16, while Smith is at Vassar College as writer-in-residence, vandals burglarize and burn her bedroom and studio on the mountain, destroying thirteen thousand letters, personal papers, unpublished manuscripts, all notes on India, and notes for disabilities anthology. Receives Georgia Writers Association's award for *The Journey* in December.

Publishes "Prayer for a Better World," *Parents*, December.

1956 Spends four months at Neptune Beach, Fla., trying to recover from shock of fire by walking long hours on the beach. Publishes "Negroes in Gray Flannel Suits," an essay review of Walter White's *How Far the Promised Land?* in *The Progressive*. Begins the novel *One Hour*.

1957 "The Right Way is Not a Moderate Way" (speech for first anniversary of Montgomery Bus Boycott), published by Atlanta University's *Phylon* and the Fellowship of Reconciliation's *Fellowship*. For the speech, she is awarded the Franklin D. Roosevelt Citation by Americans for Democratic Action.

Receives Doctor of Humane Letters from Atlanta University and responds with speech, "The Winner Names the Age," which *The Progressive* published and cited as "Best Speech of the Year."

"No Easy Way, Now" (speech given in Arkansas after federal troops enforce desegregation in Little Rock) published in the *New Republic*. Continues work on *One Hour*. Spends spring months in Washington, D.C. and on eastern shore; summer at East Hampton.

1958 "And Suddenly Something Happened" published in *Saturday Review*. Works on *One Hour*.

1959 *One Hour* completed in May; published in September. Receives Freedom Award of Women's Committee of Roosevelt University.

1960 Spends spring months in Washington, D.C.; makes speeches at colleges in East, Midwest, and South. Much reading in theology and philosophy. "Novelists Need a Commitment," in *Saturday Review*, December.

1961 Writes new foreword and last two chapters for revised edition of *Killers of the Dream;* "Ordeal of Southern Women," in *Redbook*. Writes *Memory of a Large Christmas*. Short version published in *Life* magazine.

1962 "Miss Smith of Georgia," a television documentary, produced by Time-Life Broadcasts. Publishes *Memory of a Large Christmas*.

Records selections from *Killers of the Dream.*
Receives Sidney Hillman Award for best magazine writing in 1961 for "Ordeal of Southern Women," and responds with a speech, "The Awakening of the Heart," later published in *Redbook.*
"Now the Lonely Decision for Right or for Wrong," in *Life*; "The Mob and the Ghost," in *Progressive*; "A Strange Kind of Love" and "No More Ladies in the Dark," in *Saturday Review.*
Doctors find cancer in her lung.

1963 Treated for cancer.
"To Tame the Shrew" and "Thoughts as My Travels End" published in *Saturday Review.*
Spends winter in Jacksonville, Fla.; gives speech "Woman Born of Man," at Stetson University; lectures in Los Angeles.

1964 Home again on the mountain. Writes *Our Faces, Our Words* about the non-violent civil rights movement of the early 1960s, published in fall. "The Day It Happens to Each of Us" published in *McCall's.*
Receives honorary Doctor of Literature from Western Maryland College.

1965 Records *Our Faces, Our Words* for Spoken Arts.
Joan Titus records Smith reading from *The Journey*; receives first Queen Esther Award from National Women's Division of American Jewish Congress; responds with speech published in *Saturday Review*, "Poets Among the Demagogues."

1966 Receives the Charles S. Johnson Award from Fisk University. Writes letter to the editor of the *Atlanta Constitution,* which is reprinted as "Miss Smith on SNCC" in *New South.*
Is recorded reading selections from *Strange Fruit,* produced by Spoken Arts and released in 1968.
Dies September 28, in Emory Hospital, Atlanta, Ga.

1999 Inducted into Georgia Women of Achievement.

2000 Inducted into the Georgia Writers Hall of Fame.

2000–2013 Lillian Smith Foundation establishes Lillian Smith Center for Creative Arts; offers summer residencies and workshops; artist in service awards; establishes Lillian Smith House Museum and becomes part of Southern Literary Trail; partners with Piedmont College to use the Center for Maymester courses.

2013 Piedmont College acquires Lillian Smith Center. See www.piedmont.edu/lilliansmith-resources

A Lillian Smith READER

INTRODUCTION

A hundred years ago in the summer of 1915, Lillian Smith's father, Calvin Warren Smith, turned financial disaster into a grand adventure, a creative response to adversity that would shape and inform many more lives than those of his immediate family. Perhaps his third daughter, Lillian, would have become a writer even if her father's business had not failed and he had not founded Laurel Falls Camp. However, the what ifs are not as interesting as the consequences of the family's move from the prosperous life they had known in Jasper, Florida, to their summer cottage on Old Screamer Mountain near the rural community of Clayton, Georgia. Over forty-five years later, in *Memory of a Large Christmas*, Lillian Smith recalled her father's perspective on that move:

> There was nothing dismal about that moving, for my father departed like an explorer setting out for an unknown continent. He actually succeeded in convincing everybody but Mother that our new life was going to be more interesting than our old, that mountains were more beautiful than swamps and lily-covered ponds and oaks heavy with moss, that we'd never forget our first spring when we would see dogwood in bloom on the hills. (And of course, we have never forgot the beauty he spoke of—nor the deeper, mythic fascination of the swamps and cypress and sand and great oaks where we were born and where our memories still live.)
>
> The move to the mountains, by the time Dad had planned it, had acquired all the drama and tension and highlights of a Great Hegira. He leased three big freight cars and stored the household furniture and the piano and the dishes and trunks full of Mother's linens and our things in two of them. [. . .] In the third freight car were the cow and the horses and the dogs and crates of pure-bred Leghorns from his farm plus feed for the long journey, plus farm implements plus tools and toys plus two of the brothers—and two of the young Negroes from the farm who were com-

pletely entranced by our father's stories of mountains and red earth and the great gorge at Tallulah Falls and asked to go along on this adventure. (MLC 49)

Memory of a Large Christmas contains some of the happy, humorous experiences of the Smith family's bountiful Christmas traditions in Jasper, poignantly contrasted with one Christmas in the mountains when their father invited forty-eight prisoners and their guards to have dinner with the family. After their guests had returned to "their quarters on the railroad siding," Calvin Smith spoke to his family:

> We've been through some pretty hard times, lately, and I've been proud of my family. Some folks can take prosperity and can't take poverty; some can take being poor and lose their heads when money comes. I want my children to accept it all: the good and the bad, for that is what life is. It can't be wholly good; it won't be wholly bad.... Those men, today—they've made mistakes. Sure. But I have too. Bigger ones maybe than theirs. And you will. You are not likely to commit a crime but you may become blind and refuse to see what you should look at, and that can be worse than a crime. Don't forget that. Never look down on a man. Never. If you can't look him straight in the eyes, then what's wrong is with you.... This world is changing fast. Folks get hurt and make terrible mistakes at such times. But the one I hope you won't make is to cling to my generation's sins. You'll have plenty of your own, remember. Changing things is mighty risky, but not changing things is worse—that is, if you can think of something better to change to.... But I don't mean, Sister, you got to get radical. (MLC 56–57)

Lillian Smith's memory of her father's remarks that Christmas night reveals much that inspired his children to fulfill his dreams even as they created their own. Clearly, her father was Lillian Smith's first and most enduring role model of resilience in the face of adversity.

In the years following that Christmas of 1918, Lillian Smith devoted her life to finding and creating "something better to change to." First as "Miss Lil," director of Laurel Falls Camp, and then as a nationally known magazine editor and best-selling author, Smith found creative ways to challenge racial segregation and all the dehumanizing injustices produced and tolerated in defense of maintaining white supremacy. As examples from camp plays and magazine contests reveal, she created spaces where those old practices could be unlearned and replaced with new ideas for relating to an always unknown future.

Lillian Smith died on September 28, 1966. She chose to be buried not in the graveyard with her parents but on the mountain by the chimney she had designed, a lasting monument to the theater where campers and counselors helped create and perform their responses to internal and external forces that threaten human life and growth. On her grave marker she left these challenging words from *The Journey*: "Death can kill a man. That is all it can do to him; it cannot end his life. Because of memory . . ." (201). Since her death, those who knew her, loved her, and valued her work have given their creative energies and resources not only to promote her books, letters, essays, and her recorded voice but also to preserve and sustain the place where she lived and worked as a center for the creative arts. Now under the auspices of Piedmont College, the Lillian Smith Center is opening up new possibilities for students of all ages to dip into the vast pool of human wisdom from which Lillian Smith drew and to which she contributed. The old campsite is again a place to gaze at the top of Old Screamer Mountain, to feel the spirit of renewal and hope the Smith family found there, to touch the huge rock chimney, and perhaps to hear Lillian Smith's challenge from the last words in *The Journey*: "to believe in something not yet proved and to underwrite it with our lives."

Responding to the challenge implicit in Smith's life and death, the editors of this collection hear echoes of some of her questions. Are we creating a world where all children are encouraged and enabled to grow? Are we still finding ways to resist others' demands for human justice? When we read her novels set in the 1920s and 1950s and speeches given in the 1940s, 1950s, and 1960s, we find them not dated but prophetic. In Smith's work we find our usable past, what Imani Perry calls our history of resilience and new ways to "practice undoing historical injustice" (107).

This collection is designed to invite new as well as returning readers to journey with Smith through a sampling of her writing organized chronologically from the 1930s to the 1960s. A chronology of significant events in her life provides a framework. If you want "just the facts," see the chronology on pages xiii–xix. If you want to see and hear how and why Lillian Smith became a writer for our time, keep reading.

Trembling Earth

On many occasions throughout her life Lillian Smith introduced herself with a story from her childhood home in Jasper, Florida. Accordingly, her words reintroduce this new collection of her work. Because she was terminally ill, on July 14, 1966, in Atlanta, Georgia, she dictated this reminiscence. It was recorded and transcribed by Joan Titus, who was planning to write a biography of Smith titled *Trembling Earth.* Although Titus specified the title "Trembling Earth" when she later submitted the reminiscence for publication in the *Virginia Quarterly Review,* it was published in the autumn of 1982 as "The Old Days in Jasper: A Reminiscence." In remembering the first place she left, Smith also recalls her first treasured friendship, actual and symbolic of that most desirable relationship between storyteller and listener. Implicit in this reminiscence, which may be considered her last writing, is her message to future writers, storytellers, and the creative spirit in everyone: each of us needs collaboration to continue creating the world we want to live in. None of us lives fully or creatively alone. To hear Smith's recorded voice, go to www.piedmont.edu/lilliansmith-resources.

> I was thinking of old days in Jasper this morning. It's funny how your mind goes back and stays and you don't realize it's there. You are planning things with your conscious mind and sometimes even reading a book; and yet this old memory is like a ghost just flitting around from the big camphor tree to the banana shrubs, on to the big oak tree and the magnolia and so on. And suddenly I saw two little feet and one of them was mine and one of them was Marjorie's, and they were wiggling up and down in the sand and each of us was digging a hole with our hands but we were also half-digging with our toes and making what is called a toad-frog house. And we'd dig and dig and dig. This is strange land down there in North Florida. If you dig 12 to 14 inches you always come to very

wet earth and sometimes even at six inches you do, so it's wonderful to play with. There we were digging away and these little toes just flipping, flapping up and down and we made a hole and then we took the dirt and dried it out with some dry sand and built it all around our feet. In other words, each of us used her foot as an armature and built up a house that was actually more like a little Eskimo house than anything I can think of. But this was our way of building what we called toad-frog houses. Then after it had dried a little bit around our feet we'd slip the feet out and there would be this nice mysterious dark hollow place inside. And then that night we were sure a toad-frog would come. I don't know why we called them toad-frog—we didn't say frog and we didn't say toad, we said toad-frog. Somehow that made it more important and more mysterious, too. And then we'd look inside, hoping to see two little glistening eyes staring back at us next morning. It's a wonder we didn't find a little snake staring at us instead. But we didn't. And Marjorie and I would play like that by the hour or stringing red seeds out of the magnolias. After the petals have fallen there is something that looks almost like a pinecone, I suppose you'd call it a magnolia cone, and it has these beautiful, beautiful clear red seeds in it. And we'd string them and wear them around our necks.

But Marjorie and I did things more important than stringing magnolia seeds together and making toad-frog houses and climbing the great trees around us. We told each other stories. And for years I thought we actually told each other stories. I didn't know that I told the story and Marjorie was that important person, the listener, and in that way we made the story together. That came as a surprise to me, although of course I had learned it the hard way as a writer—a book is nothing until you find the reader who can listen and really hear everything you're saying in the book. And most readers hear very little of what you're saying. But Marjorie was apparently the perfect listener and when I was five, six, seven, eight, nine years old, according to her memory and mine to a more dim extent, I told the long stories and she listened and in that way we collaborated. What these stories were about neither one of us can remember for the life of us today. I think they were about a world that was better, though, than the one we had; and of course we had an enormously good world compared to most children—full of fun and full of things and full of comforts. But each of us was growing the hard way, and there were times when we were furious with our families and with our sisters and brothers and with everybody but each other. I don't remember that we ever got furious with each other. And we were friends from the time we were four years old until she left Jasper at 15. Then I left there at 17, and since then we have seen almost nothing of each other.

But coming back to these stories. Apparently she and I would walk down the railroad track walking the rails, falling off, but stopping to pick wildflowers—violets, irises: the irises grew down there by the thousands in the ditches, along every railroad track and along every path and road. We'd be stooping, picking flowers and here I would be going on and on and on with this continued story, which I don't think stopped at the end of our play day but was picked up the next time we were together. And yet neither of us remembers very much about it, except she said that she was always just hypnotized by it and I think it was because it was her story too. I think I rather remembered her as collaborating, I would say, more actively than just listening because it *was* her story. I was telling the story of two little girls who loved each other very much and yet were lonely children somehow: surrounded by big families and yet each of us cut away from those families by our fantasy life I suppose and our dreams.

Anyway, it was like that. And I've often thought of it since then, this collaboration of the dream: how no one—no writer, no painter, no sculptor, no musician even can perfect his dream or even carry it out or create it in full until there is a listener or a looker to collaborate with him. How we find these dreamers who can collaborate with us is a strange and wondrous and magic sort of thing. I don't know how we find them; we never know. I write a book, say a book like *Strange Fruit*, and it sold into the millions; and I would say that maybe, just maybe, not more than fifty thousand of its readers really collaborated with me as listeners on that book. The rest thought that the book was about something it wasn't about; they had heard these fantastic tales of how scandalous it was and how obscene and how controversial and that it was written to help Negroes and so on and so on. So all kinds of people came to that book to read it; and it was almost as if they were deaf and blind because they never saw what the book really was about. They had already created a book in their minds before they picked up my book, and my book was just a hunk of pages to them. They whiffed over those pages never really knowing what they were reading, never listening, because there's so much more to a book than the printed words on that white paper, so much more. Every word casts a shadow and every word makes an echo. Sometimes a word casts ten shadows and sometimes it makes ten echoes, and a good listener, a good looker will get all of this, and when he does, or when she does, the collaborator has been born that the writer needs. But if that doesn't happen then your book has been read by a deaf and blind person. He has gotten only the sounds that he had already heard from gossip and in book reviews and newspapers and he never knows what your book's really about; and that leaves you feeling very sad and lonely. And that is the way I felt as a very grown-up, sophisticated person when *Strange Fruit* was published and not read but bought and the pages turned by millions of people. Some of them were looking for a four-letter word, as though they couldn't find four-letter words scrawled on the sidewalk. There was a four-letter word—one—in the entire book if I remember rightly, if we are using that word to mean something that has to do with the body and sex. It's something so pitiable to me about the hunger of many Western people, especially Anglo-Saxon people, who were restricted by Puritanism from really understanding the hungers and needs of the human body. This is another form of segregation which has always seemed to me even more important than racial segregation: we have segregated the body into evil and good parts, into dark and light, and there are some things about the body that we think of as being sinful and wrong when nothing could possibly be sinful and wrong about the body.

Well anyway, as I thought about *Strange Fruit*, I remembered Marjorie, the little listener who did collaborate with my dreams because her heart was lonely for what my heart was lonely for. Her mind was very keen and I think mine was, and she could reach out and understand my vocabulary and what I was trying to say even as a small child, so we did have that beautiful collaboration and it was the strongest part of our friendship. It was an enormously rich and creative friendship for two little girls to have had. There was nothing nasty or mischievous about it. It was a very natural thing. It was tremendously mental and spiritual and also it was physical. We loved to play the same games, we adored not so much group play as we did what you would call lonely play. Each of us liked to dance around. Each of us loved to do acrobatic things and we were always risking a cracked skull by doing wild and awful things on the high limbs of the trees and then daring each other to try it too. We'd climb as high as we could and get out on little tiny limbs where we were really dizzy and we wouldn't admit our dizziness—daring the other one to do the same. Then sometimes we'd climb out of the window of her grandmother's house—a big big house—and creep over to a very giant size chinaberry tree whose limbs overhung the roof. Then we'd swing up to those limbs and get on and then keep climbing. And there were tree houses in all the big oak trees and chinaberry trees and we'd play in those. And we both read at the same time but not the same book. I would go over to spend the day with her and we'd read all day long. She would read one book and I would read a book and we were having another community of the daydream there, in that we each knew the book that the other one was reading and had we not already read it we were going to read it immediately when the other one finished with it, and therefore our reading was shared on a deep level just as my storytelling was shared with her.

This collaboration of the dream is such a strange, strange kind of thing. And yet there'd be no art without it. And without art I can't imagine there being such a thing as the human being, the person. We think of many important things about being a person and we tend in this political age we live in to think about our civil rights and our so-called human rights. But in a way the most important right we have, I think, should be the freedom to collaborate in each other's dreams. And that means the freedom to look at a painting and see there what we want to see. Sometimes the critic tries to keep us from seeing what we want to see. That's an interesting thing: how there's always a segregator around trying to block off a view. And maybe when I look at a modern painting I see something a little different from the abstraction that the critic is talking about. Well, that's good, that I see something different. But if I'm not careful I shall feel a little uneasy about it because he has told me that I should see what he's seeing. Well, that isn't true. Each of us should see what the artist has whispered to us, and there are all kinds of echoes in every painting. He hears some of them, I hear others. There are all kinds of shadows. He sees some, I see others. And that is the way it is, of course, with a book. Sometimes when you think about what creating really is and why it's so needful, you begin to grope on those dark levels; you get into what we call the labyrinth of the spirit and of the mind and the memory and go down deep deep deep deep. I don't know why we use the word deep because the word out out out out is just as good. You go distances, anyway. Deep down or far out and into worlds that our ordinary senses don't perceive easily. And there is where the creation is done by the artist. There is where the collaborator is born. And there are so many people who can't paint and who say I don't know anything about painting, I know what I like. Well, if you really know what you like, of course, that would be the most important thing in the world. Sometimes, though, we are liking only what our five senses tell us because we haven't gone down into those dark, deep or very very brilliantly lit places where we perceive something quite different. And when people ask me how I dream up something of course I don't know. I know that I use materials that have accumulated in my life. I know that's true of my own writing.

I was born in fabulous country and I've always been so glad I was, although I left there when I was seventeen years old. But on that edge of Florida where it joins to Georgia and where the great swamp is it's not very deep; it's not a very thick piece of land. It really is just a thin little island that is hung on to the Okefenokee Swamp and hung on to the Georgia Islands and hung on to Alabama. But to have been born near the swamp was a wondrous thing to have happened to me. Actually I was born about forty miles away from it, but little fingers and little driblets of it streak out in all directions and the land near Jasper was a part actually of this formation. There were lakes and ponds around and there was one called Shaky Pond. We'd go there for picnics—Sunday School picnics.

When I say the word I see all kinds of images of beautiful damask linen table clothes spread on the ground and with sandspurs almost poking up through them and on them spread a dozen different kinds of cake, baked ham, and roast chicken and fried chicken and sometimes even fried fish and deviled eggs and all kinds of sandwiches and chicken salad and ham salad and salmon salad and all the different kinds of salads that our mothers and grandmothers had learned to cook down in that area of our country. And that would be fun. I mustn't forget the big barrel of ice lemonade that would have a two hundred pound block of ice in this huge barrel. It didn't leak; I don't know why but it didn't leak. I remember that would surprise me. It would be full of lemonade with the lemon slices floating all around in it nice and sweet and acid and ice cold and a dipper there. We drank out of the dippers and gourds and if you have never drunk out of a gourd there's nothing quite like it. It has a little echo of a taste from the dried gourd material and they would scoop this out and leave an opening and it makes a beautiful thing to drink out of.

Well, aside from the food which all kids remember, what I remembered really and what drifted down into that area, that dark deep area of one's creative life, was the trembling earth around the pond. One could get within twenty, thirty feet of it and suddenly one knew that one was walking on earth that was probably no more than a few inches thick and that all this was floating on water of endless depth, a depth that could never be measured. I would walk softly and feel myself almost floating up and down—wondering. If you stayed still you would begin to sink so you didn't dare stay still: you'd keep walking and wondering and you'd wonder about that. And you'd wonder: Is the earth like this, and is all that we do—all I do and all my mother and father do and my sisters and brothers and my friends—is it on just a little thin level of something? I didn't use the word reality then but later, you see, this is what happens to you: you extend the sentence. You say first when you're little, I wonder, and then you say I wonder if this is like so and so, and then you begin to extend that sentence. It gets longer and longer and longer and wraps around the whole earth—just around and around and around as you keep saying: I wonder if the whole, everything that happens to a human being is just like trembling earth? Is it all floating on something that we'll never know, something unknown and mysterious, and is this reality—this little thin floating thing that I'm now standing on? But as I said, you don't think that at five or six; you feel it and you keep feeling it and you feel it more and more. You add word after word, sentence after sentence, until there's no end to the millions of words as you continue to wonder what this thing is that we call human reality and where it extends to. And then what? And it tied up with my sense of time, that was really my sense of space—the beginning of how I began to feel about space. So I wasn't really surprised to find that the planets and the stars were millions and millions of what they called light years away, because I had begun to say I wonder when I walked around Shaky Pond.

I also began to say I wonder about time. But that came to me in a different way. That came to me through the graveyard because I went to the funerals. It was the custom in our little town for little children to go out to the graveyard to the funerals. Death was not something that people then thought was dishonorable. They just thought it was sad and mysterious, and therefore they let children attend this sad and mysterious human occasion when someone seems to have gone to sleep and is not going to wake up any more. You know that there is more than that. You learn it the hard way, because in those days there was no way to preserve bodies and we lived in very hot country. So by the first day there was the slight odor of the dead and by the second day the odor was stronger and by the third day it was quite strong. It wasn't repulsive, it was strange and mysterious and frightening. It didn't smell like something spoiled; they had some ways of keeping the body a little bit. But the body would darken and the face would turn gray and so you knew in those days what death really was, that it was a disintegration. I didn't know that word but I know that what had put us together and made us whole and alive was not keeping us together whole and alive but that we were going to pieces. And it frightened the very life out of me almost as a child. But at the same time it didn't do to me what it has done to many children of today—make them feel that it doesn't really happen and doesn't have to happen. We knew more about death than we knew about birth, much more—which was of course due to our puritan upbringing. Ridiculous that we were made so ashamed of birth that we couldn't even ask questions about it, while we were invited in to watch death take its full effect on the person who had once been alive. But I think this is when I began to think of time, when someone would die and I would hear that beautiful liturgy of the dead which the Episcopal Church has and which the Methodist Episcopal Church also has and then you come to the dust to dust part which seemed elegantly beautiful to me as a small child. And so I tied up death and poetry together as being almost equally wondrous. I was afraid of death. I was not afraid of poetry but somehow they had much to do with each other, much to do. And so I began to think about time and why a life ends and what eternity means. Of course I drove everyone crazy when I was about nine or ten years old with my questions—my existential questions. I didn't know *that* word at that time but every day I asked: When does eternity end? And my Sunday School teacher finally told me that if I couldn't stop asking that question I couldn't come to Sunday School anymore, that she just couldn't bear it any longer. Poor dear, what could she have to say to those two big eyes looking at her? They weren't going to accept any easy answer and she knew it. And who has ever been able to answer that question about time and eternity?

No one could read my books without finding these early signs of my childhood—the trembling earth, the moss swinging on the trees and making strange shadows, the enormous size of the trees so that you knew a lot about age and years and hundreds of years. All these things—and Shaky Pond, the graveyard and the telling my little friend stories as we picked flowers down the railroad track or sat on a tombstone in the graveyard are what maybe turned me into a writer.

Letter to Mr. Hartley

In the following letter, Smith recalls her experiences in China and the many ways she was educated there that would inform her life as a writer. Written in response to a high school teacher whose students had asked whether formal education helps a writer, her reply provides a fine summary of her educational experiences and also reaffirms her commitment to lifelong learning, all of which are evident in subsequent selections of her published work. The letter was later published in *Redbook* as "Bridges to Other People."

December 1, 1959

Dear Mr. Hartley:

My reply is slow because I have many things to do, many responsibilities, and seldom find time to reply to a letter such as yours—not that it is not interesting but simply that teachers write so many of them! You would like to inject a little sweat and blood of a faraway writer into the deadness of literature, I know; I understand; but if we writers replied to all the letters we got from teachers, we would never never never write a book again! But—I am replying to you because your particular way of putting your questions rather scratched me. Now, you know and I know, and all but the morons in your class know, that education is a private matter between the person and the world of knowledge and experience and has only a little to do with school or college—after one learns how to read, write and figger. It all depends on what one does with one's mind outside the classroom. I don't think college ever helped a creative person, but I don't think it often harms one. It is all a gamble. If you meet two or three real persons at college, then it is worth the tuition, the toil and the trouble. I'd settle for one real person, real and sensitive and gnawed with curiosity. High school? Well, there are techniques, skills, et cetera one gains at high school that come in handy—no matter what one does, whether it be janitor's work, garbage collecting or writing a novel.

What really matters is this: learning; wanting to learn; yearning to know; craving knowledge; eternally scrabbling through the past to find out what interesting minds have thought; eternally exploring the present to see what interesting minds are now thinking.

I was in a Georgia college one year: there I met a remarkable man who happened to teach literature. Harvard-bred and yearning to read everything in the world, he made us read as much of this everything as he could. And I have always profited from that year—from talk with him, from the books he made me read, and made me want to read later when I had more time. I have now and then seen him and have always been glad. Then I spent four years at the Peabody Conservatory of Music, in Baltimore, and took private lessons from a wonderful Dane who always asked me first: "What have you read this week?" And we'd talk novels, poetry, short stories, philosophy, and then he'd say, Now play for me . . . show me what you understand. And I'd play, and he'd say, Yes, you feel; you are growing; you are imagining; you are hungry. . . .

Then for three years in China I taught music in a girls' school. Here I had a principal who was intelligent, modern in her approach, liberal in her philosophy and open to China's richness and wealth. And she helped me open up to China too; and there was a fine English teacher who lent me her books and she had a fine collection; and there were the sights and sounds and rhythms of a changing China; and I learned from everybody: the Chinese girls, their families, the city of Huchow, the people on the street, the English papers I read out there.

And it was there that I heard of Gandhi and of Tagore—and suddenly while in China I was also in India, in the minds of its two greatest leaders. And I read Gandhi's magazine and I learned of what was happening in South Africa, and slowly, and yet almost suddenly, the whole earth opened to me and I saw us as one people, as human beings, all aching for freedom, all longing for knowledge and understanding, all reaching toward the light of truth, all wanting to love and be loved.

And there were slow Saturdays spent in a little houseboat on one of China's canals where we five American teachers rested and talked and learned of human anguish and longing and dreams from one another. And of course I heard of Li Po, the great Chinese poet, and read him; and I heard of Lao-tze and read a little of him and much about him; and I heard of Buddha and read about him and wandered through Buddhist temples looking at Buddhist sculptures and wondering about this religion and the Christian religion and the Jewish religion and all religions.

And there were revolutions and counterrevolutions and the war lords were in full command of things while I was there, exploiting rich and poor, terrorizing. And I read about the 1911 revolution and hurt inside to think that it had become a debauched thing and a degraded thing after all the fine dreams of men. And I heard whispers of Communists and I met Sun Yat-Sen's sister-in-law and I had a long talk with the girl who was to become Madame Chiang Kai-Shek, and we, two 25-year-old girls together talked and talked and talked.

This is the way I was really educated. Then I came home and worked for my brother, who was city manager of Fort Pierce, Florida, and at the city hall I learned of politics and intrigue and graft and I saw my brother show courage when it was difficult to be brave and I saw him refuse big sums of money from big industries who wanted his help—and so I learned again. I was close to the police departments and the fire departments and I learned from these men, who used to hang around my small private office, which led into my brother's. So—one goes on.

Later I took over my father's summer camp for girls, which happened to be the first private camp to open in Georgia. And realizing I knew nothing much about children or grown people, I read psychology and anthropology and psychoanalysis and I observed the kids and observed myself and observed the counselors and I learned this way too. I read systematically because I respect a subject and I think a little reading here and there is a poor way to try to understand something so complex, so fascinating, so involved, as the human mind and the human soul. So I read Freud carefully for eight years until I felt I knew his writings and understood them, the great points of success in them and the abysses of failure. And I have kept reading him now and then: but I read on too: his pupils' writings; Jung and Rank and Hans Sachs and Ferenczi and others—the American psychiatrists and child specialists.

But I learned more from the campers themselves because I tried not to put barriers between me and them and we talked together about everything: our bodies, sex, death, life, God, our parents, hate, love, fear, anxiety, guilt and beauty. We talked music and poetry, we watched the mountain and its wild birds, we danced. We created things together. We had a craft shop and a sculpture shop and a painting shop—and because I did not know much about sculpture and painting, I read and looked at paintings and sculpture and whenever I was in New York I looked at paintings and sculptures in the galleries and museums and read and looked and watched our young painters paint.

So it went: artists . . . painting . . . sculpture . . . looking at, reading about, talking to the creators themselves. And so I learned. Then music: I had studied it for 18 years but actually I had heard very little of the world's music, so I began to collect records and we listened to music at camp, in the big, beautiful old library there and out on the hilltop. And I learned more and still more.

Then my counselors knew so much; an expert swimmer had things to say to me; an expert horsewoman or horseman had experiences to tell me and things to show me about horsemanship. So you see, it just went on and on. Nature lore . . . camping out—at night on top of a wild mountain you learn things. You learn things too when kids are sick in the infirmary and their parents are far away; you learn how to be a friend to them, how to persuade them that you really care and are there close by to help; all this—and a kid's courage when hurt and so far away from home. All this. And always more and more——

Then I suddenly decided that although I was a Southerner, I knew very little about my South. There are so many levels of our life; we are separated from each other by color, by wealth and poverty, by learning and ignorance, by city and country, by white-collar jobs and mill jobs. And so I went out to learn. I met for the first time in my life men who worked in coal mines, and men who worked in steel mills, and men who worked for a sharecropping portion in cotton and corn fields. I met union men and big industrialists and talked to both. I went to union meetings and talked in great, ornate offices. I went to the campuses of Negro students and talked with them, again and again and again; I invited into my home Negroes whom I liked and accepted invitations to their homes. So I kept learning.

And then food. I liked it and I found I enjoyed the food in every country; this interested me and I have tried to cook quite a bit of it. All kinds of food: gourmets' food and simple folk food. And this was learning, too.

And the Theater: we had one at camp and we made it into a very lively place, indeed; and once more I was learning as I wrote plays for our theater and so on.

So? Well, I think all of life is learning. If you want to close up, you can close up; but if you open up, you will be bound to learn, to become aware, to reach out for others and toward others. And then, of course, having traveled across the earth, having swung high into the air, I had to come home and go down deep into my own heart and mind and memories and find out what is there; and this is sometimes hard learning but beautiful learning too. And then there is always what you learn when you build bridges to other people: to one, then to one more, and on and on.

I don't know when learning stops. But I know a writer never stops learning, not ever—until she is dead as a creative being. When you stop learning, stop listening, stop looking and asking questions, always new questions, then it is time to die: time to crawl into that small room and pull the cover over you.

So tell your pupils—well, tell them this, this that I have written you.

Sincerely,
Lillian Smith

PART ONE

A Chain Reaction of Dreams

1936–1945

> "Though they lived in communities indifferent or hostile to these ideas, the smaller groups who were her audiences were hungering to hear such words said aloud. Had they not been spoken by someone, in such manner as she said them, and at such times and places as they were said, the acceleration of change that has occurred in the last quarter-century could not have taken place."
>
> —PAULA SNELLING, "Preface" to *The Winner Names the Age*

These selections from Lillian Smith's writings published from 1936 to 1945 exemplify the breadth of her political and cultural concerns as well as her multifaceted literary talent. Significantly, these examples of her early fiction, editorials, columns, book reviews, essays, speeches, and Laurel Falls Camp plays also demonstrate the importance of collaboration in Smith's theory and practice as a writer. Lillian Smith published her early writings in the magazine she created and coedited with Paula Snelling. Like her development of Laurel Falls Camp, from which it grew, the magazine provides another example of Smith's creative response to adversity.

Lillian Smith and Paula Snelling had worked at Laurel Falls Camp in 1921 and 1922, Snelling in athletics and Smith in music; but they did not become friends until they met again on the train to Clayton, Georgia, in the summer of 1925. Smith was returning from three years as director of music at a girls' school in Huchow, China, and Snelling, from a year at Columbia University Teachers College where she had earned a master's in psychology with a minor in English. After her first summer as camp director, Smith hired a new camp staff and put Snelling in charge of athletics. In 1928 Smith bought the camp and named Snelling her assistant director. Both women were intellectuals, and their relationship grew beyond their work at camp because of their mutual interests in psychology, literature, and the political and literary ferment that began in the 1920s South. After Smith's father died in 1930, and when her mother was able to spend winter months with relatives in Florida, Smith shared an apartment with Snelling, who was then teaching high school math in Macon, Georgia. When not working on camp materials, Smith began writing fiction based on her experiences in China and her childhood in Jasper, Florida. Of Snelling's influence in their early years together, Smith wrote: "She was intensely interested in books and poetry. We read together, we discussed literature a great deal, and it was through those discussions that I began to turn my creativity toward writing instead of music [. . .]. Without her encouragement I doubt I would have had the courage to go through those first four or five years of groping." Between 1932 and 1935, Smith wrote two novels, *And the Waters Flow On* and *Tom Harris and Family*, and two novellas, *Every Branch in Me* and *Julia*. Although these manuscripts were never published, their subjects permeated Smith's later writing (*HH* 9–11).

In the winter of 1935 both Snelling and Smith were confined to a small cottage on Old Screamer Mountain. Smith was responsible for the care of her invalid mother, and Snelling remained to recuperate from injuries she sustained in an accident with one of the camp horses. To relieve their boredom and isolation from life in Macon, Smith suggested they start a literary magazine. Conceived as an outlet for Southern American writers and as a review of Southern American writing representing a more recognizable and inclusive South, their magazine would include and review—for the first time in the region—the work of black as well as white women and men as subjects and authors. The magazine first appeared under the title *Pseudopodia* (1936), then *North Georgia Review* (1937–41), and *South Today* (1942–45); it grew from 12 pages and 27 subscribers to 110 pages and 10,000 subscribers (White and Sugg, xi).

To enliven their social life and in lieu of monetary payment for contributions to the magazine, the editors established a tradition of inviting contributors to spend a few days as their guests at the camp. Their guest lists expanded through the years to include a variety of people—editors, journalists, educators, political activists—mostly Southerners, whom Smith and Snelling thought would be interesting to know and whom they viewed as being involved in changing the South. They had their first biracial dinner party with guests from Atlanta in the fall of 1936. Through the magazine, as with Laurel Falls Camp, Smith was able to create on her mountain, at least periodically, another aspect of the South she wanted to live in: a place where intellectuals and artists could gather to exchange ideas, examine their society, and perhaps find ways to influence the development and direction of its future (*HH* 12–13).

The following selections of Smith's early fiction, book reviews, and editorials exemplify the editors' intent as stated in the Spring 1936 issue. The magazine would concern itself with the South and with "whatever seems to us artistic, vital, significant"—the goal was not to perpetuate "that sterile fetishism of the Old South" but "to expose rather than gloss over vapidness, dishonesty, cruelty, stupidity" (White and Sugg xii). All items originally published in the magazine are taken from the first posthumously published volume of Smith's work, *From the Mountain*.

The Harris Children's Town—Maxwell, Ga.

Published in the magazine's first issue, *Pseudopodia*, in spring of 1936, the "Harris Children's Town" was excerpted by Lillian Smith from an early draft of her novel, *Strange Fruit*. In this sample of her early fiction, Smith demonstrates her criteria for honest, truthful portraits of her region's culture and people, which she hopes the magazine will promote. Refusing to separate the personal and the political spheres in her analyses of the American South, Smith intentionally draws into consciousness what she unconsciously absorbed as a child. The influences of race, religion, money (and how it is made), and the mysterious relationships between people she saw every day, appear again in *Strange Fruit* and *Killers of the Dream*. Her sensory verisimilitude invites the reader to enter simultaneously her physical and psychic sense of place. Also evident and more fully developed in her later work is Smith's attention to her physical environment, which complements and deepens her observations of the people who inhabit that space.

There are ten thousand other little towns of the size of Maxwell, Georgia, all very like Maxwell, all a little different but it happened that the Harris children were not born in any of these. They were born in Maxwell. And Maxwell was the warp on which the small patterns of their lives were woven. From which they could never cut themselves loose. Though some tried. Tried and found that they were only carrying Maxwell with them, wherever they went. As every child grown in a little town carries it forever with him until the threads rot and fall to dust.

Maxwell claimed a population of eighteen hundred, eight hundred whites, one thousand Negroes. The Harris children knew that. Knew too that cotton, lumber and turpentine made money for folks, or broke them—that people should have diversified crops, but didn't—that their papa was the busiest man in town and maybe the richest—

But these facts were less than the sand which slipped unnoticed into their shoes during the day and as carelessly was emptied out on the floor at night. For folks as they had heard all their short lives had to make money or lose it. Their papa did both so being the richest man in town—if he was—did not give them more or less spending money than their friends had. And Maxwell's eighteen hundred inhabitants were very simply people they said howdy to when they met them on the streets and they said howdy to every one of them, black and white, even though a face or name now and then might be unknown to them: because their papa did.

But out of the flux of Maxwell's eighteen hundred human beings swirling in little slow eddies on the business streets on Saturday, about the Methodist and Baptist churches on Sunday, to and from school on week days, about the Woodmen of the World Hall, the Masonic Temple, the Knights of Pythias Hall on lodge night, out at the cemetery every week or so when there was a burying, on rare entertainment nights in the Opera House, at the baseball ground near the African Methodist Episcopal Church where a ball, eluding the outfielder, would crash into the Black God's ramshackly temple to the gasping delight of the White God's children—out of this fluid mass faces, and bodies, became three dimensional, solidified into sharp lines, and threw their shadows on the Harris' hearts.

Hardly more than a *shush* of long, gray moss across your face as you ran on the white sandy paths beneath great oaks, hardly more than the crunch of acorns under bare feet, or the prickle of sandspurs, or the feel of cold iron on blowy days when skates jamming into sand you fell breathing hard and laughing against the new metal fence put up after the old pickets had rotted down; hardly more, but there, to remain there forever, as moving in its slow orbit Maxwell swung from God's Sabbath to Nigger Sad'dy night, and gathering up its strength began anew.

Mr. Pusey, on Sunday the Methodist Sunday School superintendent, on week days manager of Maxwell Supply Store, at night the husband of a wife invalided by "female trouble"—Mr. Pusey five feet one inch in his shoes and a trifle pudgy about the belt took charge Sunday morning as well as he could of the squirming hot, clean, murmurous youth (he called them youth) sent or accompanied by parents anxious that the by-product of their weak moments learn so much about God that they'd never get in jail, never be talked about, never be radical, always make a good living, and die a respectable death in such a respectable manner that whoever the minister might be at the time he could convince their bereaved, broken, desolated hearts in firm, comforting, unassailable words that their dead child was safe in the arms of Jesus. That is what they wanted. The children wanted to be close together, hear each other's voices, watch the grown folks and show off their knowledge—or their ignorance, as their mood might be—of the Golden Text.

After the classes, small chronological clusters scattered about the pews and hovered over by pretty young school teachers who talked gravely about vague segments of old Jewish history, Mr. Pusey would strike hard the iron bell on his table and reassemble the disintegrated congregation to hear old Dr. Munson expound the lesson according to Josephus. Old Dr. Munson from the North, curly gray beard reaching far below his belt, walked stiffly down the middle aisle each Sunday morning, knees popping in and out as he walked, opened a heavy book and resumed with the mysterious words, "Now according to Josephus . . ." the running commentary he had been making all the years of the Harris children's lives on the Sunday School lesson. Only as the years passed his voice grew more quavery until sometimes you could not make out the words, and the book shook up and down in his hand until sometimes you could not tear your eyes from the shaking. They thought he looked exactly like God and they thought Josephus must too and it made it easier somehow for them to think of the Trinity when they thought of Dr. Munson, Josephus and God.

Only sometimes as they listened, they wondered what he did to Miss Ada when she ran wild-eyed and mumbling into the back door of his office in the drug store and (if you hung around the corner playing stick frog long enough) came out flushed and quiet and bright with happiness. Miss Ada, starey-eyed, black hair straggly-loose about her white face, biting and licking her fingers as if they were all-day suckers, laughing quick-like, as quick-like frowning, walking up and down back streets, her shirt waist on backward or a Mother Hubbard tied about her with a patent leather belt, walking, walking through Nigger Quarters, across the ball ground, sometimes in palmettos on the edge of the hammock, walking, walking, and then slipping into the back door of the drug store.

She lived in Old Town with her mother whom encroaching Nigger Quarters and ever enlarging cemetery could not drive into the newer Maxwell. If you walked about a bit after a burying reading old tombstones and wandered over to the West Side past the pauper lot where the thin edge of the swamp creeps up close to Maxwell—the hammock it is called, being dryer and higher here—you would see the old log house built by Miss Ada's great-grandfather and you might see Miss Ada but you'd be sure to see Miss Ada's old, old mother sitting on the stoop, shut in by an ancient greenness of tall box hedge and moss covered board roof.

Or you *might* meet Miss Ada face to face as you came around a tall tombstone and then, if you did, she would smile sweetly and laugh softly and you would laugh with her and suddenly you both would stop; and she would look through you and haughtily pick up the train of her white wedding gown and carefully pick her way among the crowded graves, while you watched her move stately among tall marble tombstones, cool and dim under big oaks, through the gray mist of softly floating Spanish moss. They said he died of typhoid a day before the wedding and she had buried him on her wedding day twenty years ago—before you were born—but she would say differently if you dared ask her, and once you *had* dared, whispering as your eyes slid smoothly over yellowed satin but never quite reached her face, "Miss Ada, are you married?" and she half whispered back "Yes, dear . . . are you?"

Miss Ada never came to church, nor her old mother grown too feeble to walk the distance from Old Town to College Street where the churches were. But almost every one else came to church. Even Mr. Prentiss Reid, publisher of Maxwell's weekly newspaper and an infidel. He came to listen to the sermon in order to have something to argue about the next week, the Harris children's papa said, always adding "But Prentiss Reid is a superior man, a superior man" and mama would always answer "No man can be superior who does not believe in God."

On the first Sunday of the month old Opie Culpepper, syphilitic and mangy, uncombed gray hair dribbling down his neck, some of his sores bandaged, some left open "fer a breath of God's good air" he'd tell you out of swollen, cracked, pus-thickened lips, "ain't no need" he'd tell you "ter be ashamed of yer ail*ments* when the good God gived 'em ter you"—on the first Sunday old Opie Culpepper took Holy Communion kneeling first at the altar rail, taking the first draught of the Lord's Blood out of the big silver cup which would in turn be offered all communicants, while the bowed congregation watched and tried not to see, tried not to think, tried only to sing *Break Thou the Bread of Life*, tried only to beg of their God forgiveness for their manifold sins.

Among those who besides zealous old Opie responded to the first invitation to partake of the Lord's Supper were the prominent citizens: the school superintendent, the Board of Stewards of the church, the cashier of the Maxwell National Bank, and the newly converted. Whenever big, hulky, red-faced Gus Rainey, butcher and owner of the meat market, was newly converted he went up promptly, very simply kneeling next old Opie Culpepper—for never was a creature of God more humble than Big Gus after a conversion. Like a clumsy, overgrown yearling, he'd fall down beside the altar, his protuberant belly squeezed against the carved slender rails, knees on the raised carpeted ledge, bottomside of number 12 shoes blaring out in the faces of the children on the front pew, big bottom blaring out too, while he humbly mumbled vague penitences to God for His having made him the weak, forlorn, sinful creature he was. But he was not always there. There were the months each year when he sat on the back pew of the church wriggling around, pew creaking, until in utter confusion he would rise and tiptoe out of the church, often in his stupefied embarrassment running straight into the bell rope in the vestibule, causing a faint clang of the great bell above to shiver through the stillness of the service. And there were other months when he would not come near the church; sitting out in front of his market on Sundays, whittling, his big, red, chuffy face still set in its good nature but ready at one hopeful glance from a church member to sull up; or hidden from the eyes of the town, sleeping off one of the jags for which a few months later at the annual revival the good God would have to forgive him . . .

"While these retire let others come" was the signal for the ladies of the congregation to move forward. A few men came then too, it is true, lukewarm members who went to be a good example to their families. But this second group was made up largely of the wives of the church officials, the Sunday School teachers and those good women who, while eager to repent of their transgressions felt that there was, after all, a ladylike way to do everything.

The third invitation from the minister brought a rush of children who tried to walk slowly but fell against each other awkwardly, stung by the impact of a hundred pairs of grown-up eyes on their backs, and finally in a sudden huddle flopped down on the altar ledge.

On Sunday afternoon in Maxwell you walked down the railroad track where lilies bloomed in late spring in the ponds and ditches on either side the embankment and violets grew in deep blue patches on the grassy slants and yellow jessamine filled the hammock with sweetness; or out to the cemetery where inscriptions were read again and again:

Born 1830–Died 1865
Born 1903–Died 1904
Born 1895–Died 1900
Born 1814–Died 1890

until death rang its slow bell in your heart and God seemed close, and eternity very near but none of it dreadful for you were young and no one you loved had ever died and old green moss on cool marble felt good to the touch and phlox blooming at your feet were pink-sweet and the laughter and talk of companions crisp and sure, and the sun was still bright and glimmery.

But when the three tall, magnificent monuments of the dead Harwell family had thrown thin shadows far across the tiny baby grave which had no headstone, only a mound of old dirt hardly longer or bigger than some of the toad-frog houses you had built when you were little, when shadows touched the poor little unknown baby's grave, it was time to walk back to College Street and home. The way you liked best to return wound between two old family grave lots. Twisted green-old iron fence ensquared crumbling brick tombs, falling apart until big gaping holes beckoned curious eyes and one by one bright sure voices hushed, you passed through ancient creaking gate and knelt beside the last feeble gesture at immortality of some one's dust, peering through dark vacancies, smelling dank moss, old lime and unsunned dirt but believing you smelt decayed flesh (half hoping you did). Here death laid bony fingers on young, warm shoulders and pressed cool pains to the heart. And suddenly the cemetery was a place of mystery and gloom and dry rot, heaven far away and inaccessible, and only the familiar square of home on College Street held warmth and security and life.

It was not until the archway of the cemetery was left far behind and the African Methodist Episcopal Church was near where good pungent earthy living Negro odor drove away the smell of death that hearts beat young again. Thick, musky body odor mixed with musky Hoyt's German cologne, gay laughter, wiggling black bodies of young girls dressed in white folks' castoff finery, nuzzling against big, black, flashy bucks fresh from the turpentine stills. They had a way, these bright-faced, high-smelling couples of pushing you off the sidewalk. Laughing hard, avoiding your eyes, they would walk straight ahead, as though through you, giving in not an inch to your physical presence, until with a sudden nudge of turpentine-hardened muscle you were off and walking in deep sand. You knew in a muddled way that this made up to the wenches for wearing your big sister's cast-off dresses or some other white girl's dresses, but it made you mad, and once mad, life grew immediate and real . . .

Bright, like striped stick candy they looked, gathered in little clusters in front of the old ramshackly A.M.E. Church or coupled off, walking with Sunday arrogance up and down the sidewalk. On Monday they would be once more quiet, respectful laborers and as laborers comprehensible and well-liked but now, maddened at the insult of being pushed into sandspurs, an insult you knew well was intended for your white color and not a personal you, you felt Them as you felt Them in the thick, black mobs on Saturday nights down town where you never went if you were a Harris girl, or any other nice white Maxwell girl, unattended by an adult white male. There threading your way through the black strong-smelling mass of flesh and bone and muscle clothed in blue overalls worn alike by mill hands, cotton hands, turpentine hands, you knew that unnamed always untalked-about fear of the Negro . . .

Fifty blacks to one white, they were on Saturday nights, when all the cotton hands had come in from the farms, scrouging each other, laughing loud, talking big, sometimes silent, sometimes shy when picking out a piece of calico fur de ol' 'oman, showing gold teeth (the dandies), buying tight, new shoes that they'd slit across the top next day to make room for crowded toes, buying pink suspenders, buying a little candy, buying a little snuff, a little flour, a little likker, handing over to white men in stores all the money other white men had given them for a long week's labor.

Later in the night there would be razor fights and by Sunday morning the calaboose would be full . . . some nigger gal's throat would likely be slit from ear to ear, or a buck knifed to the heart. But that, unless it happened to be your family's house girl or cook or your washwoman's daughter, you would hear little about—or nothing. Only after the sun had gone down beyond the Great Swamp did the streets of Maxwell turn full black, when the saw mill shut down, when the logging teams loaded with men came in from the camps, when the turpentine hands, grayed and smeared with rosin and pitch, walked the four miles in or rode the big mules, and field hands in wobbly wheeled wagons lighted by pitch torches came through twisting sand ruts from faraway shanties . . . Then the white race, save for the vendors and the keepers of the peace, quietly disappeared. It was nigger night. It was Sad'dy . . . And the streets were theirs.

Eighteen hundred people moving in a small town procession and you knew them all by name, or most of them. Some you saw buried, heard the dull hollow *plunk* of a fresh smelling clod of dirt dropped on the coffin lowered already in the hole. *Dust to dust* . . . you heard the minister say gravely and always the bereaved family caught their breath in quite audible sobs at this betrayal of immortality and always your heart was caught too in the strangling age-second of misery, a little for the dust in that new spaded hole but mostly for that clear, empty knowledge of the end to all things . . . so soon again to be forgotten. Some you saw so fresh-born that shame surged through you at the sheer ugliness of birth and in your embarrassment your tongue thickened so that your words to the exhausted prideful mother were inaudible and you were glad when her smile released you and you could run from the room . . .

And as Maxwell moved in its swinging orbit from God to money, dying, giving birth, marrying, laughing, hating, drinking, fornicating (only that word the Harris children knew to be a Bible word and one not used by real people, though they often wondered what word real people did use if they used one, knowing only the short words scrawled on the school privy), the Harris children ran here and there, watching, listening, touching, smelling, drawing in great draughts of life, unknowing that they drank.

[Spring 1936]

Dope with Lime Columns

Visit to Margaret Mitchell

Referring to the popular nickname for Coca-Cola and its overly sweet taste being cut with lime juice, Smith's Dope with Lime columns featured wide-ranging personal commentary that differed in tone and style from her more formal book reviews. Almost bloglike by today's standards, chatty, witty with a bite, the first column's account of the editors' visit with Margaret Mitchell (who reportedly greeted Smith and Snelling with the question, "Which is which?") creates a provocative set-up for Smith's later review of *Gone With the Wind.*

Perched high up on Old Screamer swinging our legs over "space and the twelve clean winds," good fun that it is, doesn't make for literary tittle tattle. Squirrels and whipporwills [sic] don't like it and our mountaineer friend Joe says thar ain't no sech varmint roun' thet he's heerd tell of, but thar's a sight of mournin' doves and he's been aimin' ter name it ter us ter look out for a uncommon summer.

As indeed we are: for not since Caroline Miller's *Lamb in His Bosom* have Georgians shown so much anticipatory excitement as *Gone with the Wind* by Margaret Mitchell of Atlanta has aroused. Edwin Granberry, reviewer for the New York Sun, writes us that his enthusiasm, soon to be expressed in much print, is boundless.

So... Dope with Lime took off their mountain boots, put on their town clothes and after an interval of space and time knocked on Miss Mitchell's door. A very small keen-eyed red-headed attractive person asked, "Which is which?" said immediately, "I'm scared to death. Do come in." But curled up on a divan, drinking black coffee, she really did not look scared but very alert and intelligent and vivacious with the situation well in the hollow of her hand, and seemed far more interested in discussing Faulkner, Cabell, Emily Clark, Wolfe, and some mutual friends than her own book. "I'm sick to death of it," she groaned. "You would be too if you had spent six months checking ten thousand references—or was it twenty?"

"Were they all wrong?"

"They were right. But you see, I didn't know they were. I wrote the book never expecting to publish it, from my memory of the thousands of conversations I have listened to all my life about Lee, Sherman, Lincoln, Longstreet, Appomattox, the Battle of Atlanta . . . I didn't write of the past," she laughed, "but of contemporary happenings. Time has stood still hereabouts." Again she laughed. "I had to check. I don't dare face some good old Confederate soldier, whiskers bristling with indignation as he points his finger at me and says 'Sister, you said Lee was in that cornfield north of the old cow pasture on the morning of July 14, 1863, when by God he was in the cornfield a mile south of that one.' You can't . . . not safely."

She calls her book "a Victorian novel," insists that she has no theories of style, trying only to avoid journalese. But she says she wrote the first chapter seventy times. She is very modest, seems to prefer visiting her friends in little Georgia towns to New York literary teas, declares her book unimportant, herself unimportant, has no desire to be a "writer" and hopes the Lord will protect her from writing another book.

[Summer 1936]

On *Lanterns on the Levee*

Smith's columns grew increasingly bold in attacking all forms of white supremacy, especially the hypocrisy of the South's and the nation's defense of racial segregation as America prepared to go to war to defend democracy. In her winter 1941 Dope with Lime, she critiqued the "sham gentlemanness" of William Alexander Percy's *Lanterns on the Levee.*

Lanterns on the Levee, a best seller in Southern states, is an anachronism with a highly rubbed patina. Those who enjoy surfaces without looking at substance can read this book without pain; those who wear the aura of racial superiority will acknowledge with satisfaction the halo which the author has woven so delicately around his own head. Others will lift eyebrows at a tasteless though muted expression of white arrogance in an unhappy year when white men, if ever in their existence, should be bowed down with humility for the chaos they have brought upon themselves. Some, reading the book and pondering its immense popularity South and North, will grow sick at heart for the future of a people who can write and read with pleasure words which burn candles at the shrine of racial and class superiority at the very moment they are sending their sons to die for democracy and the brotherhood of man.

A book like this is more disturbing to L.E.S. than a Georgia demagogue's cheap tricks. It is easy for intelligent people to reject violent and vulgar expressions of race chauvinism; it seems more difficult for them to resist the seductive chanting of those same words if modulated and muted to a well-bred softness.

The 'lyrical longing to be a gentleman'—how it aches in the hearts of southerners! That it is a sham gentlemanliness we long for is no matter. . . . Driven by our insecurities, aching with unconscious and conscious fears and dreads and frustrations, we feverishly continue to blow ourselves up from miniature dimensions to the magnificent proportions of a super race and a super class.

It is a grotesque and comic thing. One could forget it in a great gust of sane and healthy laughter were it not so malevolent in its effects upon mankind.

[Winter 1941]

Book Reviews

The following book reviews illustrate the magazine's clear challenge to the establishment writers of the 1930s, the New Critics, the Agrarians and Fugitives, and their generally racist and masculinist reading of Southern history and culture. Smith's exemplary review of work by Claude McKay and about Paul Laurence Dunbar further supports her understanding of African American literary history as integral to any discussion of Southern and American letters and culture. The reviews also reflect Smith's intentional inclusion of the Southern and national record of lynchings and gross injustice, as well as currents of awakening to different ideals. Significantly, Smith revealed her own ideals as a writer when she wrote of McKay: "He refused to be a 'race man' though uncompromising and fearless in his pride of race; refused to be a Communist though in sympathy with workers; refused to be a reformer; he is, he says with disarming simplicity, a poet."

One More Sigh for the Good Old South

Gone with the Wind, by Margaret Mitchell, Macmillan Co. $3.00

Because of the author's unsure psychological grasp of character and limited historical perspective the 1037 pages of Scarlett's amorous and monetary adventures seem to this reviewer in their essence hardly more than a sentimental effusion enameled with box-office candor and debunking bluster. Regretfully it is said, for we too had long looked for the "great novel of the South" and had hoped that this was it. It isn't.

The book of course has numerous surface merits: written in a nervous vivacious colloquial manner it swings the reader along at a rapid and effortless pace—its plot concocted of the new and old stock-in-trade of melodrama (murder, attempted rape, childbirth with all details, deaths, passionate and not so passionate love scenes, flights from danger) laid against a background clear-cut in its authentic detail, of war, Ku Klux activities, Carpetbagger regime, has all of its strings with their little beads of suspense tied neatly and skillfully—the whole overlaid with witty comments and a gruff humor which stiffens up the sentimentality. Miss Mitchell's sense of comedy is strong and she handles deftly those scenes where it predominates—in sharp contrast to the woodenness of her "emotional" passages. Her knowledge of the Civil War-Reconstruction period is admirable and so precise and comprehensive is her acquaintance with the customs of the time and the scenes of that early, young Atlanta that she achieves an atmosphere of contemporaneity (despite hoop skirts and stays) which is in the nature of a *tour de force.*

Yet as a whole the book wobbles badly like an enormous house on very shaky underpinnings. For although Miss Mitchell's knowledge of the period from 1850–75 is adequate she does not seem to possess the understanding of distant historical backgrounds and social origins necessary for grasping and evaluating the complexities inherent in the period and its people. Too often she seems to be one with her characters in accepting and acting upon premises which, however valid they once seemed to people of a certain narrow culture (albeit a gracious and in spots pleasant one) surely now we can hold no longer important. As we protest the interpretation of our American life today solely in terms of Capitalistic (or of Marxist) ideology so we protest the interpretation, however unconscious, of Southern life seventy years ago in nostalgic terms of old Planter-ideology. An artist comprehends the social-economic-intellectual assumptions of a period, their implications and effect upon personality but surely he must remain detached and critical of them. Just as it would be difficult for most of us today, when half the world is starving or killing or preparing to kill each other and many of the other half tangled up despairingly in their own emotional problems, to take seriously the feuds, conventions, snobbery and ambitions of Atlanta's Society Set (or any other town's) so it is difficult for us to read without boredom of the trivial social snobbery of the Atlanta of Reconstruction Days. Yet the author gives us the impression that she, despite her laughter, thinks it somehow important. Perhaps inadvertently. Perhaps it is a fault of method rather than assumption, due to a vacillation between the satirical and sympathetic attitudes. Consistent satire might have avoided the appearance of straddling the fence—and turned into a comedy of manners, against a legitimately exciting background, what so often edges on sentimental twaddle.

As wavering as her comprehension of historical realities is her understanding of the inner life of her characters. To attempt the creation of character, the probing of personality without recognizing and comprehending the dynamic force of the unconscious as it plays upon and determines so powerfully the external manifestations of personality is, frankly, to be naïve. Whether we wish it or no, the findings of Freud and his followers have not only made for us enormous extensions of knowledge in the realms of the spirit but by their very nature are changing the intrinsic quality of that spirit . . . While there have been from time to time since the existence of novelists and poets rare individuals who could penetrate the depths of the soul with intuitive, profound insight without the assistance of Freud, most past writers have been impoverished by the lack of the knowledge he has given us and its point of view; for contemporary writers it is very simply a *sine qua non.* And Miss Mitchell is no exception. The absence of this subtle and sensitive comprehension of the motives and feelings of her characters places her work on the level of slick, successful but essentially mediocre fiction; and no amount of high spirits, "God's nightgowns," and witty comments (entertaining as they undoubtedly are) can compensate in the opinion of this reviewer for the lack. But perhaps we are treating too seriously a book which has no claim surely on literature but is rather a curious puffball compounded of printer's ink and bated breath, rolled in sugary sentimentality, stuck full of spicy Southern taboos, intended for and getting mass consumption. Harmless enough. Unless it has done what its publishers claim—"set a brand new standard for fiction." *That* we should be inclined to take seriously.

[Fall 1936]

Along Their Way

A Long Way from Home. By Claude McKay. Lee Furman. $2.50.
Paul Laurence Dunbar. By Benjamin Brawley. Univ. of N.C. Press. $1.00.

In the mellow year of 1891 when tender-hearted Americans choked up over *Little Boy Blue,* batted moist eyes at the cadences of *An Old Sweetheart of Mine,* and lynched two hundred and fifty citizens mostly Negroes, male and female, there lived in Dayton, Ohio, a young boy who had composed the song for the graduating class of Central High School. Paul was the only Negro in the class. He was president of the Philomathean Literary Society and editor of *The High School Times.* He admired the song he had composed, the other members of the class admired it, and many people in the audience thought it remarkable. It began thus:

Why stirs with sad alarm the heart
For all who meet must some day part?

So let no useless cavil be;
True wisdom bows to God's decree.

There were seven more verses like this one, or practically like it.

Paul Laurence Dunbar had begun his literary career and although it was destined to follow the spongy path of the Heart Throbbers which Eugene Field and James Whitcomb Riley were rapidly widening into a highway broad enough for all democracy to travel in comfort, it was not to be an easy way for him. For Paul was a Negro. This fact confronted him with its usual firmness. He gave up his cherished plan for a college education and took a job at four bucks a week as an elevator boy. He continued to write verse, continued to send it away to magazines. And after a time bits of it began to be published here and there. In 1893, with the help of a physician of Dayton, his first book *Oak and Ivy* was printed. It was a little thing, crude in format, containing verse no better, but no worse, than that of his contemporaries, Frank Stanton and Ella Wheeler Wilcox.

Down in Georgia, Governor Atkinson had shocked several million southerners by making his sportsmanlike suggestion that prisoners be unshackled from handcuffs and permitted to defend their own lives if sheriffs were unable, as so many sniveled they were, to protect them. Such realism was too coarse for the stomachs of people nourished on *Mighty Lak A Rose, Over the Hill to the Poorhouse*, and two hundred and fifty lynchings a year—and they turned away from it in nauseous disgust. What Paul Laurence Dunbar thought of it, we do not know. What he thought of his race's misery, we cannot discover from his verses. His biographer declares his sympathy and he is doubtless right. But Dunbar was a singer, a maker of pleasant rhymes, an artificer working in the materials of those everyday surface experiences which euphemize the word 'human.' Simple, sincere, not troubled by intellectual complexities, Dunbar sang his songs; and singing, quietly unloosed the handcuffs of white skepticism which, more than white hate, had locked his race so desperately fast to their American heritage.

For Dunbar was not only a Negro; he was black. Black, pure African—and yet he could sing. No better—and that was fortunate for his race for there would have been few ears to hear in the last decade of the 19th century—but no worse than the white singers of the period. There had of course been others. Since Jupiter Hammon's *An Evening Thought, Salvation by Christ With Pennettential Cries* appeared in 1760 and little prim, pedantic Phillis Wheatley's first volume was published in 1773, there had been no less than thirty-odd Negroes who had published volumes of verse, none of which had been widely read. But now America was listening. The Negro race had found its poet.

In 1895 courageous Frederick Douglass died, ingratiating Booker T. Washington made his famous Atlanta speech, and Dunbar published his second volume of poems called *Majors and Minors.*

If one will look closely at the soul of that decade, raw and bleeding with its 1800 lynchings and the most bitter labor exploitation this country had known, obscene in its greed for more and more riches and power, and then turn aside and touch the lavender and old lace of its sentiments, one can read *When Malindy Sings* and *When the Co'n pone's hot* and not censure too harshly a young Negro poet who could not, despite talent, rise above the silly drool of the times and its white leaders.

The day had not come for honest words.

But there were in Atlanta even then three Negroes who later were to speak clearly to their own race. Dr. Burghardt DuBois was teaching in Atlanta University and writing that poignant book *The Souls of Black Folk* which later challenged black and white with its bitter, heart-breaking candor; James Weldon Johnson was completing his studies at the same school before beginning a career phenomenal in its success of ragtime writer, collector of Negro Spirituals, U.S. consul to Nicaragua, writer of many books among them the beautiful *God's Trombones* and that thoughtful and provocative address, *Negro Americans: What Now?*; Walter White, a small child then, was drawing into himself those impressions which were later to give him the courage to risk his life many times while investigating and publicizing scores of lynchings.

But the time was not ready as young white Theodore Dreiser was discovering and it was perhaps well for the black race that Dunbar preferred to write of co'n pones and courtin'.

He died of tuberculosis in February 1906, having published many books of verse, several novels and numerous essays in the magazines of the period.

Because I have loved so vainly
And sung with such faltering breath,
The Master in infinite mercy
Offers the boon of death . . .

Hardly had these words faded from America's ears than there pounded like iron strokes of a bell of mourning, piercing the heart, the stark anguished cry of *The Litany of Atlanta*:

". . . Bewildered we are, and passion-tost, mad with the madness of a mobbed and murdered people; straining at the armposts of Thy throne, we raise our shackled hands and charge Thee, God, by the bones of our stolen fathers, by the tears of our dead mothers, by the very blood of Thy crucified Christ: *What meaneth this*? Tell us the Plan; give us the Sign!

Keep not thou silence, O God! Sit no longer blind, Lord God, deaf to our prayer and dumb to our dumb suffering. Surely Thou too art not white, O Lord, a pale, bloodless, heartless thing!

Ah! Christ of all the Pities!

Forgive the thought! Forgive these wild, blasphemous words. Thou art still the God of our black fathers, and in Thy soul's soul sit some soft darkenings of the evening, some shadowings of the velvet night...."

With passion and dignity, no longer simulating the grin of a clown to please 'white folks' or the humility and meekness white Christians demanded of black, *The Litany* bravely rang in a new period for Negroes. Dunbar had quietly unlocked the handcuffs, DuBois gave the courage to live.

The old-timey Negro was dead; long live the new. There was a quickening of blood in Negro veins, new energy, fresh hope, versatility of talent, exuberance of spirits. And there began movements as diverse in results as the Negro theater activity flowering in such artist-comedians as Bert Williams, Bob Cole, Rosamond Johnson ... and later such serious actors as Paul Robeson, Richard B. Harrison ... a succession of musical shows which reached their peak in the 1920's ... the quick fame of the Fisk Singers ... numerous collections of spirituals and work songs ... the Memphis Blues and, long after, its child 'Swing'... the Urban League and its magazine *Opportunity* ... in 1910, the magazine *Crisis* which so quickly acquired a nation-wide circulation ... the National Association for the Advancement of Colored People.

In 1912 was published James Weldon Johnson's *Autobiography of an Ex-Colored Man*, a novel revolutionary in its frankness but rarely read by whites until it was re-issued in 1927.

And all this time Negroes were moving into Harlem....

Into this ferment of progress, hope, fear, came a Negro from Jamaica, very eager and very black. Claude McKay had published a slim volume of poems *Songs from Jamaica*. They had been reviewed in the West Indies, in England, France, Germany, but America had not noticed. McKay wanted to find his American audience and, very simply, came to it. Two years he studied at Kansas State University, a short period at Tuskegee and then went out and met America face to face, as a laborer. Longshoreman, Pullman dining-car waiter, butler in tails ... McKay took his jobs in his stride, made friends white and black, a few enemies, loved, listened, played, laughed, wrote poetry.

He begins his autobiography with an amusing account of a meeting with Frank Harris in 1918 and in few pages with admirable selection gives a deft portrait of 'the great editor.' There follow in quick succession sketches of Max Eastman, his sister Crystal, Floyd Dell, days on *The Liberator*, the publication in it of the sonnet "If We Must Die" which was reprinted in every Negro paper in America, recited from Negro pulpits and taught to Negro children. Those words:

If we must die—let it not be like hogs
Hunted and penned in an inglorious spot . . .

stirred American Negroes as they had never been stirred before.

In time the book covers that most interesting and active period of Negro achievement known as the Negro renaissance. But while James Weldon Johnson calls McKay a leader of it, McKay, perhaps modestly, says he has had little or no part in it. He has consistently refused to be a 'race man' though uncompromising and fearless in his pride or race; refused to be a Communist though in sympathy with workers; refused to be a reformer; he is, he says with disarming simplicity, a poet.

Such heresy the Communists and propagandists spue out of their mouths. You must go the whole hog or not a squeal. Eugene Gordon declares writers like Fauset, DuBois, James W. Johnson worked only for special rights for themselves . . . Eugene Clay says there is a great need for Negroes to grow "more revolutionary" and brightly proceeds to discount the work of DuBois and B. T. Washington . . . He says Langston Hughes has taken a 'decisive step to the left.' His works from 1926–1931 were 'linked in his evolution with only occasional retrogressions.' One re-reads the beautiful "I have known rivers" and that lovely little lyric "De railroad bridge's/A sad song in de air" and gives thanks for the retrogressions of our poets.

Young Langston Hughes, influenced surely by McKay, once said, "We younger Negro artists who create now intend to express our individual dark-skinned selves without fear or shame. If white people are pleased we are glad. If they are not, it does not matter. We know we are beautiful. And ugly too. The tom tom cries and the tom tom laughs. If colored people are pleased we are glad. If they are not, their displeasure doesn't matter . . ." But recently he has said ". . . Negroes should be writing to expose racial discrimination and evils . . . join with white workers . . ."

At all this orthodoxy McKay laughs a big black laugh and goes on his way.

His first novel *Home to Harlem* (1928), attacked by self-conscious members of his race who believe—and one can understand their reasons—that only admirable, intelligent Negro characters should be put in novels, is an interesting, honest book, and perhaps the most widely read of novels written by Negroes during the past fifteen years. In sensuous imagery it is excelled by Jean Toomer's *Cane*, a book which fits no category; in movement and vitality, by none. Jessie Fauset's novels are more analytical, are as sensitive, as intelligent (McKay calls them 'little primroses') but lack its power. Zora Neale Hurston's are richer with folklore but stiff, and somehow unmoving. Rudolph Fisher is as detached, as honest; John Matheus is more versatile and has superior technical brilliance. But none of these has had the influence or gained the audience which is McKay's.

The truth is, there has not yet come from the Negro race a first class novel. Honest ones, yes, and colorful and dealing with intrinsically interesting material, but lacking power of characterization, perspective, beauty of prose. They have done better with their autobiographies. *A Long Way from Home* is more personal, more colorful than James W. Johnson's *Along This Way* but lacks the close touch with Negro movements and the Negro intelligentsia which gave Johnson's book its interest and value. McKay is a more ingratiating writer, achieving the miracle of talking continuously about himself without seeming to; and he touches penetratingly upon people and movements in Europe and America which are worth reading about.

In its exuberant candor the book is sharply contrasted with Benjamin Brawley's biography of Dunbar. Mr. Brawley has done a plodding, unimaginative job with his study. One sniffs the faint odor of an obituary. It is a pity. Surely the first Negro in America to be acclaimed with nation-wide enthusiasm as a poet deserves franker treatment. While one suspects that Dunbar's mind was as conventional as his verses, one is certain the man's life digressed from beaten paths. Perhaps this little book was indeed just a 'job' for Mr. Brawley between more important works; he can write well when he is interested, as he has often proved.

[Spring 1937]

Reminiscences of China

Before Smith began writing *Strange Fruit*, she wrote a novel called *And the Waters Flow On* based on her own experiences and those of people she knew while teaching at a girls mission school in Huchow, China, from 1922 to 1925. Because the original manuscript was destroyed when Smith's home burned in 1955, the following sketches selected and edited by Smith for publication in her magazine are all that remain. However, these sketches more than adequately illuminate and justify her repeated reference to knowledge gained in China. Having written about the abuse of power, hypocrisy, and cultural blindness exhibited by white American Southerners and other Westerners in remote China, Smith turned her critical vision more directly to similar abuses of power and hypocrisy in America's failure to ensure democratic freedoms at home.

The two sketches appear together in *From the Mountain* under the title "Reminiscences of China." Originally "He That Is Without Sin . . ." was published in *North Georgia Review* in the Winter 1937–38 issue, and "And the Waters Flow On" was included in the Summer 1938 issue. Smith's original endnotes are denoted by asterisks within the text.

He That Is without Sin . . .

On the afternoon of Saturday, May 30, 1925, we sat in a boat on a canal in Chekiang province and talked of China. My companion who had lived many years in the interior was explaining to me—a novice of three years' residence—the origins of the intense and then wide-spread anti-British feeling.

And as she talked I listened, but only politely, for my thoughts were of Chinese friends from whom I had parted that morning, and my eyes were lingering in reluctance to leave forever the countryside through which the small boat pushed so slowly.

"The first open hostility," she was saying, "was in 1839 over opium which the British against the laws of China persisted in selling. The Chinese lost that war. Another followed in 1856. From these two wars the British gained a big slice of China: Hongkong, extraterritoriality, concessions, fourteen open ports, 'most favored nation' treaties, legalized opium, access to the Yangtze river, special indulgences for missionaries, indemnities."

The train of boats crept slowly under an old arched bridge, paused in a narrow village canal edged with shops and homes where the elders sipped tea from beautiful fragile bowls and beggars whined for alms and young girls with thin arched brows peeked through embroidered curtains of sedan chairs.

"A nice haul. They get what they want, these British." Smells of fried food, and *tsai*, and bean-curd and incense slipped from the street above us to the boat. Nearby a man gravely sat on a big toilet pot, his silken gown gathered carefully about his hips.

"Usually. In 1895 the Japanese succeeded at last in wresting Korea from China. They had had their eye on the little peninsula from the 16th century but had made no attempt since that time to invade it. In the 60's and 70's however Japan went modern, reorganized her entire country, resources, habits, and girding up her modernity plunged into Western aggressiveness, found that she liked it, and snatched Korea away from China. Now China had no real claim on Korea, save an anomalous suzerainty which she had established over the unwilling Koreans and had no intention of handing to Japan, unless forced to. Japan easily and quickly defeated her. To save Peking Li Hung Chang signed a treaty which gave the Japanese about all they could think to ask for including 200,000,000 taels in indemnity. That was the bankers' cue to appear on the stage. They came, British, French, German, each wanting his share of the loans which China was forced to make in order to pay this 'debt' to Japan."

The boat moved on. A wayside shrine with its paint peeling off... a window's arch curving blackly against the late afternoon light...

"And the United States, all this time?"

"Was using tact. Whenever the British pushed the Chinese against the wall and forced her to sign a piece of paper, the U.S. was just behind her asking for an autograph too. And got it. As did France. Whenever something was wanted, they merely waited until a missionary-incident occurred. Nor did they have long to wait. In 1870 a massacre at Tientsin, in 1875 the death of an interpreter, opened four more cities to the British; in 1890 and '91 anti-Christian riots in the Yangtze paved the way for more privileges. In 1897 several German missionaries were killed in Shantung. Germany at once seized Tsingtao, asked for and received a 99-year lease on the port and land controlling Kiaochow bay, and railway and mining leases. This was all the excuse Russia needed to occupy Port Arthur. Great Britain obtained Wei-hai-wei for 'so long a period' she said 'as Russia occupies Port Arthur.' France took Kwangchow-wa."

"And the United States?"

"Uncle Sam was busy with other matters, Hawaii and the Philippines, but called to the boys to be sure to keep the door open . . . Then some one thought of spheres of influence and immediately, like ants running to and fro over a big juicy worm, the Powers busied themselves allocating the country to capital. Until China grew afraid and suddenly turned furiously upon the foreigners who had already so weakened her. And that brings us to the Boxer Rebellion."

"It goes on and on like a Chinese play, doesn't it?"

A small houseboat with five ragged, dirty, redcheeked children on its deck, and a pot of pink geranium, drew up close, suddenly darted out into the stream. The train of boats circled a small island on which stood an old crumbling pagoda. A junk with red-brown sail bellied out by the breeze glided by. The stream grew narrow again. On either side were dull blobs of graves, here and there the yellow of a fresh coffin.

"The Chinese lost their composure and for once forgot their good manners. There had been much unrest due to aggression of foreigners, the reforms of the Chinese themselves and the sudden reactionary edicts of the Empress Tzu Hsi. Secret societies of 'Boxers' composed largely of rowdies much like our Ku Klux Klan were multiplying. Then on December 31, 1899, an English missionary was killed, and the country was in an uproar. Even so, matters might have been smoothed over had not an international force taken the Taku forts which opened the way to Peking and Tientsin. This was the last straw. Empress Tzu Hsi against the advice of more levelheaded counselors issued an edict to kill all foreigners. The German minister was killed, numerous missionaries and business people, thousands of Christian Chinese, the legations besieged. The Powers while not declaring war put down the riots with their usual efficiency, captured Peking, and looted the capital. For this attack of nerves and loss of temper the Chinese were charged up with 450,000,000 taels as indemnity* to be paid in 39 years, required to suspend civil examinations for five years, required to punish by death

*In 1908 the U.S. announced its policy of returning a portion of its share of the Boxer indemnity. Sums remitted were set aside for Chinese scholarships for study in America. U.S. remitted unpaid portions of indemnity May, 1924. Other Powers made preliminary plans for remission but all plans called for allocation of funds to educational and cultural projects which merely raised a new danger of educational "spheres of influence." [Original note.]

certain officials held responsible for the affair, to erect memorials to the German minister and others, and to give the foreigners the right to fortify and police the legation quarters. Disorders had spread now to Manchuria so Russia promptly sent large numbers of troops ostensibly to protect her subjects but actually to occupy—which she did ruthlessly—much of three provinces. At the same time she secured an agreement from China whereby she came into control of much of southern Manchuria. Immediately Japan and Great Britain became alarmed, formed the Anglo-Japanese pact, with the help of the U.S. exerted pressure on Russia who promised to withdraw her troops. But Russia procrastinated, showed more temper and greed with the result that in 1904 Japan felt that for the good of civilization she must go to war with her. Russia walked out of southern Manchuria; Japan walked in. Trouble began again. The U.S. did not like Japan's unfriendliness to her nationals, sought a railway concession herself, and proposed to neutralize the Manchurian railroads by a joint loan from the Powers. Immediately this brought Japan and Russia swooning into each other's arms against their common enemy, the Western Powers."

A soft rain had begun to fall. The stream grew wide. On either side as far as one could see stretched the cool green paddies of growing rice crisscrossed by darker slits where narrow canals ran. A cluster of thatched huts, enclosed by a mud wall, lay near the stream; a dog barked furiously at the boats as they passed. Someone on the roof above us coughed, cleared his throat, spat. A baby whimpered. A blind beggar played his *gi tzu* as he tapped tapped down the narrow run-way of the boat.

"Well . . ." she who had talked so long suddenly smiled. "You know the rest yourself. In 1911, the revolution. China became a republic. The seeds sown by foreign hands began to bear fruit in upheavals and confusions which have placed China today at the mercy of war lords. Tibet, Outer Mongolia took the opportunity to withdraw from China, never having felt a real part of her, and were pounced upon swiftly by Russia and Great Britain. In 1913 Yuan Shi Kai obtained what was called a 'reorganization loan' from Great Britain, France, Italy, Russia, Germany, and secured it by a lien on the salt monopoly. Sun Yat Sen, his radicals—the Kuomintang—protested bitterly but to no effect, and this salt has burned in the open festering sore of governmental chaos ever since. The World War began. Japan immediately seized Tsingtao 'from the Germans' and forthwith as much of Shantung as she could wrest from the Chinese. In 1915 she presented her infamous and secret Twenty-one Demands which practically gave her control of China. The terms of the treaty leaked out, the other Powers roared, Japan smilingly kowtowed to bigger bullies than she, until once more their backs were turned.[**] Then China reluctantly and under heavy pressure from the Allies entered the World War. At its close, believing she had proved herself worthy of a place in the family of nations, she sent to the peace conference a group of men, brilliant, astute, save in their expectations. They asked for the restoration of former German properties to China, for cancellation of spheres of influence, withdrawal of foreign troops, postoffice, telegraphic communication; restoration of foreign concessions and settlements to Chinese jurisdiction. They did not get it. So indignant were the young educated Chinese that the Japanese-controlled Peking government dared not sign the treaty. In 1921–22 the U.S. called the Washington Conference and having a twinge of conscience gave China the opportunity to lay her case before the world. Many promises were made. A few carried out. The foreign postoffices were abolished. Extraterritoriality was to be abolished 'if and when.' Since then the war lords have held the stage."

"And the British?"

"Are still the British. The Chinese believe they do not intend giving up extraterritorial rights or any other rights they now possess. The old treaty of 1902 has rankled a long time: British goods exempt from likin duty; a Britisher in charge of maritime customs. Thorns. It is perhaps their lack of tact that has caused much of the recent feeling. You've seen the sign on the Shanghai park 'Dogs and Chinese not allowed.' Rather humorless, isn't it?"

"You make out quite a case against them."

"I don't mean to. Japan is as culpable, and nearer. We have done our bit of dirty work (as have France and Russia); though we use better manners than the others."

The cabin was now dark. A candle was stuck on the narrow ledge above the door. The alcohol stove was lighted and coffee prepared to accompany the good food Ah Oo had put up for us. The poukais were unrolled and blankets spread on the two broad shelves that would serve as beds. Queer odors of coffee and cheese and wood-alcohol crept from the foreigners' cabin and mingled with familiar smells of fish and tsai, urine and opium. The Chinese said, "Foreigners are aboard," and the peasants stretched on the roof of our cabin peered below curiously to catch a glimpse of the foreign devils. In the next cabin some one coughed and

[**]Feb.–Mar., 1917, Japan made secret treaties with Great Britain, France, Italy whereby these Powers assured her their support at the peace conference to her demands for the former German holdings in Shantung. In Nov. 1917 the U.S. entered upon the Lansing-Ishii agreement by which she recognized that "because of territorial propinquity . . . Japan had special interests in China." That this was terminated in 1923 after the damage had been done is almost beside the point. [Original note.]

spat, coughed and spat without rest. The boat grew quiet. Only the slush-slush of the water against its sides and the low cough of the passenger next door.

By the time we had our coffee next morning the little launch was weaving its way through the traffic of the Whangpoo, very importantly whistling and belching smoke; now darting across the path of a Dollar steamship, now bullying the sampans cluttering around it. At last it could go no further. The boats were detached and we were poled through Soochow Creek to the launch office.

It was Sunday morning. We found a path across the crowded house-boats to the street and there called rickshas. As we waited we looked about us, glad once more to be in Shanghai. The street seemed very quiet, strangely deserted. And suddenly we felt it, the tension, and saw it in the eyes of the passers-by, in the forced smiles of launch-office clerks. "Something has happened," we said. And as we rode down Nanking Road toward the French Concession, past house after house closed and barred, shop after shop with drawn blinds, we said again to ourselves, "Something must have happened."

It was quickly told us. On Saturday afternoon a thousand or more Chinese students had paraded up Nanking Road carrying banners denouncing extraterritoriality. With such slogans as "Free the Students" ... "Give us back control of salt revenues" ... "We Demand Living Wages for Factory Workers" they had marched and thousands of spectators, Chinese and foreign, had watched them. Our friend who stood across from the British yamen had just said to someone near him, "It is like a football parade in America." Now they were in front of him. The students paused. Leaders conferred together. Then in a dog-trot they ran to the iron gates of the yamen, shouting, laughing, in sudden determination to free their fellow-students who had been imprisoned a short while before for leading a Chinese strike in one of the Japanese-owned cotton mills. In a great white mass they pushed toward the gates. The British officer in command gave a sharp order. Guns were raised, leveled into the mass of youngsters, fired. Six fell, instantly killed. Others were wounded. Confusion, uproar, screams, cries. And then abruptly, silence. Empty streets. Save for the six dead and the wounded.

Americans asked that night, why, why had not the British—if they felt compelled to repulse the crowd—turned the fire-hose on those kids? British imperialism replied that 'they had not thought of it.'

All Shanghai was very quiet that Sunday. There were conferences of Chinese behind closed doors. There were conferences of foreigners behind closed doors. A few mutual friends, Chinese and foreign, conferred together, determined to find a way to avoid this "crisis."

Doggedly the British as a group—with notable exceptions—maintained that the police were only doing their duty. The Americans were divided: business men were inclined to think "it's pretty bad but it's time something was done to show these fool students where to get off"; the missionaries, by no means unanimously, believed it a shocking and terrible piece of stupidity.

Mission schools in the nearby provinces closed. St. John University had its now-famous flag incident.

Tuesday I went to the Bund to buy gold for the trip to America. Exchange had taken a steep decline; there were rumors that the Chinese banks were suspending. On the way home I fell into line to board a street car. In front of me was a British woman of upper middle class status, in front of her a well dressed Chinese gentleman. As the Chinese started to board the car, the British lady kicked him, snarled, "You damned Chinaman, haven't you the manners to let a lady get on first?" The Chinese bowed, stood aside quietly, and let the female on. I followed her. On the way home, the street car was rocked. Windows were broken. A passenger cut on the arm. The conductor cut on the cheek.

On the steamer to America I was placed at a table with two American missionaries. The second day out, I invited a Chinese girl, graduate of Gingling College, who had been put at a small obscure table by herself, to sit with us. The missionaries barely acknowledged the introduction. The next meal they did not appear until my friend and I had finished. The following morning a dining room steward asked me to tell the Chinese student that the missionaries did not care to have her at their table.

Well... why go on? It was the beginning, as every one knows, of two years of intense anti-Chinese, anti-foreign feeling... of childish retaliations, of foolish defenses, of the rise of the Nationalists, culminating in the Nanking Affair where several foreigners were killed and others would have been, had not the foreign gun-boats in the Yangtze shelled the city.

And now tonight, January, 1938, as I write, the pictures of the Panay incident are being shown throughout the country and once more anger and hate and prejudices are being fanned into flames. To what end? This time it is against the Japanese. Three men were killed in the Panay incident, ruthlessly, without excuse. But remember, twelve years ago six Chinese youngsters were killed by the British, as ruthlessly, as needlessly. "The Japanese have no right in China; we can't sit by and see them steal her wealth and kill her people!" You hear it every day. But we Western imperialists have been stealing her wealth and killing her people for 100 years. "We can't sit by... there's our national honor..." No? We sit by and let our neighbors' children starve and do nothing about it. We sit by and see Negroes lynched and make no effort to punish the mob. We are not outraged when textile workers are killed, when miners starve. Here where we could defend our national honor with no bloodshed, with no risk of a collapse of civilization, we do nothing.[***] We've closed our eyes to the depredations Great Britain has made upon India; Gandhi has been for most of us only a stooge for our wisecracks. We forget Africa; we forget Mexico; the Philippines.

I am thinking of the spring of 1917. Of the war to end war. Of violated Belgium. Of the *Lusitania*. Of the American boys whose lives were wasted because munitions must be made, loans must be protected, cotton must be sold, faces saved. I am thinking of Wilson re-elected because "he will keep us out of war"; of April 6, 1917. I am thinking of Franklin Roosevelt who says, "We want peace" and begins an armament building program never equaled before in this country; of Landon who wires hysterically, "I am standing by you"; of the recession; of low-priced cotton; of unemployment so easily solved by the draft—and the upward curve of munitions; of the 'menace' of fascism; the 'menace' of communism; of the new cry, and its old death-echo, "Make the world safe for democracy."

[Winter 1937–38]

And the Waters Flow On

(*These glimpses of China are taken out of context from Miss Smith's writings.*) [Original Note.]

OLD PATTERNS

The city scarcely breathed in its quiet sleep. Only the dull beat of the priest's drum in the temple. Down on the river below the hospital hundreds of little houseboats crowded close together lay still, the black water smooth and tranquil under the pale light of the moon. A thin breeze pushed a few waves toward the shore, stirred slow ripples. There was no sound save the soft rubbing of wood against wood.

Gathered close by a crumbling wall built when Bethlehem was young, Lincheng lived on in the warm spring night, its crooked dark streets breathing in the old rhythm of love and hate and birth and death:

Across the city in an inner apartment of a wealthy silk merchant's home sat his wife and little wife gambling at mah jong. Fat, sleek, crafty,

[***]No isolationist am I. I believe in a consistent foreign policy that will promote peace. In 1931–32 we could have done something. In 1917 we could have done something. In 1919. Even in the 19th century. But during a war, when insanity prevails, how can one reason? And force only begets more hatred and inevitably war. L.E.S.

with black hair smoothly drawn back from their faces, they sat across from each other gossiping amiably and smoking cigarette after cigarette. They had been thus since late afternoon. Near each sat an old amah fanning her mistress—for the evening was warm and they had eaten heavily at a birthday feast at noon. Two bowls of tea now grown cold were nearby. The old amahs sleepily watched the moves made by their mistresses as they tirelessly played on and on . . .

. . . Down a dark narrow alley filled with the stench of a public latrine, trotted a servant boy lighting the way with his oil paper lantern while behind him clumped an old mid-wife scolding him for walking so fast. The boy not lessening his pace, laughed and said there was need of haste . . .

. . . In a private room of the hospital Tsang Ling Oo, of more than four-score years, lay staring at the shadowy wall in front of his bed. It had been a good life. An honorable member of the silk merchants' guild, a gentryman, he had kept the wealth left him by his venerable father and had added greatly to it. His wives had given him four sons and a number of daughters who were now married with children of their own. The last few years had been brightened by a plump merry-eyed concubine who tormented and teased but always gave herself to him softly and completely. Such smooth round thighs . . . A half smile played on his face. Yes, a life such as Kong Fu Tze would have approved: money, wives who had borne strong children; sons carrying on the business; good friends most of them gone now; good wine, good food. He gave a little sigh, turned over on his side and died.

. . . Under the matting roof of a small boat wedged in among hundreds of others on the canal at West Gate, a small child whimpered restlessly. The mother sleepily felt around in the dark, found the crying child from among five sleeping ones at her feet, picked it up, gave it her breast, patted the shoulder of another near her head who had stirred—and again fell asleep. . . .

. . . Up on the city wall a dog, mangy, half starved, barked furiously at the moon as he sniffed this dark corner, that, hoping to find a real feast as sometimes he did hidden away in wooden boxes. Then there would be a tearing of warm flesh, a crunching of bones, a trampling underfoot of a tiny dress. . . .

. . . Sprawled on her bed lay a young girl sobbing. She had cried all that day and the day before. She would continue to cry until her father gave her permission to return to the Mission School out of which she had been taken peremptorily when she had written of attending morning prayers. She had such good times in that school. Such good friends. They had parties and played basketball and sang queer foreign songs. She increased the volume of her wails. Listened again. Her father gave a low groan and turned over restlessly. Her almond eyes glinted with satisfaction, as she continued her sobs. . . .

. . . Lu Ong quietly let himself in the back gate of the Compound, walked soundlessly in his cloth slippers to his little room behind the kitchen of the Ladies' home. They would not like these nocturnal adventures of his. But what was he to do? He could not marry on his cook's wages of fifteen dollars Mex a month when he had not yet paid for his father's funeral. Only today the coffin maker had spoken to him. . . .

China softly breathing. . . .

The moon sank behind the Purple Pagoda. A breeze rustled the fresh new leaves of the mulberry trees. The night-watchman beating his drum to warn night prowlers passed in the street below and disappeared.

Out of the stillness sounded the whistle of the night launch from Shanghai. Cries of chair coolies shattered the quiet as they ran to the canal hoping for passengers. Servants with lanterns hurried out of tea shops where they had been gossiping while awaiting their masters returning on the launch. Laughter, shouts, *walla walla* of disputing chairmen filled the air. In a house near the canal a child half wasted with tuberculosis awoke and began to cough. A low whistle as the launch passed under South Gate bridge.

. . . The deep, low clang of the gong in the Temple of the Five Virtues, a sound as soft as the dawn, stirred the sleeping city. Dung carriers and house servants and all others who attend to lowly work arose and began their tasks.

In a small, dark cell in the second court of the temple a man whose name has been forgotten lifted himself slowly from thc hard rock floor and groped his way toward the pale square of grey in the blackness in front of him. He clung to the iron bars of the small aperture and peered through them at the world beyond—a world not as large as the court of the temple, holding only the wall opposite his cell, half of a door leading into the inner temple, one column carved in red and blue and green, which melted into a soft black in the faint light, and the tall black incense burner in the center of the court. His eyes, sunk deep in a face pallid from years of rice and tea moved slowly here, there, until they had accounted for every object in his world. A breeze touched his long black hair, which hung over bony shoulders, covered by rough, grey, priest's cloth. For thirty years he had kept his vow of silence. A bird stopped in flight, balanced for a moment on the tip of the incense burner, began to sing. A pause, then a crescendo of sound pressed deep into the peace of the temple court. The bird darted quickly over the roof. Silence again. The solitary had not moved. Now he fingered his beads restlessly. . . .

. . . Down the street from the temple, across the narrow canal, past old

Tung Lo's coffin shop stretched the thin rectangle of the foreign Compound, alien and unsubstantial in the mists of early morning. Only the church steeple cut a black triangle against the pale light.

—BEARING GIFTS

She sat in her office. On the desk the mission school's financial records lay before her. It had been a good year, as far as the money was concerned. And now nearly finished. A good year too in other ways. For she had managed to secure some decent textbooks on science, for the first time. And the English had gone better this year. Now if she could find some one who could teach Chinese classics as they should be taught—the young Chinese man she had had this year—

A tap at her door. Her *lai* brought a very young pupil into the room, advancing hesitantly, breathing a little quickly.

Rapidly she tried to place the child—for she took pride in knowing her pupils. Oh yes . . . the Zi child . . . Zi Ssu Ming . . . from the wealthy Zi family of Kashing . . . a little anti-foreign she believed they had been, until recently . . . sixth grade . . . no, the seventh.

She looked up and smiled at the young girl, and raised her eyebrows in interrogation.

Ssu Ming drew in her breath, made a quick bow in politeness to her honorable principal, spoke rapidly, her voice hardly more than a whisper, "I no more go to church," she said, "I not care to hear more about Jesus."

The thin hands moved slightly. "The term is almost over, only next Sunday and that is Commencement Sunday. I don't quite understand." Eyebrows raised.

Ssu Ming made another little abrupt bow. "I wish to come back next year. I like school—and you" her voice was a whisper now "but" her head came up bravely "I not like Jesus." She bowed again.

"Perhaps next year . . . you will feel differently about it. We shall see." The principal smiled at the flushed face.

Ssu Ming reached into her wide sleeve. "I bring you a small gift" she said and bowed again. "It is nothing." She laid a little package on the desk, suddenly smiled, drew in her breath, and darted out of the room.

"THE ROAD TO SHUH"

They left the Compound by the side gate. As they went through the narrow streets the new foreign teacher practiced her Chinese on the children at play who laughed at the odd sounds and said to her and each other "*Yang sia sang*." On the city wall the two missionaries turned, taking the west path.

Beyond the wall, across the river which stretched like a curved band of metal in the still air, clusters of thatched baked mud huts caught a glint of gold in their roofs.

Below them, the soft green plots of spinach and *tsai* in which peasants scratched with wooden implements turned black as the sun dropped behind the mountains. A thin dust, driven in from the Gobi sands, hung between them and the red clouds.

A bugle from the yamen sounded.

Grey figures of soldiers moved about in the court of a temple outside the Wall.

A dog sniffed here and there for food, and growled at them as they passed.

The sky faded.

They turned toward the Compound, stumbling a little on the dark path which led them back to the city. And then, as they were leaving the Wall, the young missionary crushed something under her foot. A little dress, a broken skull, a few soft bones, all that was left after the dogs feasted . . . She began to cry softly, tried to hide her tears with a laugh.

The older missionary smiled. "We have to get used to these things," she said quietly.

They had gone on rapidly until they had come to streets bright with sputtering gasoline lights and cheerful with the busy din of shopkeepers, the cries of coolies bearing incredible burdens, of chairmen pushing aside pedestrians to make room for a wealthy silk merchant who sat, eyes looking beyond the crowd, as he was borne quickly down the narrow street to his home; past small foodshops where coolies exchanged bits of 'cash' for hot fried rice cakes and ate them at once there on the street wiping their mouths on their broad sleeves; and on until they turned abruptly into a dark and quieter street where the soft slam and burr of the silk looms in the small houses was a familiar sound to their ears.

Unobserved they stood at a doorway watching the man at the loom as he deftly worked in the satiny figure which gives brocade its lustre. Stripped to the waist he sat before the loom. In the soft light of the lantern thick strands of muscles under yellow skin played quickly here, there, as he made the swift strong movements necessary to the pattern. Flat-chested and stooped he sat before his work, while the burr and slam of the loom beat out its rhythm, and over his thin wasted body muscles coiled and twisted and stretched until a small flower grew on the smooth ground of silk.

The girl looked up quickly at her companion. But the older missionary's face was tired and drawn and her eyes were staring far away beyond the man, the little house, the silk.

As quietly and unobtrusively as she had lived, Miss Harrison died in her sleep. Mrs. Tsung told the foreigners about it. The evening before, she had read a chapter from the New Testament, made the bed comfortable and bade her patroness good night. Early the next morning she went in with a cup of hot coffee to warm her up—Miss Harrison's only luxury—and found her, like this.

The body was buried in the little Mission cemetery; the consul notified; her possessions divided among her embroidery women as her will dictated; a notice of her death cabled to the office in America; and Mrs. Tsung temporarily put in charge of the embroidery school until the mission committee could make further plans.

The Compound felt only relief for all had dreaded Miss Harrison's approaching retirement, knowing too well her fear of it. It was so much simpler, this way.

Sometimes, like this, one's problems are solved so easily, the young missionary was thinking as they left the little burial plot. And she had lingered behind the others, murmuring that she would come later. She walked slowly, paused at each of the graves. Here, the Merediths' baby; already so old the stone looked, as if it had taken on the great weight of China's age. She remembered the hot damp day when they had followed the small box to this place . . . Martha's white hard bewildered face . . . So seldom she wrote to any of them . . . as if she would like to forget those years out here—if she could forget. Julie said she was keeping house for her Uncle Bob and her mother . . . that she had given a talk to the Junior League on Chinese art . . . Under a gnarled camphor that must have been a sprightly tree then was the darkened slab which bore the date September 13, 1898, and the name Sadie Martin. Sadie Martin had died of cholera . . . 1898 . . . that was before the Boxer Rebellion . . . Sadie . . Somebody named Sadie had come far across the ocean to bring her ideas of right and wrong, of God, of humanity, to a heathen people . . . to a people who had built a civilization and maintained it for thousands of years. And Sadie had given her life for them . . . that they might learn to live like people in Dobbs, Mississippi, lived . . . The girl tried to envisage Sadie . . . how tall she was, or fat, or fair . . . quiet, or talkative . . . And here near a clump of bamboo was the first Lane child, Robert Lane, Junior, the worn inscription said. Someone had told her when little Martie died that the Lanes had lost their first baby in the same way, though the Lanes had never mentioned it. Encircling the small plot was an old stone wall. The fresh dirt of Miss Harrison's grave looked raw, crude, in this place of age, and death and silence and peace.

She slowly followed the little path into the city. At the gate she turned suddenly to the right, climbed the crumbling steps which led to the top of the wall. The wind was raw and she searched for an old coffin where she could sit in shelter. At the turn of the wall she found one, crawled gratefully behind it. Beyond her stretched the river, dull and turgid. The wind had made it rough and the small boats scuttled past her with incongruous speed. A fisherman on the opposite bank was stretching out his seine. Back of him the fields were yellow and grey and dead, and beyond them the wide stretches of bare mulberry trees dissolved their solidity into tenuous, low-lying grey smoke.

More than six years out here. Years which had passed swiftly, uneventfully, save for sudden tense moments; splashes of color against a dullness. A little life. Martha—Jack—Jane—Julie—grey Mrs. Lane taking Doc's crumbs, what he had left after serving the heathen—kaleidoscopic memories of teas together, of tennis games, merged one into the other—her music—her old tubercular neighbor—Ssu Ming—China . . .

China . . . how she had tried to feel the authentic China—to grasp the reality of this old civilization. And always whatever knowledge she had gained turned into a dull lump of facts, slipped away, leaving her clutching only a few wisps of personal experiences. To these her mind would cling forever. Swiftly, rapidly, came faces of foreigners she had known; business people, Standard Oil—British-American Tobacco—Dollar Line—consular attaches—missionaries . . . old 'China hands.' And out of the multitude of faces one came and went, came and went, at last rising out of her memory:

She had been spending a few days in Shanghai, going to attend Mo Siang Ying's wedding one late afternoon. She had come from the wedding back to the Missionary Hotel. And in the large dining room she had been placed at a table with a Swedish missionary, a woman perhaps forty years old, with the inward look of those who have lived much alone. Over their mutton and potatoes they had talked casually.

"In Shanghai for a vacation?" she had asked to make conversation.

"No, only for a few days." The Swedish woman replied. Then added, "I brought my friend. My friend is not very well. We are sending her to Europe for a while." She cut a piece of mutton.

"Where are you stationed?"

"In Szechuen, China Inland Mission. We have been much alone. The two of us in a station. No other foreigners. We go months without seeing a foreigner. The Chinese are good to us. But Olga felt the loneliness. God sent us there—it was His will. I was glad to know that I was where He wanted me to be. But Olga said," the woman's hand trembled as she cut the mutton. "Olga said the wall pressed in upon her—the wall pressed in—"

The tense calm drawn tightly over every feature of the woman's face, over the immobile mouth, startled the younger missionary. She knew a little of these China Inland missionaries, who went to the farthest corner of the land with no means of support save their faith in God. She had heard of their bigotry and their selflessness.

She found that she could only murmur stupidly, "I am so sorry."

The woman went on. "Olga says she has forgotten Swedish and she wants to talk in her own language. She tries all day long to remember Swedish words, but all that will come to her is Chinese. She is very sad . . . We think she will be much better after a good rest at home." The Swedish woman's voice brightened.

"And you?"

The woman was surprised.

"Her boat sails tomorrow. There will be friends aboard. After I get her off I shall go back."

"Alone?"

"Yes. The work must go on. I must hurry back. It will take me five weeks to make the journey. I have been away a long time from my work."

The younger missionary could think of no reply.

The morning after she returned to Lincheng she read in the Shanghai paper a brief notice of the death of Olga Olsen, a missionary returning to Sweden. She had jumped through the port hole of the S.S. Maru while her companions were at dinner . . . Reading it she had wondered how long it would be before the other missionary on her lonely journey to Szechuen would hear of the death of her friend.

And now she was wondering once more about her . . . where could she be . . . what was she thinking far out in Szechuen as she saved souls for Jesus.

Big drops of rain spattered and stung her face as she sat on the old coffin and watched China slip slowly past her.

She wanted to hold each bit of it, to let it cut so deep into her memory that it could never be smoothed out by time. For it seemed to her that she looked upon the passing of a civilization. Something good and fine and still vigorous, ugly as is an old woman grown too wise to hide her ugliness, and beautiful as is all tried strength.

The old life would pass. In its stead would come the new. And no man could foresee what the heat of youth in its impetuous lust would conceive.

And her friends . . . She knew they would stay on and on, believing they were needed here.

A sail blackened itself against the sky, disappeared around the bend. Dogs near the village of Laochow barked furiously, as suddenly hushed.

She listened to the slow spatter of rain on the old wooden coffin, listened to slow memories stirring as if a hand had touched the strings of a Chinese harp and softly they had sounded and softly echoed.

[Summer 1938]

Mr. Lafayette, Heah We Is

As a means of educating the editors as well as their readers and attracting more contributors, contests and surveys became one of the distinctive features of the magazine. In announcing an essay contest on the causes of war, Smith's framing of the subject seems significant in terms of restrictions (e.g., not to use "war cries of democracy and fascism") and suggestions (e.g., "tracking war back to its hole is likely to lead . . . into paths through a briar patch or two back to man's kitchen and his cradle"). Her appeal especially to women to submit essays on the subject and her hope that women might offer a "recipe for peace" indicate Smith's ongoing struggle with an essentialist view of "man's enmity with woman" as the cause of war. (For further examples of Smith's analyses of this subject see "Man Born of Woman" and "Woman Born of Man" in WNA.)

Although Smith did not consider herself an isolationist, her opinions on America's intervention in the war—both before and after the attack on Pearl Harbor—set her apart from most white Southerners. As her biographer Anne Loveland astutely observed, Smith's views were more in agreement with those of black Americans. To talk of saving democracy abroad when they had not realized it in their own country was sheer hypocrisy to Smith. Continuing her earlier observations from "He That Is Without Sin," Smith attacked the "foreign missionary zeal" of the interventionists in the following editorial. As Loveland also noted, the editorial's attempt at irony was not entirely successful, for in comparing the lot of Jews in Nazi Germany with that of Negroes in the United States, Smith displayed insensitivity toward the former and a patronizing attitude toward the latter (35).

> A prize of $50.00 is offered by *The North Georgia Review* for the most interesting article on the causes of war with special reference to the current controversy in Europe. The only restriction is that the war cries "democ-

racy" and "fascism" not be used. Since the process of tracking war back to its hole is likely to lead up and down the main roads of civilization and into paths weaving through a briar patch or two back to man's kitchen and his cradle, the Editors feel compelled to limit the mileage to 6 pages of the *Review* (approximately 3,500 words).

The Editors also, while agreeing that war is a serious business, would be delightfully surprised to receive a few manuscripts of less solemn mien than those one habitually reads—and writes.

Though the day may come when an increasing war spirit will require of American women heroic Lysistratan measures if another debacle be averted, there are at present available less rigorous remedies; and of these 'simples' the Editors wish a few women would speak in their own terms. The man who nearly 2,500 years ago said, "Nay, never play the brave man, else when you go back home you own mother won't know you" understood well the canny realism of the female. And though the old playwright had his tongue in his cheek when he cried "... the very sheet-anchors of our salvation may be those yellow tunics, those scents and slippers, those cosmetics and transparent robes," his words could prove themselves a literal truth in this year of 1939. It is because women have fewer illusions about human nature than men, are less in their souls romantic, and hold more lightly to ideals, that in matters of war and peace they may possibly be more clear-eyed. This is a mere conjecture—and one that seems partially invalidated at the outset by woman's notorious myopia of character and mind. But perhaps because of this very foreshortening of interest and vision she may stumble on a solution right under her nose and thus play a very interesting if belated role in world history. Regardless of these delusions of female grandeur with which this editor is momentarily beguiled, we in all seriousness hope that women will submit articles in this contest. For undaunted by their well-known weaknesses, undiscouraged even by the spectacle of Dorothy Thompson brandishing her hard-boiled idealism just like any romantic male, and Mrs. Roosevelt growing more hesitant as she draws near the cross-roads, we still look hopefully in the direction of women for a recipe for peace. (In the midst of our peroration we pause to mention that the contest closes on June 25, 1939.)

Though scared by it, one cannot but admire the amazing foreign-missionary zeal of the proselytizers of the Democratic Religion who are so anxious for us to give your bodies and our souls to spread the gospel in heathen Europe. "Go ye into all the world" they cry and their eyes shine with a light never on land or sea but often on the brows of those who habitually focus on far-seeing places. It would be a shabby trick to distract their attention, to dash the dew from their illusions by muttering about the need for home work. And so (becoming a little fired by their evangelical enthusiasm ourselves), we suggest that we send our grimy home work to Europe. We suggest that we contribute toward the foreign mission fund—little mite-boxes as it were—all the lives that are a blotch on our fair democracy, all the human beings who persist in casting their shadows on our gleaming purity: the sharecroppers, the unemployed, the slum-dwellers, the undernourished, and the Negroes. That would be a fair-sized 'bit.' And it should not be difficult to persuade them (remembering how readily propaganda turns all tricks), to sacrifice themselves in order to make democracy safe for the rest of us. A simple solution, and one possessing a logic that should commend it to the proselytizers. We'd send the Negroes as our shock troops, since they have the longest and most persistent record of being splotches. They could go, calling out in their deep mellow voices: "Mister Lafayette, heah we come! Leastways, all of us cept the 5,000 or so who was lynched a while back. Mr. Lafayette, heah we is. They don't call us mister back home and they don't let us ride in their railroad cars or eat at their tables or sleep in their hotels or let us vote;—and they give us what scraps are lef as to jobs and we knows to say 'thankee Boss.' And we take what's lef over in the way of schools and hospitals and houses and sewer systems and sech liddle things like that, and tips our hats. But we live in Gawd's country en that's a fact, en it's a fine place to live in ef yo knows yo place, and we knows our place, yeah Lawd! Now we'se come to lay down our lives for those Jews Mister Hitler's been pickin on. We hear tell he takes their property and their money and kicks them about and spits on 'em and burns their books. An' all that makes our democratic blood about boil over. Yas suh! For hit sho must be terrible to live in a country whar yo has yo money tuk (our ways a lot better cause we has no money to be tuk—jus a little furnish which is et up and gone fo yo can say scat) and it sho must be awful sight to have yo books burned—hit's a lot better never to learn how to read and write like us, we'se tellin you. And to be spit at in the face! That just shows the awful wickedness of that fascism business. Now in our country things are worked out mighty well, a sight better'n that. Theah's plenty of back streets to walk on in every town and back doors what you can go in and out of. And theah's always the Quarters. Yo don need to scrouge up close to folks, close enough for 'em to spit at yo! You kin always step off the sidewalk. And if worse comes to worst you kin run yo tail off and make it to the Swamp. Yeah Lawd . . . there ain't nothing so plumb democratic as a good cypress swamp. . . . Ef them Jews hada jes had a coupla cypress swamps it'd sho helped them get rid of fascism. Yeah man. . . ."

[Spring 1939]

Behind the Drums

(*With a Long Preface to a Very Short Play*)

Developed and performed at Laurel Falls Camp in the summer of 1939, this was the first and only Laurel Falls Camp play to deal specifically with race. Its appearance in the Fall 1939 issue of *North Georgia Review* emphasizes the complementary creative processes at work in Smith's simultaneous development of the magazine and the camp.

In addition to using contests and surveys to educate themselves, in 1939 and 1940 the editors applied for and received travel grants from the Julius Rosenwald Fund. Founded in 1928, the fund had focused primarily on developing black education until 1937, when a fellowship program open to Southern whites as well as to blacks was established to broaden the fund's efforts to improve race relations. In her February 1940 application for a renewal of their Rosenwald grant Smith reported that *Drums* was "being rehearsed for presentation by the drama department of Atlanta University," and that partial recordings of the play had been made and had been "received enthusiastically by various groups, including the Ga. Div. of the Southern Conference for Human Welfare" (*HH* 31, 37). Over sixty years later, a daughter of one of the campers who remembered the play and the way Smith used drama to teach black history wrote: "Here's one of the Miss Lil lessons I inherited: We're all products not only of the past, but of what we learn about the past. Do the history. And remember that black history is white history, too" (Schmich).

It would be simpler to set down the words, music and stage directions of our rhythm-montage and let the reader assess the result for what it is worth. But in so doing, we should ignore values, larger perhaps than those inherent in the play, which grew out of the making of it.

It is a play created by eighty-five young girls and adults and it was begun long before some of them came to live on Old Screamer.

It began years ago with the singing of the spirituals, with a sudden cheapening and jazzing up of the tunes, with a "swinging" of *And He Never Said a Mumblin' Word*—and a shamed silence. Later, someone talked about the Sorrow Songs, and Frances sang them. She sang for an hour while we lay on the floor and listened, candles throwing shadows on her face and ours, beyond us Old Screamer throwing its shadow on the roofs of our little cabins. Shut in by mountains, cut off from the world of trouble and conflict beyond us, we lay secure in our peace and listened. And while we listened, we entered, without knowing it, another world of trouble, of black-dark trouble, and the shadow of it fell on young white hearts. And no one forgot that evening.

It was a summer later perhaps when Frances sang old ring-shouts to us, and interested by Rosamond Johnson's *Rolling Along in Song*, we began to drum out on the floor primitive rhythms while she searched for ring-shouts to match. And this was fun—a new game.

Then one day someone spoke of a lynching in South Georgia. "Is it true?" "Yes, it is true." "But surely they did not pour gasoline on him and burn him?" "Yes." "Why?"

Why? Question old as the white man's and Negro's life together; young as each new South-born child.

A greedy question that will not be satisfied with one answer. Or two.

But we tried. We tried to untangle the tight strands of the Negro's and the white man's lives, discarding blame as one would lay aside a knife, knowing that if we cut one strand we cut both—strands grown together as two grape vines that have twined and intertwined and twined again from roots old and tough and big to new fresh tendrils.

And afterward most of the girls went easily back to tennis and riding, play and laughter, but one young girl said softly, "I am ashamed of white people. After all . . . we have the power" she added.

And then one night this past summer, someone half idly, but not wholly so, tapped on the floor, beating out African rhythms, beating out a story in her mind. And, as if they felt it, too, others sitting around making nightly reports laid aside their charts, and suddenly one of them said "Let's make drums. Let's make as many drums as we could possibly want."

We knew that we would like to do this. So we made drums. We took nail kegs and old inner tubes of tires and made drums. We searched the farms in the near-by coves for skins, soaked them, scraped and dried them, found hollow logs, made more drums. Our driver had his idea of how a drum should be made—and sound—and so he made drums, back of the kitchen; our stable man had different ideas about the making of drums—and how they should sound—so he made drums, down at the stables.

There came a day when three drums were finished—nail kegs and inner tubes. We heard the sound when we were far away: low, like the sigh of some great creature. It couldn't be a drum, someone said, it is the drone of a plane behind the mountain. But soon we were gathering and soon we were beating. Thereafter, each evening when the sun dropped over the peaks beyond us and the valley turned blue, someone would bring out a drum, and then someone else, and another, and another, with few words—for drum beating is not often a riotous affair but a grave pleasure, in which one takes austere satisfaction, if one is a real drum beater.

We were in the library one night, eighty of us, beating drums, singing work songs, spirituals, making new songs. Slowly a girl rose to her feet, stood unmoving for a moment, began to dance. No one spoke. Another stood. Another. The beating went on. Then everybody laughed, feeling good and at ease and relaxed, and we went to bed tired and sleepy.

But not all could achieve so facile a synchrony of body and emotions and drum beating. One little girl who found it hard to give up the security of home, who still felt difficult and pressing the demands of her new environment to which others adjusted so smoothly, said one day suddenly "I don't like it," lips trembling, "I don't like the beating." And so we changed to a modern swing rhythm and watched the ease come back on her face. There were others, too, who fought the pull of the tom tom, resisting, as if they felt walls crumbling, behind which lay dammed up unconscious memories of a personal and phylogenetic past—and feared lest their immediate conscious selves be drowned in its torrents.

One day, unaware that she was observed, a little girl with sensitive thin tight face and eyes holding that lost look one sees so often on the young went up to one of the drums. She stood for a long time looking at it. Slowly she picked up a stick and softly beat it. Once, twice. Listened. A little clumsily groping for rhythm she tried again. Listened. Sighed. Softly laid down the stick and walked away. . . .

And so, the valley overflowed with the sounds of our drumbeating, while Old Screamer loomed above us like a giant sounding board, giving back the rhythms again, and within us another sounding board, old as Old Screamer, received them and made of them new strange patterns. . . .

But now we must get on with the play. For inevitably out of so much excitement and pleasure came a desire to give form to feelings.

We would make a play. We would make a play about the Negro because though we experimented with many kinds of rhythm patterns we were always drawn back to 'primitive' patterns; though we sang many kinds of music, we liked best the Negro songs; though in our search for rhythms we came close in our minds to many races, only the Negro and the drama of his three hundred bitter years of living with white men moved us deeply.

With little talk we knew that we would use the tom tom beaters, the singers, the dancers, the speakers (our choral speech group) the mask makers—groups already functioning in our life on Old Screamer—shaping the pattern of our play to these available human materials as well as to the inherent dramatic necessities of our theme. Because most of us were young, some of us knew that we would make a simple, naïve play but, we hoped, an honest one.

And we began, all of us, for everybody was in this play, feeling our way step by step, feeling no sense of haste, although it was done in two weeks.

We added a solo speaker whom we called the Voice and we tied the units of this rhythm-montage together by the tom toms which beat, sometimes in background, sometimes in foreground, throughout the play. Scene after scene we worked through together.

We decided to use for the first set a grey cyclorama on which in the center-back would be a large mask of a Negro face. When it was finished, the mask was about six feet by four feet in dimension, a simply modeled face of strong Negroid features, a face of austerity, of passion and sadness and thought. We used what the girls call 'tropical colors,' sharp greens and scarlets and browns, and blues and greys. The planning of this was easy and seemed to us right, for the Africa scene and the stockade-slaveship scene. Then we discussed the slavery scene. What kind of set should it be? Asked this question, quickly fifty hands were raised, fifty young white voices cried "a big house—white columns—mammy—pickaninnies—somebody singing old songs—"

"But remember—you are not white girls talking, you are now Negroes. Think a minute. If you were a slave, what in slavery would hurt you most, would mean most to you? Remember, only a few slaves were house-servants, some perhaps never saw the big house . . . what would mean most to you . . . what would stay on your mind the most. . . ."

Little girls, big girls gravely pondered, sitting there on the floor, some of them bewildered, a little puzzled by these words. And then a fourteen-year-old spoke. "It would be the separation," she said. "That fear never leaving you of being separated from your family, from your husband or your lover, or your children. Afraid tomorrow they'd sell you or those you love."

The room was quiet. And there followed grave talk of this fear, of the importance which the mother held in the Negro family, how she came to symbolize the only security it had, how later after legal slavery, she still symbolized this security . . . how she lost her children. . . .

"You're crying," one girl whispered to another, "and I am, too," she sniffled and tried to laugh.

Then we talked of cotton . . . and we built this scene using for a set the same grey cyclorama with an enormous boll of cotton (painted) on a backdrop; using for the pantomime, an old mother sitting hands wrapped in apron, eyes looking at the stars, while the Singers sang "Tramping" and "Hush, Hush, Somebody's Calling My Name," and a procession of slaves, field hands, artisans, old men, and young, children, house servants, passed slowly across the stage in the shadowy background.

A girl from one of the densely Negro-populated counties of Georgia waited afterward. There were not tears in her eyes but anger. "We cry," she said, "and then we forget. I am today ashamed of being white, but that doesn't help the Negro. I wish I knew something to do. How could my people have done it? They are kind. They try to be good. They pray. Everybody in my family prays." . . . her lips were trembling now, "*everybody*. . . ."

The play grew. And suddenly one day it was finished. In three days we would give it. In three days—"Lordy, Lordy," someone cried, "we have no audience! We're every blessed one of us in it! What'll we do?" It was no idle question. A play without an audience . . . oh no . . . So it was suggested that they ask their parents to come if they thought their parents would enjoy it. "You see," this was a time when you felt your way, "we are all southerners, we love the south, we each in our own way think we love the Negro, too, but we do not agree. Some of your parents will like this play. Others will not like it. We shall not say that they are wrong. We shall not think it either. Emotional maturity means, in part, forming your own opinion. You try to be 'emotionally mature' up here and you have a right to form your own opinion, but remember, so have your parents this right. Remember, too, that as we do not blame each other here but try instead to understand each other and change a situation so as to avoid that same mistake again, so we are not interested in fixing on any one blame about the Negro. We would like to understand him better and ourselves better, and do what we can to change the situation. That is all."

One girl said, "My parents will like it. Father says 'the search for truth is a great and brave adventure.'" Some of the girls looked at the speaker a little wistfully. Another spoke quickly, "There is no need for me to fool myself a moment. Mother gets hysterical, simply *hysterical* if you talk about Negro equality, or labor! So count my folks out." And there were others who did not know, who were not sure. . . .

And then somehow the day came, and the night, and the audience. . . .

The chorus (the Singers and Speakers) are in the balcony to the rear of our theatre facing the stage. The Voice stands in the shadows below the stage, and with her in the semi-darkness are two, sometimes three tom tom beaters. The curtain is closed when the Voice speaks, and opens only for the brief dance-pantomime scenes, during which we rely on lighting, stage sets, music, costume and designs made by moving bodies of dancers for dramatic impact. The tom toms are beating softly, then more loudly, dying away to a whisper:

(The script follows, incomplete for we have omitted words of songs, music, tom tom rhythm patterns, and dance patterns):

The Voice: Beating . . . ten thousand years. . . .
And even now, in silence, making bright patterns of laughter
Making black patterns of pain
Making life.
And you and I
Listening
Hear as we hear our own heartbeat, a people
Telling an old story.
A story old as falling rain—

Speakers: Old and cruel as a tiger's mouth
Old as the beginning of all things
Old as sorrow

(Tom toms beat on)

The Voice: Behind the drums—Africa:
Burning the eye with bright splendor
Lashing the skin with danger,
Heating the blood with beauty—

Speakers: A drowsy copper snake, slipping through the centuries.

(A pause—tom toms beating on)

The Voice: Behind the drums, lovers:
Hands smooth to the touch as weathered ivory
Thighs soft as lapping water in night-time
Whispers warm as jungle sands in sun-heat.

(Tom toms continue to beat on softly, as the Voice pauses)

Behind the drums, laughter:
Pounding the blood

Quickening the pulse
White teeth . . . wide mouth . . . brown bodies—

Speakers: Singing laughter
Sobbing laughter
Dancing, dancing
Pounding
Beating
Lashing
Burning. . . .

Scene 1.

(Tom toms drown out Speakers, as curtain rises on African tribal scene. A ceremonial is taking place before the warriors go out to battle, in which a purification rite is suggested—the tabu idea used—a suggestion of religious ecstasy. There are five dancers, twenty tom tom beaters, an old woman possessed, a dance around a drum in which a spirit seems to be imprisoned, ending as two grotesque figures eight feet tall in masks rush out from the wings and, their white robes swirling about them, dance madly. The curtain falls.)

(The drums grow faint, strong, slow)

The Voice: Behind the drums, death:
A creeping cat through the jungle
A crunch of bones in hungry mouth
Shadows. . . .

Whisperers: (from various spots in the theatre):
Shadows . . . shadows . . . shadows. . . .

The Voice: White man's chains
White man's gold
White man's lust. . . .

Speakers: Black man proud
Strong black man
Man of laughter
Travel a long road—

Speakers: Travel a sun-down road
Travel three hundred black-dark years
Down a lonesome road. . . .

(*Singers* hum "Lonesome Road" as the *Voice* continues)

(Tom toms . . . very soft here)

The Voice: Black girl looking
Black girl loving
Black girl losing her man
Down a lonesome road
Across the seas—
Speakers (very softly): Across the centuries

(One of the *Singers* carries the melody of *Lonesome Road,* while others softly hum the harmony.)

Scene 2.

(Curtain opens on the dance of the captives which symbolizes the long hard journey from stockade to ship. Only tom toms are used. Curtain falls, tom toms continue with a change in rhythm pattern.)

The Voice: Across the South
Across the years
Proud man grow humble
Black man find his place;
Find chains
Find Jesus.
Speakers: Yes, Lawd, find Jesus.
The Voice: Lost and lonesome
Black lambs ahuddling
Speakers: Waitin' for de Lawd
Waitin' for heaven. . . .
The Voice: Down the black-dark road—
Speakers: Down the black-dark road awaitin'. . . .

(Light and dark voices are used here effectively with a strong high voice speaking 6th line. All voices for last lines dying to a whisper.)

Awaitin'
Alovin'
Alosin'
Aprayin'
Sweet Jesus
Ah'll see ma baby in heaven . . .
Sweet Jesus
Ah'm awaitin'. . . .

Scene 3.

Curtain opens. (A spotlight on the old mother.)

The Voice: Mother of blackness
Mother of lost sons
Mother of misery
Awaiting.
Hands wrapped in apron
Body wrapped in patience
Heart wrapped in God—
Looking at the stars
Looking at Heaven. . . .

Singers: (Sing "Tramping." . . . "Hush-hush." . . . Tom toms beat softly as procession of slaves passes.)

(Black-out. Curtain).

The Voice: Like the deepening waters of floodtime
Like the mumble of toothless old men
Like a furrow plowed long and unending
Days come . . . days pass away. . . .
Years . . . curve into centuries.

Speakers: Rubbing the hands in labor
Bending the spirit to white pride
Stooping the heart to shame.

The Voice: Rain and sun. . . .

Speakers: Sun and rain
Rain and sun
Sun and rain. . . .

The Voice: Greening the cotton fields
Fluffing the stalks with richness
Making a full sweet breast for white children's mouths. . . .

Speakers: Making a salt sweat-taste on black lips.

(Tom toms change pattern).

The Voice: Like the crack of a giant tree falling
Like the snap of lightning on hot nights
Came the breaking of shame bonds
Came the breaking of chains.

Speakers: Black man laughed
Black man clapped big hands
Threw back head and SHOUTED
FREE . . .

AH'M FREE . . .
BLESS GOD . . . MAN AH'M FREE. . .
FREE. . . .

The Voice: But cotton so soft
Cotton so fluffy
Covered the fields with white silence
Smothered black man's shouting.

Speakers: (Faltering) Ah'm free . . .
Bless God . . . Ah'm free . . . Ah'm free. . . .

The Voice: Black hands labor on
Black bodies sweat on
Black hearts ache on. . . .

Speakers (half whispering): Ah'm free . . . Ah'm free . . .
Ah'm . . . Lawd Gawd . . . have mercy on black
man . . . mercy.

(Tom toms beat softly).

The Voice: Misery . . .
A hound dog
Beating the dust with its tail.

Singers: (Sing work song "Gwine down" . . . and as curtain is raised, they sing "Workin' on de Chain Gang," and Chain Gang dance is done in a slow work rhythm with the tom toms. For backdrop we use the same cotton boll on grey cyclorama. Dancers are dressed in chain gang stripes).

(Curtain falls.)

Singers: Ah've got misery.
Speakers: Yes Lawd!
Singers: Ah've got misery.
Speakers: Yes Lawd!
Singers: And Ah've got song. . . . (this is chanted on two tones).
The Voice: A gold tooth in trouble's wide mouth—
Speakers: A-brightenin'
A-shinin'
Wide mouth a-singin'
Wide mouth a-shinin' with song!

The Voice: Black hands a-strumming
Black feet a-stomping

Speakers: Stompin' out the sadness
Stompin' out the blues. . . .
Cake-walkin' crost de misery line. . . .

Cake-walkin' to heaven....

(Curtain rises. Brash gay cake-walking scene
Curtain falls. Tom toms change to slow rhythm,then to
quick low rapid beats).

The Voice: Blood hounds a-panting
Panting down the years—
Speakers: Nigger in de cypress swamp
Nigger in de shadows....
Whisperers: Shadows ... shadows....
Shadows....
Speakers: Hush your feet from stompin'
Hush your mouf from laughin'
Hush your mind from thinkin'
Hush your heart from beatin'

(Tom toms, soft but rapid)

The Voice: Hate with tongue a-lolling
Panting down the road—
Speakers: (dark voices): Death is a white man
Holding high a torch!
(Light Voices): Death is a nigger
Swinging from a limb!
(All): Swinging crost de misery line
Swinging ... into heaven....

(Curtain rises on lynching scene. The shadow of a noose is swung on the back drop. Right, backstage, stand four Ku Klux Klansmen, motionless, with torches burning. Upstage, facing the noose shadow, backs to audience, are the same group we saw as slaves, in varying attitudes of prayer, terror, horror, grief, anger).

Speakers: (Whispering) Gawd ... Jesus ... Gawd have mercy ... Sweet Jesus....

(Curtain falls).

Singers: "Nobody Knows de Trouble Ah've Seen" (all of the song).

(Tom toms gradually quicken, change finally to jazz rhythm).

The Voice: Swinging ... from the cotton fields
Swinging to Harlem.

Jazzing cross the misery line
Jazzing cross Jordan
Jazzing to heaven. . . .

Speakers: Hotcha . . . Baby!
Ah've got song
Ah've got music
Ah've got ma baby
Ah've got ma man. . . .

(Curtain rises immediately on Harlem Scene. Back drop for this scene is a painting of a swing orchestra leader madly waving his baton. Tom toms change pattern as curtain falls).

The Voice: Jazzing to hunger
Jazzing to waste
Jazzing out of black jobs
Jazzing to fear. . . .

The Voice: Hard times for black man

Speakers: All the same old tune
All the same old singing

The Voice: With a new word here and there

Speakers: All the same old rhythm

The Voice: With a new step here and there.

Singers chanting: Ah've got ma music

Speakers: Who got yo baby?

Singers: Ah've got ma blues
Ah've got ma free time

Speakers: Sho—white man got yo job.

Singers: Ah've got ma liberty

Speakers: Sho—yo know to read and write.

Singers: Ah've got—

The Voice (calmly with a kind of long range hope): Jungle night is ending
Black night a-passing

(*Singers and Speakers* make side comments but *Voice* continues calmly, unfalteringly).

Singers and Speakers: How come yo say—

The Voice: Sun is a-creeping up
Gold tooth a-shining

Singers and Speakers: Man!

The Voice: Trouble's mouth a-shutting
Hope is a-stomping
Cross the misery line.

Stomping cross to heaven
Through a half shut door—

Singers and Speakers: That's right! (bitterly) . . . *Jim Crow heaven . . .*

The Voice: Stomping cross to freedom
Stomping cross to liberty. . . .

Singers and Speakers: Jesus! . . . Sure, free to starve . . .

(Tom toms keep on as *Voice* pauses a moment).

The Voice: Drums in your black heart
Drums in your soul

Singers and Speakers (in half whisper): *Yes?*

The Voice: Beating out a new song
Beating out a life. . . .

Singers and Speakers: Pray Gawd! . . . Life for what . . .

The Voice: Beating out a new song
Through a half shut door—

Singers and Speakers (half whispering)*: Yes . . . Jesus. . . .*

The Voice: Beating out a new life
Through a half shut door

(Tom toms beat on as voices—expressing varied Negro opinion—die away. All is again quiet save for the soft drum-beating).

The Voice: . . . Even now . . . making bright patterns of laughter
Making black patterns of pain
Making life . . .

Speakers (softly): Shadow of life

Whisperers: Shadows . . .

The Voice: And you and I listening
Hear as we hear our own heartbeat
A people
Telling an old story . . .
Old and cruel as a tiger's mouth
Old as the beginning of all things
Old as sorrow.

The end.

So You're Seeing the South

As White and Sugg noted, while the effects of the Rosenwald travel grants pervaded the magazine, they were most explicit in the following sketches or vignettes by Lillian Smith, which appeared in *North Georgia Review*, Winter 1939–40 (326). The questions referred to in the truck driver's response were published in the Fall 1939 issue as "Do You Know Your South?" The contest offered a reward of "$250.00 in cash, or $300.00 in books (these to be selected by winner) to the *North Georgia Review* reader who answers accurately and most adequately its *One Hundred Questions about the South*." Of the one hundred questions, the following accompanied the initial announcement:

> Do you know its needs and its opportunities?
> Do you know its books and its writers?
> Do you know its great fortunes, who possess them, how they were made?
> Do you know its business, its political leaders and their opinions about social and economic and political problems?
> Do you know its churches and their programs?
> Do you know its schools and their aims?
> Do you know its mores? Its folk songs, its dances, its crafts?
> Do you know its swamps and its mountains?
> Could you draw a spot map of its crime centers? Of its disease centers?
> Do you know its music, its food, its superstitions?
> Do you know "the Negro," "the tenant-farmer," "the textile laborer," "the mine worker," how he lives, and where, what education he has, what cash income, what play facilities, what kind of health?
> Do you know its sports, its parks, its resorts?
> Do you know its peaches-and-cream complexion, and its warts?
> DO YOU? (*FTM* 361)

The last sketch, "Break Their Hearts . . . ," is a prayer Smith heard at a gathering of black sharecroppers who had been thrown off a plantation in Arkansas for joining the Tenant Farmers Union. Smith referenced the experience repeatedly in later writing. "Give Them Tears" was her first title for *Killers of the Dream* (*HH* 124–25).

Lady, Ask Me Something Hard

Know the South? Me? Know ever inch of it! Truck you see there—it and me's covered ever inch of it. Bet you couldn't think up a question I couldn't answer quick as that! Tell you the thing you'll worry about most goin round. It's the coffee. Yeah . . . you get to studyin about it—reckon it'll be worse or better than last cup you got down the road. Yes, mam—sure like to take a look at them questions you been tellin me about. Lady—you couldn't think up a question bout the South I couldn't answer fore it was out of your mouth . . . Next time, if I was you, I'd not offer big money for a thing easy as that. Know folks has to learn and I don't mean to be criticisin. Well, better be limpin along. Old wagon and me gotta clip off 300 more little miles come dark. Sure . . . we're on the stretch-out. Who aint these days! So long . . . an make sure to have a big time on your trip.

Stars over Jordan

So you're seeing the South? Well, well, and you're a Georgian. Will you let an old man give you a little advice my dear? Try to see something *good!* Easy to see bad things. Everywhere there're bad things. World over. Now if you were crawling on all fours, your nose would pick up stale and mighty unpleasant odors which it doesn't get when you're standing straight, but it would miss the smell of good clear air with the sunshine in it, and the sweetness of blooming things, wouldn't it? There're blooming things in the South . . . everywhere. Don't ever let yourself forget that. Can't prove it, any more than I could prove I loved my old mother. But I know it . . . you know it . . . everybody born down here knows it . . . Bend of grass in the wind there, ain't it a thing now to look at . . . suck of water gainst lily roots . . . way a hickory leaf eases to the ground in sweet giving up of its place in the sky . . . way the moss hangs on that old oak there—day after day—months—years—right moment comes—drops like a sigh . . . way the air blows cross your face soft and slow like most folks' talk . . . way . . . Sitting here . . . nothing to do but knock the ash out my old pipe, put in new fillins knock the ash out again . . . keep thinking . . . You don't think much about the hard times you had . . . ten per cent, twelve, sometimes twenty per cent interest you had to pay the banker ... you forget how you hated him for it, hated him because he made you push your tenants hard as he pushed you, hard as somebody was pushing him ... hated them cause you knew there was nobody neath em to push down hard on to ease the hate inside *them* ... Come a time, you stop thinking about it ... yes ... Look over there ... front of that cabin. Old Mose ... sitting there ... same as me. Old black man ... old white man. Color don't mean much now to Mose and me. Not now. Just two old men sittin in the sun. Eighty-five years we've lived, Mose and me. As bad years I reckon as folks ever lived through ... But we've seen spring come ... yes, mam, the prettiest sweetest way of coming a man could wish for. No bustle. Nothing flashy. Kind of like dreaming about a woman you've loved. Sit dreaming ... look up ... and she's there ... smiling at you ... right there by you ... That's the way spring comes down here ... eighty-five times I've seen it come ... like that. Yes, I know ... Old Trouble's had us all down here squeezed mighty tight in his hand. And no way out without hurting somebody ... bad. Used to worry about it when I was young. Must be a right way out, I'd say. Must be. Ought to be a way out that won't hurt nobody. Used to think that. Well ... one day knew better. Knew better ... Knew a man could get himself in such a fix he couldn't get out, without hurting somebody bad. Yes ... reckon that was time I realized I was getting old ... reckon so ... Well—we sit here ... Mose and me ... shadow crosses the grass—we know a buzzard's gone by ... slosh of water in the pond there, the old gator's moved from one side to t'other ... And when that clump of palmetto starts turning black in the evenin we know its about time for old men to be going to bed. So you're seeing the South ... It's a fine thing to do. But remember—mire's there. Yes, it's there. Plenty. Plenty. And if you keep looking too close at it, you'll not see the stars overhead—and they're a pretty sight to see ... a real pretty sight ...

I've Just ... Lost Control

Yes, I've heard my husband speak of you. Please rest your coat, won't you, and sit down? ... that we can be of value to you on your trip? I don't know that we can but we'll be glad to help. Introductions to ... yes, of course ... my husband will see about it for you I feel sure. Yes. It's good that you want to see the Negro South too ... Yes ... I beg your pardon—I didn't hear ... No. No—I'm not sick—I—I—Some of your work is with children, isn't it? What do you do when you have—a child—who has had a bad—shock ... who ... Today my little girl ... maybe we've been wrong . . . but we've thought . . . my husband and I . . . it seemed best to us not to let her run into—things until she was older. So she's never been—around white people. We—we wanted to give her faith in herself first—and pride—and belief—in her own race. It seemed to us—we read the child psychologists and they—it seemed if we could make these first years secure and happy for her—maybe she could take the world later—even here—without bitterness . . . you must forgive . . . me . . . for . . . crying . . . like this . . . I've never . . . lost control . . . before . . . I've—always believed . . . a person—ruins her life if she lets hate in . . . My husband and I both—learned to—laugh—at—things . . . and not let them hurt . . . too much. This year we put her in the University Laboratory School—and usually I take her back and forth. But it's only a block or two . . . and lately I've been letting her—walk home . . . Today—a white boy stopped her . . . called her—called her—words . . . told her . . . things. . . . I'll get myself together . . . in a moment . . . I've just . . . lost control . . . you see—she's only six . . . I don't know what—to tell her . . . I've been trying to think—all afternoon what to—tell her . . . Yes, please come back—I'm sorry to spoil your visit . . . this way.

And Plenty Money

You want to hear me play? Sure! Move over girls, and let the lady hear me play. Now what'd you like to hear? . . . Can I play boogie woogie? Can I! Listen to this . . . What do you think of it? . . . I'm good, don't you think? Maybe you'd like to hear me sing too . . . You would? . . . How was that? Thanks. Oh, I'm good all right. Maybe I'm not good as Marian Anderson in some ways, but I got plenty Anderson hasn't got—just burnin me up inside. Sometimes feel like it'll burn me to a cinder if I don't . . . Some day I'm going to have my own orchestra and they'll break down and cry and beg me to hush—I'll be so good. Yeah . . . they'll—Books? I don't like books much. Rather sit at the piano and make things up. You don't have time much to read in college. But I liked *Gone With the Wind.* I liked it a lot . . . Yes—but lots of colored people too sensitive. They make me laugh! White people's ways don't bother me. Phoof! Sure! You know all that—but you don't think about it—see? And all that in the book happened long time ago. You can't take history personally—*see*? All I want is to have an orchestra and make people so crazy with my music they can't sleep nights. And plenty money . . . If you have a car and clothes and plenty money, and folks knowing your name everywhere—what you care about anything else for? What you care?

When You've Stood About as Much Bad Food

So you're traveling through old Dixie . . . Wonder what you'll see? Wonder what you've got eyes to see? To most folks going round it's a lot of pretty scenery and bad dirt and shanties and cracker talk—and the damnest food on earth—if you'll excuse me, mam. Sloppy coffee . . . grease. Sorter covers the South, don't it, like the dew. Yeah . . . Best cooks in the world in our homes when we've got a little money to buy rations with and have had enough to be used to rations. But we don't like to cook for the public. Think they ought to fix their bacon over their own camp-fire, don't we? Who's that all time talking about the disappearance of our last frontier? Somebody who goes home to supper every night, lay my last dollar on it. Why mam, everything about us nearly is frontier. May be wore out but it's still frontier. Reminds me of a woman I heard talking not long ago about Caroline Miller's book—what she call the dad-blamed thing?—that's right. Well, she was talking this woman and her voice twanged like a guitar. She wanted to know if South Georgians weren't still furious with Mrs. Miller about that book. 'There couldn't have been such crude people in Ware County,' she twanged—herself about as refined as an oyster shell. 'Even in South Georgia there must have been some aristocrats.' Good Godamighty . . . I ask your pardon, mam. So I turned to the lady and I said 'Madam' I said, 'good Goda—.' Well, never mind about that.

If you've got to go on this wild-goose chase—and what you doing it for anyway, you haven't told me that yet. Now if that's not the—All right! When you've stood about as much bad food as you can stand, tell you what to do. Forget all your worries about our poverty and racial problems, and unemployment and too many children, and too many churches (you're dad-blamed right there) and soil erosion, and too few hospitals and bad housing (My God, we're in a bad mess, aint we)—turn your car into Alabama and drive to Talladega. When you're five miles from town, stop your car, get out and walk the rest of the way. Countryside's mighty pretty—hills, vistas, all that, and plenty of battle markers. But that's not why you're walking. No mam. You're walking up an appetite for a dinner you're going to try to eat at the Purefoy Hotel. All right. You get there. They make you register. Then they show you the old silver wash bowl and pitcher and slop jar in the guest room and some old furniture that'll do, and a lot of old mirrors ugly as hell—you'll have to excuse me mam—but don't let that antique worship discourage you. You know well as me we have to kow tow a little before the shrine of the South. After you've bent the knee, they'll take you into the dining-room. And you'll sit down to a table set up in old southern-novel style. You'll drink out of a silver goblet and eat off of fine china and there'll be colored servitors bowing and scraping to make you feel like a big-bellied aristocrat, and handing you dream food. Yes mam. Dream food . . . chicken and turkey . . . braised mushrooms . . . asparagus with almonds . . . ham salad . . . oyster pie . . . watermelon preserves . . . brandied peaches . . . sweet potatoes and pecans . . . celery hearts . . . fluffy little biscuits tender as—now you got me, don't know what they're tender as . . . and a dozen more vegetables and salads, and then you finish off with ice cream and three kinds of cake, and a piece of pie and some coffee. After that, if I were you, I'd ask God to forgive me, and I'd find me a quiet spot in the shade under a tree somewhere and sleep it off till sun-down. Then you go back to your car, get in and drive real slow through the twilight, because it's a pretty thing in that country, a twilight.

Maybe I'm Just Easy to Cry

Reckon you don't belong round here, do you, stopping like this to hear niggers sing. Sure it's all right! Stay long as you want to. Glad to have you. Won't you come in and sit a while? Sun's right warm here on the porch. Yes'm. Getting things ready for planting. Trying to. They say ground's awfully wet . . . So you're visiting around, seeing the South. Must be fine to have a trip like that. Always wanted to travel somewhere. Not much to see round here. You ought to go down to Natchez in the spring or down to New Orleans or Gulf Park. Yes'm. Fraid you didn't pick much when you came here. You don't happen to be from Georgia? You are? Always wanted to go to Georgia, ever since I read *Gone With the Wind.* Know you're proud to be a Georgian, to live in the same state with Margaret Mitchell . . . Say you like that song they're singing? . . . No'm, don't suppose it's got a name. Just what they sing when they're working. Ever hear a bunch of darkies sing "Sometimes I Feel Like a Motherless Child"? Gosh . . . makes you feel queer. Makes you want to cry—don't know why—just want to cry. Now what's in a song like that to make you want to cry? Ever thought about it? Maybe I'm just easy to cry. Sit here of nights . . . on the porch . . . when they're singing down there at their cabins—always end up crying . . . like I'd been to a movie or something. Yes'm. Times always hard on a plantation. Most years. . . . I hope to go to college next year but Papa says not to count on it too much. Cotton hasn't gone up near what they expected when the war started. Folks thought it'd go high and we'd have a boom or something . . . Everybody round here felt real cheerful for a while. Mam? Yes'm. I'll probably teach. Bout all a girl can do unless she goes to New York or somewhere . . . Sometimes I've kinder thought I'd like to be a missionary. Yes'm. But with so many wars everywheres, don't reckon they've got much need for missionaries now. No'm . . . our farm's not so big. Yes'm, big for this part of the state but mighty little compared to the plantations down to Greenwood and Greenville. Yes'm. You sure must go see some of them. Twenty, thirty thousand acres, some of them. Mam? Biggest one I reckon is the one at Scott, over on the river. There's a big one they say in Mississippi County, but that's in Arkansas. Yes'm. Nearly fifty thousand acres . . . eleven hundred nigger families on it. Yes'm. Does seem right big. No mam! Not a union in this county. Folks wouldn't stand for unions here. See we couldn't. Minute you let niggers start thinking they're running things . . . it'd be nothing but bad trouble. You've heard about the big man-hunt down in the swamp? Yes mam, down below Natchez. Biggest in years. Yes'm, they'll get him I reckon. Yes mam, I think so too—a lynching's a bad thing. But what you going to do when niggers kill people? There's so many of em—you got to keep them in their place, haven't you? Least that's what my dad says.

Break Their Hearts, Oh God. Give Them Tears

Break deh hearts oh God. Give um tears. Fill deh froats wiv sobbin cries and don let um hush. Don let um hush oh Gawd until dey feels deh sins. Rech down oh Gawd and break deh hearts. Break um all tuh pieces Gawd. Let a tears flow. Flow across da lan until da fences fall down. Flow across a delta. Flow across a past. Flow across a earth til it saved at last. Mek a ribber rise Gawd. Mek a floods come. High above a levees down tuh bottom lan. Wash away de doodlum, wash away de sto, wash away de chaingang, wash away a lynchin, wash away da ridin boss—*Lawd do dat for sho!* Rench out deh fears God, wash out deh hate. Git a hands clean of blood befo it too late. When deh hearts is broke Gawd, tek yo white chile up. Tell im hush his frettin. Tell im try an smile. Tell im he feel better in a liddle while. Tell im folks jes has tuh learn tuh treat his black brudder like a real fambly what belongs tuh one anudder. Tell im he been stubborn fo a long long while. Tell im better dry his face an try an smile. Tell im lot of work—don he want tuh do his share? Tell im loads been powerful heavy jes fo one tuh bear.

Growing into Freedom

Published in the Autumn 1943 issue of *Common Ground*, this article is an early version of "When I Was a Child," Smith's opening chapter of *Killers of the Dream*. The editor's note referenced Smith's previous contributions to *Common Ground* and her forthcoming novel, *Jordan Is So Chilly*, (Smith's original title for *Strange Fruit)*. Clearly, by 1943 Lillian Smith was known widely and recognized for boldly declaring that segregation harms white children as well as black.

I am a southern woman born in that region of all the earth where race prejudice is sharpest, where it has its bitterest flavor, its deepest roots, where the relationship of the two races has become so intertwined with hate and love and fear and guilt and poverty and greed, with churches and with lynchings, with attraction and repulsion that it has taken on the ambivalent qualities, the subtle conflicts, of a terrible and terrifying illness.

And because I was born there and have lived most of my life there, I find it difficult to think without emotion about my South—and race. *Segregation, White Supremacy, the Negro's Place* are not words to me, nor theories, but a way of life, a tragic way which I, and others like me, white and Negro, have lived since birth.

It is not easy to pick up such a life and pull out of it those strands which have to do with color, with Negro-white relationships, for they are knit of the same fibers that have gone into the making of the whole fabric; they are woven into its most basic patterns and designs. The mother who taught me what I know of tenderness and love and compassion taught me also the bleak rituals of keeping the Negro in his place. The father who rebuked me for an air of superiority toward schoolmates from the mill settlement and rounded out his rebuke by gravely reminding me that "all men are brothers" also taught me the steel-like inhuman decorums I must demand of every colored male.

Neither the Negro nor sex was often discussed in my home. We were given little formal instruction in these difficult matters, but we learned our lessons well. We learned the intricate system of taboos, of renunciations and compensations, of manners, voice modulations, words, along with our prayers, our toilet habits, and our games. I do not remember how or when, but I know that by the time I had learned that God is love, that Jesus is His Son, that all men are brothers with a common Father, I also knew that I was better than a Negro, that all black folk have their place and must be kept in it, and that a terrifying disaster would befall the South if ever I treated a Negro as my social equal. I had learned that God so loved the world that He gave His only begotten Son that we might have segregated churches in which it was my duty to worship each Sunday and on Wednesday at evening prayers. I had learned that white southern people are a hospitable, courteous, tactful, and warmhearted people who treat those of their own color with consideration and as carefully observe Jim-Crow customs, segregating from all the richness of life—"for their own good and welfare"—thirteen million people whose skin is colored a little differently from my own.

I knew that a member of my family would always shake hands with old Negro friends, would speak gently and graciously to members of the Negro race unless they forgot their place, in which event tones would grow peremptory and icy, drawing lines beyond which only the desperate would dare take one step. I knew that to use the word "nigger" was unpardonable and no well-bred person was quite so crude as to do so—nor would a well-bred person call a Negro "mister" or invite him into the living-room to eat with him.

I knew that my old nurse, Aunt Chloe, who had so patiently nursed me through long months of illness, who had given me refuge when a little sister took my place as the baby of the family, who comforted me, soothed me, delighted me with her stories and games, let me fall asleep on her deep warm breast, was not worthy of the passionate love I felt for her, but must be given a half-smiled-at affection similar to that one feels for one's dog. I knew that the deep respect I felt for her, the tenderness, the love, was a silly childish thing which every normal child outgrows—that such love begins with one's toys and is outgrown and discarded with them. I learned to give presents instead of esteem and honor; I learned to use a soft voice to oil my words of superiority; I learned to cheapen with tears and sentimental talk of "my mammy" one of the profound and tender relationships of my life.

From the day I was born, I learned my lessons. I was put into a frame too intricate, too complex, too twisting to describe here so briefly, but I learned to conform to its slide-rule measurements. I learned that it is possible to be a Christian and a Southerner simultaneously; to be a gentlewoman and an arrogant callous creature in the same moment; to believe in freedom, to glow when the word is used, and to practice slavery from morning to night. I learned it in the way all of my southern people learn it: by closing doors that lead into honest thinking and feeling, by turning away from new ways of living.

I closed the doors, or they were closed for me. Then one day I began to open them again. Why I had the desire, or the strength, to open them would require in the answering a self-analysis too long, too stark for me to make here. And perhaps I would not have the honesty that such an analysis would demand of me; nor the will to make it. I know only that somewhere along the uphill path we all travel from babyhood to maturity I learned in my heart and imagination what it means to be rejected by one's fellow men. How or why one learns this is not so important as that it is learned. Perhaps it comes to a little child in the family when it feels deprived of a love which it wants; perhaps through experiences when tender human relationships have been betrayed; sometimes when one feels one's self the object upon which an adult misuses his power.

These profound hungers of a child and how they are filled must have much to do with the way in which later experiences are assimilated. To excerpt, therefore, an experience from a life, from a family background, and describe it as an isolated phenomenon, surely is not only a distortion but an act without real significance. Yet I believe, as I travel the road back to childhood, that there was one race experience which I had that may have left a lasting effect upon my personality. I should like to preface an account of it by giving a brief glimpse of my background and my family, hoping that somehow the reader by entering my home with me will be able to blend the sharp ragged edges of the experience into the full life picture.

I was born and reared in a small Deep South town whose population was about equally Negro and white. My life began as one member of a large family whose material environment was made smooth by moderate wealth. The nine of us grew up freely in a home of many rooms, surrounded by spacious grounds, lawns, backyard, gardens, fields, and barn. We were given the advantages of schooling, music, art which are available in the South, and our world was not limited to the South for always travel to far places seemed a simple and natural thing to contemplate, and usually there was at least one of us in some distant part of the world.

We knew we were a respected and important family of this small town, but beyond this knowledge we gave little thought to status. Our father made money for the fun and excitement of making it, not for what money itself can buy, nor the security that it sometimes gives. And I do not remember at any time wanting money for its own sake, nor do I remember that thrift and saving were ideals which our parents considered important enough to urge upon us. We were trained to think that each of us should have a profession in which we were interested primarily because of its usefulness to the world, and the family thought it the right thing to make sacrifices, if necessary, to give each child adequate preparation for his life's work. We were trained to think books are important, and music and art, but above all else the urgent thing was what each of us planned to "do with our lives." That we must "do something" seemed as natural and inevitable as breathing. While many of our neighbors spent their energies in counting the limbs on their family tree, or reliving the old days, or refighting that bitter Civil War which has haunted us for so long, my father was pushing his nine children straight into the future. "You have your heritage," he used to say, "some of it good, some not so good; and as far as I know, you had the usual number of grandmothers, grandfathers, etc. That is that. The past has been lived. It is gone. The future is yours. What are you going to do with it?" Although he asked this question of his children, and sometimes one knew the question was but an echo of an old question he had spent his whole life trying to answer for himself. For always the future held my father's dreams . . . always he expected to find there what he spent his life searching for.

We lived much as do other Southerners, but our parents talked in Christian and democratic terms. We were told ten thousand times that "all men are brothers" . . . that we are a part of a democracy and must act like democrats . . . that the teachings of Jesus are real and could actually be practiced if one were to try. We were taught that we were superior to hate and resentment and that no member of the Smith family could stoop so low as to have an enemy. No matter what injury was done one of us, we must not injure ourselves further by retaliating. We had family prayers once each day . . . all of us as children read through the Bible once each year . . . we memorized hundreds of Bible verses, said "sentence prayers" around the family table, or repeated verses at breakfast. God was not someone we met on Sunday at church but a permanent member of our household. And it never occurred to me until I was fourteen or fifteen years old that He did not see every act and thought of mine and chalk up the score on eternity's tablets.

Despite this somewhat burdensome strain of always living with God, the nine of us were strong, healthy, energetic youngsters who filled our days with play and sports and managed to live much of our lives on the animal level at which young lives should be lived.

Our mother was a wistful creature who loved beautiful things in a vague inarticulate way and who took good care of her children. We always knew this was not her world . . . but one she accepted under duress. Her private world we rarely were permitted to enter, any of us, but the shadow of it lay at times heavily on our hearts.

My father owned large business interests, employed hundreds of Negroes and white laborers, paid them the prevailing low wages, worked them the prevailing long hours, built for them mill towns (colored and white), built for each group a church, saw to it that religion was plentifully supplied, that there was a commissary at which commodities were sold at a high price—and, in general, managed his affairs much as ten thousand other southern men managed theirs. I can still hear him chuckling as he told us how in his fight for prohibition he lined up the entire mill force of several hundred, gave each a little money, marched them in and voted liquor out of Hamilton County. It was a great day in his life. He had won the Big Game—a game he was always playing with himself against some evil. It did not occur to him to scrutinize the methods he employed in his fight against evil. Evil was to him a word written in capitals; the devil was smart; if you wanted to win you had to outsmart him. It was as simple as that to him. He was a practical hard-headed, warm-hearted, high-spirited man, born during the Civil War, earning his own living at twelve, struggling through the bitter decades of Reconstruction and post-Reconstruction, through the Populist movement, on into the 20th century, with only scorn for those who pitied themselves or the South—scheming, dreaming his dreams, expanding his business, making and losing money, with never a doubt that God was always by his side whispering hunches to him as to how to pull off a successful deal. When he lost, it was his own fault; when he won, God had helped him. When the telegram was placed in his hands telling of the death of his beloved favorite son, he quietly gathered his children together, knelt down, and in a steady voice which contained no hint of his shattered life, loyally repeated: "God is our refuge and strength, a very present help in trouble. Therefore will not we fear, though the earth be removed and though the mountains be carried into the sea." On his death bed, he whispered to his old Business Associate up in Heaven: "I have fought the fight; I have kept the faith."

Against this backdrop I want to tell a story of two children who learned to love each other and then saw each other no more.

A little white girl was found in the colored section of our small town, living with a Negro family. This family had recently moved to our town and little was known of them. The white clubwomen busied themselves in an attempt to do something about this child, and the Negro family was interviewed somewhat persistently for several days, until they grew frightened and, finally, evasive and silent. This only served to increase the suspicion of the white group, and at last the child was forcibly taken from her adopted family despite their tears and protests. She was brought to our home, mother having consented to look after the child temporarily since one more could so conveniently fit into our ample family pattern. Julie roomed with me, shared my bed, sat next to me at our table, wore my clothes, played with my dolls, and followed me around from morning to night, happily dazed by so many comforts and conveniences and pleasures. She was an affectionate little thing, and I was pleased by her adoration, and quickly a warm personal relationship grew up between us.

Then one day things changed. Word came from an orphanage. There were meetings and whispered conversations with my parents. Julie was quickly whisked away. There were no explanations. I questioned my mother. "Why did Julie have to go back when we have plenty of room? She likes us—she hardly knows them." "Because," Mother said gently, "Julie is a colored girl. She has to live in colored town." "But why? She lived here for three weeks." "She is a little colored girl," Mother repeated. "She's the same little girl she was yesterday," I remember saying to my mother, "and you said yourself Julie has nice manners. You said that," I persisted. "Yes," my mother said, "Julie is a nice child but she is colored. A colored child cannot live in our home." "She did live with us," I said, "and she is the same little girl she was yesterday. Can she come to see me? Spend the day?" "No." "I don't understand." "You're too young to understand," Mother said and turned away.

Yes, I was too young to understand. But I was not too young to feel the pain of separation from a little friend whom I never saw again, nor too young to make an identification with her shame and bewilderment, nor too young to begin to doubt my parents and the sincerity of their religion. I knew they had done something which did not fit in with their teachings, with what they said they held dear. I could not put this into words. I was too young, too inexperienced with the vocabulary of economic necessities, with that jargon of folkways, mores, slow change, which can dull the imagination so successfully. I only felt a profound reluctance ever again to accept something simply because it was told me by my elders. But though I felt burdened by doubts, by a loss of faith in my family's integrity, I practiced the customs of my people just as I had always done. I had not the strength as a child to do otherwise.

The doubt remained, and the hurt. When people talked of love and Christianity, I knew they did not mean it. That is a hard thing for a child to learn. And as I grew older, as more experiences collected around this faithless day, tying on no doubt to far earlier and more profound (though forgotten) experiences, I began to see myself and others like me as crippled people. I began to see that in trying to shut the Negro race away from us, we have shut ourselves away from the good, the creative, the human in life. The warping distorted frame we have put around every Negro child from birth is around every white child from birth also. Each is on a different side of the frame, but each is there. As in its twisting distorted form it shapes and cripples the life and personality of one, it is shaping and crippling the life and personality of the other. It would be difficult to decide which character is maimed the more—the white or the Negro—after living a life in the southern framework of segregation.

For the humiliation of the Negro is matched by the dull complacency of the white; Negro fear by white arrogance; hate by the cruel cheapening of human worth; ignorance by willful hypocrisy and blindness. Every illiterate Negro shut off from schooling is matched by a white who deliberately shuts himself away from knowledge and honest thinking; every sensitive, loving, perceptive Negro's hurt is equaled by the aching conflict between conscience and culture which the civilized Southerner endures all his life.

I began to see that even though, as we (white and black) acquire new knowledge, live through new experiences, we may, individual by individual, gain the strength to tear the frame from us, yet we are still stunted and crippled and can no more in our lifetime grow straight again than a tree put into a distorted steel-like frame when young and tender can grow tall and straight like free trees, when the frame is torn away at maturity. We may try. We may do clean, simple, decent things, we may say them, but we never do them or say them with a light heart, with a mind serene and sure. But always with a mind and spirit burdened with fear, fear of "doing harm," fear that maybe the others who are so certain they are right may be saying the truth, even though our intelligence, our knowledge, our heart, our spirit cry out that they are liars and cowards—just crippled people like ourselves who have not the strength to break the framework, even a little.

This deep inner conflict, this wearing fear of bringing disaster to the innocent is the price we pay for the privilege of being human in the Deep South. Some of us have made the choice and are willing to pay what is required of us.

But the price is too high. It must not be exacted of another generation. Somehow we must find a way to make it possible for a southern child to grow up now in freedom, to grow a personality strong and honest and creative and loving—and without fear. No child today in the South can grow that kind of personality. It is not possible in the rigid framework we put around them at birth.

Somehow we must realize that in keeping the black man in his place, we white Southerners are lynching the spirit of every one of our children. We don't believe that now, down here. When we once believe, when we look at these children and assess the injury we have done them, we shall change. We shall stop talking so glibly about a vague democracy, a good life which we must bring about slowly, very slowly, for the future's children. We shall want it now today for our own—and we shall get it.

Growing Plays: *The Girl*

The ideas given form in the story of the Girl and her emergence from the pink egg evolved over many summers before they appeared in *South Today* (Spring–Summer 1944) and in *Educational Leadership* (May 1945). Various aspects of growth toward maturity were discussed at Laurel Falls Camp, and Smith continued to speak and write about the barriers to growth that all individuals create out of fear and insecurity. The meaning of maturity for the Girl—accepting responsibility for creating her own life and helping to shape the world in which she lived—is another recurring theme, especially important in Smith's challenge to the white Southern lady image. She made Laurel Falls Camp a lab school for human growth and understanding unlike anything else in the socialization of the young Southern women who attended. Her concern for opening doors to the girls' internal awareness was always related to a corresponding effort to open doors to their awareness of social responsibility. In a letter to one camper's parents, Smith described the essence of her intent for the camp: "So much of our effort here is spent in trying to wake up these little sleeping beauties that our Anglo-American culture has anesthetized, or rather put in a deep freeze. We have tried to help them feel deeply, fully, and to do something interesting with those feelings and fantasies. At the same time we have tried to give insight and understanding" (qtd. in Gladney, "Lillian Smith's Hope" 283–84).

A STORY OF HOW CHILDREN MADE A PLAY OUT OF THEIR OWN LIVES

The Girl was part of our lives on The Mountain ten years before we put her in a play. No one remembers her beginning and no one believes she will ever end. She is part of every girl who spends a summer up on the Mountain; she is every little girl. Into her have gone the struggles, the growing pains, the fears, the hates, the failures, the guilts, the understanding, the pleasure, and the love that each girl feels.

No one quite remembers just how but she began to seem real to us, long ago.

It happened like this:

The counselors have a daily discussion group in child guidance, where theories of psychoanalysis are discussed, special problems analyzed, play projects initiated, and opportunities given to air and evaluate the natural human conflicts that arise now and then between people living closely together. One day two campers came in to talk to the director.

"What do the counselors do at those meetings?" one asked bluntly.

The other said quickly, "Of course, don't tell us if you'd rather not. But we would like to know."

The director said, "They talk about you and themselves. They talk about growing up, the things that keep us from growing, the things that help us grow. They talk, sometimes, about such things as temper tantrums, ways to get attention; and hate, and love. Things like that. We call it 'psychology'."

"Well gee," said Katie, "if that's what they talk about, seems to me they're the wrong ones doing the talking. It ought to be us! Look at me! I've grown four inches this year. Mother says I'm a mess to live with, shooting out in every direction. You know how hard I find it to get along at home . . . why don't *I* have a chance to learn how to grow! Those counselors are already grown, aren't they? Or are they?" She grinned, pushed her bangs off her freckled face.

"You see," the tactful one said softly, "some of us worry so. If we knew what made us feel the way we feel inside, maybe we'd know more what to do about it . . ." She smiled to soften her words, always the girl who sandpapered the rough edges and made them smooth to the feelings.

Katie grinned again. "We aren't vegetables. Not really. A carrot just grows, doesn't it, if folks fix the ground and fertilize it and keep it moist? All that kind of thing. Folks *grow* vegetables. But counselors and parents can't grow us. We do our own growing. I mean—I know I'm more than a beet or a carrot! Though I can't prove it."

"I remember one day when I first came to camp," the gentle one said, "I was homesick. I felt awful inside. Terrible. And I didn't know why. You took me in your room and petted me a little and explained to me what homesickness is. We talked an hour or two and you talked to me as if I had sense and I understood you. I remember I felt bigger than the thing that was bothering me," Jennie smiled. "I felt I had the draw on it."

Katie sighed. "Golly, that's what I need. Only it's not homesickness with me. It's a heck of a lot of—other things."

So, led by the girls themselves, we began to have "psychology" hours at camp, just as we had hours for tennis, swimming, riding, sculpture. And no girl ever missed these hours. If she had to choose between horse-back riding and her 'psychology', the horse would be left in the stables . . .

Their curiosity was, and is, a startling thing. They seem never to learn all they want to know about their bodies, their feelings, their problems and how to come to terms with them. With fresh, wiry minds, not too strongly trained to resist knowledge (as are most of our older minds) they take a grip on psychoanalytic theory as if it were a tennis racquet. They are not afraid of the right words for feelings, for situations. They accept with beautiful simplicity and honesty what grownups call the 'ugly' facts of life, just as they accept the pleasing facts. They have not learned yet to shroud these facts in secrecy and fear. To them, they are as much a part of life as the house you live in, or the color of your eyes.

We began talking of ourselves as we were when we were babies. How we were born, how we felt, what we wanted, what we learned to love. Often these talks had to be suspended while each girl reminisced, telling the 'cute' things about her babyhood; every other girl listening as long as she could, then breaking in with an account of the 'cute' things *she* did . . . and on and on. The hour would often end before we could move on from these beloved stories of ourselves.

But the talks did move on, slowly, with no sense of hurry, for we were not covering a textbook, or doing a unit of study or trying to pass an examination. They were talks that became in themselves creative experiences, as new insights were gained, as sudden expressions of pent-up feelings stirred our imaginations, our sense of the drama of growing. We talked about the plain, ordinary things: thumb-sucking, weaning, toilet habits, playing with our bodies; how these experiences affected us, kept us from growing or helped us grow. And we talked as simply as we talk at camp about form in riding, strokes in swimming. One was as honorable a part of our life as the other; all, the play, the sports, the emotional insight, the growing, being integral to our experiences in living together.

As the years went by, the Girl began to seem real to us. SHE, from the day she was born, had to climb step by step by step, toward emotional maturity, as we did. And we climbed with her through our own experiences. We began giving nicknames to our experiences; making our own special little jokes about growing difficulties. "Babyish" became an adjective that even the youngest of us no longer wanted to be labelled with.

"Mature" was a cherished word in every one's vocabulary. To be cited at Council Fire for having shown emotional maturity in some difficult situation was as high an honor as any one could receive on the Mountain. It rated with recognition for expert riding, for expert swimming, a fine piece of sculpture, a beautifully wrought ring.

We found out who the Girl's "enemies" are, as we discovered our own. The hate feelings which had accumulated in our lives, had accumulated in hers; she had to find ways of using them up, so as not to use them on people, as did we. When we discovered that a good hard sweating tennis game was a wonderful way for us to get rid of our resentments, we knew the Girl had found it too. When we made a piece of sculpture and found ourselves in a loving, sympathetic mood toward folks, we knew the Girl felt the same way.

We decided that guilt tired us out more than an overnight trip; that failure was like having your feet chained together. We finally decided that hate, fear, guilt, failure are our mortal enemies and the biggest job in life is to find ways of outwitting them. Growing up emotionally, maturing, became an adventure to us. It was not easy, but it was good fun. We all decided one day that you are the center of attention only once in your life, and that is the day you are born. That day is your day. You are First, a little queen, for one day only. After that, you, if you grow, have got to get out of that center and go places. . . .

GROWING PLAYS

Each summer at camp we grow a play out of our experiences together. Usually it develops out of something we have talked about, done together, or something in the outside world that we are trying to understand. One summer we grew a play about the 300 years the Negro has spent in America; another year, it was concerned with the war and peace; one summer we grew a play about America. We called it *I Am American*, believing America is no better than each of us in it. It was concerned with the way our country grew, its conflicts, its little towns, its people, its fun, its gay, busy, frightening cities, its greed, its shining good deeds and dreams, its churches, factories, unions, poverty and wealth.

One summer, the campers decided the play should be about themselves. It would be, they said, a kind of modern pilgrim's progress. Its drama would be the drama of growing up. At first they tried to find a name for it. No name pleased us all. But as the play grew, we began to speak of it as *The Girl*, and at last we knew we had its title.

The girls built her story. She must come out of an egg: a beautiful, pink wonderful egg, large enough for her to step through the opening.

"Of course that is not science; that's poetry," one said hesitantly.

"I should say it isn't science," another said briskly, "Dr. de Schweinitz says in *Growing Up* that the egg you came from is no bigger than the point the sharpest pencil can make—"

"Oh well, Dr. de Schweinitz wasn't making a play. How could you have a tiny—"

"Yes, but art to be art must be true—"

After a little work-out on that ancient controversy, we all agreed that a play was better with more poetry than science in it, though it must be essentially true. Every one agreed that the Egg was true.

So they built the Egg. Such an egg you have never seen. Large, pale pink, lighted from within, the opening covered by layers of pink chiffon. Girls would come in after a hard tennis game or from the stables or the rifle range, and work a little while on the Egg. It was fun to go inside it and suddenly come forth into the World. Every one had to try it to see how it felt... Yes, it really was poetry.

Then what? The children pondered. Well, the Girl had a lot of fun when she was little, lying down all the time, rolling around, playing with her toes, cooing, sucking—

"The little egotist!"

"Seems to me," another youngster said, "she really did play practically all the time just with herself."

"Sounds awfully silly," an eight-year-old snickered.

"It was silly but it must have been fun. We all did it."

"I bet I didn't," a stolid browned tennis player snorted. "I bet I never stirred until they put a ball in my hand."

"Born, weren't you," scorn dripping, "with the world's tennis championship pinned to your chest!"

"Go ahead, let her have her pleasures!"

We did. Five of the smallest girls decided to be Little Pleasures. When the Girl came from the Egg, the Little Pleasures were to run out of the Egg with her and play with her and they were to make her have so much fun that she would hate to leave them and move on toward more mature levels.

"Now what happens?" one ten-year-old said, looking up from the piece of clay she was modeling—into a Little Pleasure.

"Well," somebody suggested, "she has to learn the rules, you know."

"Golly," one breathed, "I say the gal had better!"

"Aw—poor little ole thing. Let's let her skip em."

"Skip em? And do what? Be a baby all her life? She *has* to learn em!"

We settled down for another long discussion.

"Let's let her hate something," a tall, rangy girl said and laughed, then turned a handspring, landing as lightly as a cat; turned another, to make it even.

"Don't worry, she will—if she learns all the rules *I* learned."

"Shucks—you had such a hard life, didn't you, darling," another purred. "Poor itsy bitsy—"

Time out while itsy bitsy fixed up the purrer.

The Girl learned the rules, but not easily. No, again and again, she would run back to her baby ways and refuse to grow a bit. There was a little trouble about this. Some of the girls thought she should not run back more than once. "Honest, you shouldn't. Maybe one time, you could, when you're nine or ten years old," a fourteen-year-old said, smiling patronizing at the younger girls, who glared back. "Maybe then you could get aches or pains and go to the infirmary to spend the night because somebody's hurt your feelings, or maybe have a temper tantrum or something—"

"Oh yeah," a ten-year-old defended her group, "I've seen fourteen-year-old girls in this very camp pick up a tummy-ache when they'd lost a tennis set. I've seen—"

Firmly, we went back to the Girl and her regressions. "The point is," somebody suggested, "she's likely to have a lot more fun growing up than growing in reverse, unless her path is blocked. What's going to block it?"

"Hating other people, getting jealous of your sister—that kind of thing—"

"Keeping things on your conscience too much—"

"Feeling guilty after you're big about little baby things you once did, like—"

"Believing you're no good. Can't do nothin'."

"Being afraid—afraid to love folks—"

"Shutting yourself off so you can't believe the truth even when it's told to you—"

"Oh dear," somebody else wailed, "*how is she going to learn the truth!*"

We were silent.

"Maybe you don't ever learn all of it." A big awkward girl, who seldom spoke in the discussions, now said softly.

"Yeah, maybe we don't. But she's just got to understand. Poetry—not science, you know." Everybody grinned. "She's *got* to know how important it is to love people! She's got to."

We decided that we must have a Speaker in the balcony, who would symbolize understanding and truth and love; who would symbolize our parents' help and sympathy and all the grown folks who had encouraged us to grow, and all the knowledge we gain about ourselves.

There would be two voices for the Girl; one her little baby voice and one her voice when she was older. There would also be the Girl herself, a dancer.

There would be much dancing, much music, and not a great many words. We must therefore have groups: a group called the Loves who would try to lure her up the steps toward maturity and who would win her away from the Hates and Fears and Guilts and Failures who must try to keep her from growing up. Now we had our focus of conflicts and our characters. The girls chose their roles, helped create their costumes, and all the Hates, Fears, Guilts, Failures, made big hideous masks to wear, for we decided that these feelings were not really 'human', but destroy human feeling. The Loves showed their own sweet, shining faces; and how those faces beamed out on the audience!

The play was almost ready. We used a simple grey cyclorama for all the scenes. There were no curtains; only dimming or blacking out of lights. There was a ramp up which the Loves persuaded the Girl to go on her path toward maturity; the Egg was on a level below the stage; the various levels of the stages symbolized progress and regression, as the Girl pushed on or turned back in her growing. We used a background of music which the children chose from the large repertoire of music they love: Cesar Franck's first movement of the symphony in D Minor was the theme music of Life itself. The Egg music was taken from the Sea Mood of *Scheherazade* by Rimsky-Korsakov. We used a sinister little thing by Villa Lobos (bassoons only) for one of the regression dances; the 'demon' music from Stravinsky's *Fire Bird* for the big struggle when the Hates and Fears and Failures tried to destroy the Girl. The wonderful music from Scriabin for the triumph of the Loves.

The play was ready. We all lived through it to its triumphant end and there was no girl, big or little on The Mountain who did not feel that this was her 'biography', that she was the one who had triumphed, that the successes were hers, and that her strength had increased from living through and projecting in a beautiful and thrilling form her own feelings and dreams.

[The words alone do not give more than half of the play, for by means of the choreography, much of the story and the conflicts were told. Throughout the play, there is no interruption. The pattern is always in flux, the dancers (who symbolize the Girl's creative and destructive impulses) are on the stage, off the stage; sometimes surrounding the Girl, sometimes blocking her path to maturity, sometimes (as in the case of Love and Understanding) leading her away from her babyhood toward a rich full mature life. We decided that an attempt to describe the dances, movement, even the pantomime, would only be confusing. We are therefore giving the words, believing your imagination can fill in some of the

Frances Bear, a scene from *The Girl*, *South Today*, 1944.
Courtesy of Piedmont College.

Frances Bear, a scene from *The Girl*, *South Today*, 1944.
Courtesy of Piedmont College.

Carolyn Gerber, costume sketches for *The Girl*, *South Today*, 1944.
Courtesy of Piedmont College.

blank spots. The costumes were in rich, beautiful glowing colors, the lighting and music gave an extra emotional dimension to the whole project. It was in the opinion of the parents the most satisfying, theatrically, of any play we have done.]

THE WORDS

(Curtain is raised. Dim light by Speaker. Stage is dark. Floor space between Egg and balcony lighted by dim blue-green light. First forty measures of Cesar Franck's symphony.)

The Speaker: I speak of Life!
Not of the dead but of the living.
Not of the silent
but of that which whispers and shouts and laughs and sings and sobs,
bending sound,
twisting and bending and shaping sound to its image.

I speak of Life!
Not of tombs, not of cool, dark tombs,
not of death, not of cool, silent smooth tombs,
not of old moss and stone and stillness and darkness,
but of light.
Of the bend of trees, the beating of boughs,
of buds swelling and snapping twigs under running feet,
of a silence crushed in the fist by laughter and words
. . . and tears.
Of stamping hooves upon the ground
and the rush of wings,
the great rush of wings through the air,
the mighty rush of wings through the air,
strong wings
through the bright air,
shining through the air,
beating against the brightness.

It is of these that I speak.

It is of all that make the living strange to the dead;
strange to the stillness,
strange to the silence,
strange to the motionless,
strange to the darkness.

It is of you that I speak;
of your life and my life . . . and the girl's life.

(Music from Scheherazade. Very soft. Light comes on in Egg until Egg is glowing.)

The Speaker: Out of the darkness,
out of the soft warm darkness,
out of the soft warm dark stillness,
out of the still warm dark . . . soft . . . soft . . .
out of a shell left empty,
comes life!

Out of the egg,
smooth and round
smooth and round and floating floating and smooth and
 round round curving and round,
out of all that is round and smooth,
floating between death and life
out of the egg
out of all that is warm and soft and round, we come.
And the girl will come—when it is time.

When it is time to break the stillness,
to push through the warmness and the darkness and
 the roundness into light and sound and the
 rushing of wings.

And she will not know that hate is waiting,
That fear is waiting,
that failure and guilt are waiting to pull her back
 to silence and stillness,
back to old moss and stone and tombs and darkness,
back to death.

She will not know.

She will not know that love is waiting,
she will not know that love and truth are waiting,
that all that is wise and beautiful is waiting
 to lead her to life,
to make of her the living, the bright living,
to fill her with the bend of trees, and the beating
 of boughs, and the rush of great wings through
 the air, the bright air.

She does not know. She does not know.

(The Little Pleasures play with the girl, romping and teasing, they roll and tumble through the dance. The stage is gradually lighted, area by area, and the light goes out in the Egg.)
(After the Girl has played too long.)

The Speaker: Aren't you ashamed!
You mustn't do that! Don't you know, don't you know!
You must grow, you must grow!

You can't stay and play with the little pleasures
I say you can't stay there and play day after
day after day so carefree and gay kicking up your
heels in play you can't stay there and play little
girl all day!

(said rather rapidly in one tone)

Come, you must learn your way
through the city,
the big city,
the tall city,
the busy hurried tall big city
that mankind built.
You must learn how to cross the streets—
The Girl's baby voice: No!
The Speaker: when to stop,
when to go—
The Girl's baby voice: No!
The Speaker: You must learn directions.
You must know
when to stop and when to go;
when to go fast,
when to go slow.
You must know your way through the big city streets—
The Girl's baby voice: No no no no!

(Music from Petrouchka . . . soft and quiet and comforting as voice speaks.)

The Speaker: You must go until you find the tallest place
where you can look down and all around
seeing all that eyes can see.

Where you can look in every face and say
"It cannot injure me."
Where you can say, "I am not afraid of anything
that man has made."
Where you can feel strong and tall as the tallest tree,
as the tallest tree.
Where you can say, "I have faith in me."
Love will give you strength.
Don't be afraid to say,
"I have the strength that love gives, I have that. I
have love for my own. It is good to be grown."

The Girl's baby voice: No!

The Speaker: But the girl turned toward the city,
the big tall busy city which mankind built;
turned away from the meadows,
from pleasures—play, play so gay all day—
turned away from the soft warm darkness—
soft and dark and still and round round floating
floating and round—
to find her direction through the big city streets
the long streets,
twisting and busy and full of sound,
full of sound and movement, so furious, so swift;
the big tall busy city that beats and pounds and
shapes those who build it,
that beats and pounds and shapes the direction of all
who walk in it.
And she could hear Love speaking, "Come my dear,
this way."
And she could hear Understanding say,
"Beyond you lies all that is beautiful and wise."
But the Girl was afraid.
Afraid of the streets,
the twisting turning busy streets;
afraid she could not remember when to stop and when
to go, when to go fast, when to go slow,
afraid of streets that come to a dead end, dead end,
dead end...
afraid of streets that do not bend, but bend you to
their end, to their end.
All she could remember was a meadow where she could
play play all day gay gay.

All she could remember was smooth and round and soft and dark . . . floating floating. . .

Voices of Teachers of the Rules: Stop! Go! Go slow! Go fast! Go slow!
Stop! Go! Stop! Go!
Stop—Go—Stop—Go
Stop go stop go stop go stop!

The Little Girl's voice: I am going back . . . I am going back . . . I will not stay here . . . I do not know when to stop and when to go . . . I shall go back and play in the meadow and play . . . I shall go back where all is smooth and round and soft and dark and floating . . . floating . . . floating . . .

(The girl resumes her baby ways, turns, plays with the Little Pleasures. Moves toward the Egg while her baby voice speaks from the balcony.)

The Little Girl's voice: Everybody's bad. I hate them! Yes I do . . . I hate everybody. Wish they would go away . . . never come back . . . wish they'd all go way and never come back . . . they'll be sorry . . . they'll be sorry they're so mean to me . . . I'll die . . . yes I'll die and then they'll be sorry! They'll be so sorry . . . they'll cry and cry and wish they'd been nice to me. . .

(Now the girl dreams a beautiful princess fantasy.)

I'm a princess . . I'm a beautiful princess and I'll wave my wand . . . Down on your knees! My unworthy subjects. Down on your knees! (she laughs a little) (she sighs) I hate them! Hate everybody . . . wish they'd die . . . wish they'd all die and leave me alone. Everybody's mean to me . . . everybody's doing things to me . . . (cries a little) I feel so bad . . . maybe I'm going to be sick . . . maybe I'm going to die . . . they'll be sorry. . .

(The Little Pleasures are softly pulling the Girl back toward the Egg. She goes with them, step by step, slowly)

The Girl's baby voice: (Laughs) Love to suck my thumb . . . Hey, little toe! Hey . . . (sighs) hmmmm . . . feels so good . . . like to be little . . . like to be a baby . . . and not drow up . . . don't want to drow up . . . want to be itsy bitsy baby . . . (talks baby talk now)

The Speaker: Stop! You cannot go that way! You cannot play and play the livelong day. You must learn directions . . . You must know when to stop and when to go . . .

(And as the Speaker speaks, the Loves come on the stage, move down toward the Girl, block her way back to the Egg, gently lead her on toward maturity. But as she moves on to another level, little Fears creep out, Failures grow big as she stares at them, Guilts slip around her, crowd the Loves back. And for a moment the Girl hesitates. Then suddenly she laughs at them all, at all the stern business of growing, forgets everything now but joy in being young and having fun. Sees her reflection in the big mirror, feels good, wants only to be gay for life is suddenly like going to a party!)

The Speaker: But even guilt and fear, even guilt and fear and failure
even dread
can bow its head
to one who is young.
And the Girl,
the Girl laughed, "I don't care!
whoof! I feel light as air,
I feel good!
I am young. I feel young. I Am Young.
What do I care? I feel so free!
    I am in love with ME."
And through her there was a rushing of wings through
    the air, the bright air.

(Now follows the mirror dance. The Girl dances, admiring her own image, suddenly care-free and full of herself.)

The Young Girl's voice: "I am in love with me,
so beautiful . . .
I am in love with all who love me,
    so beautiful. Pretty . . . pretty . . .
Listen, you hear? You are lovely, my dear.
My dear, myself, so lovely you are,
    lovelier than anyone else, by far.
I make a lovely light . . . and all the world is
    beneath my feet. I'm sweet . . . you hear, dear?
And all the world is far away. I go my way!
I go my own way! This is my day. I can play and

play . . . What do I care? Whoof! I feel light as air!

(The Loves come and try to lead the Girl away from her mirror but the Guilts and Fears overpower the Loves and during this struggle, the Little Pleasures come once more upon the stage and try to induce her to play with them. She starts slowly down the steps toward the Egg. Then suddenly as she begins to play with the Little Pleasures who look as babyish and "cute and winsome" as she did when she was a baby herself suddenly they whisk out masks, put them on, and she sees what once was babyish and cute turned before her eyes into something obscene and ugly and regressive. This frightens her. She hesitates, looks up toward the Loves, who now have been pushed almost out of her sight.)

The Speaker: Stop! You cannot go that way! That is an empty shell,
the dead-end way.
That is a page on which no word is written;
music which has no sound.
That is stillness and darkness and stone and death.

(the music here is that of eight bassoons, a strange little piece by Villa-Lobos; suddenly it changes into more primitive sounds and rhythms. The Girl is deeply troubled by she knows not what. And as she hesitates, she hears within her her own fear, failure, rage, guilt, whispering to her, and she turns away from the path to maturity to listen to them.)

Chorus of Destructive Feelings:

Fear: *You are afraid. You are afraid.*
Failure: *You can't do it, you hear!*
Fear: *You're filled with fear.*
Rage: *Hate them! Hurt them! They hurt you-you hurt them!*
Guilt: *Everything you do is wrong . . . wrong . . . wrong . . .*
Don't you wish you were dead!
Failure: *Your heart is lead.*

(Now the Failures come out on the stage, approach the Girl where she is sitting on the steps between the Egg and her own age level. With little struggle on her part, they take the cords from around themselves and tie her arms close to her and bind her feet, and leave her there, helpless. A dialogue follows now between the Speaker, who symbolizes love and understanding, and the Girl's own destructive impulses. While this battle of words goes on, the Guilts, Hates, Fears, Failures are struggling to keep the Loves away from the Girl, quietly pushing them farther and farther away from her.)

Her Destructive Feelings:

Rage: *Hate you! Hate them! Hate all of them! I'll hurt them!*
Yes I will. I don't care! I'll hurt them!

The Speaker: Your hate will destroy all that you prize and love—

Rage: *I don't care! I want to destroy. I do not love.*
I hate them all—you hear!

The Speaker: Yes, dear.

Rage: *Then save your breath!*

The Speaker: To destroy what one loves is a way to death.

Fear: *I don't care. I'd just as soon die.*

The Speaker: I think perhaps you lie.

Rage: *No! No! I hate them, I want them to die—*

Guilt: *I mean, I want to die! You hear?*

The Speaker: Yes, dear. Listen, don't you hear the rush of wings
through the air, the bright air? Strong wings
shining and beating . . . Don't you see right before
your eyes so much that is beautiful and wise?
Don't you hear sound, so lovely, so lovely and clear,
don't you hear? Don't you feel—

Rage: *Always telling you to grow! Telling you*
to stop and go.
Always telling you—

Fear: *I'm afraid . . . you hear? I'm afraid!*

The Speaker: You have strength for the living. You must go
until you find the tallest place where you can
look down, seeing all that eyes can see,
where you can look in every face and say,
"It cannot injure me."

Fear: *I'm afraid . . . afraid—*

The Speaker: Fear leads to a dead end, dead end. And it will
bend, bend, bend you to its end!

Failure: *I have no strength. I cannot go. I cannot go.*

The Speaker: You can try.

Failure: *No, no, I'd only die!*

The Speaker: I am here, dear. Listen, love is here. Love will give you strength. Just say, "I have the strength that love gives. I have that. I have love for my own."

Failure: *I'll only die.*

The Speaker: You lie! You hear, you lie! You want to destroy all that is good and wise. Your heart is full of lies! You turn away from the light . . . the bright living . . . the wonderful rushing of wings through the air—

The Girl's Voice (sobs): They are all against me now.

The Speaker: You turn to the blackness . . . to old moss and stillness, to stone and tombs—and death.

Listen, dear, I am here.

Love is here: *this way*. Beyond you lies all that is beautiful and wise. All that is light, all that is of the living. You have the strength!

The Girl's Voice: I've tried.

I've tried and always I fail. I've tried!

The Speaker, (calmly): There are two ways. You must decide.

(With tremendous energy, the Loves push through to the Girl: untie her, give her the ropes with which she has been tied. Slowly she smiles. She understands. She knots the ropes into a whip, and in sudden freedom she drives the destructive impulses off of the stage and out of her life. Music becomes strong, triumphant, powerful.)

The Speaker: And she could hear Love speaking,
"Come my dear, this way."
And she could hear Understanding say,
"Beyond you lies
all that is beautiful and wise."

(The Girl turns, a Love on either side of her, and walks steadily, steadily, steadily up that stage ramp—toward maturity, while every girl in the play and every girl watching from the wings, in her own heart marched steadily with her. . .)

The End.

Putting Away Childish Things

Significantly, this article also appears in the Spring–Summer 1944 issue of *South Today*. Smith's message for the campers informs her analyses of adults' resistance to social change. Smith calls "racial thumb suckers" those white people, North and South, who continue to say that racial segregation cannot be undone. They are in effect regressing in their behavior out of insecurity for they "still think and feel as white people" and fear if segregation goes, they will lose the "priorities" that go with white supremacy. Regardless of genre, Smith is shifting the prevailing narrative about race from one that says segregation cannot be changed to one that says what you fear is keeping you from becoming human and from living the life you say you really want.

In 1943, men dreamed of brotherhood and filled the American calendar with days of rioting and bloodshed, with obscene talk of White Supremacy, with bus fights and death, with smear stories and rumors, with all the fury that destroys men's good feelings for each other and makes understanding so difficult.

But it is not of these acts of violence that we need to talk now. It is of ourselves. There is no one reading these words who took part last year in a race riot, who killed a Negro, who used the foul words of a demagogue. Men who kill, riot, use foul words in the name of race will kill, riot, use foul words in the name of anything that safely provides outlet for their hate and frustrations. They are our criminals, our delinquents, our psychopaths, our sick and miserable people. Whether they wear frock coats or overalls, the toga of leadership or the stripes of the chaingang, they are the casualties of a culture which promotes hate more assiduously than love, which makes it so hard for men to live in dignity with each other that in despair they sink to the level of animals, tearing to pieces the good and the bad, hardly knowing one from the other, as they search in great hunger for something they lost in their childhood, and which nothing in their culture gave back to them.

Theirs is another story. A story hard to listen to. A story beginning with a man's mother and father and his childhood, weaving itself in and out of a culture which pressed here, pulled there, until there was no way for the personality to fit itself together in one piece; no way to find human, creative goals to work toward; no way to feel at ease with itself.

They are the 'bad' people. And we? We are the people who dream the good dreams and let the 'bad' people turn them into nightmares. Horrified, yet with a feeling of strange helplessness, we watch their violence, wanting to do something, wanting to stop such things from happening, but blocked from action by paralyzing fear. Our minds fill with compulsive phrases, "You'll do more harm than good . . . You'll only stir up trouble . . . This isn't the right time . . . You can't change customs quickly; only education . . ." Or we gasp in relief, "Race prejudice is economic, only by abolishing poverty . . ."—in other words, "Let the unions do it." We turn away, feeling that there is nothing much that we personally can do about it, except perhaps observe Race Relations Day once a year in our churches (though that does not, of course, mean that we must give up our segregated churches!), or join an interracial committee (if it is a cautious one), or talk a little about giving "equal opportunity" and a little about housing. Doing the little things so that we can forget that we are not doing the big things.

All most of us want, deep within us, is to be assured that there will be no more race riots; no more lynchings; no more killings on buses; no more public exhibitions of race-hate obscenities; no more flares of violence calling attention to a way of life in which we all willingly participate and are willing to continue to participate, if only the Negroes will be more contented; if only the psychotic, the delinquent, the criminal, the sick will not use "race" as a way of expressing their frustrations, although we give them a green light to do so.

We, who call ourselves the 'good' people, the intelligent, even the wise, accept without protest the spiritual lynching of Negroes which goes on around us daily, in every town, every city, every part of our nation. We accept the quiet killing of self-esteem, the persistent smothering of hope and pride, the deep bruises given the egos of young Negro children; the never-ceasing humiliations which Jim Crow imposes upon human beings who are not white. We willingly say—almost all southerners and many northerners say—that segregation can not be abolished; whatever is done "for" the Negro must be done under the very system which lynches his spirit and mind every day he is under it.

For most of us are still thinking and feeling as white people. Most of us still want the priorities which we have under the White Supremacy system and we fear when segregation goes our priorities will go with it. Most of us are incapable—having calloused our imaginations with the daily rubbing of one stereotype against another—of realizing what we are saying when we say calmly that these things must be changed very slowly, that the Negro must 'prove' himself and then he will be 'accepted' by the white man. We drop the heavy millstone of Jim Crow about the Negro's neck and turn away from seeing what it does to the man beneath it. We are saying in effect: the system of White Supremacy means so much to us, the pattern we are living under has given us so many compensations, that we are willing for each little Negro child born into the world today to have the Jim Crow yoke placed around his shoulders, we are willing for black children to be humiliated, bruised, hurt daily, subjected to a psychic brutality that would arouse us to fury if our white children were subjected to it; that *has* aroused our fury when it has happened to Jewish children in Germany. We are willing for these things to go on and on because we can not endure the thought of facing the basic fact before us: the white man and his love for himself and his skin color.

Our trouble is, we cannot feel deeply these words we are saying. Our emotions are blunted concerning Negroes as human beings. It is as if we had segregated an area in our minds, marked it Colored, and refused our feelings entrance to it. And when we do begin to feel, as lately some of us have been feeling, when there springs up in us that deep, thrilling desire to tear off this steel frame of segregation that is warping both white and black lives, that is distorting everything fine and good which we prize and believe in, then suddenly we are pulled back, held by a chain that will let us go only so far and no farther. The old fear begins its old compulsive whisperings, *Yes, but this isn't the right time to do it. You'll only do harm, not good . . .*

As a white southerner, born in a Deep South town whose population was predominantly Negro, reared under the segregation pattern, still living today under it, I know the fears by heart. I know the placid taking for granted of a way of life so wounding, so hideous in its effect upon the spirit of both black and white. I know the dread of change; I know all the rationalizations by which the white man eases his guilt and conserves his superiority; how he concentrates—as if *he* were unchangeable, as if *he* and *his* pattern can never be changed—*not* on his own problem of white superiority, *not* on his own sick obsession with skin color, but instead on the Negro, hoping that somehow the Negro can be changed to fit the pattern more harmoniously. That is what most of us mean when we talk of race relations: a more harmonious adjustment of the Negro to the white man's pattern. And we have sold the idea to the North also.

In times of harmony, of ease, this fear grows less, the chain loosens, and we become more amenable to the teachings of Christianity, of democracy, of science. Even in the Deep South, in times of ease, men grow more 'liberal' toward the Negro, feeling then that he may safely be 'given more privileges.' But as tension increases, the old fear increases with it, and action is paralyzed by old taboos against speaking of human relations in terms of human equality. All else may be discussed but segregation; all else but the basic question: *are Negroes human, or aren't they?* The taboo of silence restrains such discussion in a way that only the hardiest, the most independent, dare defy it.

This is well demonstrated now in the South by many liberals who in their private lives do not practice the segregation they compulsively proclaim in public, who often eat with Negroes (unostentatiously), who, when away from the South—and often while in it—break many of the old segregation taboos, but who now insist publicly upon their belief that *for the South the pattern can never be changed*, and who punish, by ostracism and belittlement, other southerners who dare speak out plainly for a way of life that is Christian and good for southern people. And by this public insistence on segregation, they tighten the bonds of fear, they deepen prejudice, in all people; they strengthen the position of demagogues, who have never lacked courage to speak *their* piece on race; they make it easier for every man of good feelings to regress to less humane ways of behavior. They do this evil, they think, in the name of 'expediency.' They are not aware of the more profound reasons which compulsively make them act—not according to the demands of reality, but according to the demands of unconscious fears and guilt which they have no name for and which they can not come to grips with.

We need to understand these fears. And though we have little space here to go into it fully, perhaps a few suggestions might give us insight into a problem which is one all white people, rich and poor, South and North, share in common.

We would all agree that around this subject of race have gathered the southern man's deepest fears: that only about God and sex do we feel so strongly. Religion ... sex ... race ... strangely tied up together in our minds and hearts! All that we feel deeply about them we began to feel as small children. We learned about God, about sex, about race, before we began to speak words, we learned at the same time, we learned from the people who were dearest to us: our mothers and fathers and nurses.

We were trained to feel a certain way about God; a certain way about sex; a certain way about race. We were trained to feel, to act out these feelings. The words *race, sex*, were not often used by those who trained us, though we learned early to talk easily of God; but attitudes *toward* sex and race were more deeply engrained in our personalities, perhaps, than were our feelings for God. We were taught that we did not play with our bodies at the same time that we were taught that we did not play with Negroes. We learned early to feel that incest was wrong; we learned as early to feel that segregation was right. We learned these matters, as children always learn, by deep feelings. We felt profound guilt if we betrayed our learning, and we felt it as deeply about one as about the other.

As we grew older, went to school, read books, traveled, some of us acquired new and scientific facts about race and sex, some of us acquired more mature ideas about God; and sometimes we seemed to believe them . . . but deep within us, we continued to feel much as we felt when we were little children. We acquired the façade of an educated man living in an enlightened world. We use, even now, intelligent words and phrases, we behave under most normal conditions as educated, well informed people should behave. But deep within us, we feel much as we felt as little children. Any new feeling, any profoundly different feeling, would seem to our unconscious minds a betrayal of childhood love for our parents—for most of us have never learned to separate this love from the 'right' and the 'wrong' which our parents taught us. All are tied up together and to all we react with indiscriminate emotion. Much of this we never put into words, not even in our minds do we think it. And yet a reminder of this fact may suggest the ease with which men regress under strain and pressure to earlier, less rational, less appropriate feelings.

There is not one of us who has not seen this regression happen to children. A child who long ago stopped sucking his thumb gets sick; begins thumb-sucking; regresses to an earlier, more secure, less strained period in his life and its habits. When we are put under racial strain, when confronted with the need to make new adjustments, we find it easier to become racial thumb-suckers, easier to give up our more 'liberal' and mature ideas; afraid now to do what the needs of reality demand, afraid (in the intense way children are afraid) to break the taboo of segregation. And our northern liberal friends find it easy to thumb-suck with us. They, too, are using the rationalizations we have so persuasively taught them—though with far less excuse for using them than have southerners, whose training in race was begun earlier in childhood and carried on more persistently.

Now we hear talk of one world, of one brotherhood of people. We know there will be no peace on earth as long as skin-color makes enemies of men and divides them one from another. We see the evils of segregation in our own country, the harm our preoccupation with white superiority is doing; we fear the riots, the murders, the lynchings in our home towns; but we find it hard to change our obsessive thinking, our fear (stronger than the fear of race riots) of meeting old needs in new ways. We find it so easy, as conditions grow hard, to regress to our childhood racial feelings, even though they are grotesquely inappropriate to the demands of the present.

It is true that we have stereotyped the Negro but we also have stereotyped ourselves and our actions. We need to learn to think of the Negro as human; we need ourselves to *become human.*

There are of course, areas in which all of us are 'human,' in which even delinquents and criminals and the mentally ill function as humans. Although we begin life loving only ourselves, most of us do not stop there. There are few individuals who do not have some ability to identify their sympathies with other people, some willingness to place the needs of others, of at least one other, on an importance with their own. Only the schizophrenic has completely lost his ability to love and to make human identifications. But when we reserve this humanity of ours, this precious quality of love, of tenderness, of imaginative identification, for people only of our skin color (or our family, our class), we have split our lives in a way shockingly akin to the way schizophrenics have split theirs; and we develop—as whites have developed toward Negroes—a personality picture strangely like theirs: of blunted emotions, delusions of persecution, feelings of 'aloneness,' extreme irritability when efforts are made to change our white ways; projections of our conflict upon the Negro himself, making him the 'menace,' the 'problem'; and a desire to shut ourselves off by segregation not only from him, but from all science, all influences that are disturbing to the picture we have made of ourselves and our "persecutors."

It is not a pleasant picture that I have drawn of the white race. There is not one of us who can take pleasure in thinking of ourselves in a way so disturbing to complacent self regard. Yet, if we do not resist it too much, if the aroma of psychoanalytic words does not offend us too deeply, perhaps we can begin to gain insight into the damage race prejudice has done to our personalities and culture. We need to assess this damage, for it is more than poor wages, wasted soil, poverty, race riots; it is more than the damage done to Negroes themselves; it comes close home to each one of us white people.

There is a problem facing all of us, black and white, but it is not the Negro Problem. It is the problem, for Negroes, of finding some way to live a good life with white people. It is for each white the problem of learning to live a good life with himself.

From *Strange Fruit*

With the publication of *Strange Fruit* in February 1944, Smith suddenly found herself a famous (and then infamous) author of a "big" best seller. Selling at the astonishing rate of 25,000 to 30,000 copies a week even before it was banned in Boston, the interracial love story set in the post–World War I South sold a million copies in hardcover and over three million copies during her lifetime. Translated into fifteen languages, and made into a Broadway play, *Strange Fruit* brought Smith international acclaim and greatly expanded her sphere of influence as a social critic.

Readers of Smith's earlier fiction, essays, and plays may find familiar characters and settings in the following selections, which serve primarily to introduce the Andersons and the Deens, whose lives and relationships embody and symbolize the American South Smith knew and dared to question. Listening to her recordings of some of these passages (www.piedmont.edu/lilliansmith-resources), as well as reading her answers to contemporary readers' questions about *Strange Fruit*, should further enhance any reading of the full novel.

Chapter 1

She stood at the gate, waiting; behind her the swamp, in front of her Colored Town, beyond it, all Maxwell. Tall and slim and white in the dusk, the girl stood there, hands on the picket gate.

"That's Nonnie Anderson," they would tell you, "that's one of the Anderson niggers. Been to college. Yeah! Whole family been to college! All right niggers though, even if they have. Had a good mother who raised her children to work hard and know their place. Anderson niggers all right. Good as we have in the county, I reckon."

"Stuck up like Almighty, Nonnie Anderson," some colored folks said, "holding her head so highty-tighty, not like Bess. Bess common as dirt, friendly with folks."

"You forgot Ern Anderson's ways?" others said. "Spittin image of her pappy in her ways. Shut-mouth jes like him, dat all. Pity ain mo like her! Too many folks letting off their moufs bout things they don know nothin about, poking their noses in—"

"Biggety thing," white women said, "I wouldn't have her in my house with all her college airs." But most said it enviously, for women on College Street and the side streets knew that Mrs. Brown's servant Nonnie was the best servant in Maxwell unless it was her sister Bess. And so good to little imbecile Boysie. Everybody knew how good she was to the little fellow.

"Sometimes I wonder," Mrs. Brown would say, "how I ever did without her! She's so good to the baby, Frank! He cries so in this hot weather and she never gets cross with him. You can tell a good nurse by her hands. Way she touches a baby. No matter how bad the poor little fellow is, Nonnie's never rough with him. Always so easy, picking him up. Wish we could pay her a little more. I'm afraid she'll leave us."

"Nonnie's a good nigger, all right," Frank would answer, "good as we'll find, I reckon. You pay her enough, three dollars plenty! Already more than anybody else on College Street. You'll have the women on you if you start raising wages."

"Her shy as a little critter," Tillie Anderson used to say, long ago. "Won't talk to nobody. Who got yo tongue, Nonnie? Come out from behind my skirt, can't spen yo life apeekin from behind yo Ma! You know dat, honey!"

And white boys whistled softly when she walked down the street, and said low words and rubbed the back of their hands across their mouths, for Nonnie Anderson was something to look at twice, with her soft black hair blowing off her face, and black eyes set in a face that God knows by right should have belonged to a white girl. And old Cap'n Rushton, sitting out in front of Brown's Hardware Store as he liked to do when in from the turpentine farm, would rub his thick red hand over his chin slowly as he watched her wheel drooling, lop-headed Boysie Brown in to see his papa, sit there watching the girl, rubbing his hand over his chin, watching her, until she had gone back across the railroad and turned down College Street.

Nonnie pushed her hair off her face as she looked across White Town. Strange . . . being pregnant could make you feel like this. So sure. After all the years, sure. Bess wouldn't see it. You hated to try to explain. Bess would feel disgraced. Ruined. The Andersons ruined, Bess would say. You live in a dream world, she'd say. Sometimes I almost think you're crazy,

Non! she would say. I almost wish you were crazy, she'd say in her bitterness.

Sharp words rattling like palmettos.

Nonnie sighed.

Across the town came the singing. A white singing to Jesus. An August singing of lost souls. A God-moaning.

August is the time folks give up their sins. August is a time of trouble.

Whiter than snow . . . yes whiter than snow . . . oh wash me and I shall be whiter than snow.

Her thoughts swung with the Gospel tune.

Around the curve from Miss Ada's, where the trees open up, clearing the path, she could see him coming. A drag of left foot, a lift of shoulder, half limp, half swagger. Limp, swagger . . .

She would tell him, now that she felt certain. Though she had known since that night at the river. Somehow she had known since then.

He would say, "You all right?" and look at her as if he saw her for the first time. And the sound of it would hurt in her throat. Funny, how you don't get used to things.

He had said it first when he picked her out of the sandspurs, long ago; so long, it seemed now as if she must have dreamed it. She had fallen when Nat pulled up her dress, pulled at her underpants. Nat's freckled hand had reached out for her and she had jerked away from him, but more from the look on his sallow face, new to six-year-old eyes. His words already old. Words scrawled on circus posters, on privies, on fences, said with a giggle, carrying no more meaning to her ears than the squawk of guineas running crazily along ditches in search of worms.

"You all right?" Tracy had said; and then, to Nat, "Beat it. She's not that kind. And don't let me catch you around here again."

"Haw, haw, haw," Nat showed tobacco-stained teeth and lolled his tongue. "I didn't know she was yourn."

"She's not mine," Tracy said and reddened. "Now git—before I knock the liver-an-lights out of you."

Nat Ashley put his hands in his pockets, sauntered slowly away to show he wasn't afraid of nobody! Increased his nonchalance by jumping a gallberry bush. Grew in manliness by shouting to the boys on the distant ball ground, "Hi, how about some shinny?" Faded from their sight and from their lives.

The swamp had thrown deep shadows. Hounds barked in Nigger Town and beat the dust with their tails. The smell of scorched cloth from shanties clung to the sweet, near odor of honeysuckle in her hand.

Slowly she took a step toward him. "I am yourn," she whispered, and held out the grubby flowers.

Twelve-year-old Tracy took them. "You'd better run home," he said. "Your mama oughtn't allow you to run round alone. What were you doin, anyways?"

"Picking flowers and—" She hesitated.

"And what?" he probed.

"And visiting." She stooped, pulled a sandspur from her foot, pushed her toes deep into sand.

"Visiting? Who?"

"Everywheres. The swamp, mostly."

He spat and studied her face. "What you do in that swamp?"

"Nothing. Just goes." She paused. "It says, 'Come here, come here, come here.'"

He squinted his eyes.

"You hear it?" she whispered.

"Nope. Nothing but frogs croaking, and dogs."

She smiled, pushed her black wavy hair from her face, drew in a deep breath.

Tracy spat again, looked away. "Silly way to talk," he chided, "it's silly. You've got no business going near that swamp. You might get lost. Who you belong to?"

"I'se Tillie's child."

"Tillie?"

She searched for a meeting ground. "She's Miz Purviance's cook."

"Yeah, I know. Now run on before it's pitch-dark."

"Who is you?" Voice shy in its first social exploration.

"I'm Tracy Deen. Dr. Deen's son."

She looked at him gravely.

"Now run along! Ought to tell your mama on you."

She started toward the old Anderson place, walked a few steps, stopped, watched him cut through the gallberry bushes. In the dusk she could see him limp a little, could see his shoulder twist. He stooped over a bush. When he went on again his hands were empty. She sighed, began to run hard, dreading the scolding her sister Bess would give her for staying out so late.

In the dusk he stood now before her, tall, stooped. Took her hands from the gate, held them. "You all right?" His eyes searched her face, moved from her hair to her eyes, to her throat.

"Of course." She laughed softly.

"Cool. Your hands are cool, and it's hot as hell."

"I know. Boysie's cried all day."

"Boysie! How do you stand the slobbering little idiot day after—"

"I don't mind. It's a fine job for a girl like me," she said and smiled at the white man.

Tracy did not smile.

"Come in," she said. "I'll fix you something cool to drink. It's better in the arbor."

"No, I promised Mother—promised a lot of people—to go to the meeting tonight. Think all Maxwell is praying for me. Goddam em."

He opened the gate, came inside. Slim and white she stood there before him in the dusk. He pulled her behind a spirea bush. "I'm too hot to touch you," he whispered. "Sweet and cool . . . always sweet and cool . . . you smell so good to me. Non," he said unhappily.

"I'm glad."

"All right. Tell me quick. What's happened?"

She looked up at him steadily. "I'm pregnant, Tracy."

She felt his hand tremble on her arm. "And I'm glad," she whispered.

"Glad? You can't be!"

"I'm glad."

"But—"

"You see," she spoke quickly, "I want it. I'll have something they—can't take away from me." Voice low, hard to hear the words.

"What do you mean?"

"It's like thinking something for a long time you can't put into words. One day you write it down. You always have it after that."

His face eased into the old quick grin. "Might have been better this time to have written it down, Non."

He frowned, ran his fingers slowly over the fence pickets. "Let's don't think about it," he said.

"All right," she whispered. She looked at him and smiled, and he stared into her eyes as if he had not heard a word that she had ever said. "I wish you were glad," she said and felt her body shaking against his in sudden betrayal of her calm.

"Reckon we ought to talk about it, or something—" He looked out toward the swamp, forgetting his words. *In the dusk she's as white as Laura. God, if she weren't a nigger! Lord God what a mess . . .*

"No, we don't need to talk about it."

"Well, good-by, honey." He touched her hair, turned away, stopped, faced her again. "It's Mother. She—you know how it is! Nothing I've ever done has pleased her, as you know." He laughed abruptly. "Now the damned meeting's got her worked up. After dinner she—I don't know what's happened. Seems—well, she said—lot of things—about joining the church, settling down. Other things—Laura's lack of interest in church—seems disappointed in her children." He laughed. Non waited.

"Nothing new as far as I'm concerned. First time I ever heard her put Laura in the red." He laughed again. "Well . . . better be going."

He stared into the evening. Turned suddenly, opened the picket gate, closed it. "I may come back tonight late. All right?"

"All right," Nonnie whispered, knowing he would not come.

From Chapter 3

[. . .] Once, when they were little, Bess and Ed, Non tagging along, had been in the field hoeing the okra. Mama was home from work that day, bothered with her rheumatism. It was so hot that they had flung away their straw hats, choosing the blaze of the sun to the heat steaming against straw and skin. Sand burning feet but unmindful of it, Bess and Ed were playing a game, swinging their hoes between the chopping, to a tune they had made up, clashing the blades against sound, swinging hoes up as they moved down the rows. It was a gay game, and the heat was forgotten as they twisted their bodies between hoe and song and earth, stepping along. And then by a hill of squash the next step away lay a big cottonmouth, stretched out gold-brown-black and shining against the sand, eyes on them, unmoving.

They turned their song into such a wild scream that their mother had come running. She'd taken Bess's hoe and cut that snake to pieces, beating its head to a pulp against the sand, and then beating its body until it was nothing you could say you knew the name of when she finished with it.

"Hit's nothin but a cottonmouth," she'd said, handing the hoe back to her daughter and wiping her face. "Nothin to go screaming about," wiping her hands on the corner of her apron.

But her children stood there, a killing in their minds, staring down at it, fitting blood and pulpy flesh back into the long gold-brown-black skin that had lain there a moment ago, so smooth in its shining length, so threatening, now gone forever.

Tillie looked from one half-opened mouth to the other and the other. Followed their eyes to the sand. "Tain't nothin but a cottonmouth. Nothin to make such a whoop-doodle over," using words to take that look off their faces as she would have used her apron to wipe their noses.

"But they kill folks," Bess whimpered.

"They can't kill you efn dey don strike you. Member dat. Jus mind where you puts yo feet. All of you, you hear!"

Ed had not taken his eyes off the blood and pulp in the sand. He looked up at his mother. "I woulda kilt it if Bessie had let me," he said. Wiping his face now on his sleeve, spitting vigorously.

"You durned little liar! You little old chickenhearted story-teller. You couldn't kill a roach. You too scary to kill a roach even! You too . . ."

"Bessie! Mind you manners! And don go calling yo family names!"

Ed turned sullenly from the sound of her voice. "I just don like dead things," he said, and deliberately pulled up an okra plant.

"I don like um neider," little Nonnie quavered.

"Well, I don't like em neither!" Bess screamed. And now she and Eddie were glaring at each other, hoes raised, and quickly, hardly knowing why and without taking her eyes off her brother, she gave Non a hard push, toppling her over in the squash vines.

"Hush yo moufs, all of you! Us Andersons don raise voices. We belong, you hear! Hurt one of us, you hurts us all. Member dat. Now git to yo hoein."

But the hoeing seemed hard to get to. For Nonnie had wandered off into the squash rows during the talking and was bending over a vine, sticking blooms in her hair.

"Look at her, Mama! Pulling all the squash blooms!"

Mama, inexplicably, seemed pleased. "Ain't she purty as a picture?" Tillie stood there, mouth a little open, lines easing around her eyes. "Bessie," she whispered, "ain't she a purty little sight!"

Bess was finding it hard to breathe. "Ain't I pretty a bit?" she squeaked.

"Yes, Bessie," Mama never took her eyes off the yellow blossoms flopping over Non's ears, shadowing the child's pale face. "You're real purty. Eddie's all right too. All my chudren fine, upstanding chudren. But purty is as purty does. You all member dat!" The moralist looked her family in the eye.

They had stood there in the hot blaze of a summer sun: Tillie and her children. Squash and okra and tender pea vines and corn and children growing together in the South's hot summer, drawing their life from its dark soil. A wind came out of the swamp, slapping young stalks of cane together, bending corn tassels, ruffling big squash leaves, plumping a tomato to the ground, cooling hot faces; as quickly left them to their quiet growing. And Tillie's children looking up into the brown strong sweating face above them, listening to her words, thrust their roots more firmly into that soil out of which they had come.

"Now, Eddie, git yo hoe an help yo sister. And next time you all sees a snake, go atter it. Don come callin me. An next time you wants to holler at each other you to stop still. You hear! You to stop and swallow your spit five time, you hear! And you ain to say it. Whatever hit is, you ain to say it! Nonnie, come out of dat brilin sun. You is too little to set out in the sun all day. Come along."

And Tillie had turned toward the old house, planting each foot firmly on the deep warm earth, pressing every grain of sand in place. You'd felt it wouldn't dare move, not one little grain would dare, after Mama had put her foot down. But you had dared hiss, too low for her to hear, "Throw dat squash bloom away!" You'd put a threat in your voice which Non's ears heard. "Chunk it down." Bess remembered to this day the way Non had turned and looked at her, chin shaking, eyes swimming in tears, making no sound. Slowly she took the blossoms out of her hair, chunked them to the ground, ran down the field after her mother. Bess had watched Non's slim heels prick the soft sand furrows and the scrawny tendons move in the back of her knees as she ran, until the glare of midday blended them with the light and the field. And then in puzzled misery she and Ed slowly picked up hoes, went back to their weeding.

If she had dared tell Tillie, she would have taken a hoe and driven that white boy plumb out of their lives. And would have done it in the right way, minding her manners in the doing.

From Chapter 5

[...] All these years Laura had given back to Alma what Tracy had taken away.

And now as she sat in Laura's room, holding the little clay torso, a hideous thought swept through her mind. *Tracy is destroying Laura.* Not directly, but by the subtle influence of his failures. Tracy's tight lips, his silence, his withdrawal from the family, his refusal to be someone worth while, the long hours spent... Wherever he spent his time it was wickedly spent—this she knew. And Laura must surely be aware of this, now that she was grown. Because of it, was she losing faith in her mother? Did she believe it *her* fault, that Tracy was no good, a failure? Could she be so unfair, she who had always been so close, so loving? Could she not see that all her life Alma had slaved to make something out of that boy? Was she going to take *his* side now—

She felt, for the first time in her life, that she might faint and sat down. "It's the heat," she whispered. The room turned black, and for a moment she could see nothing.

Then, with the infallible weapon of her belief in herself, she fought back doubt. She was right. She could not be wrong. With infinite patience she had planned Laura's life. She had built it with care. Nothing—no one—could tear down what had been built with such thought and prayer. She began to breathe more quietly. Affirmation, soft to her bruised spirit, gathered about her:

Laura's *Yes, Mummie* trailing through the years, like a little song... the baby Laura's quick rush into her arms after being punished—the young

Laura's *Mother dear, I have a good book, let's read it together—But what kind of dress would you wear, dearest?—I'd rather stay home with you . . .*" And then, fearing that the child was growing too dependent upon her, she had been firm about college and Laura had proved her right again, winning honors each year.

Alma breathed deeply, let her fingers relax, resting the figure on her lap. She had noticed lately that she was a bit nervous. *Change of life makes you like that.* She must not permit herself to go to pieces over something trivial. *After all, this is a little thing. After all, it is a matter of idle hands.* These months in Maxwell had made Laura restless. She quite likely copied this thing out of a book without realizing its—its—well, that it wasn't so *nice.* She remembered now a book around the house on Greek sculpture. Though this didn't look much like Greek sculpture. No Greek sculpture she had ever seen had looked so *naked.* Odd too, because of course it was naked, but there was a refined look about it, while this thing, with its great bulges, looked as naked as—once she had helped her old fat grandmother out of her chemise and she had looked—well this thing looked like that. And there was no art about Grandma.

She remembered that the young Laura had gone through a foolish period when she thought she wanted to be an artist. It had begun with the reading of a book. Laura rushed in to her one day, eyes shining, "Oh, Mother, I'm going to be an artist." Mrs. Deen had taken care to smile sympathetically as she replied, "I am sure, dear, that your book must be interesting." "Oh yes, it *is,* Mother! It makes me want to try—it makes me believe I can *do* something—really *something!*" Mrs. Deen smiled into the eager face, "You *can* do something. Mother has a plan for you." And as Laura listened, Alma told her of college, of university, of teaching in some girls' college. "You are all I have to count on, darling," she'd whispered, and had smoothed back Laura's light brown hair from her wide forehead and told of her wish for her to work for a Ph.D. "You would like that, wouldn't you? And I should be so proud of you. It is what I have always wanted to do myself." No more was said about art. And later Alma quietly burned the book.

But this summer at home . . . it had been a mistake. They should have made the effort to keep Laura at the university for the summer. She should not have listened to Tut's talk of wanting his daughter at home. Laura said she didn't want any more degrees. But of course she did! Anyone who had as much sense as Laura would want a Ph.D. They would have a little talk about it. They would establish the old nightly exchange of confidences. It was foolish of her to let herself get so upset over a little lump of clay.

Mrs. Deen's eyes traced the curve of breasts, of rounded belly; moved inexorably downward, lingered, seeing the figure dimly now through the opaque film of confident motherhood. She had met every exigency of Laura's life. This, too, she could take care of.

She stood. Her face was calm, her jaws squared. Only the nostrils of her high nose quivered as she drew a deep quiet breath. Then, taking the figure more securely between her plump white hands, she kneaded and pressed and pounded it with slow deliberateness until it was reduced to a shapeless wad; and, walking swiftly through the hall, past Eenie in the kitchen, to the back porch, she dropped it in the garbage can. It lay there among corn shucks, okra stems, tomato skins—no more than the mud pies Laura used to make years ago; just another of the messes Alma had cleaned up after her young daughter.

She lingered, looking out upon her back yard, blinded by the glare, feeling nothing, as if physical processes had stopped, blocked by some obstacle to which their pattern could not bend. Words moved through her mind, stripped of feeling. *Laura must go back . . . she hasn't enough to do . . . he can't do this to her . . . I won't permit it.*

"Miz Deen," Eenie called from the kitchen, modulating her voice to a bland mixture of subserviency and reproof, "hit's way atter 'leven by the clock and dey's singin deh heads off over at dat tabernacle."

Mrs. Deen turned to enter the kitchen. As she passed the garbage can, like a shadow come and gone Laura's face trembled before her eyes.

"I want you to make Miss Laura some fig ice cream," she said, her eyes focused now on nothing; "and get my hat, please, I'm late."

In the dim hall before the old pier glass that had belonged to her mother, Mrs. Deen carefully adjusted her broad-brimmed white hat, carefully powdered her nose, smoothed her heavy black eyebrows while gray eyes looked steadily back at her from the mirror, picked up her white pocketbook and linen handkerchief, took her hymnal from the console. At the front door she called to Eenie to tell Laura, should she come in, that she was at church.

Chapter 17

Laura turned over in bed and ran her fingers softly across the screen of the window. From where she lay she could see the narrow stretch of their side lawn and the street adjoining. The big pecan tree at the corner of the house had grown limbs that stretched across her window and beyond. Lying so near, she could look up through the dark branches at the sky. Now, if she wished, she could step easily from her window to a big limb, when as a child you had to cling to the ledge until your feet obtained a safe hold on the gutter and from thence climb to the roof of the sun porch and over to the small tree. It had grown imperceptibly, steadily, sap pushing up, up, with stubborn rightness, obeying all the intricacies of an inner pattern, in its good fortune so little cramped by this house, or other trees, or Maxwell. Growing old, maturing as it grew, putting out leaves and clusters of green nuts, dropping them one by one as they ripened, taking the winter in its bare strength. She wondered if human beings could grow and mature. All the people she knew seemed not to grow through life, but merely to move from year to year, as a small child plays on a stairway, taking all its playthings with it as it goes up from step to step, not knowing what to leave behind. If you knew what to leave behind . . .

Laura moved restlessly. Lying awake, like this, did your feelings no good. It was childish to be so upset. To keep putting your finger on a sore place does the hurt no good! You opened the drawer to get the clay. It was gone. Such a little thing. You could get more clay.

She hates what I like! she had thought as she stood there looking at the empty drawer. It seemed now that she had been knowing this for a long time without telling it to herself. That her mother had destroyed the little clay figure, Laura took for granted. It was one of those things you take for granted. But asking herself why was like going through old trunks for something lost. She had not found the answer, though she had found other answers.

You can get more clay. But there are some things you cannot get more of. She had wanted to say something, to make a scene as Tracy sometimes did. But she had no words that could safely be used. Words that, unspoken, seem so harmless would, once said aloud, become dangerous explosives containing hidden feelings that would flame into something you dared not set free. They would begin with the little chunk of clay. They would not end there. No. That little piece of clay would merely be a lighted fuse which would lead, circuitously perhaps, but inevitably, to everything in your life that you cherished. That the clay was going to be discussed soon, Laura knew. When her mother walked in Friday night after Tracy had had words with her, it was on her face. She had sat down on Laura's bed and Laura had slowly laid her book aside, dreading the look in her mother's eyes.

"We have so little time these days to talk, Laura."

"Yes, Mother. I know."

"I miss the little Laura." Her mother had smiled, but the muscles in her throat had trembled.

"You'd want me to grow up, wouldn't you?" She'd see if she could turn it into more casual directions.

"Of course. But somehow I have an idea that you still think, and feel, even if you are grown. We used to talk about—those things."

"Yes, I know. I suppose college makes a difference. If I ever have an important thought, Mumsie, I'll tell you." That sounded so glib.

"All you think is important to me."

They sat there for a moment, neither speaking.

"Laura"—Mother had looked around the room—"do you think it wise—to go around with older women so much? After all, Jane Hardy is so much older than you. Why do you like—that type of woman? Don't you like your old friends? Don't you like Harriet and the others?"

"Yes, Mother. I like them. Very much." She'd hesitated. "Jane's fun, Mumsie. She's interesting."

"But what do you talk about? You always seem to have so much to talk to her about."

Laura tried to smile easily. "Oh, I don't know. Books, I suppose. All kinds of things."

"There're—women, Laura, who aren't safe for young girls to be with. Of course you are young and inexperienced—" Mother was finding this hard going.

For heaven's sake, what do you say now! "I've been to college, Mumsie, and things are talked about there. I think I know what you are trying to say."

"Laura, it would kill me . . . if anything—happened to you."

Her mother sat there looking at her, and Laura felt naked under the gaze.

Laura said, "It's nice that Dottie is going to marry Tracy, isn't it?"

"Yes, it is." Now Mother lowered her voice: "There're women who are—unnatural. They're like vultures—women like that." Mother's face had grown stony. "They do—terrible things to young girls."

"Oh, Mother!"

"I don't believe a woman is the right kind of woman who talks about the naked body as Jane does." How did she know that? What did she mean? Laura did not try to answer her.

"Good night, Laura," Mother said, and stood up to leave the room.

"Good night, Mumsie."

After her mother left, Laura slipped out of bed and went over to her desk. What did Mother mean? Slowly she pulled the letter drawer open, picked up Jane's letters. Yes, they did write to each other even though they lived in the same town. They had so much to say. There was so much you could say to Jane that you had never before been able to say to anyone. Laura's heart was beating heavily—she did not know why. She picked up the top letter. No, it wasn't the last she had had from Jane. Then Mother had been in her letters. Mother had read them. Mother knew Jane had posed for the figure. Jane had talked about it in that letter. The letter was gone. Mother had it. Mother had this friendship in her hands now, like the little chunk of clay.

Laura had gone back to bed, but not to sleep.

And now again tonight she could not sleep. You waited. You knew Mother was biding her time. Waiting for what she called the "psychological moment."

That her mother had discarded her own life, as you throw away a dress you don't like, and had chosen to live hers instead, Laura knew. It was as if, having once nourished Laura within her body, she now claimed an equal right to feed upon her whom she had brought to life. And maybe she had the right. She had done so much for her, more than most girls have done for them.

Laura turned until the moonlight was bright on her watch. Three o'clock. Tracy had not come in. She could not have failed to hear those steps. Eighteen steps from her door at the top of the stairs to his door. Eighteen stealthy slow steps, every other one dragging a little, a little slur against the hall carpet; then a door would open and close softly. She had been hearing it almost since she could remember. It was late tonight, even for him. Yesterday he joined the church, gave Dorothy a ring; tonight he had not come in.

She sighed. He didn't have it in him to go straight. Always he would be doing things—like this. It was as if he had to fail—as she had to succeed. Or was she succeeding? And now he would fail with Dorothy. Poor Dottie. She would never understand him. Who did? Always she would worry over him and try to reform him, pushing him further from her with each reformation, for he'd hate her for it. And as the years passed she would give up, and her lips would wrinkle up tight over her teeth like her mother's, and she would spend more and more of her time in church work.

Once when Tracy had come in late—she had left her door open and was reading in bed—he had stopped in the doorway and looked at her. She'd never forget that night although nothing happened. "What you doing?" he'd said, and smiled, and for the first time in her life she noticed how deeply blue his eyes were and somehow how sad, and his quick amused smile. His thin face had relaxed and in relaxing had grown assured.

"I'm afraid, just another book." She had closed the book and laid it aside and had smiled back at him, wanting to ask him in, feeling that maybe, this once, they could talk.

"There're other things in the world, Sis," he'd said gently, "but maybe you don't want them."

"Maybe I would want them—if I knew what they are." She knew, yes she knew. He was hinting that she should go with men, maybe get married. Men didn't like her. Thought her too smart, folks said. But maybe it was because she was a little gawky. That was the real reason, she'd always known it—a little gawky and shy.

"You aren't asking me to tell you, are you?" And he had thrown back his head and laughed softly, and his teeth had flashed in the lamplight. She realized this was the Tracy that Negro girl knew. He had come so quickly from her that he had not had time to take on the protective coloring he wore in the Deen family. "Well . . . good night," he had said, and had limped quietly down the hall to his room, leaving her feeling deprived and restless. This was the Tracy Nonnie Anderson knew. The Tracy women loved. She had often wondered why women liked Tracy—all the Miss Belles, the old maids, and the young married women, and the very old ladies. She saw it now. His gentle, affectionate manner, unhappy eyes, enough tension in his voice to make women want to soothe him. They called it his beautiful manners . . .

Why had he always failed and she succeeded? It made you, lying here like this tonight, feel that you had climbed to success by standing on his failures. It made you want to throw it all away, throw your whole life away and begin over again, and let him begin over again. Far away from Mother—and Jane.

Jane was an orphan who lived on in Maxwell teaching school, living with the Harrises, but living always alone with herself. For no one knew Jane. Folks always said, "Fine woman, Jane. But she won't let anybody know her. Fine girl, though," and had been awed by Jane's learning and Jane's book-lined walls. And then one day they had been playing tennis and suddenly had begun to talk. And you knew you could talk to Jane, you could tell her about your sculpture and your verses, about your fears and your feelings. And soon you were feeling with her a security that you had not felt since you were a little girl with your Mother. And you loved her. Yes, you loved her and wanted to be with her. And now Mother was labeling it with those names that the dean of women at college had warned you about. Yes, you knew. You knew and you did not know. Your mother knew and did not know. The dean of women knew and did not know. But you also knew if Mother made an issue, if she labeled this feeling for Jane with those names, there'd be no more feeling . . .

The moonlight picked out the roofs of the houses across the street, showing little crannies and angles one never saw in the daytime. How often she had lain there and looked out on that small segment of her town.

You'd hear people drive slowly down the street; sometimes someone walking would whistle a measure of brash sound against the street's quiet breathing; sometimes across town you'd hear the colored folks singing, and the slow rise and fall of it would be as sweet to your ears as Mamie's slow deep breathing used to be when you lay against her soft breast. It would be nice to see Mamie again. Eenie had never been like Mamie to either of them. Mamie so gentle and anxious to soothe her white folks. And how Tracy had hated Laura for taking his nurse away from him! She remembered little of it, of course, save what Mamie had told her later. But they said that for a long time he would eat nothing that Mamie did not give him out of her own fingers. And once he had run away and hidden behind a big pecan tree in the back yard and refused to come in and go to bed until Mamie went out and wheedled him in and put him to bed herself. Mother had let Mamie go back to nursing Tracy, and she herself had looked after Laura. Yes, the colored nurse you've loved so passionately goes away—to another job maybe or to another child. And you're supposed to forget all about her.

Down the street where Mrs. Viola Smith, the dressmaker, lived somebody must have been thirsty and stepped to the back porch for a drink. For in the stillness the rasp of the pump screamed out and caught her nerves and bit deep into them, and her heart jumped and pounded hard in her throat. Yes, somebody wants a drink of water and in the getting of it, somebody else a half block away is frightened until the body's metabolism is abruptly changed because of it. Mrs. Smith would not give up the pump, declaring no city water could equal the water pumped right there from the ground beneath her own back porch. "Yes," she'd say, and ease her snuff a little under her lip, as she knelt to chalk the hem line of your dress, "people have their likes and people have their dislikes. And city water is my dislike. I abominate city water," she'd say. Laura had always wanted to ask Mrs. Viola Smith what her likes were, but her tight sallow face as she bent over the sewing machine, or crouched close to the floor chalking your hem line, invited no such question.

There'd be no more feeling. Just another of the little messes Alma cleaned up after her daughter.

Maybe you could go away. Maybe you could go away and never come back. Never come back to Mother—and Jane. You wouldn't want it. You wouldn't want your relationship with Jane when Mother finished with it. You wouldn't want—anything.

Lillian Smith Answers Some Questions about *Strange Fruit*

The following selection appeared in the *Georgia Review*'s 2012 special issue honoring authors from the Georgia Writers Hall of Fame with the following editor's note: "Smith received several thousand letters concerning *Strange Fruit*. . . . In the Winter 1945 issue of *South Today* (Vol. 8, no.2: 75–87), Smith printed excerpts from several of these letters as "Author of *Strange Fruit* Shares Her Mail." Of reading the letters, Smith wrote, "It has been sometimes a heart-breaking experience . . . yet it has been fun; thrilling sometimes too, and often hilarious. . . . However this may be interpreted by others, to [me] it means that there is need to face truth that hurts, and thank God, there are plenty of human beings ready to face it."

1. *Why do you think Boston banned the book?*
ANSWER: Not because of "the word," of course:—a word known by every school child and grown-up in the United States, and used in the book with the serious purpose of showing how a small girl reacted in horror to an experience in real life. Most modern novels have dozens of similar "words;" some modern novels have hundreds and with less reason for their use—yet Boston has not banned these books but instead banned *Strange Fruit* which had only one such word in it. The real motive can more surely be found in the reactions of the anti-Negro forces in Boston. The forces in Boston who banned the book are the same forces that fight democracy on all of its levels: anti-Negro, anti-Semitic, anti-union, anti-freedom of the press, etc.

2. *But some people who do take democracy seriously, who actively work for better race relations were also shocked at the book. Why?*
ANSWER: It is probably true that every reader is shocked at the book. Shocked at realizing that a way of life, in which we all participate, is so

destructive of that which is fine and creative and rich in human relations. Some readers who have been reared from childhood to think themselves "superior" to Negroes, are shocked to realize that segregation has injured the white race as much as it has the Negro race. Some are shocked at the writer for breaking the taboo of silence concerning certain matters which we have thought about but have seldom spoken about. Feeling shocked, they seek to find an acceptable reason and, the "word" being obvious, seize upon it as the excuse for disturbed feelings.

3. The Church is sharply criticized in Strange Fruit. *Are you opposed to Christianity?*
ANSWER: As the author of *Strange Fruit*, I should like here to speak in the first person. I accept the teachings of Jesus Christ with profound seriousness. I believe we should practice, in our lives, these teachings. I think the Church has seldom practiced these teachings in the South, and seldom preached them. I doubt if the Church has practiced them widely in the North. And because of the Church's refusal to face the implications of Christianity it has become, South and North, often a cheap and hypocritical thing, and has betrayed the basic teachings of Christ. I was reared in the Church and my family are today prominent churchmen. It is because I believe the Church has great possibilities for leadership which it has lost temporarily, that I consider it important to our culture for it to be analyzed and pictured as it functions in most small towns and cities of the South. Here and there, we have a minister and a congregation who takes seriously the teachings of Jesus. Not often do we find either, South or North. For it is almost impossible, under the system of segregation, to *be a real Christian* no matter how much one wants to.

4. Why did you call the book Strange Fruit*?*
ANSWER: A few years ago I wrote an article in which this phrase was used:

"The church in the South has been in the main a gregarious expression of lonely, impoverished, hard pressed, sometimes dangerously situated, rural people. It has been a mirror of their tastes, their feelings, their conflicts and their needs. . . . It has been a religion of a people who are at once exploiting and exploited. It is filled with ambivalences, inconsistencies, hypocrisies, and hard bargainings with the Lord. . . . It is all its people are; no more, no less. . . . This religious feeling—the complexity and strength of which are barely suggested here—restrained and encouraged alternately by economic pressures and historical incidents, has borne strange fruit . . ."

Later, I heard Billie Holliday sing her "Strange Fruit" and was deeply moved by it. Last year I wrote "Two Men and a Bargain" in which I used the phrase again in this manner:

"... I'm that which splits a mind from its reason, a soul from its conscience, a heart from its loving, a people from humanity. I'm the seed of hate and fear and guilt. You are its strange fruit...."

"Strange Fruit" seemed somehow the right title for the book—not because it symbolized a lynching, but because it symbolized a people. We, the people, white and colored, are the strange fruit which our culture has produced.

5. Why do you let Bess and Nonnie, who are college graduates, go into domestic service? Does this not indicate that you are prejudiced against Negroes?

ANSWER: In *Strange Fruit* the South is shown as it is, not as we would like for it to be. Unfortunately, under a system of segregation and racial discrimination, a college education does not solve the Negro's problems. Many Negro college graduates are in domestic service in the South *because they cannot find anything else to do*. Sometimes, as in a period of transition like this, education is a necessary step to take in this process of integration, but it is not the full answer to the Negro's problem, and does not, in its present form, solve the white man's problems either.

The *right kind* of education would do much—but remember that Gene Talmadge also has a college degree. College degrees are hardly "the answer."

6. Why did the author bring out again in the open the old question of intermarriage? Does she not realize that it always upsets people, and causes a reaction against the Negro?

ANSWER: Are Negroes human or aren't they? That is a question we must face, all of us, black and white: as Christians we must face it; as democrats; as people who value sanity. It must be faced, no matter how much it upsets us.

Freedom to form one's profound emotional needs, is the "psychological" freedom we must add to our list of basic freedoms. The choice of a mate is and always has been a personal, individual matter. We marry the woman we love, the one who fits our needs, the one we want to be a mother to our children; the one who can fit most richly and harmoniously into our particular social group. There should not be arbitrary barriers to our personal relationships. The real barriers are, and should be, only those within ourselves.

What is really important in our life today is not so much the choice of a mate (for that is something each human being settles according to private and family criteria) but the effect of segregation upon the personalities of all children. For all children are injured by it. It is as harmful to a child's personality to *segregate* as it is to *be segregated*; as injurious to emotional growth and sanity to think one's self superior as it is to think one's self inferior. Arrogance injures character in a different way but as seriously as humiliation injures character. The cultural pattern of segregation is in different ways crippling every child who grows up in it, white and colored. What kind of people will our children grow up to be, is the most urgent question we can ask ourselves today.

7. How long did it take the author to write Strange Fruit*?*
ANSWER: Seven years. The book grew slowly. It was conceived as a whole, and then the details were slowly filled in. Sometimes I worked on the third chapter; sometimes on the twentieth. The book was an organic whole in my mind all the time I was working on it, but it was not written consecutively. Once, for two years, not a word was written about Tracy. It was necessary for me to think of him for long months, to see him in his relationship with his mother, and grandmother, his nurse, his sister, his father—to experience with him his fears and his dreams—in order to understand his relationship with Nonnie, and his failure to adjust himself to his culture.

8. Why did the author—a woman who has, for twenty years, made a study of children and worked closely with them—consider it necessary to break the rules of good taste and use the "word" which has caused so much controversy?
ANSWER: Good taste is necessary to the rituals of living; and in many areas of life, good taste is the legitimate arbiter of our conduct. There are, however, areas where "good taste" cannot operate but is forced to relinquish its authority to necessity. It is not good taste in social situations to expose certain areas of one's body. In illness, it is a necessity, at times, for these exposures to be made, for the purpose of examination or treatment. In literature and art, words and discussions that are not legitimate at a tea-party, are necessary for the purpose of mature understanding of our selves and our culture. The "word" was not used to make the reader snicker or to cause him to yearn to participate in the sexual violation of a child. The word as used, the scene as written, would have no effect on any decent reader except that of producing in him a deep sense of pity for the child who suffered the harsh experience. No one but a mentally ill person would have any other reaction. Young adolescents would be helped, not injured, by the serious study of such a scene. I, as the author, am shocked and troubled by the assumption of many adults that young boys and girls are so perverted, so unclean, that they would misinterpret an intelligent, grave, compassionate study of human problems. I know children well. I have worked with sick and well children for many years, but only in adults have I found unclean, lascivious attitudes toward life.

Never in a child; he is always willing to face life gravely and honestly if given encouragement to do so.

9. What do you want Strange Fruit *to do?*
ANSWER: I hope it will give its readers a more profound understanding of human relationships; that it will quicken their awareness of the complexities of personality; that it will arouse their imaginations so that they will think of our people, white and colored, as human beings, not as "problems." It was written, not for a short-range "purpose." It was written because its author wanted to put on paper her feelings, her knowledge, of a little southern town and its people; to set down the "truth" about human relationships as she sees it; to re-state in simple, contemporary terms that ancient, three-fold struggle between man, and his home and his world; to state, perhaps more explicitly, the paradoxical question: how can a man be sane in an insane culture?

Lillian Smith and childhood friend Marjorie White in window; Wombolt Paulk underneath window, Jasper, Florida. Permission of Piedmont College; courtesy of Hargrett Rare Book and Manuscript Library, UGA Libraries.

Lillian Smith with students at the Virginia School, Huchow, China. Permission of Piedmont College; courtesy of Hargrett Rare Book and Manuscript Library, UGA Libraries.

Paula Snelling and Lillian Smith at Laurel Falls Camp, 1933. Permission of Piedmont College; courtesy of Hargrett Rare Book and Manuscript Library, UGA Libraries.

Lillian Smith with Kelton Watts planting ferns on a walkway roof at Laurel Falls Camp. Courtesy of Georgia Archives, *Vanishing Georgia Collection*, rab355.

Campers from Nantahala Cabin on steps at Laurel Falls Camp, 1933.
Clockwise: Seated in front, Frankie Knight; standing, Laura McManus;
seated, Sara McManus, Marge Scott, Marge Helm, Chelle Furlow, Kennon Henderson.
Photo from Kennon Henderson's photo album. Courtesy of Henderson's daughter,
Susan Patton Hamersky.

Lillian Smith, Mary McLeod Bethune, Eleanor Roosevelt at a reception in Washington, D.C., given to honor the National Council of Negro Women's 1944 Honor Roll.
Published in the *Washington Star*, February 17, 1945.
Reprinted with permission of the D.C. Public Library, Star Collection,
© Washington Post.

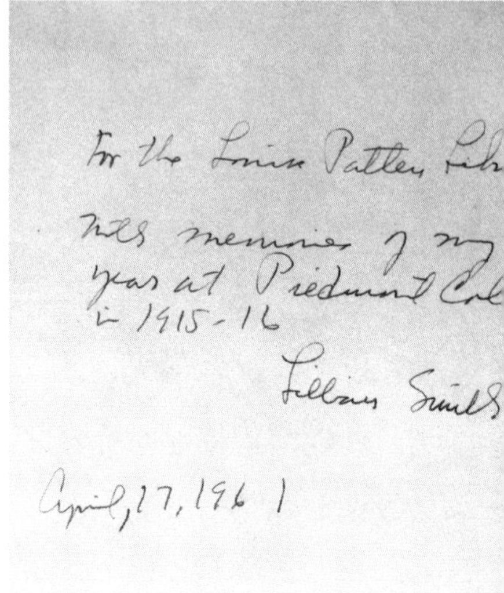
For the Louise Patten Lib
with memories of my
year at Piedmont Col
in 1915-16
Lillian Smith
April, 17, 1961

The book jacket for *Killers of the Dream*, first edition, 1949, with handwritten inscription. Courtesy of Piedmont College.

Protesters in Little Rock, Arkansas, 1957. Library of Congress.

Lillian Smith by the chimney at Laurel Falls Camp. Photo by Peter Powell. Reprinted by permission of Joan Titus.

"the Chimney."
this is all that is left of the big camp playhouse and theater. It was a very large building with big stage, a huge fireplace, and room to dance, play games etc. Underneath was where finger painting and etching were done. We had the building demolished a few years ago.

Lillian Smith's handwritten description of the chimney. Courtesy of Piedmont College.

Lillian Smith's grave marker beside the chimney. Courtesy of Piedmont College.

Entrance sign: Piedmont College Lillian E. Smith Center, 2015.
Courtesy of Piedmont College.

Children Talking

Published in *Progressive Education,* October 1945, this article epitomizes in style and content Smith's accomplishments as Laurel Falls Camp director and renowned author. Furthermore, her responses to the questions Laurel Falls campers asked the day World War II ended would inform Smith's writing for the next twenty years.

It was supper time on the mountain when we heard that the war was over. A counselor picked up the last few words of a commentator and told the campers near her. And they shouted wildly to cabins and trees, "The war is over," and little seven-year-olds playing in the Magic House laid down their dolls and screamed, "The war is over," and there were running foot-steps and sharp, confused voices and, as suddenly, every one hushed and spoke in whispers. They came to supper slowly and quietly sat down. The blessing was sung. I told them briefly that President Truman had announced the end of the war. There would be more news tomorrow, I said, and finding it hard to say more, I did not try.

They ate almost in silence. A few children and counselors kept their eyes on the old mountain whose peak is so close to us and so familiar a thing to look at. And two or three wiped the tears away as they sat there. When supper was ended, I followed them out to the ridge where they gathered in small groups or stood alone, looking across the valley. In the little town beyond us, the siren was screaming its mad pleasure. One girl began to cry and whispered, "I'm scared. It may be the siren. I think I'm scared about peace and the future. We know more about war." Another said, "I'm crying for my brother, I'm so glad he's safe. But when he comes back—he has a terrible temper—I wonder what he'll do at home with all he's learned about killing." And an eight-year-old came up and said, "My daddy says there'll be bread lines when the war ends. Will they begin now?" And an older girl said, "Is this the peace that the papers said the atomic bomb would bring us?" And another one said, "Do you think we would have dropped it on white people? Or was it because they're yellow and don't matter much to us who are white?" And still another said, "I thought I'd be glad but now I feel it's the end of the world."

So I called them together, these girls of the deep South who spend each summer up on our mountain, for it seemed time to talk things over. There is nothing new to us about talking. For many years we have been feeling around with our minds and hearts and imaginations for the roots of things, and putting into words what we find there, sharing with each other these words, sometimes awkwardly but always with honest good humor.

We gathered on top of the ridge where our eyes can move across the sky to the ends of the earth and come back home again. And sitting there close together, I told them an old story, as familiar to them as each other's nickname. A story we like to tell, for though it always begins the same way, it never has quite the same ending.

This is the story I told them:

"Once upon a time, each of us was born. We came out of our mother's body after living with her for nine months. And some of us were eager to come, feeling strong and ready to be born, and some of us came slowly, hating to leave the warmth and the softness and the sweet content we had found there."

(One little girl was staring far away, her eyes on the deep blue of the peaks. She turned and smiled, "The pink egg," she whispered and went back to her mountains.)

"We came out of the 'pink egg' and began growing. But there is not one of us who does not want, sometimes, to go back to it, when we are hurt, or lonely, or afraid, or feeling small and useless—"

("Or like tonight," a tall girl said slowly, "when war has ended and peace has not begun.")

"Or when the future stretches out like a steep path—"

("It isn't the steepness we mind," she said. "If we only knew the path led somewhere!")

"Or when we are not sure that we believe in the place that our path leads to. After we came out of our mother's body, we began to reach out, little by little, toward the world of people and things and sights and sounds, climbing one by one the steps to maturity, drawing back when we got hurt, sometimes sitting on a step a long time, or running back toward the pink egg when we grew too afraid of what was ahead of us, or when the steps came too close together, or seemed too steep."

("Like giving up the nipple for the cup," one camper murmured. "I sat on that step so long I almost grew a new eggshell around me as I sat there.")

"Sometimes, a step is harder to climb for one of us than for others. But we all have steps that are hard to pull up to."

("Mine was bed-wetting. Still is," an eight-year-old giggled and looked around with composure. "And mine was my first year in school. Oh, it was terrible!" another said.)

"Whatever the cause for each one of us, the day comes when we want to go back to the pink egg and curl up there forever, forgetting the world outside and the wonderful fun of growing; forgetting it ever had been fun to grow. All we want is to shut ourselves up and stop growing. But usually, it doesn't last long—and we go back to our climbing.

"There are a great many steps to be climbed as you know, before we can reach maturity. Like the steps here at camp that lead from the parking space up to the top of the ridge, they wind and twist until it is easy to lose our sense of direction."

("I did that—the time I decided that nobody liked me. I was lost a long time," an older camper said and smiled at the others. "I got lost too," another said, "when I used to hate my brother so much I wouldn't try anything!")

"Sometimes it is hate that makes us get lost; or sometimes hate uses up all our strength pushing other folks off the steps so that we don't have any left for our own climbing. And sometimes, because we feel inferior and unimportant, we brag and boast of how much better we are than other people—"

("Like we do, down South, about Negroes.")

"Yes, like we do, down South, about Negroes and some times about other folks also. Bragging and boasting take a lot of breath when you're climbing. It's easy to stop where you are and stay there. Some of us do that. And because we don't want to see all the steps we've failed to climb, we grow a shell around us to shut the sight out."

("So if you don't want to go back to the pink egg you have to keep moving, don't you?" a solemn ten-year-old suggested.)

"You have to keep moving. You have to grow so fast that no shell has time to stick to you. Trouble is, there are so many ways in which we must grow. It begins to get complicated. First, our bodies must grow. Most of us have learned to keep them growing with milk and play, sun and sleep and vitamins. We know a lot about children's bodies. But we have to grow sexually too. And most of us don't know much about that—not nearly as much as we should know."

("Because it embarrasses our mamas to tell us. If they would only act natural!")

"Though it embarrasses some of us to remember it, we still have to climb every one of those steps: thumb-sucking, and playing with our toes, and masturbating and—"

("And don't forget, falling in love with ourselves, like Narcissus!" someone reminded the story-teller.)

"And falling in love with our own image. Some of us stay a long time there—"

("White folks are still in love with their image, aren't they?")

"Some white folks are still in love with their image. But unless we are hindered by feelings of shame and guilt, we learn to take the next step and become interested in other people. Because people are fun. It's easy to love them—"

("Not always." One camper spoke with finality.)

"Not always. But finally we learn to love them and then we learn what falling in love with boys means and when we grow up fully, we marry and have babies of our own."

("I guess that's why we have wedding rings," a thirteen-year-old suggested, "because it all makes a nice round circle.")

"It makes a good and honorable circle, every bit of the way, just so we keep moving."

("My mother wouldn't agree with us that masturbation is part of the circle. She thinks it's a terrible disgrace. She used to tie my hands each night—." Another interrupted, "My mother didn't. She always said, 'Here dear, here's a nice toy to play with.' Of course I knew what she meant.")

"The only disgraceful thing about growing is to stop growing. Every step of the way is honorable if we don't linger too long."

("Some of us still play with ourselves, even here at camp. That's lingering a long time before we round out the circle, isn't it?")

"I know. It takes time but as long as we remember where we're climbing, most of us will keep on, until we get there."

("Then," one girl said, "when people marry and wear a wedding ring that means they've made the circle?" Another child spoke up excitedly, "Sure! That's why they wear wedding rings to show everybody they've finished growing and are ready now to have babies. That's it, isn't it?")

"It would be fine if it were like that. But some folks marry before they've made the circle."

("Oh, but they couldn't!" another said earnestly. "That would be cheating.")

"Some do. Some grow up in their bodies and think they've grown in other ways, when they're still far down the steps."

("I have an aunt like that. My daddy says she loves just herself and nobody else. Her husband is getting a divorce.")

The children were silent for a little and we sat there quietly, feeling the cool soft wind blowing across our faces.

("Oh I do hope I make the circle," one girl sighed. "I can wear my ring then and feel I've earned it.")

"Growing up sexually is part body-growing and part growing up in our feelings. But just as bodies must grow in different ways, so our feelings grow, stretching until they can reach around a lot of people. At first, we don't reach far. Just to our mother and father, or nurse, and then to the rest of our family. Reaching out, just to have something to hold to. But gradually, our feelings reach deep down into the heart of the people near us and we begin to feel we are part of them and we learn to feel what they are feeling. Almost as if we were one person. But we can't do this unless our imaginations grow too. So you see, it is complicated."

("I always think of imagination as the making up of stories like we do here at camp.")

"Making up stories is both reaching back into memory for things we've stored there and reaching forward into the world we've heard about. It takes imagination to do both. I like to think of it also as spinning a bridge which connects my world with your world, and with other people's worlds."

("Inside and outside worlds?")

"Inside and outside worlds."

("There's some people it's awfully hard to spin a bridge to," one of the older girls said. "I have a brother I don't believe anyone has ever spun a bridge to." "He must be very lonely," some one commented. "Yes, he must be," another said quickly, one who has just begun to spin bridges herself. "But he can't wait for people to spin bridges to him. I know," she looked at all of us and smiled. "He must spin a bridge himself. Of course it's lots of trouble.")

"Spinning bridges is a lot of trouble. And your feelings and imagination won't spin them unless they have food to give them the energy. We wouldn't expect much of our bodies if we didn't give them food and sleep and sun and play. Your personality can't grow much either without love and special vitamins that make you feel important, and you need something to warm you, like feeling enjoyed."

("The same way we need sun baths.")

"When we spin a bridge, it ties us together so we can go back and forth into each other's feelings. Then what happens to you seems important to me, and what happens to me seems important to you."

("I like the idea," an older camper said.)

“We all like the idea. So we reach out with our imagination and actually become other people to such an extent that what happens to them is important. That is, if we feed our imagination and emotions enough love and vitamins. If we don’t, then of course we don’t spin bridges.”

(“I wonder how Mother feels about the war ending,” a child said softly, looking far away to south Georgia.)

“Wondering about our mother and her feelings is the beginning. After a while, we keep on reaching out and including others and wondering about them also, until it matters to us what happens to a great many people.”

(“But we don’t care what happened to those people in Hiroshima, do we? At least, I try not to. Ever since I read about the atomic bomb, I’ve tried not to.”)

“Sometimes we don’t care.”

(“But why should we?” An older girl spoke sharply. “They’re our enemies. We couldn’t have enemies if we cared how they felt.”)

“Sometimes we reach out and include only our family and friends and the people who go where we go, or those who look like us or who dress like us. After that, we stop reaching and then we grow a shell around just the few we care for. And nothing else matters.”

(“Like the way we grow a shell down here and shut out the colored folks.”)

“Like that.”

(“That’s an awfully thick shell, isn’t it, the one we’ve grown to shut out the Negroes.”)

“It’s a thick shell for it has been growing and thickening for a long time. So long, that most folks are afraid to try to get through it.”

(“I’ve never thought about it until this minute but, I guess I’ve never spun a single bridge to any Negro, though I’ve lived near them all my life. Have you?”)

“I’ve spun a few. Not nearly as many as I want to.”

(“But coming back to our enemies,” the girls who spoke first about Hiroshima said, “suppose we felt everything our enemies were feeling, it’d be terrible! You’d never be able to fight them. It’d be like bombing your own family!”)

“We’d find it hard to have enemies if we cared about what happens to them. War makes us cut a lot of bridges we’ve been spinning all our life.”

(“I guess that’s why some of us are scared of peace. We’ve got so many bridges to spin back and we’ve almost forgot how folks spin bridges.” She paused for a moment. “If we had been in Hiroshima at a summer camp with other children that bomb would have fallen on us, wouldn’t it?”)

"Yes."

("Yet we didn't have a thing to do with this war, nor did those children over there either. It doesn't seem quite fair to children.")

We sat without talking as some of us tried to spin a bridge across the earth to Hiroshima.

"Sometimes geography—and distance—make it easier not to care."

("The men in the plane who dropped that bomb must have been glad they couldn't see below them. Or maybe they'd never known a Japanese child, or maybe they just called them 'yellow monkeys' and that made it seem not to matter—like folks down here say Negroes don't matter.")

("That's what I mean," the camper said who had first mentioned Hiroshima. "When I say I try not to think about it, I mean I've cut my bridges. Because if I did think, my conscience would hurt too much, I couldn't stand it.")

"We grow a lot of egg shells to shut the sight off, so our conscience won't hurt. I've done plenty of that kind of egg-shell growing."

("Do you suppose that's why we put up White and Colored signs down here, to keep our conscience out?")

"It sounds likely."

("Maybe that's why I've never spun a bridge to a Negro, though I'd like to. I wonder what would happen if we did spin bridges and felt what they are feeling.")

We southerners sat there, thinking, and wondering.

("We'd take the signs down first," our best athlete said with her usual energy. "And then we'd break the shell between us, and then what happened to each other would seem important. My goodness!" she cried out suddenly, "that's what segregation is, just another pink egg, isn't it! I don't know what I really thought it was;" as we all began laughing, "I guess I thought it was a natural law or something God decreed." She hushed suddenly. After a moment, went on. "Though God wouldn't have decreed segregation . . . he couldn't have—for Jesus talked so much about love," she was groping now in her thinking, "Jesus must have understood all about pink eggs and how we need love to hatch out of them. I guess every real religion does.")

"Every real religion understands."

("But some folks are scared not to have shells around them. They would feel too lonely.")

"Yes, some are scared. Some are so scared that they grow a shell inside them and try to crawl in it and stay there."

("Like my brother who won't spin bridges to anybody.")

"A little like that, though he hasn't gone inside completely. When we go inside and stay there, we get sick, or die, or live almost like the dead. For when you crawl inside and grow a shell, you shut out love and people's pride in you and their enjoyment of you and your personality starves."

("And you have no way to get rid of your hate so you keep it inside you until it poisons you. You told us that, long time ago. I just remembered.")

"Yes, it poisons us and makes us sick just as it would if we never eliminated the waste from our body."

("Then to keep healthy, we ought to have daily elimination of hate, shouldn't we? Why don't our counselors check us on that?")

"It should be frequent elimination anyway. When we are little, we don't know toilet habits and so when we feel the need to eliminate, we do so, regardless of the inconvenience it causes other people. Savages are like that too. But as we grow, we learn physical toilet habits. And knowing makes our world a much pleasanter place to live in. Not to speak of safer."

("I should say! Suppose here at camp we never bothered to observe toilet habits. It would be terrible! Typhoid and things—and our drinking water. Gol-ly!")

"People developed good toilet habits because they became sensitive about such matters. And because they learned how bacteria spreads. And because we have Boards of Health to make us be careful. But when it comes to hate, nobody seems to have thought much about it. We go right on having temper tantrums and pinching each other."

("Oh here at camp we're learning to pinch clay instead of people. Look at all the nice sculpture we've made this summer.")

"But I have seen lots of campers have temper tantrums right in the middle of the floor, before all of us."

("I'm getting embarrassed, for I had one yesterday. Reckon my emotional toilet habits aren't so good." Another girl spoke tensely, "I don't think we should hate at all because it's wrong to hate.")

"I thought that too, until I learned that hate is like waste from the food we eat. When we live with people and love them, we are nourished by our human relationships, but our personalities can't assimilate all of it, so there's bound to be waste. The only problem is to learn what to do with it so that it won't offend other people or harm them."

("And that's why you can't stay inside yourself in a shell. If you didn't starve for love, you'd be poisoned by all the hate you'd have no way to get rid of." She went on after a little. "Seems to me, the whole earth is full of eggs, isn't it, rolling around, breaking each other. It's crazy! Because when we were born and began to grow, that meant we were to keep out of eggs. Growing is pecking your way out of shells, isn't it? How do you peck? I know love warms the shell on the outside but you have to do some pecking inside, don't you? At least that's the way our biddies hatch.")

"That's the way. Understanding helps you peck out, and it comes from spinning bridges to other people, and from knowledge. And that's another way we have to grow. When we come into the world, of course we don't know anything. This ignorance of ours is a shell too, shutting us away from the world we live in. But day by day we learn more, and year by year, until our minds begin to stretch in all directions, just as did our bodies and feelings and imagination. Long before we were born, people had been collecting facts; just as soon as they could, they fed us these facts, though slowly—"

("But just soft facts, at first, like our pablum. Later I bet it was arithmetic and things like that.")

"At first they fed us soft facts, things we really wanted to know, and later the hard facts that we ought to know."

("More spinach and carrots. I bet it's the same old story," she began to laugh. "When we learn facts that we don't like or that will make our conscience hurt or will make us stop doing what we want to do, we grow a shell, don't we, and pretend the facts aren't there.")

"That's right. It's a curious thing about growing. Sometimes our bodies grow faster than our minds or our minds grow faster than our imaginations and our feelings. And that is what has happened to us lately. Our minds have grown faster than our feelings for people. And our scientists have given us airplanes before we have learned to spin bridges to the people the planes will take us to. And they gave us the atomic bomb before we got rid of our egg shells."

("So," one of the campers took up the story, "we get in a plane and take an atomic bomb and drop it on the Japanese because they've built an egg shell out of fascism and we think it's a dangerous shell and should be broken. Of course it is a dangerous shell!")

"It's a dangerous shell, as all shells are dangerous, and like all shells, should be broken."

("But if you try to break it by dropping a bomb on it, you'll kill the people in it. And people are always important.")

"Of course as long as there are egg shells, somebody will want to drop a bomb on them."

("Then it seems to me," our little athlete was speaking again, "there's nothing to do but get rid of the egg shells. You can't have pink eggs around and not expect them to get broken. And especially now, with this atomic bomb . . . Well, we can't have it and eggs both on one little earth, can we?")

"It doesn't seem so. That is why we are all so frightened."

("It seems to me," a nine-year-old said slowly, "that we could have an egg if it's the size of the whole earth. That would be a nice size egg to have, anyway.")

"If that happened, we'd really be grown. We would have reached the top of the ridge, in body, in mind, in emotions, in imagination, in human understanding."

("And there wouldn't be a bit of the shell sticking to us.")

"Oh there might be a little—just to remind us that once upon a time, we came out of a pink egg—"

("And if we don't watch out, we'll go right back to it.")

"But you see, that's the exciting thing. That we *can* watch out—now that we know how to watch, with love on the outside and insight on the inside."

The children were silent.

"A few years ago, we didn't know much about how minds and emotions grew. We guessed at it. Though some of our guesses were good, some were bad. But science found out. Like penicillin. A few years ago, we didn't have penicillin. And people died for the lack of it. Just as people die today because of lack of insight and understanding. Scientists discovered penicillin but people still died because there wasn't enough penicillin to give it to everybody. They knew how to make it, but they couldn't make it as fast as it was needed. But the war came, and it frightened us so, that folks everywhere got busy making penicillin until they had enough for everybody. The psychiatrists and psychoanalysts have discovered the important things we need to know about people's feelings. But not enough people know it. There just isn't enough insight for everybody. It has to be manufactured in quantity"

("I think we ought to teach children emotional toilet habits. If they knew what to do with their hate, that might keep a lot of people from crawling into shells to keep out of the way.")

"But we'll have to work fast just as folks did with penicillin—now that there's an atomic bomb hanging over every shell. But it will be a wonderful job to do, if we do it together."

("Let's get at it, in the morning" the athlete said. "I don't believe in putting off things.")

We sat there in the night and looked at the sky, thick with stars. The wind was blowing cool in our faces, and somehow seemed nearer.

"I wonder if the earth really looks like an egg to the rest of the universe," one little girl whispered.

"A bad egg, I bet after this war."

"A bad pun" some one said and everybody was laughing. Then we began to sing for we felt like singing and somehow we felt better about the future as we sang there and peace seemed nearer, though we hardly knew why. We just felt that way about it.

PART TWO

Sanity in an Insane Culture

1946–1966

> "[T]he human condition is not a Neolithic stone [tying us] down, but a condition of continuous change taking place inside and outside the human spirit."
>
> —LILLIAN SMITH, "The Role of the Poet in a World of Demagogues"

Lillian Smith found the phenomenal success of *Strange Fruit* bittersweet. From the spring of 1944, when she signed a contract with José Ferrer and Arthur Friend to produce a play based on her novel (*Strange Fruit*), until its final production at the Royale Theater on Broadway January 19, 1946, Smith was intimately and exhaustingly involved with every aspect of the play. When an accidental fire in late fall of 1944 destroyed the *South Today* office at Laurel Falls Camp, Smith had money to restore the building but no time to manage the magazine. Consequently, she and Snelling ended publication of *South Today* with the Winter 1944–45 issue. Dividing her time between her apartment in New York and her home on Old Screamer Mountain, Smith continued to direct Laurel Falls Camp through the summer of 1948. By then, however, she had begun writing *Killers of the Dream*. To continue writing the major work she wanted to do, she had to close the camp. In her February 1949 letter to parents, Smith acknowledged how important the camp was in her life:

> My writing, the bit of success I have had with it, the somewhat stormy and exhausting years that have followed the book [*Strange Fruit*], all these have only made me more certain that from children come one's richest and most real experiences in life and one's final contribution to

> this world's welfare can be measured most truly by what one does for children everywhere. (*HH* 123)

In her March 21, 1949, letter to parents, she closed the camp with these memorable words:

> In a troubled world, whose children are in many lands lost and lonely and hungry, it is good to remember those years on Old Screamer Mountain and the dreams we dreamed there, so many of which have come true in the lives of girls now grown and mothers of children.
>
> I hope that the idea of Laurel Falls will not die. I want to believe that we have started a chain reaction of dreams that will go on touching child after child in our South. (*HH* 124)

Although she gave up the responsibilities of managing editor for *South Today* and director of Laurel Falls Camp, the theories and practices she developed through both projects remain central throughout her writing. Accordingly, selected writings for part 2 of this collection embody seeds of ideas and characters introduced in her earlier fiction, speeches, and editorials. Such is the nature of that creative process Lillian Smith called "a chain reaction of dreams."

A Southerner Talking
Chicago Defender Columns, 1948–1949

From October 1948 to September 1949, Smith wrote a weekly column for the *Chicago Defender*, one of the nation's premier African American newspapers. Each column was framed at the top with the title "A Southerner Talking" and at the bottom with the legend "Adventures in Race Relations." The following editor's note accompanied her initial column:

> The Chicago Defender is happy to welcome to its family of columnists a distinguished daughter of the white South who has risen above the prejudices of her class and section. Miss Lillian Smith of Clayton, Georgia, first won recognition as editor of the magazine "South Today" and still greater fame with the publication of her first novel "Strange Fruit." (October 16, 1948, 1)

Continuing the style and range of subjects Smith had developed earlier in Dope with Lime, the columns illuminate her reputation as a white liberal Southerner whose mind covers the world while her feet remain firmly planted on home ground. Whether traveling from her mountain home to the West Coast, to art galleries in New York, or to rural south Georgia, Smith sees beauty and ugliness always intertwined. As she observed in 1920s China and in 1930s and 1940s America, practicing white supremacy undermines any and all efforts to promote democratic ideals at home and abroad.

A Southerner Talking, October 30, 1948

When I have become too weighed down with the world's misery I go to the kitchen and cook. I whip up a cake, or make a chicken pilau—a wonderful new version of this was served me in a Moslem home while I was in India last year—or curry shrimp or make an old-fashioned vegetable soup with plenty of okra in it. There is something good about the feel of raw vegetables; and sometimes it helps my spirit to get messed up with flour . . . Even cleaning up dishes afterward is not bad therapy!

But alas, the day has passed when a decent person can eat a stomach full without conscience aching afterward. Sending CARE a check for food packages is the best medicine I know to take—if you don't want your night haunted by 230 million wan faces of children, to every one of whom our garbage would be a tea-party. It is a shocking thing to know that the United States, rich and full stomached, has given only one-tenth of its United Nations quota to the starving children of the world.

Sometimes the burden of the world's misery is almost too heavy to bear, when there are so few people bearing it. One wonders how long we can keep at it without losing our humor, our balance, our tender concern for our own personal relationships; and more than all else, how we can feel compassion for the very ones whose sins are destroying our earth's children. It is so easy to hate; it is so much harder to understand. Yet only understanding can rid the world of the EVILS WHICH MAKE YOU AND ME EVIL, and the "others" evil also. Like every one else, I grow discouraged but not for long; always it comes back to me: the indestructible faith that men can find a way out of the worst human dilemmas if they WANT TO.

We have two big jobs today: one to make our world whole by healing the splits between people, the other is to make our selves whole by healing the splits within our own minds and hearts. Both are tough, hard jobs; both require courage and humility; and both are necessary. For there can be no real unity outside until there is integrity within men's hearts. So simple and so terribly complex! It is not easy to face up to the bitter fact that democracy cannot work unless its citizens are mature; that citizens cannot mature unless they are free to grow; that they cannot grow unless they are whole; and they cannot be whole as long as they are segregated on any level of their life. There should be signs up all over the world: TAKE CARE, CHILDREN GROWING.

A world of growing children . . . growing in body, in mind, in emotions, in imagination, in social relations, in ethical values. Think of it! All of our children in Dixie, in Chicago, in New York and Detroit, and Europe and India and Asia, growing freely, unprisoned . . . free to reach out and accept the whole earth as theirs, to accept all of its people as human, to reach inside and accept themselves as human also. Children, free to love . . . to play . . . to laugh . . . to think . . . to move . . . to learn . . . to work . . . to dream.

To me, the growth of a child is the essence of morality: what makes a child grow is good; what kills a child's growth is bad. When men and women come to their senses enough to understand that no belief, no idea, no thing, no ideology, is worth killing one child for, then we shall have peace in our hearts and perhaps even on earth.

The Mountain is golden now and blazing with reds in the coves; it is colder than it was last week; the air is sweet with the smell of apples; there is a stillness down in the valley. It is a pity that men's hearts cannot mellow also in this ripening autumn weather.

A Southerner Talking, November 27, 1948

I have been re-reading *Masters and Slaves* by that distinguished Brazilian writer, Gilberto Freyre. In many ways it is a better book on the strange relationships between races and cultures than the excellent study of Gunnar Myrdal's. Better, because Freyre, refusing to consider segregation and its evils and the white man and his economics out of context with the whole of the life of the people, went to the roots of culture to find what he sought.

Religion, ideals about death and birth, child care, food habits, even food recipes seemed important to him in studying the total capacity for living and the patterns by which the Brazilians (Portugese [*sic*], Indian, African) defined their life. Thinking of the whole life it was logical for him to put under his microscope the sex habits and attitudes of the people, not in statistical columns of "outlets" in Kinsey style but as matters of extreme psychological relevance to this mammoth puzzle we call "race relations."

His study showed his awareness of the profound effect which attitudes toward sex and body have on a people's attitudes not only toward so-called "inferior" people but toward themselves and money and death and the creative process. I have believed for many years now, that only a people who suffer from deep and irrational body-guilt can shut themselves away from others "less pure" (whether of blood or virtue) as the Puritans of North America and the Hindus of India have tried to do—each of whom have their own kind of segregation system and each of whom are a people burdened by severe guilt feelings.

That is why I was a little disappointed in the *American Dilemma* not because it told too much but because it did not tell enough. I think that Myrdal, a man for whom I have great respect and admiration, did a fine, scholarly job when one considers that he had not lived his way through the dilemma and that he was here for so short a time.

I do not believe it is possible to understand the white man in America and his strange paranoid notions about his "superiority" without considering his equally strange childhood and the training he received before he was six-years old, the heavy guilt laid on heart and body while both were so young and weak, and finally the strange fruit which this kind of training has borne, not only of White Supremacy but of mental illness, alcoholism, child delinquency, exploitation and war-making. That was what I tried to say in my novel published five years ago. The "strange fruit" I wrote of was not lynching or miscegenation (a word I hate) but the white man himself and his children and his Tobacco Roads and his own wasted life; the "strange fruit" was man dehumanized by a *culture that is not good for the growth of either white or colored children.* But quite a few people in their defensiveness saw it otherwise; some as a tract against lynching, and some as a libel on the Negro race, and some as a book against the South. It was strange to be at the receiving end of these reactions. I suppose truth is a three-edged knife that hurts everybody, especially the author!

It shames me to remember that white culture permits the beating of its children. Many of our public schools still permit whippings. I cannot help but believe that a people who will beat their own children will find it easy to justify the torture of other people who seem 'different' from them. We know German children who found it so easy to become Nazis as they grew up and to help with the gruesome mass-killing of Jews came from families that punished and exerted a heavy-handed authority over their children.

One of the tragic elements in the American dilemma seems to me to be the eagerness with which members of the Negro race take on the sins of the white race in the name of "education." Too often becoming educated has meant learning to do things the "white way" which is so often the wrong way. There are Negroes, plenty of them I hear, who also beat their children. By "beating" I do not mean the mere use of a stick or switch—we can beat a child's spirit to death without ever touching his body. I think the African groups who came to America brought sane ideas of child nurture with them. Even today in many Negro families a few of the old secrets of child training are still known and practiced. I wish these truths had not been lost in the racial storms that have swept over our land.

A young woman from the Gold Coast of Africa, trained in child psychology in England, told me that she wanted to be a child psychiatrist. "But," she said smilingly, "if I return home to the Gold Coast I shall not have any patients to practice on. Our children are not emotionally sick as are American and English children." If that is true, then our social scientists and researchers in psychiatry should take the next plane for West Africa. For secrets such as they would find there would make it a psychological gold coast that would enrich the whole world.

A Southerner Talking, December 18, 1948

I am writing this as the train swings across the Arizona desert. My eyes are not yet accustomed to the Southwest's palette of colors. It is as if a giant hand had mixed finger paints until they were a grey-pinkish-brownish green smudge of pigment and had then spread them on a flat piece of paper that stretched to the curve of the earth. Mountains do not crowd the sky here as at home but are like thin colored paper cut sharply and set up as tiny backdrops on a vast empty stage. One keeps looking for the actors. When the sun sets, the mountains glow, not warmly as do our tree covered hills in the East but with a two-dimensional brilliance that reminds me of George Jenkins' transparent stage sets. It is as unreal and fabulous, as ugly and fascinating as surrealist painting and modern music. So much space and so little depth.

San Francisco I now place first on my list of North America's most beautiful cities. It reminds me of Bahia, which is my favorite Brazilian city. Not only is it beautiful, it is small enough to love and believe in; a city which actually looks as if people enjoy living in it.

While in California, I saw a preview of that deeply stirring film, *The Quiet One*. It is an experience that I shall not forget. A camera in the hands of one sensitive to the light and darkness and movement of a child's soul can do powerful things to an adult's peace of mind. There were moments when I found the film almost unendurable, so ruthless was its exposure of our civilization's cruelties to children. Ulysses Kay's music is as successful as the photography in its avoidance of prettiness and sentimentality and in its fine subordination to the terrifying cacophonies of childhood frustration. One often forgets that one is hearing music, so perfectly is it fused with the drama. I consider Ulysses Kay a most interesting and talented young composer. Perhaps you know that he is a Negro, a protégé of Hindermith [*sic*], and now holds a Guggenheim fellowship. James Agee has written a sensitive commentary. His words, as always, are the words of a poet.

The Quiet One is a story, set in Harlem, of a rejected child, who happens to be black, who has been refused love and tenderness, and its setting could as well have been Park Avenue or North Atlanta as Harlem, for it hurts as much to be rejected by a rich mother as by a poor one. We watch the youngster as he is so nearly destroyed as a human being and we see him begin to grow again.

It is as engrossing and painful as exploring one's own forgotten childhood. Important as documentary for it shows us the blind stupidities of a culture that so often puts children last in its list of First Things. Important also in film making because here is a mature, sensitive, exciting work produced not by Hollywood's millions but by four or five devoted people who pooled intelligence and talent and $30,000, and came up with America's best film to date about children.

A Southerner Talking, April 30, 1949

Spring on my mountain top is a thing to see. It has come like the tide. Down on the edge of fields in the valley below my window the color begins: a thin pink-yellow-green line that climbs day by day from field to cove, to ridge, from boulder to boulder, tree top to tree top, until suddenly the whole mountain is soft with unfolding leaves.

Last night I heard the first whippoorwill. And at daybreak, the pilliated [*sic*] woodpecker screamed like a sea gull across the ridge from my window. If you have never seen this Lord God of the bird kingdom you have missed a very special experience. There is something so arrogant, so defiant in his scream, so wild. In spite of yourself, a thing deep within you answers him and a spiritual duel is fought. He disdains the lowly earth and flies from tree top to tree top, a beautiful blur of black and white splotched with red. I suppose we really shouldn't approve of him. He undoubtedly does not believe in the brotherhood of man. And yet the scream is exciting; and always, when one hears, one gets up and goes out to watch him as we used to do when we heard the roar of a plane in the sky.

I have just come home from the city. And the country is pulling hard at me this morning. I went down in the rain last evening, just before dark and cut asparagus in my garden and picked a mess of turnip greens—the kind you taste only in your memory in the city. A rabbit scampered out of the radish bed and another froze stiff on the edge of the path as I passed by with my basket of greens. No doubt they consider me a thief invading their territory. As I came back up the hill, through the dim winding path, a wood thrush began to sing. I stood there, listening, remembering all the springs I have spent here, beyond me the old mountains that are changeless, below me, the ever-changing valley, back of me, years of pain and joy and bright moments that unrolled swiftly in that moment as I listened.

All night the wind blew hard against the mountain roaring high above the roof of my little rock house. It sounds like a great storm coming, though it travels the sky line and one never knows whether to call it a storm or not, as it never touches the earth.

Yesterday, I looked at the South from my Pullman window. When I awoke we were in North Carolina. All day the train wound through that state and South Carolina and curved back into north Georgia. In North Carolina, at breakfast time, I saw the first of those signs. Yes, first in the diner, when I walked in and faced the glass partition. And then as I drank my coffee, I looked out and saw another big sign over a doorway. It slapped this Southerner's mind hard, like an angry hand across the face. Once, I took those signs for granted. They were over doors when I was born and I accepted them without thinking, as I accepted heat and mosquitoes and sandspurs. Then one day, my imagination awoke. It was as if it had been asleep a long time. It woke up, and I felt those signs. If only all white Southerners could feel the meaning of them. Never again could they live comfortable with them.

As the train moved down the Southern railway, through textile mill-towns and back into fields, around hills, across rivers, the South flowed over me again. The down-at-the-heel look of things . . . the unhappy empty faces . . . the slow-moving walk of its people . . . their flat talk . . . the awful mill villages, the crooked little shanties tilted over as if a heavy wind had whiffed by . . . the dull rows of tight boxes that people live in close to the tracks. Poverty is not worse than it is in northern cities, it is only more naked. You cannot miss it, for there are no skyscrapers blocking it off from view and no noise to keep the mind from feeling.

The sun was warm and soft, fields greening, trees leafing, flowers blooming . . . the clay was so red and beautiful, the earth everywhere something you love to belong to. But the people spoiled my home-coming. Their faces, so hard, so angry, so lost and empty, blocked out the spring from my eyes. I could think only of our self-destruction, of how we have chained ourselves to a servitude that we do not name but which eats up like cancer all that is sweet and good and gentle and gay in our natures. As I think about it now, even the beauty of my mountain is forgotten and I sit here, sad and troubled. It is all such a pity, such a tragic and terrible waste of human happiness.

A Southerner Talking, May 14, 1949

A few weeks ago, I visited the much talked of exhibit of paintings at the Downtown Gallery in New York. I noticed that not only I but others looked quickly at the paintings, then turned to read carefully the comments that each painter had written about his work. We betrayed the big question that moves restlessly in the mind as one looks at surrealist and primitive and infantile art. There is something wrong and the layman knows it. Not having attached his loyalty to any one of the splinter groups the layman reserves the right to keep asking this question until artists answer it in paint.

I think some of us who have looked at paintings quietly and for long hours since we were young, want to know why adult men, why the mature artist, has been forced in this age to regress to his infantile fantasies and technics, to primitive fantasies and technics, to schizophrenic fantasies and technics in order to say aloud what he dreams. Are his dreams so schizoid, so infantile, so archaic that he cannot fuse them with mature emotions? Can he satisfy the schizophrenic in him only by slicing man in thin slivers and arranging them in hypnotic patterns of color that hold us simply because they arouse the sleeping terror and dread in our own souls? Does the abstractionist have to destroy the object before he can paint it? Must he do a hatchet job on every human face he paints, on every table and chair and bowl of fruit he arranges until he makes a 'still life' look more like the work of an undertaker rehabilitating the remains of a manic murder than anything else I can think of?

This past winter I studied Picasso's work carefully from his early period on through his cubist and abstraction periods to what I would call his present myth period. Such delicate calligraphy, and skill with brush and paint, such a mathematical sense of form and balance make one bow before him in deep respect. But the ensemble of work leaves me sick with the question, "Are artists so chained to our age that they, too, cannot see things whole, they, too, are unable to affirm life and love and sorrow and laughter and tenderness?"

I don't know. But I do know that one can look at a showing of Braque and Picasso and their imitators and come away with the feeling that one has been looking at a representation in paint of the age that could exterminate six million Jews in torture chambers as if they were insects. As a literal mirror of such a hate-driven, splintered age I think modern art has done an honest and efficient job. As a mirror of man, the human being, man the dreamer of dreams who can climb to the stars by means of his own bootstrap, it is as nothing.

The paintings at the Downtown Gallery are all by American artists, if I remember correctly. American painters when they do not abjectly imitate the French schools cannot rid themselves of their natural gusto, their roving eye, their adolescent brag and daring and their laughter and tenderness. It gets in the paint somehow, even when they are trying hard to be decadent.

And there are a few paintings in this collection that are neither imitative nor decadent. Georgia O'Keeffe's Brooklyn Bridge is so tender and joyous, so affirmative and strong that one almost fears to like it so much. One almost doubts the validity of such life. It is a painting that makes your soul hurt as if it has been in the dark so long that it cannot bear so much light.

Near it, is a painting by Jacob Lawrence that does not measure up to his best by any means but is bright and lively. In the same room also is another painting that holds its own even though so near the Bridge. It is by a Hawaiian named Tam, and is a thing worth looking at for hours. Strong in composition, painted in quiet sober color that has a translucent quality that kept pulling me back to it. It makes you dream of the oldness of the earth, of the million-year age of us. It makes you feel the word 'patience' and know its meaning deep down in the mind where there are no words. It does not have the vitality of a flame but the vitality of slow-changing rock.

I liked it. I like also the people at the Downtown Gallery who seem to me real and honest men, aware of man's nature and sensitive to its varied expressions.

A Southerner Talking, May 21, 1949

I have just returned from South Georgia. Homesick for the old swamp country and piney woods I got in the car and went there. The first long leaf pine I saw was like a big wave from the past washing over me. Memories came alive like little ground flowers springing up after a big rain. Not all the memories were so bright and pretty. Some were like snakes slithering through swamp water. But the bays were still smelling as sweet as ever and honeysuckle filled the ditches and yellow fly-catchers made beautiful patches in damp places, and the fields stretched flat and warm as far as eye can see, just as they did when I was little.

They do not look the same, though. For now, there is so little cotton. I counted the fields of sprouting cotton as we went down Highway 41. The ratio was about one cotton field to four of corn, to five of tobacco, to two of oats and lespedeza. The peanuts I had to guess at, for they are not yet out of the ground enough to see from the highway.

Agriculturally, Georgia has changed to a startling degree. I wish the Georgia mind had changed as much. Perhaps it has changed more than I know.

There is a question mark, I believe, where once in the white southern mind there was only a period. People know now that they don't know the answers.

On the way back, I followed the paved roads which Ed Rivers built, tying swamp to swamp and shack to shack through his home counties. Sometimes you drive ten miles, sometimes twenty miles between settlements; often five miles between houses. Distance and darkness, those ancient enemies of good-will and intelligence, are slowly disappearing. A little twisting strip of asphalt is making neighbors of folks who've been out of hollering distance for two hundred years. And rural electrification is turning the lights on where all has been dark after sunset since

Oglethorpe's first settlers pushed through palmetto and cypress swamp to a little rise in the ground where they stopped from sheer weariness and built themselves a shack.

The lights are being turned on, in minds and on front porches. But sometimes it seems so slow, so terribly slow. As I passed through the Waycross section, the piney woods and wire grass region where my father was reared, I could see no change at all. I know things have changed, a little, but one can't see it from the paved roads. The same old turpentine stills, lumber mills, the same old shacks, the same old bony cows lying on the edge of the road, or crossing it stupidly and slowly as you speed toward them. Those old cows remind me of my South sometimes: bony, and gaunt, and tough, blocking Change as it comes speeding down the world's highways, deaf and dumb to the menace it is for itself and for everybody else.

A Southerner Talking, August 20, 1949

The fate of China leaves one with a heart heavy as lead. One can go back over the last ten years and argue endlessly about our errors and our triumphs in this struggle in the Far East. But it is a false argument.

The errors were committed by us long before this last war began. For one hundred years we had our chance in the Far East. We could have sold the idea of democracy to those millions of people but we were too busy making them buy white supremacy.

I lived in China three years, in the same province where Chiang Kai-Shek was born. In that lovely, old province of beautiful winding canals and rice paddies and great mountains, and red curved roofs and wonderous little arched stone bridges, I watched the white race do so many ugly things.

I was young then. Young and inexperienced, and from a South where I had practiced segregation since I was born. But I saw what was happening. Seeing it happen in China made me know how ugly the same thing is in Dixie. I can never forget my deep sense of shock when I saw Christian missionaries from the South (and North, and England) impose their ideas of "white prestige" on this people who were living on their own soil. Here we were, intruders, staying there only on sufferance, yet forever preening and priding ourselves on our white superiority and calling ourselves followers of Christ. It was the kind of thing that makes a young honest person sick. And I was young, and honest, and I was sickened by what I saw.

I remember that sign in Shanghai which blared out in big printed words: **Dogs and Chinese not allowed.** Yes, the British put it there; but the Americans accepted its presence with little or no protest. Once, a young Chinese teacher and I planned to go to the park to hear the outdoor symphony concert. But she reminded me, quietly, gently, of the sign. In her own country, she was forbidden to enter that park and listen to the concerts.

I remember so much that was arrogant and ugly. White voices calling out "boy . . ." **Boy . . . boy . . .** all through the Orient that Anglo-Saxon word is as well-known as O.K. Now today the communists call the Chinese "Comrade." How can any one be surprised that communism has overrun China! It is a false camaraderie, yes; and the Chinese will some day discover that "Comrade" is equivalent with "Slave." But they do not know it now. And the sound of it is like cool water running across parched self-esteem.

I remember missionaries gathering in the summer resorts, taking their vacation from their "Labors for the Lord," and forbidding Chinese from using the swimming pools. This was true at Mo Kan Shan where I used to go in the summers. All these little touches of arrogance, these false airs of superiority, these poisonous words, these terrible acts, now today are coming back to the Western World, heavy-laden with dread and death. Why are we surprised? Every wise person saw this thing coming, twenty years ago. I knew when I was there that this would happen if we did not change our ways. Even then, the Communists were in China. Even then, they were talking with Sun Yat Sen, trying to tie him and his regime close to the U.S.S.R. We who looked closely saw these things happening. We knew, then, after Sun's death, Chiang Kai-Shek rose to quick power, tied himself up with brutal fascistic forces, and "stemmed the tide" of communism. But what did it all mean? The people were still poor and starving; white supremacy still seemed to them a synonym for America and Great Britain. Why were we so blind?

I do not know. But I know today that without a big moral gesture made by us we cannot keep the Orient from accepting Communism. We can save the rest of the Far East only by laying down white supremacy as a way of life. Are we strong enough to do it? Brave enough? Honest enough? Wise enough? I do not know.

From *Killers of the Dream*

Before becoming heavily involved with the production of her play *Strange Fruit*, Smith had vague plans for a nonfiction book on segregation and white supremacy. In the fall of 1946, however, she had returned to her "Julia" manuscript, begun as a novella in 1935, and signed a contract to rewrite it as a novel. The following promotional blurb for *Julia* was written by Smith for the May 1947 catalog of Harcourt and Brace (with which Reynal and Hitchcock merged in December 1946):

> This is Julia's story and Maxwell, Georgia's story, too, for Julia lived there. It is the story of a woman, self-contained, exquisite, who stirred an old dream in men's minds and fanned old doubts in every woman for women could not quite believe in Julia though every man did.
>
> It is a love story: of Julia and her father, Julia and her husband, Julia and her young confused brother, Julia and the shadowy procession of men who came to the library of the old Massey home, and left there increased in stature. For Julia made giants out of small men and they, seeing themselves in her eyes, believed in their tallness.
>
> But most of all, it is the story of Julia's love for the image of herself, which these men made and bowed down to, and which she clung to until at last she could cling no longer. For they who make images always destroy them. The day came when in sudden, horrifying violence the image was dashed to the ground and broken and lay there with the old repressed lusts and guilt of the community. Julia, looking at the fragments, turned away quietly and died. Women were glad and relieved for once more they could believe in their own sins and their virtue.
>
> Maxwell, Georgia, is here and its people, some of whom the readers of *Strange Fruit* will recognize. The old unpainted shacks of Colored Town

> are here also, but in shadow now, for Julia walks in the sunlight of College Street alone. (HH 114)

In *Julia* Smith was continuing her exploration of the self-destructive aspects of Western culture; but this time the focus was on gender, particularly as depicted in the image of the Southern lady, that epitome of upper-class Southern whites' attitudes toward sexuality and gender roles. In a March 21, 1947, letter to her editor, Lambert Davis at Harcourt and Brace, Smith further described the novel: "It is about a woman made so empty because her men filled her so completely with their dreams that she had no room to grow. In the big sense, it is a study of the role of Madonna worship in Western culture" (*HH* 116).

By May 1948, however, her letters indicate that Smith was working on a nonfiction book as well as the novel and trying to complete the nonfiction first. In her autobiographical notes Smith recalled the turning point in her writing of the novel that resulted in *Killers of the Dream*:

> After I got to the clergyman's suicide in *Julia*, I did his letter explaining why, and there was this phrase in it: I have killed my dream. Bang—. No more *Julia*. I knew I was going to write *Killers of the Dream* first. [...] I suddenly saw the South, and the USA, and all "white culture" in a different and much more profound way. The killers of the dream are ourselves as well as "the others" and we kill our dreams on so many levels of being: this became my theme. (*HH* 115)

Not surprisingly, according to her autobiographical notes, Smith described *Killers* as "the hardest of all books for me to write; it stirred deep and dangerous memories." For six or eight months, she recalled, she "got lost completely and messed things up by trying at times to avoid the personal and use history." Significantly, it was only when she chose the personal, confessional approach that the structure became clear. That personal approach—the source of power for her writing—and her psychocultural analysis did not endear her to most literary critics of her day, many of whom were also political moderates in favor of maintaining the racial status quo (*HH* 115).

Although *Strange Fruit* brought Smith international acclaim and greatly expanded her sphere of influence as a social critic, *Killers of the Dream*, published in October 1949, affronted too many Southerners—including powerful moderates—to be financially or critically successful. Combining personal memoir, allegory, and direct social commentary, no other work so effectively psychoanalyzed the South's rigid commitment to racial segregation. This subject matter and Smith's innovative style were met with hostility (or deliberate silence) by the literary establishment, the New Critics, and the general public of Cold War America (Gladney, Introduction, 1994).

The following two letters reveal Smith's intentions for *Killers of the Dream*. In a June 1949 prepublication letter to her editor, George Brockway at W. W. Norton, Smith wrote:

> I hope to God I'm through with race when I finish this book. I feel that I have had a thorough breakdown myself and I hope it purges me of certain guilts and so on, forever! I told my secretary—southern, small-town, sweet and sensitive, and often whitefaced after a day's work on this thing—that my next book was going to be a cook book and she beamed and whispered, "Oh, yes, please!"
>
> I find it almost impossible to sum up "what to do" [. . .] because what to do about race is tied up with what to do about EVERYTHING. Can't we leave it by saying that I deal with it plainly and explicitly first on the level of the South, then the nation, that I make a big difference between human rights and civil rights, that I see no possibility of great change taking place in the South until our mouthpieces (pulpit, press, radio) are willing to take a stand against segregation which not one southern newspaper does at the present time and only a few preachers; that the rural South is the key to the problem in Dixie and much must be done for it in order for it to be willing to give up the drug-like habit of White Supremacy; that I believe the whole problem of the peasant is a world-wide one stretching from Tobacco Road to the rice fields of China and the millet fields of India; that I believe the white man's problem is a complicated thing centered at the core of our culture but that we could change the whole picture within a year or two if we wanted to and felt an urgent necessity to do so (I say in detail how I think this could be done); that I do not think the race problem is "economic" but that it reaches down to men's fundamental needs and dreams and values. I think our problem is not so much one of false beliefs but of a profound lack of any belief at all. [. . .] I talk about the symbolic significance of civil rights and why it is such dangerous strategy for us to delay and delay giving these rights once and for all to our people. [. . .]
>
> P.S. [. . .] [Y]ou are quite right, it has been only in the last 15 years that even our historians have been re-evaluating this portion of our history from the point of view of human rights. All history concerned with the 19th century is very very white with the exception of two or three recent studies[. . . .] Real history, in my opinion, has never been written and won't be until historians are willing to deal seriously with men's feelings as well as with events. [. . .] (*HH* 125–27)

After critics responded negatively to *Killers*, Smith appealed to a larger audience in the following letter to the editor of the *Atlanta Constitution*, November 28, 1949.

May I, as the author of "Killers of the Dream," tell your readers why I wrote this book and what it is about?

I wrote it because I am deeply concerned with children's moral and psychological growth. I have directed Laurel Falls Camp for 25 years and in my work with children I began long ago to question certain habits and customs of our people which destroy the moral and creative strength of the young.

One day a camper, a member of one of the South's prominent families, came to me profoundly troubled. "Why," she asked, "do our parents give us ideals that we can practice only by breaking laws? Why does the church talk of brotherhood and insist on segregation? It's hard," she said in her distress, "to believe in something that you dare not live. It tears you up inside."

I never forgot that Southern girl's questions.

And so, to try to answer them, I wrote "Killers of the Dream." I began the book by writing about my own childhood and that of my brothers and sisters for I believe that we are "typical" Southerners, and I think, too, when one criticizes one's region one should begin with one's self. I told of the lessons of sin and sex and segregation that we learned as children, of brotherhood and white supremacy. I told how the church played its role in making us segregated Christians. I told three ghost stories that have been used by demagogues to arouse the people's fears and tried, by bringing them out in the open, to convince the readers that such ghosts no longer exist. I told of Southern women, of what the ghosts did to their lives, and how, in spite of them, the churchwomen of the South have done so much to bring our people back to a Christian way of living.

Then I told the story of rural poverty. Since I am not a Marxist, I did not overemphasize the role of economics in the system of white supremacy. I happen to disagree strongly with Communism which believes that the body of man is more important than his soul and mind. But nevertheless I gave 54 pages of the book to the South's rural problems of poverty and ignorance.

I have been called "brave"; I am not brave. I am afraid, terribly afraid that democracy and Christianity and perhaps the world itself will be destroyed if we who believe in love and brotherhood and children growing do not begin quickly to live our beliefs.

For historical accuracy, and in the interest of showing Smith's evolution as a writer, the following chapters are taken from the 1949 edition of *Killers of the Dream* rather than from the revised and clearly improved 1961 edition. Smith provides another excellent introduction to *Killers* on the recording she made after Norton published the revised edition in 1961. Listening to that recording at www.piedmont.edu/lilliansmith-resources should enhance any reading of the following two selections. Both exemplify another important tenet in Smith's persistent critique of the American South. She knew her culture's attitudes toward women lay at the heart of racial segregation.

For Smith, the passionless white woman on a pedestal and the black woman with child by the white man who denied his relationships with the black woman and child exemplified related and attendant evils of white supremacy. In a culture where marriage and motherhood were women's primary roles, neither black nor white women were free to be fully wives or mothers, and neither were able to shield their children from the physical and psychic destruction of the racist society in which they lived (Gladney, Introduction, *KD*, 1994).

Three Ghost Stories

The raveling out of what had been woven so tightly was usually a slow process. One thread at a time came loose. Then another. Sometimes a great hole was torn by a quick stabbing experience. However it happened, it was not long in the little southerner's life before the lessons taught him as a Christian, a white man, an American, a puritan, began to contradict each other.

Sometimes, it was as if he were surrounded by characters in a bad dream who pull him this way and that, crowd him until he is almost smothered, then suddenly move in opposite directions, dragging him with them. And always, standing by, were his parents telling him this bad dream is life and he must accept it; telling him, gently or sternly, that this is reality.

But gradually, in the way of all flesh, the southern child adjusted himself to his world in which people said what they did not mean, and meant what they dared not say.

As I try to weigh the forces that pressed down on these children of my generation I know I am assuming an impossible task. Each personality creates its own gravitation system. A force that weighs heavily on one is without weight on another due to ten thousand differences in ego and conscience strength, in psychic energy and that indefinable something we call the capacity for survival.

Despite these differences, most of us found it more painful to adjust to the conflict set up in our personal relationships than to warring ideas or even to the restrictions put upon bodily drives, though here again one is dealing with imponderables and perhaps it is not fruitful to compare them.

The ideas, denying each other, we could bend to with relative ease, usually. Sometimes by practicing intellectual deafness we could keep ourselves from hearing, or hearing simultaneously, the antiphonal choruses of white supremacy and democracy, brotherhood and segregation, love and lynching, and so on. The human mind finds it an easy thing to split itself into what we used to call "logic-tight compartments." This separation divorced our beliefs from the energy that might have carried them into acts, but we accepted this moral impotence as a natural thing and often developed what is called a "judicious" temperament from believing equally in both sides of a question.

The instinctual drives of the body were more difficult to cope with. These were mighty feelings and no words could have stopped them. Only a fear of consequences more violent than desire could dam up somatic urges. But our early training had given us plenty of fear—both of displeasing those we loved, and of eternal punishment. And it worked. This energy of course was only deflected—had it not found a way out, the personality would have exploded in madness. But there were outlets: substitute satisfactions, neuroses, a thousand ways in which the personality, like a mountain stream, twisted and turned, went underground, came up again in a remote place, rushed over rocks, wasted itself, but finally reached, somehow, the end of its journey.

This training given my generation, and its results in the shaping of personality, is different only in degree from that given most white Protestants throughout the Western world. (I separate Protestant from Catholic just here not because the training of Catholic children was less severe—on the contrary it was more so—but because the Catholic child was given in its religion more adequate compensations for its renunciations than were given little Protestants.) But though we learned and unlearned many lessons that will seem familiar to men and women of Christian background wherever they live in the Western world, and had in common with them the same twisting love-hate-guilt ties with our parents, which psychoanalysis has made familiar to modern man as the Oedipus complex, we of the South also have had three traumatic relationships not common outside our region, that have left a lasting impression on all of us, though few, actually, have suffered them directly.

These ghost relationships still haunt the southern mind, arouse so much terror and anxiety that many of today's most urgent problems cannot be dealt with rationally, even though the outcome of the world's crisis may depend largely upon how they are solved. They are ghosts that must be laid, and I think the only way this can come about is for us to uncover them and see for ourselves the dusty nothingness beneath their masks.

These strange and twisted relationships interlock and no one of them can be understood without understanding all three. Perhaps the one that has touched most lives is the backyard temptation that pulled for a century and a half at our Anglo-American grandfathers. By the historical "accident" of slavery, our slaveholding puritan ancestors were juxtaposed to a dark people, natural, vigorous, unashamed, full of laughter and song and dance, who, without awareness that sex is "sin," had reached genital maturity. These so-called primitives (whose culture had so many sophisticated elements in it) were not, we must remember, brought into this country and hidden away in ghettos. They were brought into our back yards and left there for generations. They were everywhere, and highly conspicuous not only because of their color but because of their liveliness which the chains of slavery never subdued. From all that we know of them they seem to have had, even as some have now, a marvelous love of life and play, a physical grace and rhythm and a psychosexual vigor that must have made the white race by contrast seem washed-out people, drained of so much that is good and life-giving, and left with so little save their guilt and greed and aggression. It was natural that the white man was drawn to them. Laughter, song, rhythm, spontaneity were like a campfire in a dark tangled forest full of sins and boredom and fears. So bright, so near. . . .

But the back-yard temptation was also a menace—not so much a "menace to our women" (that poisonous idea flowered later) but a menace to the basic beliefs of white culture. In the front yard was a patriarchal system; in the back yard a matriarchy. In the front yard the lessons on sin, sex, and segregation and the value of money were taught, in the back yard the children seemed always to be having recess from lessons, and for reasons no one could understand were healthy and serene in nature, less aggressive, less greedy than the white children. In the big white house a white lady was corseting her feelings and those of her children in an effort to be "pure"—and settling back finally in flabby ignorance. But in the back yard, life went on, naked and unashamed. Little black children did all the naughty things little white children were punished for, did them and prospered in body and mind. I am not forgetting that they were slaves or that they worked long hours and were brutally oppressed. I am here concerned not with how the white man treated the Negro, but with how the Negro treated himself and especially how black mothers treated their children. For there is a story here, that we know only in fragments, which is surely worth the telling.

I think these old black matriarchs knew secrets of child rearing and secrets of sanity that our psychiatrists have been learning the hard way for the past sixty years through research, and that white mothers still know too little about. Unconfused by a church's rigid system of splitting spirit from body and injecting sin into bodily needs, unconfused by a patriarchal-puritanic system which psychically castrated its women, who in turn psychically castrated their children, male and female, by the burden of anxiety they laid on their minds—these women knew intuitively, or from old lore, the psychosomatic truths that we whites are groping awkwardly toward today. The results in their children were a stability, a health, a capacity for accepting strain, an exuberance, and a lack of sadism and guilt that no Anglo-Saxon group, to my knowledge, has ever shown.

It is a pity that we do not know more about it. For these were mothers who, under a harsh regime, worked the miracle of rearing children who grew up to be neither psychic slaves nor psychic rebels. Throughout the ordeal of slavery they remained people of easy dignity, kindly, humorous, bending only when necessary, deeply hurt and sad (as their spirituals make us know), but sane at the core as neither a vengeful nor a cringing people can be. They developed severe faults, of course, during these centuries. Easy lying, deceit, flattery became almost second nature to many of them. But they flattered with their tongues in their cheeks, and their "lies" turned into an art form that has contributed richly to our literature. There were the exceptions: crazed individuals who ran amok; others who turned their hate upon themselves and members of their own race with their Saturday night razor fights and quick killings over trifles; still others there were who brazenly exploited their own shame, pawning their dignity for profit. But as a group they retained an amazing stability throughout days of slavery and even through much of the long readjustment following it. That it is fast disappearing today is one of the ironic results of an "education" given in our country that does not fit psychosomatic needs of Negroes any more than it has fitted the psychosomatic needs of white people and which is rapidly transforming many Negroes, restive under severe restraints and humiliations, into as aggressive and bitter a people as are many of the white group.

But throughout slavery they possessed a psychological quality that could maturely withstand the temptation to take revenge. Their record during the Civil War and later during the chaos of Reconstruction is one of the most honorable in human annals. To call them cowards for not being vengeful, as some do today, is to ignore the dynamics of personality. Cowards would have been the first to let their hate feelings break through: it would not have required much bravery to kill and burn and rape helpless women and children left isolated on the big plantations. I think the answer lies in the home, in what happened between mother and child in those tiny slave cabins. Those of us who in our childhood knew a few of these strong old women—the children of slaves—can never forget their wisdom, their capacity for accepting life and people, their deep laughter, their unashamedness. They had strong instinctual feelings, not all of them loving, but they rarely let hate or fear master them. And I cannot imagine one of them feeling guilt in the way in which the white race feels it, nor do I remember their suffering from that sickness of the soul we call ambivalence.

What the white race termed "savagery" in slaves who were so much less cruel than their masters, was due to a method of child-rearing which was probably common to many African cultures and which today we moderns are accepting as the "modern way of child guidance." But to our grandfathers this "method," with its cheerful results, was a threat to their own system of punishment and sin and guilt. And yet here these black women were in the back yard, turning white beliefs into silly lies, and tempting men beyond their endurance.

Temptation and menace began to twist together as they see-sawed in the white man's mind. Attraction, fear, repulsion, attraction—so it went. After a few years, lighter faces began to appear in back yards. More and more light faces. And, at the same time that they were finding the back-yard temptation irresistible, these white men were declaring and sometimes beginning to believe that Negroes did not have souls, that they were not quite human, they were different, they were "no better than animals". . . . The first ghost had begun to walk through dark places in the mind of the South. *Mongrelizing* is a revealing word with connotations of broken taboos and guilt too terrible to say aloud.

These were rural people—rich and poor—many of them living far away from others of their kind, but close to the animals on farms and plantations, close to this alien race whom they refused to accept as human, yet they were breeding with them. Surely something akin to the dread, the anxiety that is felt by one who indulges in zoophilic practices must have nagged at their minds on a level rarely admitted to consciousness. What a strange ugly trap the white race made for itself! Because these slaveholders were "Christian," they felt compelled to justify the holding of slaves by denying these slaves a soul, and denying them a place in the human family. Because they were puritan, they succeeded in developing a frigidity in their white women that precluded the possibility of mutual satisfaction. Lonely and baffled and frustrated by the state of affairs they had set up in their own homes and hearts, they could not resist the vigor and kindliness and gaiety of these slaves. And succumbing to desire, they mated with these dark women whom they had dehumanized in their minds, and fathered by them children who, according to their race philosophy, were "without souls"—a strange exotic new kind of creature, whom they made slaves of and sometimes sold on the auction block. The white man's roles as slaveholder and Christian and puritan were exacting far more than the strength of his mind could sustain. Each time he found the back-yard temptation irresistible, his conscience split more deeply from his acts and his mind from things as they are.

The race-sex-sin spiral had begun. The more trails the white man made to back-yard cabins, the higher he raised his white wife on her pedestal when he returned to the big house. The higher the pedestal, the less he enjoyed her whom he had put there, for statues after all are only nice things to look at. More and more numerous became the little trails of escape from the statuary and more and more intricately they began to weave in and out of southern life. Guilt, shame, fear, lust spiraled each other. Then a time came, though it was decades later, when man's suspicion of white woman began to pull the spiral higher and higher. It was of course inevitable for him to suspect her of the sins he had committed so pleasantly and often. *What if,* he whispered, and the words were never finished. *What if. . . .* Too often white woman could only smile bleakly in reply to the unasked question. But white man mistook this empty smile for one of cryptic satisfaction and in jealous panic began to project his own sins on to the Negro male. And when he did that, a madness seized our people.

It began slowly. Fabulous stories began to be whispered of the Negro male's potency. And as white man visited more frequently the cabins in the quarters, and stayed more and more away from the big house, his suspicion grew of his wife left alone there with her embroidery and her thoughts. The more he left his sacred statuary while he sought warmer company, the more possessive became his words about her. "Our women" was a phrase that was said more and more glibly. And as suspicion and guilt grew, as minds became more paranoid, they threatened with death any white woman who dared do what they had done so freely. It is said—I am not certain that it has been proved—that a few white women did cross over the line and paid their penalty and that this penalty of death was dealt them by their own husband or father or brother as the case might be. I still find myself incredulous about this death legend. But, southern authorities like Hodding Carter and the late William Alexander Percy have, even in recent years, emphasized the strength of the taboo against white women mating with Negroes, and the heavy penalties exacted of them, at least by the community, though nowadays such women are more often banished than killed; it is the Negro male who receives the death penalty today as a "rapist" when such alliances are discovered. Perhaps only in the Mississippi delta do people still talk in such archaisms as "our women" and "men's honor," but there was a time when the South's vocabulary was heavy with such words and memories even yet are weighed down by them.

Men hungry for political and economic power could not resist exploiting this terrifying complex of guilt, anxiety, sex jealousy, and loneliness. By pumping from this vast reservoir—which had accumulated during long periods of stress—the mass hysteria they needed to irrigate their political and economic crops, they kept them green. And they are still green today, cultivated by the same system. It worked so well because the church and the home kept guilt and hate flowing into the reservoir, while the politician and business man had nothing to do but keep pumping it out. From this shocking partnership sprang other crops too, like the Ku Klux Klan and lynchings, and the massive anxieties which hardened into the rites of segregation.

If one had tried to dramatize the inward suspicion and guilt and fear that still gnaws on the white southerner's mind, it could not have been done more vividly than the Ku Klux Klan had done it for us. Pictorially, the Klan presents this Return of the Repressed in a stunning manner. White pillow case and sheet . . . the face covered . . . identity disappears and with it the conscience . . . a group stalks in silence through the "darkness" . . . a sudden abrupt appearance before the victim . . . and finally, the symbolic killing of a black male who, according to this paranoid fantasy, has "raped" a "sacred" white woman. It is a complete acting out of the white man's internal guilt and his hatred of colored man and white woman.

Historically, the first Ku Klux Klan originated in Pulaski, Tennessee, in 1866, formed by six ex-Confederate soldiers, half as a lark but used quickly afterward as an impromptu way of meeting an emergency situation in which the South was left without law-enforcing agencies. Had it actually been impromptu and accidental the idea would have been discarded and forgotten when order was restored in the South. But instead, it lived on and spread like an epidemic. Now today, more than eighty years later, the Klan rides in New Jersey as well as in Georgia and Alabama. It no longer limits itself to the revenging of "raping" and the "protecting" of womanhood nor is it turned solely against the Negro race. It is used against unions, against middle-class "deviationists," against people who "drink," against anyone who says or does anything the Klan disapproves of. It is becoming more undisguised and more undifferentiated in its sadism and intolerance, until now it is in the main a ceremonial acting-out of men's deeply repressed fantasies and deeply repressed needs for revenge and penance. It gathers under its hood the mentally ill, the haters who have forgotten what it is they hate or who dare not harm their real hate object, and also the bored and confused and ignorant. The Klan is made up of ghosts on the search for ghosts who have haunted the southern soul too long.

There are no available statistics on the frequency or range of biracial sex activities in the South. One has to rely on spotty bits of research, on case studies of southern mental patients, on whispers, and word-of-mouth revelations that go down in the South from white mother to white daughter and from colored mother to colored daughter, and on the garrulous reminiscence of white-haired colonels too old to care, and on the revealing but fragmentary research made by a few social scientists.

Regardless of statistics, this every one knows: Whenever, wherever, race relations are discussed in the United States, sex moves arm in arm with the concept of segregation. There is a union in minds, however unreal in terms of today's facts, that makes us know that the secret history of race relations in the South, the fears and the dreads, are tied up with the secret habits of southerners. We know too, that there are more than six million people of mixed Negro-white blood in our country and most of us are fairly certain that the stork did not bring them to little cotton field cabins—even though in 1940 a Georgia governor banned from state libraries a book for children written by Dr. Karl de Schweinitz that tells where babies come from.

And now we are close to our second ghost story, which concerns the South's rejected children. When children came from these secret unions they were rarely acknowledged by their white fathers. Usually they were wholly rejected, though now and then they were secretly clung to. Most of us know stories of a white man in our community who chose not to reject his mixed children but educated them instead and helped them find a decent life for themselves. Sometimes he left these children's names in his will and posthumously made amends for human relations which in life he had not the courage to honor. This is one of the brighter threads weaving through the dark evil design of the history of the intimate life of the two races.

But these acknowledgments, though important to remember, have been few. The stark ugly fact is that millions of children have been rejected by their white fathers and white kin and left to battle alone the giants that stalk our culture. Little ghosts playing and laughing and weeping on the edge of the southern memory can be a haunting thing. Surely one can reject a child one has brought into the world only by rejecting an equal part of one's psychic life, putting a sign over it and declaring it does not exist. White and Colored signs have had many uses down here.

This mass rejection of children has been a heavy thing on our region's conscience. Like a dead weight dropped in water it lies deep in the ooze of the old and forgotten, but when talk of change is heard, it stirs restlessly as if still alive in its hiding place and is felt by minds innocent of participating in the original sin but who for involved reasons have identified themselves with it.

The Communists have their explanation of this widespread miscegenation. They say it took place in the South because the white man wanted more and more slaves and made of slave women highly profitable economic projects in which he invested spermatozoa. These theorists do not even smile as they spin this odd little yarn. Indeed, to them, there is nothing amusing about it. It is simply a "logical" variation of the twentieth-century Story of Creation in which, according to Marxists, economics is the stork that brings all things, good and bad, to this earth. Since most of us know people to whom money and economic power have come to mean more than love and family and integrity and truth, it is not impossible to believe (though our sense of humor still finds it awkward) that money lust and not body lust drove a few planters deliberately to add to their material wealth in this shrewd, highly pleasurable, if sadistic manner. But the theory will impress most of us as more of an anal-erotic daydream than a rational explanation of group behavior.

But regardless of "why," the results are well known. The men who deviated in this extralegal way were fearful lest their sons, and especially their daughters, should feel the same attraction they felt and should perhaps continue the blending of races to which they and their forefathers had made such lavish contributions. And because they feared this, knowing the strength of temptation, they blocked their children's way by erecting as many barriers as possible, extracting energy from their own guilt to build fortifications of law and custom against what they considered an "irresistible sin." Out of their confusion came that obscene word *mongrelizing* and the sadistic phrase *enforced intimate relations*, both of which were mirrors of their own shabby past. Like all criminals, they felt compelled to confess their misdeeds and did so with the naiveté of a child by the use of these words. Now today's politicians deliberately reach for these worn-out phrases when they need them to stir up excitement and fear and fantasies. Like the South's revivalists, whose place they have in large part taken in communal affairs, these politicians plunge deep into men's minds and memories, and mixing the poison of these words with the guilt already there, they produce terror—and votes.

It is all so foolish and unreal that our sense of humor and our sanity should be able to throw it off. We know conditions have changed. There are still a few casual sex relations between the races, especially in remote rural regions like the delta and in the vicinity of a few of our southern universities, but the old life in the South that bred such deep attraction is almost gone. The back-yard temptation to the front-yard puritan has disappeared, largely due to the fact that so many Negroes have become puritans themselves and back yards are farther away. The patterns of our life have changed rapidly during the last thirty years from rural to urban because of migrations and paved roads. There are fewer personal contacts between the races. There is now in the younger generation a freer and perhaps more rational sex life between male and female of the white group and less necessity to seek pleasure down the back paths. And there is a burning blasting scorn of white men growing in the minds not only of upper-class Negro women but of nearly every woman of the colored race, making it a fairly dangerous thing for a white male to approach one of them.

Yet in spite of these vast changes the old legend persists, sustained by a stubborn memory of a now-lost life. To understand this resurgence of fantasy I think we have to remember that there was more to many of these old affairs than a passing desire for exotic experience or animal lust. Our unwritten history is full of profoundly passionate affairs, of relationships tender and rich and absorbing a lifetime. There were love affairs that made white women despair as competitors; delicate, sensitive, deep relationships in which mind and body and fantasy met in complete union. These have existed and it would make our southern past an impoverished thing were we to try to erase them because of the puritanic pride of either of the two races.

They existed because there was rich psychological soil for them to grow in. In the old days, a white child who had loved his colored nurse, his "mammy," with that passionate devotion which only small children feel, who had grown used to dark velvety skin, warm deep breast, rich soothing voice and the ease of a personality whose religion was centered in heaven not hell, who had felt when mind is tender the touch of a spirit almost free of sex anxiety, found it natural to seek in adolescence and adulthood a return of this profoundly pleasing experience. His memory was full of echoes . . . he could not rid himself of them. And he followed these echoes to back-yard cabins, to colored town, hoping to find there the substance of shadowy memories. Sometimes he found what he sought and formed a tender, passionate, deeply satisfying relation which he was often faithful to, despite cultural barriers. But always it was a relationship without honor in his own mind and region, and the source of profound anxiety which seeped through his personality. Yet the old longing persisted, the old desire for something he could not find in his white life.

Stifled, sometimes forced into the unconscious, though betrayed ingenuously by the bathos of the "my old mammy" theme, this tender and tragic relationship of childhood—the white child and his colored nurse—has powerfully influenced the character of many southerners of the dominant class. The class is small, numerically, but out of it have come politicians, newspaper editors and journalists, college professors and presidents, doctors, preachers, industrialists, bankers, writers, governors, and their wives, and in our national government many of the prominent officials who are today determining the future of the world. It therefore seems important for us to understand this primal experience which so many leaders in world affairs and creators of American opinion have undergone in childhood.

It was customary in the South, if a family possessed a moderate income, to have a colored nurse for the children. Sometimes such a one came with the first child and lived in the family until the last one was grown. Her role in the family was involved and of tangled contradictions. She always knew her "place," but neither she nor her employers could have defined it. She was given a limited authority, but it was elastic enough to stretch into dictatorship over not only children but the white mother and sometimes even the male head of the family. They leaned on her strength because they had so little of their own or because she had so much, and once leaning they could not free themselves from subjection. Many an old nurse, knowing all there was to know of her white folks, familiar with every bone of every skeleton in their closets, gradually became so dominating that her employers actually feared her power. Yet she was a necessary part of these big sprawling households; her knowledge, alone, of how to grow children was too precious a thing to throw away lightly, and her value extended far beyond child rearing. She nursed old and young when they were sick, counseled them when they were unhappy, took the problem child at least out of earshot, and in crises her biologically rooted humor had a magic way of sweeping white clouds away. She was nurse, witch doctor, and priest, conjuring off our warts, our hurt feelings and stomach-aches, all of which disappeared when she said they would. She knew wonderful simples for ailments of body and soul, and bound up both in earthy ointments. We put on undershirts, come fall, as she told us to, hung asafetida bags around our necks when there were epidemics in town, ate sulphur and cream of tartar each spring, stayed away from graveyards after dark as she taught us to do, wouldn't have dared iron anything on Sunday, and following her precepts we prospered as did her own children. Sometimes Mr. White Man himself did not deem it beneath him to call on her for help. "Mammy, come in here and talk to Miss Sarah [his wife]. Talk sense to her, Mammy," and he'd leave for the cotton gin downtown or the sawmill, hoping God that Mammy could straighten Sarah out. And usually she did, and Sarah would be as meek and gentle as a wife should be when her husband returned that evening.

In many homes, the nurse was also a wet nurse. We were children in the pre-refrigerator age and bottle feeding was a perilous business. It was much safer when mother's milk disagreed, to turn an ailing or malnourished infant over to a nurse whose ample breasts could take care of another as well as her own. It was not a rare sight in my generation to see a black woman with a dark baby at one breast and a white one at the other, rocking them both in her wide lap, shushing them to sleep as she hummed her old songs. Still swinging them from side to side in her arms, she would lay them down on the same pallet underneath a shade tree and leave them there, little black little white together, sleeping in peace. These intimacies fill our memories and do strange things now to our segregated grown-up lives.

In my home, our nurse lived in the back yard beyond Mother's flower garden in a small cabin whose interior walls were papered with newspapers. Much of my very young life was spent there. I was turned over to her when a new baby took my place in the family. And because I seemed not to have the stamina to adjust to this little intruder I protested by refusing to eat and kept up a food strike so long that they grew alarmed and called in the doctor although Aunt Chloe looked on, they say, with obvious scorn at their panic. And after the doctor left his prescription and drove away in his buggy, she took me to her cabin and kept me there. The story is that Aunt Chloe tried food after food all of which I rejected, then studying the pale young face before her for a little, she took a little food, chewed it first in her mouth, put it in mine and I swallowed it promptly. Soon I was prospering on this fine psychological diet, gaining weight and security as the weeks went by. I was once more the center of somebody's universe. What did it matter that this universe encompassed only one room in a little back-yard cabin? It filled my need and I loved her.

Such a relationship with such a woman is not to be brushed off by the semantic trick of labelling her a "nurse."

Sometimes these nurses took over the care of a baby on the day it was born. More often Mammy entered a child's life in an important way at the painful moment when a new baby had taken its place. Wounded and hurt, feeling as profound a rejection as a human heart knows, we were taken into her life, where she made us feel welcome and prized. In her own way and not wholly according to what the psychiatrists of today would suggest, she helped us adjust to the one who had taken our place, nursed us through and sometimes, not always, weaned us from this experience that grasped like nettles and threatened to hold us to it for the rest of our lives. But though freed from this, we were tied to another, even more difficult, relationship.

Psychoanalysts have made us know during the past fifty years how the deep injuries to the infant psyche can leave scar tissue that binds a personality for a lifetime. We have grown used to words we do not always understand: the Oedipus complex, "fixation," and the pictures of rejection that haunt the child memory. But this dual relationship which so many white southerners have had with two mothers, one white and one colored and each of a different culture that centered in different human values, makes the Oedipus complex seem by comparison almost a simple adjustment.

Before the ego had gained strength, just as he is reaching out to make his first ties with the human family, this small white child learns to love both mother and nurse; he is never certain which he loves better. Sometimes, secretly, it is his "colored mother" who meets his infantile needs more completely, for his "white mother" is busy with her social life or her older children or perhaps a new one, and cannot give him the time and concern he hungers for. Yet before he knows words, he dimly perceives that his white mother has priority over his colored mother, that somehow he "belongs" more to her, though he may stay more with the other. But he is satisfied with things as they are, for his colored mother meets his immediate needs as he hungers to have them met. She is easy, permissive, less afraid of simple earthy biological needs and manifestations. When naughtiness must be punished, it is not hers but the white mother's prerogative to do so; and afterward, little white child runs back to colored mother for comfort and sugar-tits. Sometimes, white child hates white mother after this ordeal, and clings desperately to his colored mother, who soothes him and gives him a tea cake as she softly asks him, "Ain' you shamed, honey, to be so bad!" And he is shamed, and confused, and sometimes very lonely also.

And now curious things happen. Strong bonds begin to grow as the most profound relationships of his life are formed, holding him to two women whose paths will take them far from each other. It is as if he were fastened to two umbilical cords which wrap themselves together in a terrifying tangle, and then suddenly, inexplicably, but with awful sureness, begin steadily to move, each in a different direction. Because white mother has always set up right and wrong, has with authority established the "do" and the "don't" of behavior, his conscience, as it grows in him, ties its allegiance to her and to the white culture and authority which she and his father represent. But to colored mother, persuasive in her relaxed attitude toward "sin," easy and warm in her physical ministrations, generous with her petting, he ties his pleasure feelings.

Big white house, little cabin, enter the picture he is slowly forming in his mind about this strange world he lives in, and both begin subtly to give pattern to it. A separation has begun, a crack that extends deep into his personality. He erects "white" image-ideals and secretly pulls them down again. He says aloud what his heart denies stubbornly. Part of him stays more and more in the world he "belongs" in; part of him stays forever in the world he dare not acknowledge. He feels deep tenderness for his colored nurse and pleasure in being with her, but he begins to admire more and more the lovely lady who is his "real" mother. He is impressed by her white beauty, her clothes and grace and charm; he feels one with the big powerful man who is his father—though he fears him too and sometimes secretly hates him—and one with the tradition that stands like the big house he was born in, always there before him as "his." But when he is miserable, he creeps away and crawls up in old black arms, every curve of which he has known by heart since babyhood, and snuggles against a cotton dress that is ragged maybe but will always smell good to his memory.... Sometimes he wants to stay in her lap forever; but he slips away shamefaced, remembering that *this* mother is not "fitten," as she says herself, to sit in the living room and eat at the table with the rest of the family. He is learning a desolating lesson that shrinks the heart when we think of its human implications; and soon he will know it too well ever to forget it.

His "white" conscience, now, is hacking at his early love life, splitting it off more and more sharply into acceptable and unacceptable, what is done and what isn't; into "pure" and "impure"; Madonna and whore; Mother and nurse; wife and prostitute; white conscience and colored pleasures; marriage and lust; "right" and "wrong"; belief and act; segregation and brotherhood. He accords his mother the esteem and respect that are hers; he feels more and more a pulling obligation to her, though he does not know why. And after a time, he feels that he "owes" her so much that he steals the adoration which he had conferred upon his colored mother long ago, and returns it to his white mother as rightfully hers. From now on, his gifts to his old nurse will be little presents, not of esteem and love, but a linen handkerchief or a check at Christmas and birthday, and all his life long, tears when old spirituals are sung....

He has almost completed the cheapening of this tender profound relationship which his culture insists upon. The segregation of his first love feelings is nearly perfected, but not quite; not ever is it quite finished. Deep down in him, he often reserves his play, his "real" pleasure, his relaxed enjoyment of sex activities, and his fantasy, for women as much like his nurse (they may or may not have colored skin) as his later life can discover. Now he has achieved his stature as a white man; he has accepted the life that his whiteness conferred upon him. But he is never at ease. The deep powerful drives of childhood will not stay in the little stream beds his culture gullied out for them. Again and again they overflow, sweeping across him like a flood. Tenderness for his mother turns into sudden cruelty for his wife which he conceals even from himself sometimes, or betrays by lightning flashes of hatred. Sometimes he loses the shame he is trained to feel about women of other color or class and admits to himself and to others his pleasure in them. Sometimes a sweeping sadistic feeling for all women overpowers him. He feels betrayed, cheated; and he despises himself and them for a treacherous partnership in which he seems always to have been the loser since childhood. And in deep repugnance, he sometimes turns away from all women, shunning them white and black, and spends his real feelings on men and his hours in companionship with them, or centers his energy on making money, more and more money.

However they dealt with it, nearly all men—and women—of the dominant class in the South suffered not only the usual painful experiences of growing up in America but this special southern trauma in which segregation not only divided the races but divided the white child's heart.

Three ghost relationships—white man and colored woman, white father and colored children, white child and his beloved nurse—haunting the mind of the South and giving shape to our lives and our souls.

And there was a fourth, poisoned by disesteem as were the others, yet a relationship that held the good qualities of one person firmly to the good of another. Back-yard though it was, lopsided by color, curiously belittled by those who valued it most, this friendship between individuals of the two races was a thing of grace and mutual concern. Begun in childhood, it sometimes was broken only by death. Shamefaced though they were in its presence, men white and colored often sacrificed themselves in its name. This friendship across barriers has been, of all bi-racial relationships in the South, the one most enriching in its human qualities; and one that has restrained the region from insane excesses of prejudice. It nourished no guilt, sheltered no hate, was not used as an escape from responsibilities. It was no ghost, but a real thing that bound men one to another though there was between them a deep chasm that drained away much that is good from the lives of both. There was no honor in that relationship but there was a secret acceptance of each other as human. And it became a green growing thing in that desert which disesteem and lack of responsibility had made of the southerner's human relations.

I remember, as a child, the bitterness on faces of my father's and grandfather's friends and other men on Main Street in the little town where I was reared. Quick, hearty laughter and so few warm smiles. . . . I remember the easy tears in hard old eyes and unhappy lips and weathered faces, reddened by sun in the sensitive way of Scotch-Irish skins. I remember mouths moving restlessly, chewing tobacco, smoking a pipe, munching a straw, or cursing, or saying low words to other men as eyes lingered on hard young female buttocks sashaying down bright streets. There would be laughter, mirthless, oozing uncleanliness. And then the old men would turn, and seeing little school children watching them gravely, they would in the way of grown-ups give them a stick of candy from the store counter or hand them a nickel and tell them to buy themselves a cold drink or a package of chewing gum. . . .

Those faces on Main Street shaded by wide straw hats are surrounded in my child-memory by hardware and ploughs, seed bags and bales of cotton, the smell of guano and mule lots, hot sun on sidewalks and lovely white ladies with sweet childlike voices and smooth childlike faces, and old gardens of boxwood and camellias, and fields endlessly curving around my small world. I know now that the bitterness, the cruel sensual lips, the quick tears in hard eyes, the sashaying buttocks of brown girls, the thin childish voices of white women, had a great deal to do with high interest at the bank and low wages in the mills and gullied fields and lynchings and Ku Klux Klan and segregation and sacred womanhood and revivals, and Prohibition. And that no part of this memory can be understood without recalling all of it.

There were other faces, and I remember them also—in church, office, library, or school, or newspaper office. Tired faces, often, and of a slow charm, and gentle, with voice soft-spoken and of profound hesitation, or sometimes urbane and witty. These were the faces you saw of men who feared the "outbreak of violence," who wrote editorials suggesting things must change slowly, who read poetry or wrote it, who said, "You can't turn the South upside down overnight," who said, "Whatever is done for the Negro—and things should be done—must be done under the system of segregation we have lived under all of our lives." These faces belonged to men loyal to their "white mothers" and loyal in a secret, deep-rooted way, to their dark ones also; loyal above all else to the conscience their mothers gave them, men who clung to their white culture as a cripple clings to his crutches; whose passion and memories had been deeply repressed, and who had put up signs long ago in their unconscious and had forbidden themselves ever to trespass them.

Tired liberals. Remembering them now and my own generation's good will and blindness, I find myself wondering if Mammy in Dixie and Nanny in England have ever been given their due credit for the rise of Anglo-Saxon liberalism—not only in its tortured form but in its best manifestations of moderation and justice and mercy and value of human life.

There were those also, who could neither successfully repress their feelings nor give outlet to them; whose minds and hearts, whose hate and love were in never-ceasing combat that drained all strength away:

our small-town failures from the best families . . . and some of the most lovable and charming men on earth.

And there were the few who were different, who somehow found a center around which to build their lives and their region. These gave us our strength, held us back from too much self-pity, reached out for the new, made great errors and achieved real triumphs. There were not many, but our region cannot forget them for they were those who carried out their beliefs, limited as these beliefs were, and refused to bow down to confusion.

But even these men did not see what segregation had done to the South's women, pushed away on that lonely pedestal called Sacred Womanhood.

The Women

Of all the humiliating experiences which southern white women have endured, the least easy to accept, I think, was that of a mother who had no choice but to take the husk of a love which her son in his earliest years had given to another woman. She valiantly made jokes about it, telling her friends that her child preferred Mammy to her and that was fine, wasn't it, for it gave her so much more time to attend to all she had to do! "I don't know how I could have done without her," she would say and laugh a light tinkling laugh which sounded like little glass bells about to break into splinters. "Mammy was wonderful," she'd say. "I just don't see how we could do without the colored folks, do you?" she'd say. "I declare! But aren't the younger ones trifling—now look at that Emmy, doing nothing but rolling a dip stick around in her mouth and humming and with her shoes off again! But when I hear men say, 'Send 'em all back to Africa,' I say *they* don't have the housework to do, why we couldn't possibly . . . Oh, my!" sighing and laughing, and trying to forget things she could never forget.

This giving up of one's men and one's childhood to colored women—for the girl-child was shaped as subtly as little boys by the nurse-mother relationship—took on the unreal, shadowy quality of a dream; a recurring dream that southern white women could not rid themselves of. One's self . . . one's father . . . one's husband . . . one's son . . . Sometimes in the old days it made a pattern like that: a stark dance which all their life they tread the bleak measures of, with heart and body too rigid to make of space anything but a thin line to hold on the way to a death that would not come soon enough.

A secret wound that can never be shown is not tragedy for tragedy finds its stature on a stage where it can feel beyond it, its audience. To these women their life was only a shameful sore that could not be acknowledged because of its origin in sin.

Sometimes they could weep. A soundless weeping that trickled down into the crevices of personality leaving damp little places for thorns to grow, and sometimes for pale ghostly flowers that gave a fragrance of death to certain women. You remember these women from your childhood, and as you remember you keep thinking of lost graveyards under oak trees where moss swings in the still air as if to the heartbeat of the dead, and small carved lambs watch over baby mounds; you keep thinking of cape jasmine in your mother's back yard, and the way you felt in the night when you awoke after dreams and smelled the night-blooming cereus below the window....

It was as if these women never quite left the presence of the dead but mourned gently and continuously a loss they could not bear to know the extent of. Unable to look at the ugly facts of their life, they learned to see mysterious things the rest of us could not see. I remember how they "felt" premonitions, counting shadows and making of them cryptic answers. They "dreamed" that a beloved one would die and the beloved sometimes died! They "felt" there would be no returning when one left on a long journey and sometimes there was no return! They chanted so sweetly the death-knell of those they loved that I remember how carefully I avoided these friends of my mother's who dwelt serenely among disasters, for I feared that one day a gentle Cassandra might hold the syllables of my name on her tongue.

The little ghost women of small Southern towns ... swishing into church, sometimes singing in the choir, slipping like their own carefully made custards down the dark maw of life. Their number was few. One remembers them because they roam even now restlessly through time.

I think, however, that most women of my mother's age, though their characters were twisted and shaped by these troubles, retained a more earthy quality and a firm grasp indeed on things of this world. The pain they denied or tried to displace. Surely this emptiness was the natural way women should feel! Like childbirth pangs and menstrual cramps, the sexual erosion of their nature was "God's way" and hence if you were sensible must be accepted. But some stubbornly called it "female trouble" and went to doctors' offices as often as to church, to moan their misery.

A few "solved it all" by rejecting their womanly qualities. They seemed to envy men their freedom from pain and their access to pleasure. And sometimes they hated their own Maker too (a blasphemy they carefully hid from their minds) for giving females the long agony of parturition and none of the male's quick ecstasy of procreation. Yet there was usually a curious loyalty to their own father, though every other man was not "fit to be lived with." In later decades, when women were freer, these protesters turned toward the cities, gathering together, a grim little number, cropping their hair short, walking in heavy awkward strides, and acquiring, as do subjugated people everywhere when protesting their chains, the more unpleasant qualities of this enemy who had segregated them from their birthright. Not daring in the secret places of their minds to confess what they really wanted, they demanded to be treated "exactly like men." They were of course a part of the psychosexual, economic, political protest of women arising throughout Western culture, a kind of fibroid growth of sick cells multiplying aggressiveness in an attempt at cure. But there was no comfortable place for such women in the South, though a few lived in every town.

The majority of southern women convinced themselves that God had ordained that they be deprived of pleasure, and meekly stuffed their hollowness with piety, trying to believe the tightness they felt was hunger satisfied. Culturally stunted by a region that still pays nice rewards to simple-mindedness in females, they had no defense against blandishment. They listened to the round words of men's tribute to Sacred Womanhood and believed, thinking no doubt that if they were not sacred then what under God's heaven *was* the matter with them! Once hoisted up by the old colonels' oratory, they stayed on lonely pedestals and rigidly played "statue" while their men went about more important affairs elsewhere.

These women turned away from the ugliness which they felt powerless to cope with and made for themselves and their families what they called a "normal" life. Their homes, often simple, were gracious and good to live in. The South—if one can forget the shabby milltowns, the rickety Colored Towns, the surrealist city tenements—is full of such homes. Places you remember—if you live on that side of town—of quiet ease and comfort and taste. In these homes, food and flowers were cherished, and old furniture, and the family's past (screened of all but the pleasing and the trivial). Sex was pushed out through the back door as a shameful thing never to be mentioned. Segregation was pushed out of sight also, and this was managed so successfully that until the last twenty years, most white southerners cheerfully said there was no race problem for it had been "solved." Out through the back door went the unpleasant and unmentionable; in through the back door came trays laden with food as delicious as can be found in the world. Though asceticism controlled the regions left out of the physiology books, and Prohibition succeeded sometimes in banishing the bottle, the groaning table was left free.

Whatever the hurt in our lives, there are these memories of food, and flowers, and of southern gardens, filled with our mothers' fantasies that had no other way to creep into life. Ladies and their garden clubs have been made by cartoonists into a national laugh, and sometimes a funny one, but some of us can smile for only a moment. We are always remembering a face we love and the longing in it as plants were set in damp ground and shaded against the sun. . . . A figure stooping, familiar hands feeling around in warm soft dirt to slip a weed out, planting and transplanting little secret dreams, making them live in an azalea, a rose, a camellia, when they could not live in their own arid lives. . . . A voice grown plaintive over a peaked little plant that refused to bloom . . . so softly scolding the flowers for not living their life to its full. In the mornings these old gardens full of lively bugs, and toads hopping among the violets, and new blow-y spider webs that never break in the memory, were like a clear mind filled with bright dewy ideas. But at night in the moonlight, a woman walking alone, up and down prim rows of camellias or in summer among the lilies, even now can make one want to close the gates against the past forever—so hurting is the realization of an emptiness that need not have been.

With their gardens and their homes, these women tried to shut out evil, and sometimes succeeded in sheltering their children from it. If you could only keep from them the things of our South that must never be mentioned, all would be well! Innocence, virtue, ignorance, silence were synonyms twining around young lives like smilax. It was not evil but the knowledge of it that injured, these mothers believed. What you don't hear or read or see surely can never be known to you. And because they did not believe things *could* change or that they should (though they could not have told you why) they had to shut their minds against knowledge of evil also. They could not let their imaginations feel the sorrow of a colored mother whose child is shamed from birth, nor once look deep into poverty, nor once touch the agony of a back-door life lived forever and ever, nor once realize what they themselves had been deprived of. They could not have borne it. And because they could not let themselves know, they were terrified at a word, a suggestion, anything that caused them to feel deeply. It was as if one question asked aloud might, like a bulldozer, uproot their garden of fantasies and tear it in a few moments out of time, leaving only naked bleeding reality to live with.

There were others whose minds perhaps were not brighter, but whose natures could not accept life so meekly. They felt compelled to question and to answer their own questions. They would not have used the word "sex" aloud, but their questions and answers told them that all a woman can expect from lingering on exalted heights is a hard chill afterward; that indeed, white women had not profited in the least from the psychosexual profit system which segregation in the South supported so lavishly; and that furthermore, no bargain had been made with them in any of these transactions. They learned that *discrimination* was a word with secret meanings and they did not like its secrets. This much of semantics they understood as clearly as their recipe for beaten biscuits. In the white southern woman's dictionary, *discrimination* could be defined as a painful way of life which too often left an empty place in her bed and an ache in the heart. Whether or not these women had themselves experienced this pain—and we must remember that many had not—they knew segregation in the South had cleaved through white woman's tenderest dreams. They had seen it turn a life drama of child, wife, mother into tragedy, or more often into plain vulgar melodrama. How could they sit in the audience and applaud their own humiliation?

So, they climbed down from the pedestal when no one was looking and explored a bit. Not as you might think, perhaps. They were conventional, highly "moral" women, who would not have dreamed of breaking the letter of their marriage vows, or, when not married, their technical chastity. But their minds went a-roaming and their sympathies attached themselves like hungry little fibers to all kinds of people and causes while their shrewd common sense kicked old lies around until they were popping like firecrackers.

These ladies went forth to commit treason against a southern tradition set up by men who had betrayed their mothers, sometimes themselves, and many of the South's children white and mixed, for three long centuries. It was truly a subversive affair, but as decorously conducted as an afternoon walk taken by the students of a Female Institute. It started stealthily, in my mother's day. Shyly, these first women sneaked down from their chilly places, did their little sabotage and sneaked up again, wrapping innocence around them like a lace shawl. They set secret time bombs and went back to their needlework, serenely awaiting the blast. They had no lady Lincoln to proclaim their emancipation from southern tradition but they scarcely needed one.

The thing was a spontaneous reaction. Mother in her old age told daughter strange truths that had gnawed on her lonely heart too long. And daughter told other women. Colored and white women stirring up a lemon-cheese cake for the hungry males in the household looked deep into each other's eyes and understood their common past. A mistress, reading the Bible to her colored maid polishing silver, would lay aside Holy Writ and talk of things less holy but of immense importance to both of them.

Insurrection was on. White men were unaware of it, but the old pedestal on which their women had been safely stowed away, was reeling and rocking. With an emotionally induced stupidity really beneath them, these men went on with their race-economic exploitation, protecting themselves behind rusty shields of as phony a moral cause as the Anglo-American world has ever witnessed. In the name of *sacred womanhood, of purity, of preserving the home,* lecherous old men and young ones, reeking with impurities, who had violated the home since they were sixteen years old, whipped up lynchings, organized Klans, burned crosses, aroused the poor and ignorant to wild excitement by an obscene, perverse imagery describing the "menace" of Negro men hiding behind every cypress waiting to rape "our" women. In the name of such holiness, they did these things to keep the affairs of their own heart and conscience and home, as well as the community, "under control." And not once did they dream their women did not believe their lies.

And then it happened. The lady insurrectionists gathered together in one of our southern cities. They primly called themselves church women but churches were forgotten by everybody when they spoke their revolutionary words. They said calmly that they were not afraid of being raped; as for their sacredness, they could take care of it themselves; they did not need the chivalry of a lynching to protect them and did not want it. Not only that, they continued, but they would personally do everything in their power to keep any Negro from being lynched and furthermore, they squeaked bravely, they had plenty of power.

They had more than they knew. They had the power of spiritual blackmail over a large part of the white South. All they had to do was drop their little bucket into any one of numerous wells of guilt dotting the landscape and splash it around a bit. No one, of thousands of white men, had any notion how much or how little each woman knew about his private goings-on. Some who had never been guilty in act began to equate adolescent fantasies with reality, and there was confusion everywhere.

This was in 1930. These women organized an Association of Southern Women for the Prevention of Lynching. Their husbands, sons, brothers, and uncles often worked by their side; many of them with sincere concern for the state of affairs, others because they had to.

Though it may seem incredible to all but southerners, the custom of lynching had so rarely been questioned that these church women's action gave a genuine shock. For this was a new thing in Dixie. The ladies' valor is not diminished, I think, by reminding ourselves that the movement could not have crystallized so early had not Dr. Will Alexander, and a handful of men and women whom he gathered around him, pushed things off to a good start in 1918 with the first interracial committee in the South. There were other yeasty forces at work: A world war had squeezed and pulled the earth's people apart and squeezed them together again;

the Negroes themselves, led by courageous men like Walter White of Atlanta and W. E. B. Du Bois and their northern white friends were making our nation aware that Negroes have rights; the group around Dr. Howard Odum—whose first study of the Negro in 1910 greatly influenced social science's interest in Negro-patterns of life—were gathering all kinds of facts concerning a region that had been for so long content with its fantasies and fears. The women's role was to bake the first pan of bread made from this rising batter, and to serve it hot as is southern custom.

After this magnificent uprising against the sleazy thing called "chivalry," these women worked like the neat, industrious housewives they really were, using their mops and brooms to clean up a dirty spot here and there but with no real attempt to change this way of life which they dimly realized had injured themselves and their children as much as it had injured Negroes, but which they nevertheless clung to.

Of course the demagogues would have loved to call them "Communists" or "bolsheviks," but how could they? The women were too prim and neat and sweet and ladylike and churchly in their activities, and too many of them were the wives of the most powerful men in town. Indeed, the ladies themselves hated the word "radical" and were quick to turn against anyone who dared go further than they in this housecleaning of Dixie. Few of them had disciplined intellects or giant imaginations and probably no one of them grasped the full implications of this sex-race-religion-economics tangle, but they had warm hearts and powerful energy and a nice technic for bargaining, and many an old cagey politician, and a young one or two, have been outwitted by their soft bending words.

They followed a sound feminine intuition, working as "church women," leaning on the strength of Christ's teachings for support when they needed it. They worked with great bravery but so unobtrusively that even today many southerners know little about them. But they aroused the conscience of the South and the whole country about lynching; they tore a big piece of this evil out of southern tradition, leaving a hole which no sane man in Dixie now dares stuff up with public defenses. They attacked the KKK when few except Julian Harris of the Columbus (Georgia) *Enquirer*, among white southern newspaper men, had criticized this group from whom Hitler surely learned so much. And they have continued this fight (known to demagogues as "northern meddling"), joining their energies with other church women throughout the nation.

But they were not yet done. They had a few more spots to rub out. One had to do with their own souls. They believed that the Lord's Supper is a holy sacrament which Christians cannot take without sacrilege unless they will also break bread with fellow men of other color. Believing, they put on their best bib and tucker and gathered in small groups to eat with colored women, deliberately breaking a taboo that had collected many deep fears around it.

It is difficult for those not reared as white southerners to remember how this eating taboo in childhood is woven into the mesh of things that are "wrong," how it becomes tangled with God and sex, pulling anxieties from stronger prohibitions and attaching them to itself. But we who live here can never forget. One of these church women told me of her experience when she first ate with colored friends. Though her conscience was serene, and her enjoyment of this association was real, yet she was seized by an acute nausea which disappeared only when the meal was finished. She was too honest to attribute it to anything other than deep-rooted anxiety welling up from the "bottom of her personality," as she expressed it, creeping back from her childhood training. Others have told me similar experiences: of feeling "pangs of conscience," as one put it, "though my conscience was clearly approving"; or suddenly in the night awaking, overwhelmed by "serious doubts of the wisdom of what we are doing."

The white women were not alone in these irrational reactions. Colored women also found it hard, but for different reasons. Sometimes their pride was deeply hurt that white women felt so virtuous when eating with them. They were too sensitive not to be aware of the psychic price the white women paid for this forbidden act, and yet too ignorant of the training given white children to understand why there had to be a price. And sometimes the colored women were themselves almost overcome by a break-through not of guilt but of their old repressed hatred of white people. One of the most charming, sensitive, intelligent Negro women I know, tells me that even now when she is long with white people she grows physically ill and has immense difficulty coming to terms with the resentments of her childhood.

To break bread together as Christians, each group had to force its way through thick psychological barriers, and each did it with little understanding of their own or the other group's feelings. When the seizures came, most of the church women, white and Negro, suppressed them firmly by laying the ponderous weight of the New Testament on their fears and hurts, declaring bravely that "Jesus would have done likewise."

In more recent years this group, united with the church women in all parts of the nation and from most of our denominations, has taken a stand against segregation in the church. The same group in Atlanta whose nucleus was for years under Dorothy Tilly's fine leadership—and supported by the Southern Regional Council—has made during the past year a brave stand against segregation in our higher schools of learning and in interstate travel. They are daring more these days, doing fewer paint jobs and more carpentry on the old Southern Mansion, adding rooms in it for the rest of the family. And because they are, they are not receiving the indulgence of newspapers and politicians they once had. Perhaps the old power of spiritual blackmail has waned. Perhaps also, these women are developing new powers, new technics, and are beginning to be feared in new ways. However much or little they have accomplished (and sometimes it seems a small thing set against the size and urgency of the job), these church women found for themselves a sublimation of the deprivations that their culture had exacted of their sex and used their freed energy and love to spread a green-growing cover crop on the South's worn-out spiritual soil. In that lovely and rare way of human nature, they pushed aside their own trouble and somehow grew strong enough to reach out with compassion toward those more miserable. It seemed almost as if they lifted their natures by their own leverage though they would say that it was their faith in the teachings of Jesus that lifted them.

It would be pleasant to stop the story of the women here, but there is a more tragic page.

Like their men, many of them found it easier to cultivate hate than love in their natures. Their own dreams destroyed, they destroyed in cruelty their children's dreams and their men's aspirations.

It was a compulsive thing they did, with no awareness of the unconscious hate compelling them to do it. Most of them felt they were doing "right." Most of them thought it was their duty to watch over the morals of their children and husbands. They did not see themselves in the ungracious role of exacting of their family the same obedience to the same Authority that had exacted so much of them. They thought they loved their husbands and children so much that they wanted them to do "right." They would have been horrified had they been accused of setting up their home as a juvenile court and themselves as the judge, though that is what they too often did.

They would have been more deeply shocked had they been accused of hate. They felt nothing but love for their families and sometimes a bit of vexation and disappointment. They nursed them tenderly through illness, planned delicious meals for them, kept the home physically pleasant, were ambitious and proud of their achievements, and felt that they were utterly devoted wives and mothers. They "sacrificed" all their lives long but they never looked clearly at what they were sacrificing.

The little thorns growing deep in secret wounds thrust up sharp points into their conscience, making it a prickly thing, but they covered it with the soft folds of affectionate concern and hid from themselves the thorn tips. When they turned this conscience against their children, or the men in their family, they thought they were doing God's will. And, as is the way of humans, in the name of "what is right" they committed as great evil at home as did their men in the name of Sacred Womanhood over in Colored Town or at the state capitals.

Many a man went into politics, or joined the KKK, had a nervous breakdown or forged checks, got drunk or built up a great industry, because he could no longer bear the police-state set up in his own home. But this would have been a hard thing for these good mothers and wives to believe, and for the men also.

As time passed, mothers went more and more compulsively about the training of their children as if it were a totalitarian discipline: imposing rigidities on spirit and mind, imposing eating schedules as if eating were a duty, elimination schedules as if elimination were a responsibility one owed to one's state, hurrying weaning as if suckling were an immoral habit which babies must give up as soon as possible, binding the curiosity of childhood as the Chinese once bound their little girls' feet.

More and more rigid became this training and more steel-like and impersonal. It was all a desperate business. If they had been asked what they feared, or to list the evils their children might "find out," they would have been deeply bewildered. They sometimes had tears but no words for their anxiety. They only knew they must keep their children pure and innocent, they must "make" them good. They felt that inside each little body, inside each mind, there was a powerful force, a kind of atomic energy; if let out, it might blast their children's "morals" to pieces. They were compelled, therefore, to spend their time walling up this danger. With a rigid training they armored their children against their fantasies and sex feelings, preparing them for human relations as if for a cruel medieval battle. Thus they segregated sex from love and tenderness and obligation, and did not see how inevitably it would slip into secret back-door union with hate and guilt.

This training, until recent decades, was often complicated by the child's dual Mother-Mammy relationship. For sometimes Mother would give orders which Mammy, more wise in the ways of childhood, would not carry out. Many a child of my generation was split as deeply in his moral nature, as in his first human relationships by a white mother's code that colored nurse intuitively knew was too rigid and unreal for the warm, pliant human spirit to adhere to. Though in many ways it was a thing to be grateful for, sometimes instinctual needs of the body were satisfied at so exorbitant a price exacted by conscience that the personality could not pay it.

We cannot forget that their culture had stripped these women of profound biological rights, had ripped off their inherent dignity and made them silly statues and psychic children, stunting their capacity for rich understanding and enjoyment of husbands and family. It is not strange that they became vigilant guardians of a southern tradition which in guarding they often, unbeknownst to their own minds, avenged themselves on with a Medea-like hatred.

In many there was a profound subservience; they dared not question what had injured them so much. It was all wrapped up in one package: sex taboos, race segregation, "the right to make money the way Father made money," the duty to go to church, the fear of new knowledge that would shake old beliefs, the splitting of ideals from actions—and you accepted it all uncritically as the Communists accept their Stalin-stamped lives. You insisted on others accepting it also. You dreaded a deviationist, you were in terror lest your children be other than orthodox southerners. You used your conscience as if it were a hypodermic needle, plunging it into the tenderest spots of young spirits, filling them with your guilt, hoping to inoculate them "for their own good" against vague, dread "evils."

But it was a tainted needle that spread through these children a poison that came out in unhealing sores.

It would be as unfair to blame the mothers of two or three generations for a way of life that began destroying its children long before they were born, as it would be to blame the men. Both men and women were born into it and of it. And because it is a culture that lacks almost completely the self-changing power that comes from honest criticism, because in the past it forced out its children who saw dangers and tried to avert them, who had insight and talents that could have contributed so richly to the South's recovery; because it bruised those who grimly stayed, unwelcomed, until their energies were depleted (we have only to recall Howard Odum's stormy years, and Arthur Raper, H. C. Nixon, William Kilpatrick, and numerous poets, teachers, authors, who were forced into exile or stayed at home under bitter attack)—because it did these things to its own men, it is not difficult to understand why these women, our mothers and perhaps ourselves, could not do other than bend to the system and think it "right" to bend to it. They did not have enough insight—where could they have got it?—to grow wary of a conscience that drives ruthlessly across natural, spontaneous needs. They did not dream the energy driving this conscience might be hate, not love. They could not have accepted the terrifying fact that their own banned desires had slipped into their conscience giving it its cruel power. They had not questioned life closely enough—for life gave harsh answers to questions—to discover that guilt and ideals are as different sometimes as the insane and the sane.

We cannot censure—who would dare!—but we know now that these women, forced by their culture and their heartbreak, did a thorough job of closing the path to mature genitality for many of their sons and daughters, and an equally good job of leaving little cleared detours that led downhill to homosexual and infantile green pastures, and on to alcoholism, neuroses, divorce, to race-hate and brutality, and to a tight inflexible mind that could not question itself.

They did a thorough job of dishonoring curiosity, of making honesty seem a treasonable thing, of leaving in their children an unquenchable need to feel superior to others, to bow easily to authority, and to value power and money more dearly than human relations and truth.

They did a thorough job of splitting the soul in two. They separated ideals from acts, beliefs from knowledge, and turned their children sometimes into exploiters but more often into moral weaklings who daydream about democracy and human dignity and freedom and integrity, yet cannot find the real desire to bring these dreams into reality; always they keep dreaming and hoping, and fearing, that the next generation will do it.

Sometimes we blame Mom too much for all that is wrong with her sons and daughters. After all, we might well ask, who started the grim mess? Who long ago made Mom and her sex "inferior" and stripped her of her economic and political and sexual rights? Who, nearly two thousand years ago, said, "It is good for a man not to touch a woman. . . . But if they cannot contain, let them marry: for it is better to marry than to burn"? Certainly that old misogynist St. Paul was no female apostle. Man, born of woman, has found it a hard thing to forgive her for giving him birth. The patriarchal protest against the ancient matriarch has borne strange fruit through the years. . . .

In speaking of millions of people and their customs, their feelings and values it is well to remember that many have not shared in experiences that have yet profoundly affected their whole lives. They have, instead, made identification with them. Experiences which others have had link themselves sometimes with our secret fantasies and needs until a curious bond is woven of the actual experiences of the few and the unconscious desire of the many to possess them. A generation, free of wounds, will identify itself with the battle scars of a past generation in a masochistic community of daydreams because it needs to feel pain. Hanns Sachs has reminded us in *The Creative Unconscious* of man's capacity to daydream in collaboration with others when each has within him a secret fantasy that can be acted out in rhythm with others. Here in the artist is the seed of a dream growing into a book, a painting, a poem, which awakens deep down in the one beholding it another shadowy dream that, like a reflection in a pool, takes on mysterious shape and substance; and suddenly there is a profound communion of dream with dream, not on the bright surface of life but in the secret shadowy places of the spirit. It may be for only a moment in time, or for all of a life, but two fantasies have met, magically bridging time and space, and whispered their secrets to each other. This is art's power over us; and art's terror, for there are dreams we do not want aroused, ash that must remain ash. And sometimes in blinding anger and fear we turn and rend a poem, a book, a painting, a truth that has blown too steadily on forgotten graves of memories calling forth ghosts whom we have forbidden to walk the earth again. This is the secret of art. And of a people's myth also. This is the secret of tradition's hypnotic power over the minds of a whole region though most of those minds may know tradition only by hearsay.

Southern tradition, segregation, states' rights have soaked up the fears of our people; little private fantasies of childhood have crept there for hiding, unacknowledged arsenals of hate have been stored there, and a loyalty covering up a lack of mature love has glazed the words over with sanctity. No wonder the saying of them aloud can stir anxieties until there are times when it seems we have lost our grasp of reality.

From *The Journey*

While Smith returned to the "Julia" manuscript for a few months in 1951, according to her autobiographical notes she also studied contemporary art and "the effect of World War II and the atomic bomb on the creative mind" and "the anxiety-inducing effect of the body image," especially the latest developments in the field of physical rehabilitation. She visited rehabilitation centers and interviewed blind, deaf, paraplegic, and amputee patients and their doctors. Out of this interest Lillian Smith and Paula Snelling began their last joint writing project: an anthology on disabilities. The proposed book, as outlined in correspondence with Earl Miers of World Publishing Company, included autobiographical experiences of a number of disabled people, a bibliography of resources, and a list of relevant state and federal laws. Although the anthology was not completed, much of Smith's thinking on the subject informs *The Journey*, begun in 1951 and completed in fall 1953 after Smith discovered she had cancer and subsequently underwent a radical mastectomy (*HH* 115–16).

The Journey may be seen at least in part as Smith's response to the growing conservatism, resistance to reform, and tradition-bound defensiveness pervading American society. Smith's correspondence with friends reveals her personal perspective as she wrote the book. Responding to a letter from Lewis Gannett, December 10, 1953, Smith wrote:

> [W]hile I still feel that I am living on borrowed time, as the months pass the surgeon becomes surer and surer that he has outwitted the malignancy, at least for a while, anyway. It is odd to be "handicapped" and have to learn to use my arm with two thirds of my shoulder muscles removed. But it has been fun to see what I can do; how fast I can find new muscles to take over old work.
>
> I was writing this book at the time it was discovered. The one that will be out in the spring, called *The Journey*. I had been working on my

novel, the one I have been on for many years when suddenly, two years ago, I laid it aside and decided I had to find out what life is about; what it is about for me, anyway. I knew what I did not believe; I thought I even knew what was "wrong with things" but I did not know what I believed nor did I know what is "right with things." So I journeyed forth to find out. This book is what I found. I was deep in it, when I began to realize that I was not well. I called it fatigue as long as I could, then went to a surgeon and was told that I had a malignancy of the breast which had gone too too long; only a radical operation could save me. I protested, wanting so much to finish my book and fearing the operation might be more than my old organism could take. As I went under anesthesia I can hear that surgeon saying: "Remember, it is going to be wonderful for the book. You will understand now what ordeal is really about." And that is all I remembered until I awoke, very much alive and part of the world.

Aren't these things strange? Cancer is the only big fear I had ever had. Always I had felt I could take anything but that. And that is what I had to take. But more strange is the strength that comes from somewhere, deep down in the soma, maybe; deep down in family tradition, maybe. I remembered suddenly, Mother; remembered suddenly Dad; both of whom when faced with tragic events had always been so quietly assured and full of faith. I did not have their kind of faith. I had to make do with what we'd call "fortitude" I guess. But it helped, the remembering of them. And I began to see a bit more clearly what death is about; just a little; I am not inclined to be mystical and I have to talk and think in human words since I know no other. But some of it came a bit more clear, anyway, during those hard lonely months, the nights . . . such plain homespun experiences these matters are, this thing, death; this thing, maiming; this thing, constant danger; but we avoid and avoid and avoid, and then suddenly here it is: "Your turn now" it says. And you have to find something, then; something to take you through it without losing your nerve and your love of life and all the rest of it. (*HH* 138–39)

In a similar vein, on February 24, 1954, Smith wrote Dr. Horace Kallen:

I think perhaps I could not have written what I said about death had I not been so close to it, one day; and were it not, that it slips in and out of my consciousness every day for a few minutes . . . We may become quite good friends, death and I, before it is all over. But the book, somehow, had to be written. I had to find out what I believe, what is meaningful in human experience for me; what is the creative meaning of ordeal. [. . .] When I want to find out something: I write a book. It is my way of searching. Not to give the world "answers" but to find them for myself. So a book, for me, is a growing season. (*HH* 144)

In writing *The Journey* Smith becomes the active collaborator in other people's stories of failure and triumph and of individuals breaking silence around taboo subjects and creating ways to relate to others' differences. Through *The Journey* Smith recovers a history of humans practicing resilience, and in the process, creates her own response to the existential questions she has been asking since childhood.

Smith's personal philosophical search for meaning is never separate from her work for social justice. Even as she continually refuses to separate the seemingly conflicting roles of artist and activist, much of what Smith discovers in *The Journey* informs her creative responses to the emerging civil rights movement in the South and all of her subsequently published work. Indeed *The Journey* contains the germinal ideas Smith continues to develop and explore in *One Hour*, the revised *Killers of the Dream*, *Memory of a Large Christmas*, *Now Is the Time*, and *Our Faces, Our Words*.

Smith's recorded reading from *The Journey* provides the best introduction for the following selected passages. See www.piedmont.edu/lilliansmith-resources.

Prologue

There is no going alone on a journey. Whether one explores strange lands or Main Street or one's own back yard, always invisible traveling companions are close by: the giants and pygmies of memory, of belief, pulling you this way and that, not letting you see the world life-size but insisting that you measure it by their own height and weight.

But you forget this. You start out feeling free. Your bags and your brain are packed full of supplies and facts for your trip, all the things you think you need. And then you get on your ship or plane or whatever, set for places you have not seen, friends you have not met—and suddenly something is there beside you, whispering, Better not look at that, better not listen; come, I know a place . . . a person. . . .

What a talent these companions have for luring us into dead ends! And yet, I could not have done without them. For though there were a few memories, an old worn-out belief or two that almost stopped me before my trip had begun, there were others that opened doors wide. And it was by their help that I found, at last, what I had gone in search of.

I went on this journey to find an image of the human being that I could feel proud of. I wanted to reassure myself of mortal strength, of man's power not only to survive on this earth but to continue growing in stature. I wanted the faith to believe that we can fulfill our role in this evolving universe of which we have been given such awesome glimpses.

We human beings. . . . What haunting words! A tune one knows and can never quite begin and never quite finish. Did they hold a real meaning for me? I was not sure.

The trouble was, I could not match the words with a clear image. Too often I could not see the human being at all, so hidden is he behind masks of political differences, of color, and spurious normalities. Long ago, I had torn those masks—they were cheap in my sight—but the person behind the mask? Had I caught more than a glimpse now and then?

It has not been easy for any of us, lately, to keep the image of man bright. Even in our own minds it has been trampled down, flattened by totalitarian beliefs that we are not aware we hold, torn by the Censors who fatten on our fears; made conforming, "normal," animal-like, machinelike, absolute.

Five words that have no place in human values. For men tied fast to the absolute, bled of their differences, drained of their dreams by authoritarian leeches until nothing but pulp is left, become a massive, sick Thing whose sheer weight is used ruthlessly by ambitious men. Here is the real enemy of the people: our own selves dehumanized into "the masses." And where is the David who can slay this giant?

I had been asking this for a long time, as have many others. One day, I realized that each of us has to find this David within himself. It is a job, like breathing, that no one else can do for us. And yet, I know too that as each discovers afresh the person within him—as sculptors and painters, dancers and writers, the poets and the prophets and the scientists put down in their unique ways what they find, the search grows easier for everyone. It is the individual's task, yes; but it is also this generation's historic mission to find and set up in a high place the human being revealed in his manifold differences and infinite possibilities, for all to see, to be exalted by, and to identify with.

And so, I went on a journey to answer for myself a few questions: What are our most human qualities? What sets us apart from animal and machine? from the masses and the monster? How can we believe in our infinite possibilities when our limitations are so conspicuous? And hope? What is this stubborn thing in man that keeps him forever picking the lock of time? that drives him to measure his puny size against the unknown—and win? The odds are against him, the odds have always been against him, and he knows it but he has never believed it. And because of his refusal to believe it, because of his crazy unconquerable hope, he alone of living creatures has learned to outwit fate and to enjoy the job so much that even on holidays from stern necessity he keeps challenging his antagonist. It is a strange talent, and strictly human.

I wanted to learn more about this mighty resource. And there were other words, old, encrusted with clichés: faith, and freedom, and risk, and that poor battered word "equality," and love, and life, and death. I needed to know what meaning they held for me.

What I sought, of course, was something to believe in; something that intelligence and heart can accept, something that can fuse past and future, and art and science, and God and one's self into a purposeful whole.

A few of my questions were never answered; others changed into new questions, for I changed as I went along. Slowly I began to understand what, perhaps, I had known a long time without understanding: That man's unique qualities and destiny begin in the unchangeable fact of his brokenness. He can never be whole though his integrity has come out of his reaching for wholeness. He is forever laying a plank across the chasm, relating himself to time, to people, to knowledge, to God, narrowing the gap between dream and reality, creating more and more ties—And yet, he still feels alone. On the milk of his loneliness is nourished everything he loves and delights in, even his future, but the ache remains.

The story I have written down here is concerned with not only what I learned but how I learned it.

I knew that what I sought was too humble, too proud and enduring and fragile to be found among generalities and abstractions. But I did not know where to look for it. I began my search by reading: poetry, philosophy, novels, scientific journals. I studied photographs of dancers, of faces, hands, for the spirit of man cannot be torn from the image he holds of his body. I went to museums, looked at sculpture, paintings, drawings. I talked with surgeons who know so intimately the brokenness of the body and the courage that binds a life together again. I read memoirs and letters. I was groping; feeling around; looking for maps that might take me where I wanted to go.

During that winter, I watched a young man whose body was paralyzed learn to move again. I had never before seen the creative spirit spelling itself out so plainly. Then it was that I learned, with a paraplegic, the passionate meaning of movement. I watched him the day they tied him to a board as if he were a mummy and stood him on end, on nerveless feet that were as full of emptiness as a wraith. He blacked out. But the next day, he stayed in this world and participated in his bright triumph. He was a man, standing up. Bound to a board but *here*. And slowly, I saw the change come. He learned to sit; to get in a wheel chair and slide out again. Inch by inch he was regaining his universe. Then came the morning when he stood on his feet, alone, clinging to the bars, but he stood.

I went away for a few months. When I came back, he was walking slowly down the parallel bars; sliding himself from end to end of that strict little path. Then, almost suddenly it seemed to me, he was on crutches, standing; not walking but standing as he learned to swing his crutches above his head, in front, behind, above his head: getting what they call "crutch balance." One day, he walked. I stood there watching him with the same deep feeling of miracle that I have each time I see Martha Graham dance. It was so beautiful a movement, rigorously disciplined, God knows, bound by an iron reality; but within the limits set by dead nerves he moved with grace, and with what I think of as an immense inner freedom.

As I watched this man I thought, Martha Graham could understand this triumph. For she, at the other end of the arc of human movement, has the same mastery of body and spirit that he now has. A paraplegic and a great dancer . . . each pushing back the frontiers of the body, and the mind, each with a free and bold imagination clearing the way for the human spirit to move to levels not yet attained.

Sometimes as I have sat in the audience watching Martha Graham dance, it has seemed to me as if she were unwrapping our body image which has been tied up so long with the barbed wires of fear and guilt and ignorance, and offering it back to us: a thing of honor. Freeing, at last, our concept of Self. Saying to us, The body is not a thing of danger, it is a fine instrument that can express not only today's feeling and act, but subtle, archaic experiences, memories which words are too young in human affairs to know the meaning of.

I went home, to the mountains. If I could understand not how nations meet ordeals, not how Man meets his, but how one man, one woman, one little boy, one girl met theirs, what defenses they drew upon for their hard moments, if I could see the human being in them, working, creating, surely I would find what I journeyed in search of, for only in ordeal is a man revealed at his most creative. Then it is that the hidden forces of a life show themselves working on the side of human growth or on the side of death.

I came upon bits of what I sought in the most unexpected places: there was an afternoon on 51st Street, at Toots Shor's; and another in an old lost graveyard on the coast of Georgia. And in a café, one night, a paratrooper who had come home from a prison camp in Germany helped me understand the largeness of life and the smallness of death. And there was Carl. And much of what I found came from my own memories, for I soon realized that no journey carries one far unless, as it extends into the world around us, it goes an equal distance into the world within.

And now, I sit here turning the pages of the manuscript. The book is almost completed.

As I read what I have set down, I see how personal a book it is. It is not my life's story, of course. It is only a handful of memories, a few experiences, mine and those of people I have known. I have used them as a sculptor uses dabs of clay, pressing them on, one by one, until finally an image is made of what a human being looks like to me. As I write, I am thinking of a morning when I was in the clay room at my camp watching the children work. There they were: each with a lump of clay, smoothing, pulling and turning, picking a little off, pressing a smidge on, until it changed slowly into an image of something they dimly saw and felt. So gravely they worked. One little girl said, "I am making something nobody in the world has ever seen." And when it was done, it was her own small face. She was right. No one had seen it before for it was herself as she felt herself, with her secrets spelled and misspelled in the clay.

And that is, of course, all I have done. I have put down here an image of the human being made from my own experience of life. Its meaning is the meaning these memories hold for me.

Chapter 3

It was Sunday afternoon. I was driving along the coastal roads of South Carolina and Georgia, trying to recover the feel of the country where my family once lived.

I had left the highway and was on the back roads. Roads that I did not know. I would see one and take it, hardly more than a sandy streak through the pines, and let it lead me back into the past if it could.

All day I had been going along slowly, fusing with the sun and swamp, the ragged swinging shadows, the ugliness, beauty, the old beat of things. A palmetto moving in the wind, the dry swish of it in the dark . . . the smell of a turpentine still . . . a wet patch near a ditch yellowed with pitcher plants . . . and suddenly one sees everything again, all of one's childhood, everything but one's self—*that* little ghost has just gone into the sand, the shadow, the bay tree.

Again and again I had come across lost avenues of twisted cedars through which the eyes travel so easily to a house that is rarely there. Sometimes the chimneys remain; now and then a garden of boxwood and briars; once through a formal avenue of century-old trees I saw a bright-painted roadhouse spraddled out like a prosperous whore sunning. And down the road, an hour beyond, there stood a gray two-story house whose Victorian gingerbread verandas were so like those I had run over a thousand times as a child that I felt as if I had stumbled across my home town.

The colored folks from the farms were going to church, walking down the hot sand road, most of them, in dresses bright as stick candy (the women and girls), in shoes not worn all week and white hats (the men and boys); a few riding up quick in a ramshackle car, shouting quick, slamming on brakes quick, then slowly opening the car door, and getting out slow and saying howdy, soft and slow, in sudden shyness.

They would stand around in front of the church set back in the shade of pine or oak, maybe in broiling sun—not anxious to go in yet, liking it there. Talking. Women shrill, men deep-voiced. Bright sounds, too far away to form words for my ears. Then they would laugh. Not only with mouth but with muscles and tendons and nerves and glands and bones and skin and memory until the whole body was rippling and washing and changing its shape into a new thing, fresh and new, cleaned of tensions, freed of resentment. Laughter that struck down the Whiteness, struck down poverty, struck down sweat and shame, laid it flat on the earth, made it nothing, made them big big big. It had been a long time since I heard anyone laugh like that and I was caught up in my past—so unchanged was this moment from all I had known long ago. Here on the coast, tucked in by creeks and marshes, moving slow as the tide were people floating in a back eddy of time. They knew so little of what has tightened the hearts and minds of the rest of the world; and yet I had the feeling that maybe they knew more, deep down in them, where knowledge is a real thing.

After a time they would go in, I thought; they would take off their white hats and tiptoe in and sit there waiting on the rough benches, and somebody would go to the little reed organ if they were fancy enough to have one, the preacher would step up front and open his Bible. . . .

And after a time, they did. Then I drove up closer, sucked into the emptiness, and listened to the singing. They had left laughter outside and hate and shame with their whisky bottles and their six-day life and were singing to God of something that He and they understood. It came out of them as if from a bottomless pit. It flowed and settled in a pool of stillness, it burst out like the thunder of water rolling over a precipice, and as suddenly was no more than a whisper. The men stopped singing. A woman was telling God now. I could see her through the window. Outside, before the service, she had stood apart from the others—a tall thin heavy-boned woman, the color of pitch pine, with big restless hands that looked like they had wrung out a thousand washes. She had on a pink straw hat, pinned back from her face, and her nose was high and thin, and she had that stern proud look I had seen on streets in Egypt and India. Now she was singing. She sang her feelings clean across to heaven, she sang her hope and her hurt and my hope and hurt, and yours, she made God bend down and listen to something that no one has ever put into words, for only in those fabulous sounds we call singing, that flow from a deeper level than words, can it be told.

And now, once more, the men were singing with her: soft at first, low; then it grew strong and loud and angry in its urgency. They were telling what it means to be human; singing of loneliness and separation, of darkness and light, of heaven.

It had come too close now, and I drove away out of the sound of it, letting my eyes drift with the marsh-grass toward the line of forest beyond, and back down the twisting creeks out to sea.

But you do not so easily drive away from memories. I kept thinking of my childhood; and of this woman as she stood there tall and straight and humbly proud, communicating with God. She might find it impossible during her entire life to talk once to a white person of what was in her heart and mind but she could tell it to God—and the white folks who heard would understand her meaning.

All my childhood I had listened to it: this never-ending dialogue between human beings and their God. Sometimes it took place in our kitchen: the woman whom we called "the cook" was hurt, there was pain that had to be expressed, anguish that needed to be understood, trouble whose limits must somehow be defined. Then would begin the singing. A voice without words would tell its story for the whole universe to hear. I have heard that wordless song, sung by women over washtubs, in kitchens, out under the oak trees when a white baby was being put to sleep. I have never heard a man sing it. His songs are different; they have words; or they are sounds that accompany body movements in work; but the women made of their voices a terrible and beautiful instrument which pierced the heart and the heavens.

I had heard it, too, in the little churches on the edge of town; only then, they sang with words for they were talking to each other as well as to their Creator. When I was a small child I would lie in bed at night listening to those sounds that pounded like the sea against an iron wall. Sometimes, lying there, I sang with them but more often I cried, not knowing why but feeling the loneliness of it, feeling too, maybe, the pressure of wrongs that could not be named in a child's vocabulary. And I knew, even then—it seems to me now that I knew—that they were talking over the white race's head to God, and in doing it, they made of the white man no more than an overseer; their Master was on their side.

Such people could never become real slaves; for in sharing his God with them, the white man made it impossible ever to keep them in serfdom. Maybe deep down in him he knew this, the human part of him, the God part, knew; and even as he snapped the lock, he handed his slave the key. It was only in those few bitter decades just before the Civil War that he tried to get the key back. Then it was, when "race" had become a three-edged thing, an economic and political and moral issue, that a part of the South made one last effort to justify itself by saying the black men had no souls. And during this time Bibles were taken from some of them and they were forbidden to come together in churches or in any place. But nobody in his heart believed it for a moment; neither white nor black believed that their relationship with God had been severed.

There is an old song which Virginia slaves used to sing at their funerals: *Come down, death, right easy*. You wonder as you listen, how they did it; how they found so naturally the simple right words for those tones that press down to the bottom of your soul and make it ache with all that is sad and bitter and tragic and triumphant not only in their life but your own. Come down, death . . . right easy . . . they'd sing, as they lowered the body roped on its narrow board down into the hole. And someone would lift the palm of his hand in symbol of "God's Book" and make up words to say, but the words often faltered for it was hard to remember what was in a Bible you had never read. Then, those standing around that hole would begin to sing; they would sing the body into its grave, sing it on up the long road to heaven . . . sing it straight into the presence of God.

And so, because long ago a few white folks decided that their slaves had no souls and hence needed no Bible and no preacher to help them die, our South and the whole world were given the most poignantly beautiful death songs a folk ever created.

How strange and lovely, sometimes, are the wages of sin!

Now in these confused times there are those who try to cheapen this rare and honorable page of man's relationship with God by telling Negroes that to sing spirituals over radio and television "stereotypes them as slaves and primitives." It is true, these old songs have left a sign on all who have sung them; they are marked—*not* as slaves or primitives or clowns or animals or cogs in a machine but as the sons of God: men who have held on through terrible ordeals to their faith and dignity. And we, who listen, have a sign left on us. We are not the same afterward; for it is not granted one, often, to come as close as this to the grandeur of man when he refuses to live or to die except as a human being.

Song and laughter, and prayer . . . I kept thinking about them on that hot Sunday afternoon as I drove down nameless sand roads. As long as our laughter can turn giants into pygmies—whether those giants threaten us inside our minds or outside in the external world; as long as feelings can be communicated in song when words are forbidden or when feeling is too deep for words; as long as prayer—our last line of defense—is available to us, the door to the future of the human race cannot be irrevocably closed.

And yet, I had taken these magnificent defenses for granted until lately; until I began to realize that the freedom to laugh, to sing, to pray can be taken away from us, too, by power-hungry censors who try to dehumanize man. Censors who may be inside our own minds, for it is not always demagogues and dictators on the outside who strip us of the resources and relationships that are most precious to us.

I was remembering a young friend. She would see no reason for this journey. She was so eager for "action." To stop for a little while and think—when there is so much to be done! "How can prayer and song and laughter be of value to us, today? To Negroes—like me? How can they be? What can they do for us in times like these? They have certainly not torn down segregation. That is what we want down: the walls."

Yes, and I want those walls down, too. I would like to see every one of them down tomorrow for I know they have almost smothered the goodness in us. But after they are down and we stand face to face—will we recognize the human being in each other? We may not. For in the struggle for something we call "freedom" it is easy to lose sight of the reason for that freedom. We (white and colored, Jew and Gentile, Westerner and Asiatic) want the walls down so that the man in us can have a chance to grow; but in our struggle we may give ourselves a mortal injury if we do not take care.

In no way are we more likely to do it, I think, than by banning from theater and television and radio what is misnamed "racial and religious stereotypes"—a phrase that is presently used to define characters who do not flatter a group's image of itself. What a curious upside-down conformity this banning could bring about! For it is not stereotypes that are disapproved of but a certain kind of stereotype. With sincere motives these self-appointed censors insist that no play, no motion picture, no novel show a member of the Negro race (however real the character may be) in domestic service or working as a "menial," or one who attempts to maintain a harmonious relationship with a white southerner, or one who is "happy" down in the South, or laughing and singing and dancing. No Negro woman may be shown in love with a white man though a white woman may be shown in love with a Negro man. You may write about a Negro intellectual however nasty in his snobbery and however poorly realized as a character but you may not show a blackfaced sweaty farmer in blue jeans struggling with the complexities of human toil and relationships and in the struggle finding an equilibrium, a serenity; no, if you do this you have made of him an "Uncle Tom" and of his wife a "handkerchief head." You may not put a Negro waiter, honest and hard-working, in a movie but you may put there a Negro businessman who made his money perhaps by exploiting his own race, who is a stuffed shirt and dull and greedy—but if he plays golf that is all right; for white folks too make their money sometimes in questionable ways and are sometimes stuffed shirts and dull and greedy, and play golf. It adds up, alas, to a parvenu gaucherie—this racial "line," this new stereotype. But no matter! Tear off the old black mask; put on the new white mask. What a sad and true thing that when we hate someone a great deal we borrow from him the qualities that gave him power to harm us, and wear them like a crown!

And the human being beneath the mask? The real person? Different from all other persons, struggling, aching and paining and dreaming and laughing and loving his life sometimes no matter how hard it is, building up the defenses he needs, trying to find fulfillment in whatever way he can, reaching out for a relationship with himself, with other people, with his earth and his God? Where is he? He is the "invisible man" made so not always by the white race but sometimes by the Negro himself, and by his friends who want to "free him."

And it seems never to occur to these would-be censors that what we need on stage and off stage, in books and in life, is people who are real; who follow no "line" save that marked out by their own life, and their hopes and dreams.

Stereotypes of course are distortions of the truth about men; never are they made of pure lies. For they have to do with the ways and means a hard-pressed man holds on to in order to survive. Caught in a trap, what does he do? If he is sane he develops defenses that will help him endure what he cannot escape. The Negro group had powerful resources within their bodies and memories and fantasy life and they used them; they found more resources in the white man's religion and the white man's ambivalence (which they reckoned with so shrewdly) and they used these too. They developed these defenses to a conspicuous degree which in gifted individuals resulted in works of art enriching the whole world, and in others bent the personality sometimes into grotesque and sometimes into utterly beguiling shapes.

And yet, as this was taking place in those old bitter years, something else was happening, too. Individuals among the Negro group knew individuals of the white group who were decent and they loved them; and these decent individuals returned that love. Ah . . . I know how humiliating it sometimes was; but not always was it a shameful thing. There was understanding; there was a shared sorrow and a shared respect; a guilt they both knew; they stood over many a coffin together—sometimes the coffin contained a body they both loved, sometimes it held a man's cherished dream.

With this profound knowledge of each other, how then were the stereotypes formed? By whom? By those who, refusing the insight and wisdom of their own personal experience, tried to justify a situation which could not be justified. By those who, finding tragedy unendurable, tried to turn it into farce and melodrama, or sometimes tried to forget it. When we want to cheapen a man (or our relationship with him, or our memory of him) we make with our words a cartoon of those defenses in his personality which have served him well, or those which have needled us more deeply. We distort them (by enlarging, by omitting, or sometimes by mating them with our own secret vices); we try to cut them down to size that cannot hurt us; we try to turn them into weapons which we can use against him (or against our own guilt). So we stereotype. It is a powerful means of carrying on a cold war—whether that cold war is with our own conscience or with external enemies. A man loses in this cold war when he is willing to throw away his defenses just because the enemy has caricatured them. He loses a second time, I think, when in his hate and confusion he tries to assume those qualities which have hurt him worst.

It is a familiar thing, this stereotyping and this identification. We see it so plainly in the warfare between parents and children; between men and women. A child becomes like the mother she fears and hates . . . so often making her own qualities that have harmed her most, discarding her identity (or perhaps never finding it). A woman wants her "rights"; she resents being stereotyped as a "female"—so what does she do? She gives up her feminine resources and tries to snatch from man his maleness, or his masculine privileges, and now and then his worst style of life.—And there are Americans today who have begun to look bloodkin to the communists whom they claim to abhor. . . . It is such a worn-out old story; why can't we human beings lay it away, bury it, and begin a new and more interesting one!

As I drove along that Sunday afternoon with the woman's singing still in my ears, I was thinking of those troubling matters. Remembering my young friend, brilliant and sensitive and lovable, who wants to "fight for her rights." "Oh, I don't want these rights given to me: I want to take them. Legally," she said and laughed, "not bowing and scraping, hat in hand, begging for something to be returned to me that is my birthright."

"Did your parents bow and scrape to white folks?" (In a lifetime spent in the South, I had so rarely seen servility in a Negro—always with the bow and the scrape there was a faint mockery; the tongue was in the cheek—and anybody who wasn't a fool knew it.)

"No. In my family we always talked back. Not in a loud voice, I've been told, but we talked back. My aunt says, we did it sometimes with our words and sometimes with our eyes and sometimes with all the bones of our body but we did it."

"I like to think that you did."

"Maybe they sound like a child, such words; but it is good for the spirit to protest. I believe that."

"I believe that, too," I told her. "And then a day comes as it did for the people of India when talking back is over. As segregation goes, and it is going fast now, we have something harder to learn to do."

"I know," she said quickly, "to forgive."

And that requires of us a deeper pride, something more real than arrogance; something both the white and colored races have to learn. Something beyond scorn and resentment—

"I wonder," I said aloud, "how many of us can find this humility—in time."

"I don't know. I know only that it is hard to forgive when you have been wronged so deeply."

"Almost as hard as it is to forgive those you have wronged."

She laughed and her eyes filled with tears. "I am all mixed up; you are; everybody in the world is, I guess. This sloughing off, layer after layer, until you find something real at the core is a terrible job. But I still say the praying and the spirituals have not got rid of segregation."

No, perhaps not. And yet the pounding of those sounds through the years against the conscience of the world—surely it weakened the barriers a little, surely a few holes were torn in the walls. But whether it did this or not, it kept the people behind the wall human through a terrible ordeal and that is an important thing. Now today, what substitutes have we for the prayer and the song?

Prayer.... I knew that I did not understand it. I recognized its great power but I did not understand how a human being relates himself on so deep a level with God. It might be a wordless relationship, as I felt in the singing of the women. It could be made with words. I am sure it is no easier to pray than it is to create music or write a poem; it must be as hard to do as it is to build a bridge, or to discover a great scientific principle, or to heal the sick, or to understand another human being. It is surely as important as these to man in his search for his role in the universal scheme of things. That role? I hoped to understand it better on this journey, somewhere.

To pray.... It is so necessary and so hard. Hard not because it requires intellect or knowledge or a big vocabulary or special technics but because it requires of us humility. And that comes, I think, from a profound sense of one's brokenness, and one's need. Not the need that causes us to cry, "Get me out of this trouble, quick!" but the need that one feels every day of one's life—even though one does not acknowledge it—to be related to something bigger than one's self, something more alive than one's self, something older and something not yet born, that will endure through time.

From Chapter 15

[. . .] No power, whether of science, wealth, guns or authority can take the place of real relationships.

We are learning this now—as parents and teachers and plain people.

The scientists are learning, too, that science becomes good only in service to human life.

I saw this happening, not long ago, in a dramatic way. It was at Toots Shor's. Late one winter afternoon. A party. In the room were men known across the earth for their distinguished medical achievements. There were philanthropists, psychiatrists, a writer or two, therapists, psychologists. A beautiful girl whose back had been broken in an automobile accident leaned slightly on her cane as she talked to a friend. There was a man in a wheelchair. A pleasant-faced woman, his wife, sat near him. Waiters were moving in and out. Toots Shor was near the doorway, beaming, watchful.

We had come to see the premiere of a documentary film made by Victor Solow and called *A New Beginning*. The story was of a paralyzed miner's rugged trip back to active life. The man, whose experience it was, sat quietly in his wheelchair waiting to take a second look at his own life. Man, watching himself. . . . We always try to remember, always paint a portrait of our experiences, distorting them, shaping, reducing, enlarging, giving them strange sharp colors or sometimes doing them in monochromes. But here a man's experience was documented on a film. What will this new potential do to the human memory, I thought, as I sat there waiting in the darkened room for the film to begin. Suppose parents were to document theirs and their child's experiences; suppose they set them down in film to look at, and talk over together, later; suppose this happened in many homes—what effect would it have on childhood, on human awareness, on memory?

The film began. Clean, swift camera work caught a mining town at dawn. Men with lunch kits going to work. Women sweeping front porches; opening windows. Sharp lines of house, roof, street. Men, more and more men going to work, down the street; down another street; another. A lyricism crept into the flow of images, as if the cameraman knew now that he was telling the world's story of men, working. The coal mine. The shaft. Men, going down, down. The sudden accident. The slow return home on a stretcher. The long wait in bed. Lying there, finished. It used to be the last weary chapter. It was not this man's last chapter. After a stretch of months, he was taken to a rehabilitation hospital. There he began the struggle back. Learning to move an inch; another; sweating it out. And we, in Toots Shor's restaurant, watched him as he picked up his inner resources, one by one, trying this one, that, to help him find a way out of the trap. And finally he got out. He can move, walk, use his hands. He has a job. He has married.

But he could not have done it alone. There are disasters no man, however determined and brave, can come out of without others to help. To get this man back on his feet and into a job required knowledge that is the result of centuries of patient scientific research. It required the pooled skills of orthopedic surgeons, psychiatrists, occupational and physical therapists, psychologists; required the use of instruments invented in the fields of electronics, electricity, X-ray, metallurgy; required discoveries in chemistry, physics—

Even this could not have done it. The science and the instruments, and the new metals and plastics, and the antibiotics would not have put this man on his feet, had not someone believed it possible for a paralyzed man to walk and cared enough to find the means by which it could be done.

But it was more than this. Someone had, also, to possess the imagination to see that a surgeon has not completed his job when he does a skillful amputation, or puts a steel pin in a hip, or operates on a spine. He is—as I have heard that great orthopedic surgeon, Dr. Henry Kessler, say—operating not on a bone but on a life. "You cannot separate a man's body from his life." When he goes under anesthesia, his life goes under, too; and all his relationships; his job, his image of himself, his dreams. And when his body heals, if his life has not healed, if he is not back in the world, working, playing, dreaming again, relating himself—"well, we haven't finished our job, that is all."

In that dim room watching the film, was Dr. Howard Rusk. Much of its story had been made at the New York Institute of Physical Medicine and Rehabilitation, of which he is the director. During the Second World War, he, too, saw this mid-century vision: a man's life cannot be broken into fragments and these fragments of body, mind, emotions, skills treated as if they have no relation to each other or to the rest of him or to his family. Science has to think of man set in the center of his life, in the center of his past and future, related to those he loves, to his job, his hopes, pleasures, childhood, dreams, values and related also to the rest of us. There is no right way for science but to use its knowledge for man's whole life. And no right way for men but to accept, in humility, the help that can come only from the knowledge and good will of other men.

It is a just thing that man's body gave him the first patterns for his tools and machines, and now, in return, these tools and machines are giving him a new image of himself and helping him connect up with capacities he did not know he possessed. Instruments thought up by his brain, giving him a view of that brain which eyes, alone, could not see. Electricity, measuring for him his electrical rhythms. Electronics, radar, X-rays, radium, isotopes giving him new means by which to perceive himself and his world.

It is a wondrous thing, too, that speech long ago gave him a giant-size capacity for remembering and storing his experience and in doing so helped him explore the universe; and now, with the knowledge he found there and the humility he has presently found within himself, speech is once more helping him explore that memory and make the return trip to a childhood he was too young to understand when he left it.

A strange and lovely thing it is, too, that we are learning to accept the body's vast potentialities by learning to accept its brokenness and differences; and in finding ways to bind the fragments into a whole life we are finding a common ground where people of the earth can meet in understanding and sympathy.

And even as we accept *relativity* as a word that has a validity for our modern world which the *absolute* no longer has, we begin to understand that the word applies neither to God nor to human values. Morality is not relative; it is a *growing* concept that has sprung from the seed of the human being's need of others and his need to believe in God in order to keep the future open. It has grown as a tree grows, dropping its "moralities" as leaves fall; greening again. The leafing and the fall of the leaves cannot be confused with the steady growth of the tree itself, as men become more and more reverent of life, more and more aware of the power of love and tenderness in human affairs, more and more sure of their interdependence and their need for a wisdom which is not science but takes to itself all that science can contribute; more and more accepting of themselves as growing creatures who change as long as they live. We begin to understand that we can never have absolute knowledge of God and yet He is not "relative." It is simply that our knowledge is incomplete and while it will increase as we grow, always there will be the impenetrable between man and God.

It is coming together, now, into a whole: the dream and the means to implement the dream. Ever since men have felt tenderness and a love of the truth they have dreamed of a good life; a good way: what the Chinese philosophers called *Tao*; what Jesus called the Abundant Life; what Buddha spoke of as moral growth, as freedom from fear, as taking thought.

But it was impossible to attain. Tenderness and love of truth are not enough: there must be knowledge; there must be the means, the technics, the instruments by which disease can be cured, disasters avoided, ordeals survived, poverty and ignorance eradicated; there must be those who care enough to have the imagination to believe something can be done about it.

Now, for the first time, we are beginning to bring together the fragments: to bind childhood to the rest of our life so that our reason can control it and thus reduce the anxiety which dictators, inside and outside us, exploit so lushly; to tie body to mind to feelings to fantasies to belief; to relate these to the rest of mankind and to the world; to relate power to humility, and responsibility to honor and freedom; to keep tenderness and truth close together.

As I sat there watching that miner make his comeback, watching as numberless friends helped him (some of whom have been dead for centuries but whose knowledge is still here for him to use) I saw this: the symphonic fullness of life as it is possible for us to live it today. Man, directing; man, playing his instruments: one, ten thousand, two billion bodies and hands and minds and hearts bringing the dream into reality as dissonances build toward climax, resolve, mount again, resolve, mount again, held in key by belief, modulating into richer beliefs—making fabulous music.

It is man's role in this evolving universe (as Auden, Shelley, Tagore, and other poets have reminded us) to teach the terrors of his nature and his world to sing, to bring order out of chaos, to create the new from the debris of the old. And he is beginning, today, to have spectacular success in doing so.

A century from now, men may think it strange that we so long spoke of our times as the age of anxiety; that we let the greed of ordinary men and the power-lust of dictators and demagogues get out of bounds even for a brief span of years; for parallel with the anxiety and the terror and the inquisitors and exploiters and the awful poverty and ignorance there is another way of life building firmly, steadily, swiftly on scientific facts and technics and on men's newly discovered humility and dignity and on their concern for each other.

There has, of course, always been more love than hate in the world—else the human race would have died out long ago. But never in the world's history has there been so much tenderness and understanding shown children, as today. Never so much concern for the welfare of the stranger and for those who are different. Never such willingness to lay aside spurious goodness and omniscience. And for the first time, we have the means to implement the good feelings, the honesty, the insight; the means of instant world-wide communication, the means of quick getting together, the means of recreating a storm-ruined town almost overnight; of eliminating poverty; of healing not only a body but a whole life.

No, our age will never go down in history as the age of anxiety, nor as the atomic age. It will be stamped with the mark of a mastered ordeal—and there will be nothing easy and pretty in that mark—but as Malraux reminds us, "always, however brutal an age may actually have been, its style transmits its music only."

I believe future generations will think of our times as the age of wholeness: when the walls began to fall; when the fragments began to be related to each other; when man learned finally to esteem tenderness and reason and awareness and the word which set him apart forever from other living creatures; when he learned to realize his brokenness and his great talent for creating ties that bind him together again; when he learned to accept his own childhood and in the acceptance to become capable of maturity; when he began to realize his infinite possibilities even as he sees more clearly his limitations; when he began to see that sameness and normality are not relevant to human beings but to machines and animals; when he learned never to let any power or dictator cut his ties to the great reservoir of knowledge and wisdom without which he would quickly lose his human status; when he learned to live a bit more comfortably with time and space; when he learned to accept his need of God and the law that he cannot use Him, to accept his need of his fellow men and the law that he cannot use them, either; when he learned that "what is impenetrable to us really exists," and always there will be need of the dream, the belief, the wonder, the faith.

To believe in something not yet proved and to underwrite it with our lives: it is the only way we can leave the future open. Man, surrounded by facts, permitting himself no surmise, no intuitive flash, no great hypothesis, no risk is in a locked cell. Ignorance cannot seal the mind and imagination more surely. To find the point where hypothesis and fact meet; the delicate equilibrium between dream and reality; the place where fantasy and earthy things are metamorphosed into a work of art; the hour when faith in the future becomes knowledge of the past; to lay down one's power for others in need; to shake off the old ordeal and get ready for the new; to question, knowing that never can the full answer be found; to accept uncertainties quietly, even our incomplete knowledge of God: this is what man's journey is about, I think.

Letter to the Editors, *Atlanta Constitution*

To readers of *Killers of the Dream* and *The Journey*, Smith's unique response to the 1954 Supreme Court's decision in *Brown v. Board of Education of Topeka, Kansas* may seem quite predictable. The following letter, published not by the *Atlanta Constitution* but by the *New York Times*, June 6, 1954, underlines the significance of Smith's stand against segregation: it was not just her timing that was important—that she spoke out as early as she did—her perspective and depth of understanding were crucial as well. Because she saw racial segregation as symbolic and symptomatic of many other aspects of human nature and society, it is not surprising that her first public response to the *Brown* decision contained broad and far-reaching interpretations of the new law.

Her passing reference to the ruling as a "powerful political instrument against communism" was not a new argument for Smith or for many others who for years had pointed to the hypocrisy of America's willingness to defend freedom abroad while blatantly denying the rights of citizenship to black Americans. While it is important to remember that Smith's anti-Communism predated the end of World War II, her use of anti-Communist language reveals her susceptibility to the Cold War rhetoric and a certain blindness in her otherwise clear vision of the relationship between means and ends in any struggle for social change. Although she may have intended to defuse the red-baiting tactics of those who labeled as "Communists" the Supreme Court justices and all others who worked to end racial segregation, her willingness to use the anti-Communist rhetoric—even against itself—left her vulnerable to charges of feeding the very red-baiting she would otherwise deplore.

In the remainder of the letter Smith's strategy was brilliant. To call the *Brown* decision "every child's Magna Carta" was at once to move the subject out of the realm of black versus white or federal government versus state and local school boards and to place it in the tradition of freedom for the individual, which even the staunchest segregationists claim to revere. Simultaneously, she pushed beyond the stereotype of race by renaming skin color an "artificial disability" compared to "real disabilities" of physically or mentally disabled children.

Smith's knowledge of the legal, social, and educational plight of disabled Americans was grounded in the extensive research she and Snelling had conducted for their proposed anthology on the subject. Her perception that the *Brown* decision would affect disabled children as well as children of color was prophetic. Few, if any, of its defendants or opponents were even considering such far-reaching implications in 1954, yet educational historians now look to that decision as a major precedent for the extension of educational access to all children, culminating in the 1975 enactment of Public Law 94-142, the Education of All Handicapped Children Act.

Smith's confidence that "millions of other southerners" would "wholeheartedly" accept the challenge of the *Brown* decision reflected her basic educational strategy for social change. Believing that people would rise to the vision of their leaders, she always tried to embody the vision she held for the South. She would develop this appeal and outline specific creative responses to court-ordered desegregation in her 1955 book, *Now Is the Time.*

To the editors, *The Atlanta Constitution*

May 31, 1954

Dear Sirs:

I have read, again, the recent decision of the Supreme Court. It bears rereading. For it is a great historic document—not only because its timing turns it into the most powerful political instrument against communism that the United States has, as yet, devised, but because of its profound meaning for children.

It is every child's Magna Carta. All are protected by the magnificent statement that no artificial barriers, such as laws, can be set up in our land against a child's right to learn and to mature as a human being.

There are, perhaps, 5 million children in the U.S.A. who are colored. There are close to 5 million other children who will be directly affected by this decision. I am not speaking, now, of "white children"—many of whom have undoubtedly been injured spiritually by the philosophy of segregation. I am speaking of disabled children:

Children who are "different," not because of color but because of blindness, deafness, because they are crippled, or have cerebral palsy; because they have speech defects, or epilepsy, or are what we call "retarded." These children we have also segregated.

There are more than 40 states with laws forbidding a child with epilepsy to attend public school—even though most children's convulsions can now be controlled by modern drugs. Little blind children are segregated in schools from sighted children; our deaf, from the hearing. Many cerebral palsy children are kept out of school not because they are unable to attend but because there are teachers who do not want to teach them. And yet, a basic principle of rehabilitation is that acceptance and a natural relationship with his human world is necessary for the disabled child, if he is to make a good life for himself.

All these children—some with real disabilities, others with the artificial disability of color—are affected by this great decision.

Then why are a few politicians protesting so angrily? Perhaps because they feel THEY will now be handicapped if the old crutch of "race" is snatched away from them.

It is true: this decision may shackle a few politicians. But it frees so many of our children. I, for one, am glad. And I believe millions of other southerners are glad, also; and will accept wholeheartedly the challenge of making a harmonious, tactful change-over from one kind of school to another. It will be an ordeal only if our attitude makes it so; there are creative, practical ways of bringing about this change. And in the doing of it, we adults may grow, too, in wisdom and gentleness.

[*HH* 145–47]

From *Now Is the Time*

Immediately following the May 1954 Supreme Court ruling on school desegregation, Smith wrote *Now Is the Time*, urging support for the Court's decision and outlining specific ways Southerners could work deliberately and calmly to end racial segregation. Written to reach a wide audience as quickly as possible, the book was published simultaneously in paperback by Dell Books and in hardback by Viking Press in the spring of 1955. *Now Is the Time* crystallized approximately two decades of Smith's practices as well as theory about effective social change. Accordingly, thoughts of how best to bring about social change dominated her writing in the mid-1950s as she dealt with reactions to her book and increasingly violent resistance to efforts to end racial segregation in the South. In December 1955 Smith learned that despite steady sales through the summer and fall, paperback copies of *Now Is the Time* were being removed from bookstores and newsstands nationwide, and Dell was not filling orders.

That month, as she tried to extract an explanation for the book's removal and fought to get it reinstated, some forty thousand black people began their year-long boycott of the municipal bus system in Montgomery, Alabama. In February 1956, at the University of Alabama in Tuscaloosa, the first major test of court-ordered desegregation in the Deep South sparked mob violence and rioting as students and townspeople protested the admission of Arthurine Lucy. Smith argued in vain for the urgent need for her book to be available to college students and the public in general (*HH* 163–65). The following selections provide a sampling of her reasoned arguments, the same ones she had made since the 1940s and would continue to make in multiple speeches throughout the coming decade.

Part I, Chapter 1

It was May seventeenth. Many of us sat at radio and television, waiting. For word had gone out that the Supreme Court would hand down its decision on segregation in the public schools, that day.

Events at home and abroad had confused and shocked us: the Army-McCarthy hearings, evasion and postponement in Congress, headline squabbles, suspicion of good men, trials, more and more investigations—and all the while, the Communist powers were moving like a tidal wave across Asia, dividing and weakening each country they touched.

China, years ago, had been lost to the free world. Korea had been divided. Now we were watching it happen in Indochina. It too would be lost or divided. The next? And next?

A feeling was creeping from person to person, group to group, a clear sense: that things need not be like this. Why was communism winning Asia? Why was this new tyranny so seductive that the people ran out and grasped it?

Until two centuries ago, the idea of freedom was only a dream; the human being's importance was only an ideal. Tyranny and slavery were the realities of man's experience. Then, suddenly, the dream, the ideal, grew into a bold and beautiful political system called democracy. Men said that never, hereafter, would human beings be satisfied with anything less. When they heard of it they would demand it as their right.

Now, here were a billion people craving this new freedom, thinking of human dignity, hungering for it—and millions of them settling for new and heavier chains of bondage.

Why? We knew why even as we asked. We knew democracy had not met their needs. Somehow, the dream had walled itself off. Somehow it had become segregated. In the eyes of Asia and Africa democracy had turned into "white democracy." They do not trust the white hands that offer them aid because, until now, those hands have given them only the bitter experiences of colonialism and white prestige. They are reluctant to accept the United States as a friend—this democracy which has never colonized any Asian or African country—because its people cling to color segregation and have laws in many states making it compulsory.

Why don't we see this? People were asking—more and more of them.

And so we waited that day, tense and expectant.

We knew what the decision would be. The necessities of our times had clearly determined it: not alone the world situation but the human situation here at home, in our children's lives, in our own hearts and minds, made it imperative that the highest authority in our land say clearly that there is no place, today, for legal segregation in a free and democratic nation. We knew. But we wanted to hear it said aloud. And when the words came, simple and plain, a deep pride swept across America.

Chief Justice Warren, who spoke for a unanimous court, did not clutter his pages with legal precedents. He based the decision on a truth more important than precedents: a child's right to learn. He stated, for the first time in the history of a country's highest court, that a child's feelings are important to a nation; that shame and rejection can block a mind from learning, hence segregation is a barrier to human growth which no state in our democracy can maintain legally in its public school system.

For a little while, that day, we forgot Asia and Africa. We were thinking of children. Of their needs. Bread, books, shoes? These we have tried to give them. But to grow as human beings they must have esteem, they must have belief in their own worth and the worth of others. Now they would have a better chance to grow. Every child could begin to feel at home here, knowing he is accepted in the American family. From this time on he will be safeguarded from those who do not care: from the bullies and the haters and the sick minds and the political opportunists who, in their greed, are willing to feed on our children's future to make their own present big.

White children were not mentioned in that remarkable document, but they too are deeply affected by it. For race segregation is a cruel frame that twists and misshapes the spirits of all children, no matter which side of it they are fastened to. Arrogance, complacency, blindness to human need: these hurt the heart and mind as severely as do shame and inferiority. We hardly need to remind ourselves of how the little Nazis' moral natures were maimed by Hitler's ideas and laws to know this is true.

White Southerners know it so well. As we listened to the decision, many of us were suddenly back in childhood, quietly walking through its years, remembering its beauty, its tender moments, its sudden joy and wonder—and its walls. Those invisible walls which we plunged against a thousand times as we stretched out to accept our human world. Walls that stopped our questions—and our dreams. We were so free . . . but we did not have the freedom to do right. For there were laws in our states that compelled us to do wrong.

Now the Supreme Court's decision would give this freedom back to the white child of the South. It is a very big gift, for which many of us are deeply grateful.

Months passed. Autumn had come. Schools once more opened. And some were for the first time in their history without segregation. The decision had made plain what the law is. The school boards decided to wait no longer. In the good American way, they went ahead on this new frontier, exploring, taking risks; with courage and independence they began to work things out.

In the border states, Delaware, West Virginia, in the city of Baltimore, in Washington, D.C. (where there is a larger number of Negro pupils than white), the school children were learning brand-new lessons together. The most important lessons they had ever learned: that had to do with freedom and its relationship to responsibility; with the meaning of human rights; with the place of law in their personal lives. They were beginning to see that our American Constitution is the steel frame that holds this great skyscraper we call democracy firmly to the earth. They began to understand that freedom can be freedom to do wrong as easily as it can be freedom to do right—unless our country's laws are obeyed.

They were vivid lessons—for suddenly, as if in a play, they were acted out: white children struck, demanding that colored children's rights be disregarded; white parents struck, telling their children they need not respect the Constitution, they need not esteem the Supreme Court and the highest laws of our land.

There were not many strikers. Only a few thousand. But enough. Enough for us to see what it looks like when American citizens put their allegiance to their color above the Constitution of the United States. Enough for us to see what anarchy could look like; enough for us to read fresh meanings into the word "subversive."

We, the American public, were back at school now—with the children—learning again lessons we had almost forgot.

With shocking clarity, we realized that no parent or child who had a regard for human rights and love of justice could have participated in those strikes.

We began to see that we have been so busy opposing communism that we have not stopped to ask: *What does democracy mean to me? to my children? Perhaps I love it as little as a Communist does; perhaps I do not understand it any better than he. Is this true?*

We began to realize that a nation is no better than the people in it; its strength is no greater than the beliefs in their hearts and the values they hold to.

We had heard it said a thousand times. Yes. But here, suddenly, it was dramatized for us, clearly, sharply. All one had to do was look at the pictures of those strikers to realize that somehow, somewhere, we have failed—and in a big way.

We began to understand that a democracy cannot do without quality in its people—and yet it cannot give them quality. It needs goodness—there is no substitute for it—and yet it cannot make its people good.

It can only protect their right to be as good as they want to be. It can only safeguard their children's right to learn and grow toward maturity. It protects everybody—rich, poor, colored, white, well-bodied and crippled, the dull and the genius, the young, the old—but that is all it can do.

To grow good human beings is the people's business: a job that must be done in the home, at church, in school; goodness seeps into a child from the books he reads, the art he loves, his play, his talk, his dreams and ideals, his awareness of others and their needs. As we watched these school children and their parents making mistakes, learning new lessons in this time of change, we saw this clearly. And we knew we had not attended to our business well enough.

Then it was that many began to realize that this ordeal of school integration can become for the entire nation a magnificent opportunity for growth, for soul-searching, for rediscovery of important things. It can become a great moment in American history if only we have the vision to see the creative possibilities in this crisis; if only we remember that it is not ordeal that determines our future but what we do about it, what we make of it.

It is a great challenge. Perhaps our one big chance to strengthen democracy here at home. If we meet it well we shall, at last, be living our beliefs, measuring up to our responsibilities. And this knowledge, this lifting of a burden which has been on our conscience so long, will quicken our imagination and release our energies. It will enlarge our sympathies for people everywhere, who, too, are changing, who, too, are searching for something real and abiding to compose their lives around.

If we succeed, it will demonstrate to the world how change, deep change, can be brought about in a democracy without violence and bloodshed.

If we succeed, perhaps our friends across the earth will be persuaded that though we have among our rights the right to make mistakes, we feel also the obligation to correct those mistakes once we see we have made them. There is no person, no group of people, no nation, that does not make grave mistakes. The test is: can they rectify their mistake? A man's honor becomes involved in how he meets this test; his sense of responsibility for the future of his children and the human race becomes involved. Honor and responsibility are a man's and a nation's greatest assets. They will carry us through any ordeal and, in the process, will enrich us and our civilization, no matter how painful the ordeal may be.

Our founding fathers understood that always there would be need for a nation to correct its old mistakes. And because they understood, they created a Constitution that was and still is a living, growing thing: resilient, flexible, sensitive to the fact that men change as they gain knowledge of their world and of themselves. Read it: you see within its pages so many open spaces left for growth. The people can do wrong, yes; we have in the past and will again; but our Constitution holds within it the potentials for doing right and the machinery for correcting our errors—and they will be corrected as soon as enough of us realize that change is needed.

Change in a democracy can be brought about quickly or slowly. The speed depends on its people's honesty of mind, their values, their humility and knowledge and insight; and, above all else, on the will to act, once they realize the need for action.

It took a long time for enough of us to see how wrong segregation is, how injurious it is to a whole nation for a group of its children in any state to be set apart or hidden away by law because of their differences—whatever those differences may be, real or unreal.

It would have taken longer—had it not been that freedom to protest and to dream of a better life are an integral part of the American way.

From 1881 to 1907, widespread enactment of segregation laws took place in Southern states. Protests from Negroes, who dreamed of a future for their people and knew they had a right to their dreams, began in slavery and increased as the segregation laws were set up. One by one, Negroes spoke out. Then more and more spoke bravely, eloquently, in prayer, song, poetry, art, books, in organized demands for their rights, in scientific accomplishments, in sacrifices for their country—using every means of communication they could get their hands on to lay their case before the conscience of our nation.

And white people, North and South, joined them in their protests. It is a good thing to remember that never has the Negro group been alone. Always there have been white people, many of them—first in the North, then in the South—who have identified with them as human beings, giving priority not to pigmentation of skin but to the spirit of man. Americans who knew that segregation divides and weakens democracy and, if persisted in too long, will destroy it and the quality of its people.

But it was another kind of speaking out—the brilliant work of the Legal Committee of the National Association for the Advancement of Colored People—that culminated in the great decision of May seventeenth.

The Legal Committee's purpose was to find means, within the American framework of law, by which Negroes could reclaim their constitutional rights. One of its first acts was to challenge the grandfather clause in Oklahoma—a clause that tried in a shrewd, twisting way to stop Negroes from voting because they had ancestors who had been in slavery. It won its case.

It proceeded to test the constitutionality of other segregation statutes. The white primary is one of the most famed.

As time has passed, as case after case has been hung up in the public mind to be looked at, the American people have grown increasingly aware of the deep wounds which the act of segregation inflicts on the human spirit.

Throughout the years the NAACP has been criticized, sneered at, called "communist" by many who seem not to know, or to have forgotten, how their own government works: what rights a citizen is guaranteed by our Constitution; what legal procedures may be used to get back his rights when they have been taken from him.

How else, except through peaceful protest, and the courts, can change come about in our country? We have no dictator to make us change. We do not resort to revolution. A democracy cannot stay alive if the people in it do not urge change when change is necessary; it cannot grow unless the people have vision. Therefore, reformers, prophets, poets, and protest groups belong to the democratic way of life. If a man does not like them, he does not like democracy.

The entire work of the Legal Committee of the NAACP will, I believe, go down in history as a superb example of the American way of correcting wrongs in a spirit of reason and good will.

It will show that this process of bringing about change in laws, or deciding on the validity of old laws, is also an important means of educating the people whom these laws affect; and that the Supreme Court, our highest authority, bases its decisions not only on the Constitution and legal precedents but on its and the people's awareness of the necessities of their times.

"The inn that shelters for the night is not the journey's end," said Justice Benjamin Cardozo. "The law, like the traveler, must be ready for the morrow. It must have the principle of growth."

The Supreme Court has made its decision. Will it become ours also? Will we put it into effect quickly enough, harmoniously enough, for it to be the means of revitalizing our own faith and restoring the world's confidence in our integrity?

This is the unanswered question.

There is so much to give us hope. The timing of the decision was so right. It is in the full current of history; it had to come—even those hostile to the decision admit that this change is an inevitable one. It is right for our children, right in terms of scientific knowledge, right for our nation's integrity, right for world peace.

And we have fabulous resources for bringing it about: instant, nation-wide communication by television, radio, newspapers; we have facts, techniques; there are many responsible, skilled people who are deeply concerned, who understand the urgent need of a quiet, immediate acceptance of this decision, and who can communicate their understanding to the people. As a nation we are prospering; no heavy economic pressures are on us; the South's old one-crop system of agriculture which, for so long, made exploitation of the Negro group profitable to many has almost disappeared—and with it one motivation for "keeping things as they are." There is a strong bond of good will and understanding between the two races, especially in the South, where there have always been many warm personal relationships. It is well to remind ourselves of this; to keep clear the fact that white Southerners do not hate Negroes. There are the haters, yes, who vent their hatred on whomever society permits them to; but though they have loud voices, they are limited in number.

Then what is holding us back?

Two things: anxiety—a taboo-like fear—which is aroused in many minds when the pattern of segregation is questioned; and the demagogues and other opportunists who deliberately exploit this anxiety to their political and economic advantage.

It may be wise to forget these opportunists for a little while and look hard at the fear.

The majority of Americans do not dread integration; but there are some who do. To many of these, South and North, the giving up of segregation seems a very hard thing; and to a few it is a terrifying disaster.

Why?

Part III, Chapter 3

From the Twenty-Five Questions

These are the questions that have won elections for politicians in the South and provoked housing incidents in the North. They are slogans which real-estate boards and home owners often use when defending restrictive covenants. They are weapons which no race agitator can do without.

They are troublemakers. Based on a few false assumptions whose roots go deep into old superstitions and folk fears of the past, most of them hold a vague, insistent threat, difficult to put into words, but there.

Everyone has heard them. Most of us have asked at least a few of them. You hear them, today, in Westchester County and in small Georgia towns, in Connecticut and the Mississippi Delta and California; Johannesburg, South Africa, may offer a few variations, but the basic questions are asked there, too; one heard them often in Asia in colonial days, in the white man's clubs; Hitler gave them a sinister twist in *Mein Kampf* but, stripped of their Teutonic verbiage, they sound much like the words Bilbo once sprinkled throughout his speeches.

No machiavellian brain thought them up. No propaganda committee formulated them. They grew slowly, one by one, out of a deep need to defend the morally indefensible, and flourished on the people's ignorance until they became thick walls in minds, shutting out what many did not want to see.

Most of these questions are dead now, killed off not only by scientific facts and our increasing knowledge of cultures and of the human body and mind, but by world events and a sharpened awareness of men's interdependence. And yet, in spite of a widespread dissemination of facts and news and values, people still use them as arguments against integration.

THE QUESTIONS AND A FEW BRIEF ANSWERS

The questions are formulated here just as they were asked me by two hundred audiences to whom I talked on human relations. Small-town club, university forum, church study group, North, South, and Midwest—the questions were the same. A curious lack of freshness was apparent—as if all the thinking on this topic of color and segregation had become stereotyped. They cluster around a few fuzzy premises which have to do with heredity and "blood" and environment, culture, economics, the Bible, the law and morals, time, and "what Negroes like." The answers given here are brief and simple. [. . .]

CULTURE

Q. 1. Don't you think each race should keep its culture separate?
A. 1. There is no culture anywhere in the world based solely on race or religion. There are groups of people living in various parts of the earth, each with a culture different in many ways from other cultures. All are phases of the human culture, which extends back to the beginning of man's history. All are indebted to other cultures for much that they now call their own. Negroes and whites in the United States are products of the American culture, which, in turn, is indebted to various European, Asian, American Indian, African, and Caribbean groups for much that is prized highly as "American."

Q. 2. The Negro has done pretty well, considering he has been out of savagery only three hundred years. Don't you think it takes time to civilize people?
A. 2. This question is a favorite with demagogues. Let us take it piecemeal. There is no meaning to the words "the Negro." There are Negroes. Most of

the Negroes now in the United States were born here. They were not born *out of* an African culture, they were born *into* our American culture. From the day they were born they began to learn quickly as do white babies. Culture is not something one inherits; one *learns* it and begins learning it the first weeks of one's life. A child learns what the family teaches him, and, later, what school, church, friends and enemies, books, the street, and television teach him. His experiences and his awareness of their meaning give him, in large part, his quality as a human being.

Q. 3. *The rate of violence and lawlessness is much higher among Negroes than whites. Isn't this proof that they are still primitive?*
A. 3. It is proof only that under a segregated regime the environment of colored town is not as good for children to grow up in as is the environment of white town. Poverty, lack of schooling facilities, discrimination of a dozen kinds, social rejection, make a poor growing climate for children. Another reason is that the law in the South is not administered with equal justice for Negroes and whites. Negroes can get by with crimes when committed against Negroes because law-enforcement officers and courts will often look the other way. This leniency encourages them to take out their violent feelings on one another. But a crime against a white is treated with extreme harshness. (This situation has improved in recent years.) When Negroes share equally in the freedoms of American citizenship they will be willing and able to share equally in the responsibilities.

INTERMARRIAGE AND "BLOOD" AND INHERITANCE

Q. 4. *If races mix, will it not result in an inferior breed of people as "mongrelization" does with animals?*
A. 4. There are no "pure" races. There are no blood types that correspond to skin color. There is only one race: the human race. The variations (such as skin color, eye color, height, shape of nose, etc.) in the appearance of groups are due to climate, food, and thousands of years of inbreeding. There are no proofs that white people as a group are superior or inferior to colored people as a group, nor is there proof that children born of mixed marriages are inferior or superior biologically. There are white geniuses and morons, and colored geniuses and morons, and geniuses and morons who are the children of mixed marriages. The differences between individuals of the same group are conspicuous. The differences between groups are relatively superficial and almost wholly those of environment.

But of this we are certain: the human race is profoundly different from animals, because of what we call "human culture." What is good or bad for a horse or dog is not necessarily good or bad for a man. We became human (1) because we learned to talk and share with each other what we learned and we can do this regardless of differences in skin color; and (2) because, in our prolonged infancy, we were given tenderness and care, and learned the survival value of concern for others. As Dr. Lawrence Kubie reminds us, every human child is a premature baby in the sense that at birth he is completely helpless. All he can do for himself is breathe. He *learns from others*. And he does so, in large part, because of human speech. Yet he is not born knowing his mother's language. He learns it. The physical differences of various groups are no more conspicuous than are language differences. Yet any child on earth capable of speech can learn, if he begins early enough, any language spoken anywhere.

By means of his ability to communicate with others and the race's skill in recording knowledge, the human being is able to learn and make use of the dreams and ideas and discoveries of strangers whatever their color, who lived thousands of years ago, or yesterday; and, in turn, to teach others. In this human context of profiting from the accumulating knowledge and wisdom of others, of giving and receiving, of the strong caring for the weak and the weak learning to grow strong, the word "mongrelization" has little meaning or validity.

Q. 5. *Would you want your sister to marry a Negro?*
A. 5. It is natural to fear that a marriage between members of groups long separated will not work. Therefore, the question should be looked at quietly and honestly. Old prejudices will linger in many minds a long time after legal segregation disappears. Social barriers will crumble slowly. But here and there a young woman, a young man, will choose to marry into the other group. Such marriages "across lines" are taking place all over the world today. Japanese are marrying Americans; GIs are bringing home brides from the Pacific islands; Indians and Chinese are marrying Americans; Jews are marrying Christians; Protestants are marrying Catholics. For most who make such marriages there are difficulties.

If a girl asked my advice I would say this: the quality of the man you marry, his values, tastes, habits, health, ability to make a living, sense of humor, intelligence, his anxieties, his interests, are far more important to you than the color of his skin or the name of his religion. It is, above all else, important that you love him. If you are mature and have chosen a mature man, you can weather the storms that will come from crossing the barriers. You will lose old friends; you will be snubbed. But you will gain much too. You will find new friends; you can create out of your ordeal much that will increase understanding among people. What happens will depend on the courage and wisdom you and your husband possess. Remember this: it will not be easy to do; but it may be worth it. That is for you to decide.

Q. 6. *Are mixed marriages fair to children?*
A. 6. Children born of married parents will not suffer as much as children born of unmarried parents. There have been millions of children in the United States, millions in South Africa, in India, China, who have been rejected by their fathers and their communities because they were born out of wedlock and across racial or caste lines. These children have suffered intensely. A child needs a secure home and the love of both parents. If it has these primary needs fulfilled, it can meet hardships outside the home. But this we should remember: there is no need for a child of mixed parentage to have a difficult time. It is our responsibility to see to it that he is accepted simply as a child with a child's right to grow and belong to his community.

The Right Way Is Not a Moderate Way

Lillian Smith was invited by the Montgomery Improvement Association to speak on the first anniversary of the bus boycott at the Institute on Non-Violence and Social Change. Because of ill health she was unable to attend, but her speech was read at the meeting of December 5, 1956. An active supporter of the boycott, Virginia Durr attended its anniversary celebration. The following day, December 6, she wrote Smith to thank her for the "most wonderful speech . . . so full of love and truth [. . .] the highest point that has been reached in any of the meetings that I have gone to." The audience's response was "almost ecstatic," she continued; fifty thousand copies of the speech would be printed and distributed (qtd. in *HH* 202–3).

The speech, "The Right Way Is Not A Moderate Way," was published in its entirety by Atlanta University's *Phylon* and the Fellowship of Reconciliation's *Fellowship*; excerpts appeared under different headings in the *New York Post* (December 13, 1956), *Civil Liberties, ADA World, Community, Congress Weekly*, and a number of black newspapers and major Southern newspapers. For the speech, the Americans for Democratic Action gave Smith the Franklin Roosevelt citation, which was presented by Eleanor Roosevelt. Eugenia Rawls received it for Smith and read her acceptance speech (*HH* 202–3).

The following copy was reprinted in *The Winner Names the Age*, in which asterisks were used to denote passages omitted to avoid unnecessary repetition of content.

I want to take my stand by your side, tonight, because I respect the creative means you have chosen to use to secure your legal rights as American citizens.

These means are non-violent. This way is the way of good will and intelligence and truth, and love. You have refused to use the crude and dangerous weapon of hate. You have refused to lie. You have not succumbed to retaliation or to resentment. You have used no harshness of word or of act.

You have behaved under stress like mature men and women—not like a mob.

But you have not been "moderates" nor have you kept in the middle of the road. No. You have shown the world that there are two extremes and they cannot be put in the same moral category.

There is the extreme of hate, yes; but there is also the extreme of love. There is the extreme of the lie; but there is also the extreme we call the "search for truth." There is the habitual thief who is certainly an extremist; but there is the habitually honest man who is an extremist, also.

Would you place the thief and the honest man in the same moral category? Would you put the person whose life radiates love in the same ethical category with the man whose life radiates hate? Are they equally harmful? Or equally good? Those who think so have abandoned the concept of morality and the concept of quality and sanity in human affairs.

So: You have been extremists: good, creative, loving extremists and I want to tell you I admire and respect you for it.

Moderation is the slogan of our times. But moderation never made a man or a nation great. Moderation never mastered ordeal or met a crisis successfully. Moderation never discovered anything; never invented anything; never dreamed a new dream. Moderation never wrote a poem, never built a skyscraper, never discovered a new drug, never made the first airplane, never painted a great picture, never wrote a great play, never explored a new frontier, never discovered new lands, never built a civilization, never dreamed a great religion. These great thrusts of the human imagination and spirit came out of daring to meet ordeal and need in a new way. It would be difficult to imagine Jesus as a "moderate." Difficult to imagine Leonardo da Vinci as a moderate. Imagine Gandhi as a moderate. Imagine Shakespeare or Einstein as a moderate. Imagine the young Lindbergh as a moderate: He may be one now but he was not one when he flew the Atlantic. It was the act of a daring extremist if there ever was such; but it was a creative act; not the act of a destroyer, nor the act of a hating man, nor the act of a violent man.

You have done many good things, down here in Montgomery. But one of the best, one of the most valuable, has been the fact that you have dramatized, for all America to see, that in times of ordeal, in times of crisis, only the extremist can meet the challenge. The question in crisis or ordeal is not: Are you going to be an extremist? The question is: What kind of extremist are you going to be?

Here, in Montgomery, you have decided what kind of extremist you are. You have chosen the way of love and truth, the way of non-violence and understanding, the way of patience with firmness, the way of dignity and calm persistence.

You have done this as others keep talking about moderation.

What do people mean when they use that fuzzy word, moderation? Why do the mass magazines keep talking about it? What makes the word so hypnotic? To answer that, we would have to write a history of the psychology of our times. But we can, at least, take a quick look at it:

In doing so, let us be as fair as we can. Many mean simply this: "We want to freeze things; we want to be neutral; we don't want to move a step either way. Things suit us as they are: why should we change them? Change is painful; so let's don't change." There are others, a few men of good will but with only a moderate amount of brains, who intend no harm at all when they lean back on this slogan. They mean in a vague way: "Let's be tactful; let's talk in a quiet voice; let's don't stir things up; let's try to sleep through it; then, maybe, someday we'll wake up and find that everything has settled itself." And there are a few sincere, even intelligent people who want moderation because the word, to them, means safety and security. They are too frightened to move or to think; too frightened to search for a new way to meet the challenge. It is known by all of us that our minds do not work well if we become too frightened, although they work best of all when we are a little frightened.

People behave this way in other crises, too; not simply in this one of race relations. There are people who react in a similar way when they are told they have cancer. They decide to be moderate and do nothing; to rock along and postpone thinking about it. Why? Because they are scared. And, because of their fright, they convince themselves that if they do nothing, if they take a few vitamins, maybe, the cancer will go away.

The tragic fact is, neither cancer nor segregation will go away while we close our eyes. Both are dangerous diseases that have to be handled quickly and skillfully because they spread, they metastasize throughout the organism. We have seen this happen, too often, to people who have delayed doing anything about cancer. We have also seen sick race relations metastasize throughout our country—and indeed, throughout the whole earth.

Because of the nature of both diseases—one physical, one social—because you cannot wall these problems in, you do not have time to lose with cancer; nor today, do we have time to lose in facing up to segregation, since the Supreme Court has spoken. The critical moment is on us. Now is the time to deal with it.

Why is there a crisis now? Why, after fifty years of segregation, has this way of life arrived at a critical turn?

As I see it, this is why:

The Supreme Court is the highest legal authority in our land. The Court interprets the U.S. Constitution for us. We are free men, yes; but we are not free in this country ruled by law, to interpret the law for ourselves, as Herman Talmadge says he does and claims that everybody can do. We have a freedom controlled by law; we do not live in a state of anarchy. Because this is true, when the Supreme Court speaks, we must obey. The Supreme Court has now spoken. It has said, segregation in the public schools must go because it is unconstitutional. The Supreme Court has said, in effect, that all legal segregation must go. Now: we are faced with a crisis.

But to say the Supreme Court's decision precipitated the crisis is only half a truth. It spoke its clear decision. The actual crisis came upon us because we did not listen. The ordeal became severe when the official leaders of our southern states spoke out defiantly and said they would not obey the Supreme Court's decision. After the Supreme Court spoke, it became irrelevant from the point of view of obedience to law, whether one did or did not want integration. The relevant matter was obedience to law. But these political leaders, many governors, many attorneys-general, many United States senators, defied the Supreme Court and began to try to force us to defy the Supreme Court (whether we wanted to or not). And in defying the highest law of our land and in compelling the citizens of certain states to do so, these politicians started a revolution against the legal structure on which our free and democratic government is based.

This is how the ordeal we are faced with, today, started. This is the situation we must now deal with: a very different situation from that of three years ago.

Three years ago, we had segregation. And it was the same old un-Christian, undemocratic way of life we had had for fifty years and have now; and people, colored and white, were harmed by it, as they are now being harmed. But the Supreme Court had not then challenged these old segregation statutes. Now: the situation is different. Different because legal segregation is against the law of our Nation. Different because, to maintain it, we must defy our own government.

How we deal with this critical situation, how we face up to it, will determine our moral health as individuals, our cultural health as a region, our political health as a nation; and our prestige as a leader of democratic forces throughout the world.

You know, as does everybody, how the destructive extremists are dealing with it in the South, and in the North. We are all aware of the mobs, of the Citizens Councils, of the Ku Klux Klans, of the quiet, stealthy injuries inflicted on those who want to obey their Nation's laws. But how are the rest of the white southerners dealing with it? May I trouble the waters, a little, by telling you?

A few white southerners—perhaps far more than you know—are dealing with it creatively and honestly and with courage. There are many white southerners opposed to segregation; there are millions who are not opposed to segregation but who believe it is more important to obey the law of the land than it is to have racial segregation. Some of these are speaking out: in the pulpits, in editorials. Others are meeting in small groups and probing deeply into this trouble in order to try to understand its roots. Others are taking, here and there, a bold stand. And some of these are losing their jobs, of course. But they think it is a small price to pay. They are the creative, non-violent "extremists" who are quietly, with wisdom and tact and good will, trying to bring change about as quickly as possible. They are attempting to meet ordeal with bold imagination, with skill and daring, but with sense and non-violence and sympathy for all concerned.

How about the others? The moderates? Those who are neither good extremists nor bad extremists? How about them?

Most of these so-called moderates are doing nothing. That does not mean they are not worried. It means they are suffering from temporary moral and psychic paralysis. They are working harder to be moderates than they are working to meet the crisis. They are driving straight down the middle of the road with their eyes shut and you know what happens in traffic when you do that. But they are trying to believe there is no traffic. They are telling themselves nobody is on the road but themselves. They are, you see, trying very hard not to be extremists: they are trying to be neither good nor evil.

And all the time these moderates are doing nothing or almost nothing, men like Herman Talmadge, men like Senator Eastland are shouting evil words at the top of their voices; and certain newspaper editors are writing violently against extremists—good and bad—and begging everybody to freeze and do nothing; and many of our mass magazines are belittling the good extremists and shouting that the "only way is the moderate way" ... And as they beg the millions to be "moderate," the mobs gather, and the crosses are burned, and the houses are dynamited, and the brave ones who speak out lose their jobs and nobody cares much, and the few southern writers who speak out against segregation are penalized and nobody cares much, and young preachers lose their pulpits and nobody cares much; and so it goes, on and on ... the White Citizens Councils mushroom, the Klan wakes up and wraps itself in pillow case and sheet—and Negroes and whites working for integration are threatened and penalized and cheated and confusion reigns.

But the big middle group turns away and tries not to see, whispering, "I must above all be moderate; I must not get worried; I must not mind when innocent people are hurt and brave people lose their jobs and lives. Some day it will settle itself, somehow."

And how are these moderates faring? What kind of price are they paying for their moderation, for this desire of theirs to keep things as they are?

It is a hidden price; it is not yet too obvious; but it is a high price. May I suggest what this price is?

In order to maintain the status quo, to maintain segregation as long as possible, even though the Supreme Court has spoken, in order to drive in the middle of the road, the white people of the South are giving up their freedoms. What freedoms?

Let me name a few:

a. The freedom to do right. * * *
b. The freedom to obey the law. * * *
c. The freedom to speak out, to write, to teach what one believes is true and just. We have almost lost this basic freedom now in the South. Teachers are compelled to sign statements that virtually strip them of their freedom to believe and to speak out. Penalties are imposed on those who speak out, anyway: jobs are lost.
d. And, having lost those three big freedoms, the precious ones that we Americans say we cherish, we are also losing our freedom from fear. In old Reconstruction days, white people were afraid of freed Negroes, or so they said. Today, they are afraid of each other and themselves. They fear. Front-door friends become back-door friends; some fear to be seen with a white southerner who wants to obey the law of our land. * * * And is this fear restricted to the South? Not at all: Magazines with mass circulation are timid about "offending the white segregationists." They fear, also. And this is very sad: to see our people, our proud, free people grow afraid to speak out and to act according to their conscience.

The risk is too big, people say. Young brave men say "the risk is too great. I'd like to do something but the risk is too big."

I say this:

> The time has now come when it is dangerous not to risk. We must take calculated risks in order to save our integrity, our moral nature, our lives, and all that is rich and creative in our culture. We must do what we do with love and dignity, with non-violence and

wisdom, but we must do something big and imaginative and keep doing it until we master our ordeal.

I was talking, not long ago, to a group of students in one of our white southern universities. They had kind of sneaked me in. Yes, really. They were a little afraid for people to know Lillian Smith was on the campus. So everything was hush-hush. I teased them a little, because of its absurdity. And they laughed, and I laughed. But we all felt ashamed.

Not only the loss of our freedoms but the loss of our old gallant courage is part of the high price we are paying today for our do-nothing attitude toward segregation. For while the moderates are staying silent, the bad extremists are shouting at the top of their lungs. And because it is so difficult for the young white southerner to hear anything good and creative said, because he sees so little courage, so little valor among his elders, he is losing his beliefs in the good, creative, brave way of life. One young man said to me recently, "I'd risk anything for something I believed in. I just don't think I believe in anything much, anymore."

Then I told these young people about your creative project in Montgomery. They had heard a little, of course. But they listened, these young white men and girls, and they grew excited and interested and thrilled.

Do you, here in Montgomery, realize that in helping yourselves to secure your freedom you are helping young white southerners secure theirs, too? This is a big thing. This is how the creative act works: it always helps somebody else besides you.

In dramatizing that the extreme way can be the good way, the creative way, and that in times of ordeal it is the only way, you are helping the white South find its way, too. You are giving young white southerners hope. You are persuading some of them that there is something worth believing in and risking for. You are stirring their imaginations and their hearts—not simply because you are brave and running risks but because you know that the means we use are the important thing: the means must be right; the means must be full of truth and dignity and love and wisdom.

Because you are doing this, I want to close my greeting to you by saying, Thank you. Thank you for what you are doing for yourselves and what you are doing also for the entire South. Thank you for dramatizing before the eyes of America that the question is not, "Are you an extremist?" but "What kind of extremist are you?" Thank you for showing us all that there is always a creative, good, non-violent way to meet ordeal.

Letter to the Editors, *New York Times*

On September 24, 1957, President Dwight D. Eisenhower ordered federal troops to protect the entrance of nine black students into formerly all-white Central High School in Little Rock, Arkansas. Smith sent a copy of this letter dated October 4, 1957, to Ralph McGill at the *Atlanta Constitution.* Neither paper published it.

To the editors, *New York Times*

Sirs:

There are valuable lessons for the entire country in the painful experience Little Rock is going through:

We realize, as we watch that situation, how dangerous silence can be. For it is the silence of law-abiding people that gives the green light to the mob and to the demagogue. No mob ever came out on the street until enlightened public opinion had left it. No demagogue will talk too much unless the good people talk too little.

We know the great germinal ideas have civilized mankind. But Little Rock reminds us that good words and good feelings are necessary every day. For when we become mutes, in the name of moderation, we slide toward barbarism with shocking rapidity.

We need, as individuals, to say aloud that we will not tolerate mob rule or disrespect for our Supreme Court. We need to speak out for obedience to our highest laws, for loyalty to our basic form of government. We need to remind each other that the welfare of our country comes before that of any state; that it is our President's sworn obligation to maintain the peace when law enforcement has broken down in a community, if the State fails to do so.

Some one said to me, last week, in New York, "But it was a terrible thing for the U.S. Army to have to take over." Ah . . . but you don't know how secure it makes some of us in the South feel to know if the demagogues in our state go berserk, if our officials indulge in the madness of Governor Faubus, that the good old U.S. troops will come in and protect us. Some of us southerners do not feel too well protected at the present moment. Those of us who stand up for human rights down here, who refuse to defend segregation are not too sure that in a crisis we would have the protection we might need.

We have a sense of sadness that it was necessary for troops to go into Arkansas. But we are proud to know, as a prominent woman of my town said yesterday, that President Eisenhower will move fast if law and order break down in our state.

The good, creative things happening in Little Rock can teach us some lessons, too: Here is a brave editor who stood for law and order, who was determined to keep down mob violence, doing all in his power to help protect those nine children who went to school because the Federal courts told them to go; here are a few ministers working day and night to awaken their church members' minds to the urgencies of the ordeal; here is one Congressman who made valiant appeals for law and order. But where are the others? where was Senator Fulbright? why did he not speak? where was Senator McClellan? why did he not go home and help? where were the civic leaders? the Jaycees? the Rotarians, etc? Could the trouble have been avoided if the leadership of the state had begun to work earlier and in much larger numbers? Is this good leadership, even today, saying enough?

I am not sure. It is urgent to say we must obey the law whether we like it or not. But a free, independent people want to feel that it is a reasonable law, that it will help their children and their country. If they obey the law without becoming convinced that it is both necessary and good for the nation, their resentment will, inevitably, slosh over.

Knowing this is so, it is our obligation now to persuade and to clarify. All of us must say aloud, if we believe it, that segregation is not a sacred way of life. It was not handed down as a revelation from God and cannot take precedence over our religious beliefs, our human rights, and the prestige of our nation.

I cannot see how segregation can be defended from any point of view. In the old days, it made money for the few; today it loses money for everybody. It certainly aids and abets the southern politicians but it has never made one southern child a better person or given him a better life. The segregation system itself puts rigorous pressures on us, strips us of freedom of speech, and above all else, of our freedom to do what is right.

It is an exorbitant price to pay simply to help the demagogues build themselves up. Then why do we let ourselves be exploited so cruelly?

For one reason only: the fear of intermarriage. As Senator Eastland said on television a few days ago, "Segregation is to keep down intermarriage and prevent mongrelization."

Yet, a glance at figures and facts, will show us that the system of segregation has always encouraged illegal miscegenation. This is an inevitable result, of a system where there is the master race and the slave race. But under the system of integration (a word I dislike very much) there will be much less illegal miscegenation—which is the result of irresponsible sexual adventures—and very few interracial marriages. Why? Because (a) educated girls who are accepted in the community are not interested in concubinage; (b) marriage is a social institution which carries with it heavy and public responsibilities. Few young couples in the South would want to assume the double load of marriage responsibilities and the burden of social taboos that would surround them were they to cross the racial line in marriage.

If the fear of intermarriage is the only reason people can find for their support of segregation, then how tragic, how truly mad it is to be risking so much for so little.

This kind of fear is not fear at all: it is anxiety. It is the result of mob thinking; the result of old memories that have festered in our minds; old superstitions that have not been analyzed, old taboos given us in childhood.

We, North and South, need to substitute for these sick anxieties a few real fears: fear of mob rule, fear of the breakdown of our national government, fear of the loss of America's moral prestige throughout the world, fear of moral delinquency, fear above all else of the demagogue who has certainly thrown the gasoline on the fire in Arkansas and will do it in Georgia, and other southern states—and in the North also—if we don't get busy now to prevent the mob from gathering in people's minds: where it always has its first clandestine meeting.

Rational fear is a technic of survival; once we fear the real dangers we can get to work to do something meaningful and constructive about them. And the first thing the North can do to help us is to open their magazines and TV forums to the white Southerners who oppose segregation and who know why they do so. Let them speak; only in this way will others find the courage to break their silence.

[*HH* 214–17]

From *One Hour*

One Hour is a novel of and about America in the 1950s, a time when commitment to surface conformity masked deep-seated anxieties and even the most sophisticated Americans seemed susceptible to witch hunting. Simply told, it is the story of a man falsely accused of attacking an eight-year-old girl and the subsequent violent and tragic consequences for his family and community. But there is nothing simple about this novel. The result is a series of psychological unmaskings and multiple subplots within a novel that reveals the complexity of Smith's thinking as does none of her other works. As in *The Journey*, the theme that life's meaning is to be found in the creative response to ordeal fully informs *One Hour*. Likewise, the novel may be read not only as Smith's analysis of the widespread oppression and censorship associated with the McCarthy era in general but also quite literally as her own creative response to personal ordeals involving the effects of mob thinking and mob violence.

In the late fall of 1955, while Smith was teaching for a month at Vassar College, two young white males vandalized her home on Old Screamer Mountain. Her bedroom and study were burned; the fire destroyed her personal belongings, thousands of letters, and irreplaceable unpublished manuscripts. A few weeks later she learned that paperback copies of *Now Is the Time* were being removed from bookshelves and the publisher was not filling orders. As Smith argued in vain for the urgent need for her book to be available, whites' resistance to desegregation escalated in the Deep South, and *Life* magazine printed a letter from novelist William Faulkner in which he pleaded for the North to "stop now for a moment" the efforts to end segregation forcibly. Smith's request for an opportunity to respond to Faulkner's letter was denied.

"When I want to find out something," Smith had written Horace Kallen about *The Journey*, "I write a book. It is my way of searching. Not to give the world 'answers' but to find them myself." In writing *One Hour*, Smith was again addressing her own questions about why her ideas about social change and human relationships were so strongly resisted.

The novel is dedicated to her friend Dorothy Norman, in whose Long Island home Smith spent several weeks while writing *One Hour* and through whom she met many of the liberal intelligentsia of New York City in the 1940s and 1950s. It was their world, in a way, that Smith was addressing, but the message she sent was a coded one. *One Hour* is set in a small city in the Upper South. Its principal characters, the town's educated elite, read modern authors, European classics, and modern theologians and philosophers; they listen to modern music, collect modern paintings, and meet in the local bookstore for intellectual discussions. Yet much like characters in *Strange Fruit* and *Killers of the Dream* (and like Smith herself) they are still haunted by their childhood memories. Their unacknowledged fear and anxieties render them incapable of dealing with the anti-intellectuals whose actions threaten to destroy their community.

Significantly, the "mere plot" through which Smith framed and analyzed the existential dilemmas of modern America involved not race but sex, and she was bound by the restrictions she was trying to probe. In the multilayered subplots (the stories of eight-year-old Susie; her Southern mother, Renie; and the repressed adolescent love affair between Grace and the Woman), we see the interaction of sexuality, gender, class, race, and region from which Smith could not extricate herself. Through the stories of women in the novel, and especially the stories of those characters whose experiences of gender and sexuality challenge the norm, *One Hour* becomes a study of what happened to the text and voice of a woman who, in the 1950s, wrote metaphorically and from multiple perspectives about our fear of difference (Gladney, Introduction).

Chapter 1

The most obvious thing about this hour is that it refuses to stay in its place in time. As I reach for minutes, I find years stretching back endlessly. When I search for its beginning, for that first tick of the first second, I hear only hearts beating.

And yet, for a long time, I felt compelled to keep at it: I must find that elusive beginning, I must find who started it. Surely someone was to blame for what happened! But the beginning only slipped further back each time I grasped it, and the face of the scapegoat kept changing as I formed name after name in my mind.

Baffled by this compulsive search for what could never be found, I turned to that even more futile *what if* business: What if I had never come to Windsor Hills as rector of All Saints? What if my parachute had opened ten seconds earlier when that plane crashed years ago? What if Mark had gone somewhere else to do research? Or had chosen another field of work than biochemistry? Or what if he had not seen Grace standing in the rain that night in front of the Royale Theater? Or suppose Dewey Snyder, senior warden of All Saints, had not known Charlie long ago? Suppose that small paragraph in his life had not been tucked away on a lost page: would he have pushed Mark so hard? Or what if Susan's mother had not been the daughter of old Congressman Addams—what if. . . .

There is no end to this kind of thinking which is not thinking at all, of course, but only a most human try at unraveling stone.

After Mark and Grace left Windsor Hills, after that final up-thrust of mad fury, there were nights when even the wrong questions could not find their way into words: when my mind was no more than a trashpile of faces, things, sounds: when I'd lie there unable to sleep, staring at an empty half-dark store I had never been in, watching two shadows slowly converge . . . hearing Duveen in that beauty shop saying, *Sugar, did the man do something real bad to you?* . . . hearing Miss Mabel's small, percussive feet following S.K. down the corridor at the lab . . . and as happens in a dream, suddenly only Susan was there, nowhere at first, then in my bedroom holding my crutches and saying, *Now, I'll tell you a story once upon a time once upon a time* . . . and as I listened I was emptying the .38 and Charlie was staring at a little schooner and the pages of his opera were sliding from the chair to the floor . . . and old Yellow Cat was sliding, too, back on the lumber pile and a rear door was wide open . . . and superimposed on these broken images and sounds was Grace's desperate *Andy must not be told all of it* . . . then Mark was in my study holding that dead cigarette and Grace and I were listening to what he had decided he must tell us, and snow was falling everywhere—

When the snow began, I'd turn on the light and read whatever happened to be on my bedside table. It didn't matter: Reinhold Niebuhr or Paul Tillich or a novel, or the ads in a magazine—whatever it was, I'd hang on to it, sometimes turning ten, twenty pages before one sentence would stick in my mind. But finally, the words would recover their meaning, my thoughts would somehow focus, and I would begin to think about what I was reading, or about next Sunday's sermon, or the fund-raising campaign or the altar guild's problems or camp for the choirboys—And then, All Saints Church would slowly rise up and surround me and the memories would crouch down behind its unyielding walls—and finally, I would sleep.

Now, two years have passed. The foolish persistent questions have grown almost silent; the trashpile has slowly receded and no longer keeps me awake at night. It would be easy to say, *It is all over. Try to forget it.* And I did say it for a time. Then, one night, I dreamed of Grace. It was more than dream: it was a large charity bestowed on me by an unknown donor: for she was standing in her living room, smiling, and slowly she laid her hand on Mark's shoulder and then, on mine. And I awoke, feeling a deep sense of reconciliation: feeling, there is meaning in it, somewhere. In all this insane chaos there is something that makes sense, something that links on to the next hour—if I can find it.

For the first time, I wanted to think about it: I wanted to bring it back, to set it down in words; that is, as much of it as I could: not in order to confess or to blame or to exonerate or to find lost beginnings; not just to stare, paralyzed, at the unmoving face of evil: but to shape those senseless, broken memories into something I could live with. Or perhaps another way to say it is simpler and closer to the truth: like Susan, I, too, have a story and the time has come when I want to tell it.

My name is David Landrum. I have been rector of All Saints Church for six years. My age is thirty-eight. I am a Virginian and attended the University—it is possible a few old-timers may remember me as the halfback who was called "Preacher." From college, I went to Union Theological Seminary in New York for three years; served as chaplain in the Air Force in World War II, and lost a leg in a plane crash two months before the war ended. Spent a few weeks at a rehabilitation center, then went to Boston for another year of study. From Boston, I went to our mission down in the old Bowery and from there I came to All Saints in Windsor Hills, as assistant to the rector who died a few months after my arrival.

Windsor Hills was once Windsor, a small century-old hamlet surrounded by a few fine estates, some of which had been there long before the Civil War. But as the city grew it reached out and pulled Windsor block by block and acre by acre into its boundaries: spacious homes began to appear in the hills close to All Saints Church, new streets opened up, more and more of them, and smaller houses were built. In recent years, the elaborate and expensive houses have begun drifting down toward the newly developed lake front. It is there, on Lake Shore Drive, that Dewey Snyder and his daughter, Katie, live. Scattered among the contemporary homes are the old landmarks: Miss Hortense's three-storied turreted gray house set back in its pecan grove, and the old Pottle place where Paul Pottle now lives and has his book and record shop. The shop is in the former servants' wing and has become a bit of a Left Bank for those in our town interested in ideas and books and art.

At the time of the trouble—a poor word but I hardly know how else to speak of it—I had temporary quarters in the Parish House on Arlington Road while the new rectory was being built. Across the street, the Mark Channings lived in a small house of great charm which had been designed for them by a friend who had studied with Frank Lloyd Wright. Four long blocks away, toward the west side, is the shopping center where Susan went, that Monday afternoon. Thirty minutes after she skated down our street, my life and the Channings' and other lives too numerous to name had changed direction although few were aware that anything had happened at all. Certainly, I did not know.

Chapter 7

As I watched the mirror, the door began to open. Slowly Susan's face crept in, then her body. She slid around the door without making a sound and went straight to the bathroom. I had not moved and apparently she had not seen me. In a moment or so she came out, darted to the closet, opened the door, burrowed through my suits and topcoats to the shelves back at the far end. I lost her for about a minute, then she slid out, darted over to the corner where my crutches were. From the way she grasped them I knew she was quite used to them. She skillfully lifted herself, handling them as stilts.

"Susan."

Crutches fell to the floor. Her composure was superb. She turned and looked at me.

"Did you come for something?"

"Yes, I came for Ali Baba. He's gone somewhere. I think he's here."

I decided to play it as casually as she was doing. "Why not look on the terrace?"

She opened the French windows as if she had done it a hundred times. Eased out on the terrace. Eased in. She walked slowly toward the bed. "Are you sick?"

As she came near I saw the dilated eyes, the stiff facial muscles. She was scared—a deepdown fear that might have driven a grownup into a heavy trembling or into flight—but her body was tight and rigid and completely under control.

"No. I'm reading."

"Is it a story?"

"No. It is a book written by some famous theologians."

She listened gravely. Her cat-yellow eyes were on my face. They shifted now to the leg lying on the rug. She swallowed hard. She said without taking her eyes off the leg, "Is it a nice book?"

"Yes, it is."

"Do you read bad books too? Like my mother?"

"What is a bad book?"

"Oh, just bad. You know what bad is."

She inched over for a view of the leg on the other side. "My daddy hates bad books. He hates them and he yells at her when she reads them and she says what you yelling at me for—"

Susan's eyes shifted again and found the black shoe on the foot of the limb—

"—and she gets real mad and says you're afraid to read psy-psychology that's what's wrong with you—"

Susan's eyes moved from the floor to the bed. They were searching for the shoe's mate—

"—and Daddy says what's wrong with me and she says you read page 148 and you'll see what's wrong with you—"

Susan had found it now on me—

"—and then my mama yelled at him and he said go get some fresh air Susan and do it right now I don't want you hearing such talk and my mama said you just won't face the facts of life that's what—"

"Susan," I said, "I have some good story books downstairs. Do you like *Hans Brinker*?"

Her eyes began at the toe of the black shoe on my foot, crept up my ankle, up my leg to the knee, up to my hip and then skittered across and slowly, carefully, crept down the deflated trouser leg and then back to the floor to the black shoe on the foot of the limb lying there and crept back to the bed to the deflated trouser leg—

"I like it OK," she said—

—and back to the leg on the floor and up to the straps and buckle at the top of it . . . and then she pointed at the leg on the floor . . . and at the deflated trouser leg . . . and swallowed hard and kept pointing.

There was an urgent question in that pointing finger. So I said it quickly and plainly: my leg was cut off in an accident and I wear that thing on the floor because it helps me walk.

"It is called a prosthetic limb. Or you can call it an artificial one if you want to. And it straps on and makes it easy for me to walk."

"How did it come off?" she whispered.

I had just told her but I said it again. "In the war. The plane I was in crashed. My parachute didn't open quick enough, the leg was crushed and the surgeon had to amputate it."

"Amp—"

"Yes. He operated so it would heal."

"He cut it off?"

"Yes."

"Had you been bad and he cut it off because you did something real bad?"

I explained again.

"Where is it now?"

She had me there. It was my turn to point. I pointed at the crutches. I said, "You bring them here and I'll teach you a funny trick."

She chose not to hear. She said, drawing in a deep breath, "Now—I'll tell *you* a story. I can tell stories, too."

Most of the time, when I look at Susan, I see a thin small face that has ferreted its way through impenetrable grown-up moods until it has become sharp and unpolished. Or, sometimes, I see a hard dry seed of a face that has never sprouted. But now, it was as if it had only one skin and suddenly it lit up inside like a stage and the bell was ringing and the play was about to begin:

She said, "Once upon a time a pros-prosthetic limb went out for a walk. And while it was walking along real politely, hopping and skipping now and then but not too much, it met a real leg that had been amputated by a surgeon. The prosthetic limb stopped and took off its glasses and said, Well well! I did not expect to find you here taking a walk. I thought you had been buried in a box in the ground and couldn't get out. And here you are! And the real leg said, Here I am—so what! This is a free country and I can go for a walk if I want to. If you want to, ha, said the prosthetic limb, if you want to. But you can't want to because you're dead, that's what!"

Then she laughed. I thought she was coming to pieces, she laughed so hard. And I was afraid, suddenly, I might come to pieces, too. For I was not seeing Susan, I was looking at a Thing I had not seen in eleven years: I was in England, forty miles outside London. Early dawn. The night had been quiet and empty with only a wind blowing through it. All night long it blew, an easy relaxed wind, but somehow it set the doors in my childhood banging . . . and I had not slept. No planes had come over for three nights. Better sleep while you can but I couldn't sleep. Now it was dawn: a July dawn, a black-green wet cool blurry hour and I went out for a walk. There was a blurry house over in a meadow and I heard a sheep's bell somewhere, a thin tinkling somewhere along the fog drift, then it came: the plane, abrupt, bearing down. This time, somehow, I did not fall to the ground. I stood there, I didn't care or maybe I had gone too far into the past to scramble back to the present, so I stood there and let it happen as a cow might have done. I simply did not react: object in the sky, siren in the village, scream, roar. Back in the meadow was that house, not far. I didn't know it had been hit, am not sure it was a direct hit. It was there, solid; something a man had built, a place people slept in and ate in and made love in and quarreled in and walked out of and back to—and then it came to pieces: walls and roof and beds and chairs and people rose up and flattened down. I don't know how long I stood in the road. My head whanged and my bones ached and I felt I was bleeding somewhere but I wasn't, later I found I wasn't. I must have walked over to the rubble and stuff and the smoke there was smoke but no fire it must have been a lamp and maybe the falling plaster put it out before it burned much. I suppose I thought maybe I could help somebody. But there was nobody to help. I found fragments—that was all. I kept pushing broken things around, turning them over, looking... and there was half a room left one half gone the other there, and on a piece of a chair was a doll, a whole doll, and as I came up to it, its face disintegrated before my eyes into bits of dust—as if it had held together only until somebody could share its final shame. It is one of my most bothersome memories for I am not sure the doll was on the broken piece of chair, I'm just not sure. But now, suddenly, I saw it again—and I knew I had better shift the present scene to get rid of that distant event. I had to and I did.

"I'll tell you another one," she was saying.

Oh no you won't. "No. We're going to have a piece of chocolate cake. We'll have it down in my study. You run along now and I'll bring it."

"But—" Her face suddenly caught on and became a greedy kid's face. "OK. I like chocolate. Where is it?"

"It's in the kitchen but you run on and I'll bring it downstairs to the study and we'll have a tea party."

She did not budge. She stood there waiting for the big scene to bang out its first note. I felt trapped. I sat up and slid over to the edge of the bed. Her eyes were on the leg on the floor. She wanted to see it hop off the floor and join its mate or maybe its mate would hop off the bed and join it or—Then, as I was trying to figure this one out, another horrible thought occurred to me. Suppose her mother were to come looking for Susan and found her upstairs, like this, with me. Then suppose Susan were to tell Renie that I had tried to—or suppose Renie were to decide herself that—or suppose Neel came in—or suppose my mother came into the nursery and found me—Did I actually think that? About the nursery? No. I felt it—the way you feel a big wave wash over you.

I was in a heavy sweat. But once more I tried to play it the casual way.

"You go downstairs to the study and wait. I'll bring the cake. You can have a Coke and I'll have coffee."

"I'll have coffee, too."

"OK. But you run on now and look for Ali Baba. He's probably in the big chair this minute. I'll be down soon."

"The story is real nice," the temptress said sweetly. "It is about a pink and a blue and a purple parasol that went walking one day just like three mushrooms—"

She almost caught me: I was about to say it, *But mushrooms don't walk.* Instead I said, "I'm sure it is. Now get out, Susan!" I yelled the words at her and she ran quickly as if I had threatened to shoot her down. I was startled by her loss of poise, the quick terror on her face. I sat there after she was gone, unable to move. Disoriented by a child's face. By my having torn—Where had I seen terror in a child's face before? In a war, yes; in bombed cities . . . but where in time of peace—in a mirror—what mirror—what peace—I wished I knew whether I had actually seen the doll disintegrate or was it something I made up in post-surgery delirium, and what was Susan actually up to—was she looking for the cat—was she looking everywhere for something she could never find?

From Chapter 26

There are two or three thousand books in Jane's library and always I find a few interesting ones I have missed on other visits. I walked around the room, looking over shelves of poetry, novels, history, psychoanalysis, drama—And then, near the cabinet, I came upon some old camp brochures. I figured quickly: Grace must have been here in 1941 or '42. I searched through the pile until I found booklets of those years, and turned the pages of pictures hoping to find her. There she was, dancing: the pose so characteristic that I spotted her before I recognized her face. Young and sad—hair long at that time and hanging loose and her eyes on the tennis court and there she was gay and sure as if nothing in the world had ever troubled her. Another Grace. Always another and another. Young one day, terribly old the next; dreaming . . . painting . . . kneeling and talking gravely with her young son . . . and then again, dancing with a wild and terrible strength as if her energy could endure forever . . . or at a party, after the drink she should not have taken, telling her wacky stories, very funny and very sad; and then another time, quiet, thoughtful, letting you see her well-informed mind, talking of important concerns; or again, off somewhere, in that imagination of hers, forgetting to wash the dishes, stacking them up, forgetting—until you wondered how Mark put up with it.

One day, during the trouble, I went over to see her. Returned a record, I think, or a book. She was in the living room, standing near the glass wall that faces the trees and ravine below. Near it, on the narrow terrace, they had planted those tulips. She turned when I called to her and I joined her at the window. We did not say much. We talked about the old beech down below, which had lost its leaves early this year. Then I said, "Grace—I keep trying to see its beginning; how it started, how it built up to this. Mark thinks I'm wrong to ask; he sees it as sheer accident; do you?" And then, she had looked at me gravely, it was one of her "old" days when she seems a million years old. "We caused it," she said. I asked what she meant by that. "There is something in us, Dave, that caused it; part of it; not anything Mark did but something we are and may not know we are." I felt she was wrong and said so. But now, as I remember it, as I see all that happened from that first day, that Monday afternoon, I think she was right, if by "we" she meant all of us.

I went out for a walk. It was too cold to enjoy it and I soon came in, still thinking of her. I could move an inch or so from the dream—the two dreams if they were two—but I could not get away from her. I did not want to think of her—it was Mark I had felt concerned about two nights ago. But now . . . well, she went along with me on that walk. And I let myself remember: her face in Baltimore, the agony I had felt when I could find no words to help them; and the next morning when I went out to tell her goodbye, in her mother's garden: She was standing by a shrub staring at it, and when I drew near she looked at me without changing expression. I could only say her name; and then I kissed her forehead and held her cold hand for a moment and left her, and joined Mark who was waiting in the car to take me to the airport. When we arrived, the plane was in. We had little time to talk more—we had said nothing on the way except the most superficial of comments—but now I asked him when he expected to be back in Windsor Hills and he told me he would stay in Baltimore a few days longer. "I need to get back to the lab," he said, "but I am not sure when I can leave." And Grace? "I don't know. I don't see how she can come back. She can't possibly go through the rest of it." Then I told him that the Newells had withdrawn the charges, last Monday, and there would be no trial. They were pushing the passengers along to the plane, and we were suddenly separated, and I was glad, for I did not want to see his eyes after I said it.

The whole place was full of her! She had spent so much time here. After Mark returned from the Japanese prison, they had built their summer cabin less than a quarter of a mile away from the camp. They and Andy had come up hundreds of times, going back and forth from library to cabin to tennis courts, to the pool, up to the peak, down to the gulch where Andy would spend hours searching for quartz and amethyst crystals for his rock collection. She had often sat in this library reading, or listening to records—And it was here, on one of these rugs that she lay that day weeping, after the Woman's plane had crashed, while memories rolled over her like a tidal wave.

She had told me of those memories long ago. One April afternoon when we were both in a quiet, retrospective mood:

I had been working on my sermon and had grown restless. I had chosen a tough theme: *Man's encounter with inner space*—one of a series I was doing on Religion and Twentieth-Century Science.—Not so much to bring insight to my congregation as to find some kind of intellectual clarity for myself. I left the typewriter and went to the window. The dogwood on her lawn was blooming, the forsythia and tulips near the rock garden were blooming—and it was raining. I suddenly wanted somebody to talk with, not to preach to. And in a moment, I saw her car turn into their driveway. I thought, I'll return a book: you can always do that. I picked up a book of theirs, I don't remember what, and went over. She was in the living room unpacking two records her mother had sent her: the work of a young composer whose name I had not heard before. Would I stay and listen to them? Andy was at Scout meeting—she was not going for Mark until five-forty-five—we could have some coffee—

She went to the kitchen to make it. I intended to follow her but as I walked through the dining room I stopped and looked at the fresco. I had often looked at it: its giant smoky shapes and curiously unstable planes had a way of holding you. And I asked her to tell me, if she would, why she had called it *Lost Memory*. It was a phrase which held meaning for her, I knew, for she had used it, also, as the name of a dance.

When she came in with the coffee, she sat on a stool near the fire and told me about her and the Woman. Relaxed and easy, most of the time; tense, now and then, as words brought back old feelings, and at these moments she would stop talking and push her shaggy hair out of her eyes and rub that left hand the way she does when fear is sliding through her veins. Then she would look at me and smile: and it was exactly as if we had eased one door shut and opened another.

"She was tall and beautiful—and could do everything: swim, ride, shoot, paint. . . ." Grace smiled. "Saying that is saying nothing. I know. It was not her skills, nor her beauty. It was her quality of imagination that made her extraordinary. Perhaps I am wrong here, too. I won't try to analyze her too much, nor me. What draws you to another human being? I don't know. It is like asking, What makes you want to look at a painting hour after hour after hour . . . she was not real, in one sense—as music is not real—" She drew in a deep breath. "I won't try it any more. She opened up the world for me, I'll leave it at that. There was an old trail at camp: I had hiked down it a hundred times but I had never seen it until the Woman showed it to me: I had never felt a rock becoming a rock through a million years changing changing . . . I had never felt time before . . . a scarlet branch of a sourwood tree—I had never seen what light could do to it. There were Indian pipes creeping out of the ground and once she knelt beside them and whispered, Come! And I knelt by her and looked at those smoky, translucent things—I didn't know what they were, not flowers nor plants, not mushrooms, not lichens—they were just themselves and they seemed miraculous. Everything had just been born: clouds, thunderheads—we'd lie looking up into them and once she said she wanted to fly through one, sometime; and I said, Wouldn't it be too dangerous, could she do it? And she had smiled and said, The trying is the fun. And I knew she was not afraid of death, that she never considered it, and it seemed to me that maybe she had come from somewhere else and didn't belong to the human race, for all of us were afraid of death. Caves . . . she loved to tell me about the caves of the world so many of which are full of man's brooding paintings and sculptures. People see so little, she'd say, in the bright light but there's a dark rim: everything has it, everybody has it, and that is where the strange and the wonderful happens. And the other: I learned from her about tenderness and passion."

And then camp closed and Grace went back to school and a doctor came and told the girls about the facts of life. And she learned during that lecture on "normal love" that this amazing creature who had seemed to her to have come out of a myth, who did not quite belong in the ordinary world, was nothing but a homosexual. "I struggled to hold on to my image of her, to cling to the validity of what I had experienced, but I couldn't. I fought that word the doctor had used, but it whipped me after two or three weeks, lying awake at night looking, listening to Her, then remembering what the doctor had said. My father was a doctor, too, and I felt this one must know; if he said what he said, it must be so. Things fell inward on me, I suppose I was ill, I don't know. Anyway, Mother and Dad decided Key West might be a good place to go, maybe I needed a change. We played on the beach, Mother and I, and fished; she was very sweet; if she knew what was happening inside her daughter she couldn't talk about it, nor could I. So we played together, took sun baths, and all the time I kept thinking of Her . . . and of the old trail, and all she had told me and it seemed good and true and wonderful, then in a split second, it seemed ugly and dirty and horrible. It would zigzag like that, day and night, day and night—

"One morning we were on the beach. I began to wade through the seaweed—hating the slimy stuff on my legs but you had to go through it to get to the good part of the beach—the water was deep deep blue and warm and there were fishing boats, some near, some far out . . . a white cruiser was out farther than the others and I kept looking . . . looking . . . it was moving . . . out to sea . . . growing smaller smaller smaller . . . and then, it was gone. And all this was gone, too."

"The memory?"

"In a sense, yes: the conflict, the knowing and not-knowing. The shell lay there in my mind—I could have told you her name, that she had been a counselor at camp, but the living part of it was gone. The pain had left, and the wonder of it; the mystery, the ecstasy were gone and the love I had felt. The new way of looking at Indian pipes and caves and thunderheads and rocks and poetry stayed, but I forgot who had opened my eyes so I could see. I existed, she existed, but the relationship did not exist."

She looked in the fire a long time. "Strange . . . two people make something, create it together—and then, it is gone and they are still here."

"And that was all?"

"Not quite. Years later, I went to Annapolis to a dance. My date and I dropped in somewhere for a drink. I saw this marvelous-looking woman with an officer from the flying field. As I passed her, I recognized her. I don't think she saw me. I didn't feel anything—I vaguely knew she had been a counselor at the camp I had gone to and I had had a silly sort of crush or something, but though this much came back, nothing else came—no feeling, no real remembering. But I saw the men and women around her reacting as people had done at camp.

"After college, after studying in New York, I came down to be a counselor in Jane's camp.

"Then it happened: I picked up the newspaper and saw Her on the front page. She was standing by a plane. Not the plane that crashed, of course; but a plane she had often taken up. Below, was the story of her going down at sea. I was on my cot in the cabin with the children. It was Quiet Hour: six of them on their cots, reading, wriggling, writing letters, trying to make each other talk and laugh. I eased off the cot, slipped out and began to run—I didn't know where I was running and didn't care, I was just running—And then a hand caught my arm. It was Jane. I was at the end of the hill. She must have been walking out there. She led me to the library and told me to sit down. She gave me a cigarette.

"And suddenly, I was crashing through to age fifteen again: back to the magic and mystery and terror and ecstasy—and the horror and the cruelty and the sweetness and beauty. Crying, as memories pushed back on me.

"I don't remember what I said to Jane except I told her I had loved this woman and it had seemed a wonderful thing to me—until I discovered it was evil and that I had been seduced; and then I had forgot it and now—

"I remember lying on the rug in front of that stone fireplace sobbing like a child, and Jane talking: I didn't hear some of it but finally this came through: she was saying, It is the quality of a relationship that counts; easy to paste a good label on something spurious and cheap, easy to paste a bad one on something fine and delicate—When she said this simple, obvious thing it burst on me like a revelation.

"I hushed my sobs and listened. She was saying: Not one incident, not one point in your life but the whole structure is what counts: what you are moving toward and away from—what you are forming altogether; not this mistake or that sin or virtue but your whole way of looking, the depth of your longing, the vision you hold to—"

"And I lay there, seeing the twisting trail and dreamlike rocks and gray translucent Indian pipes pushing out of the ground and the thunderhead in the sky and the scarlet sourwood—and all of it began to come together, to find its form: the harsh and tender and good and evil, and my heart was breaking because I could not tell Her now what it meant to me."

I gave Grace a cigarette. She smoked for a while and then she said, "And so, one day, I began to paint *Lost Memory*."

"You painted it then?"

"No. While the real memory was lost. The year before she killed herself, I did the first small canvas. And, long afterward, when we built this house, I did the fresco for Mark because he asked me to."

Mark....

I was remembering that evening when they first knew they were in love and she had felt she must tell him about it. Suppose each of us told the one we loved about the far-away memory that means most to us... what chaos! And yet, the memory is there—even though we may have pushed it far back—and sooner or later the ones close to us, and sometimes those far away, will collide with it. It is inevitable. For memories don't stay where we push them; they are travelers who are likely to appear anywhere, any time, speaking a strange language. (I tried to amuse myself with the thought but I was not amused; I saw too plainly, suddenly, how I spend my life colliding with memories and dreams—my own and those of all the others: collision after collision—)

I was staring in the fire now, not seeing much there and certainly not thinking: in that relaxed, unconcentrated mood when images... memories... ideas... float across your mind much as they must have done when you were a child: Brother Lawrence in that kitchen cleaning and praying and feeling the Presence of God within him... Grace holding tight to her fifteen-year-old memory as you hold what you prize and yet, not sure she is right, not sure, even now—She had learned the trick of pushing something that hurt her, back back back—and she had learned how to accept it again; two technics: which was she using now with Andy? I was sorry I had thought it.

I got up and brought in another log. Poked the fire and swept up the hearth. Mark: would he go to his new job soon? Or was he pushing everything out and holding to those experiments? Strange... he had never talked to me about his years in prison camp. How well did I know this man whom I loved and believed I knew so intimately? I wasn't sure . . . I saw him in my study; pressing out that cigarette . . . saw him with Eliot and the others at the cabin—

. . . Now the Woman . . . coming back . . . walking along that old trail I had never seen but which I saw now—She had begged the sea to open for her so she could be lost forever, and it had opened and closed again and there was no trace of her left. And yet, she was here in this library, with me whom she had never known. . . . I tried to see her, to understand this girl Odysseus—she seemed like that to me—who had left home to discover the dark Rim of Things—dark not with evil but dark because human eyes close when they glance that way, for mystery and wonder are dazzling and most eyes cannot bear to look. The Wanderer . . . and then, after wandering so long, after looking in caves and thunderheads and all the rest of it, did she grow a little homesick for the ordinary and the "normal"? was that why she tried to fall in love with someone who meant Coming Back Home? We shall never know. Tried to come back—and crashed, saying "tell Bill he has been wonderful," crashing gallantly. And then, this twentieth-century idea came to me: Couldn't a psychoanalyst have straightened her out? Couldn't he? Would you want her "straightened out"? would you?—And now I was thinking of Jean . . . *You know how normal I am, Dave . . . the abnormal frightens me so . . . you know this, Dave. . . .*

. . . remembering Grace's painting now: the miracle of it: coming out of the same part of her where the stricken memory lay; feeding on its death and returning to earth as its resurrection. And now I was thinking—as the Woman must have done so often—of that enormous place we call the unconscious whose dimensions never end. I try desperately, sometimes—maybe all of us do—to shut it off because I see a stiff graveyard down there whose corpses never quite die and this frightens me, although it shouldn't. But it does and I pile everything in the world against the door sometimes, forgetting all the rest that is there: the uncreated paintings and sculptures and music, the unsaid poetry and undiscovered ideas—the billion seeds swelling in the darkness . . . ready to sprout, ready to grow—

From Chapter 31

For days, I have read again and again what I have written down here, pondering it, remembering so much that did not come back at the right moment but now hovers on the edge of my mind, echoing, echoing. . . . I said when I began that I wanted to find its meaning, its form. I see now that its meaning is still in the making, its form is still being shaped by the living: For the rest of us are still here and this experience lies, even now, only half formed in the hard rock of our awareness.

I am not sure what will come next for we are still changing it: each time we feel one small movement of compassion or mercy or fear or hate, each time we glimpse a deeper level or turn away from the new vision, each time we find our courage or lose it, we are forming this hour. Someday, Katie with her talent which Charlie thought more real and sure than his may cease her mourning for the loss of his music and begin to create her own. Someday, perhaps I—But this is guessing and hoping. I am not sure what is ahead: or where the next hour lies: except I know it is hidden somewhere in this one, among quiet and noisy and uncounted possibilities. And we, the living, will find it or fail to, as we continue to shape this small piece of time we call our own.

The Crisis in the South

Throughout the mid- and late 1950s, when not writing *One Hour*, Smith devoted a great deal of energy to speaking and writing on behalf of the emerging nonviolent civil rights movement in the South. Characteristically, she had worked to increase whites' awareness of the destructiveness of racial segregation and had especially urged young people to become active in working for social change. Consequently, when in February 1960 college students in Greensboro, North Carolina, staged sit-in demonstrations to desegregate public lunch counters at Woolworth and other chain stores, Smith was ready and eager to support the students in the sit-in movement spreading throughout the South. Despite a recurrence of cancer and another round of radiation treatments in the spring of 1960, Smith accepted multiple invitations to speak to students on college campuses and to church groups, both to encourage support for the student activists and to help white students and community leaders understand and overcome the nature of their fears and resistance to change (*HH* 238–39). The following speech was given at the All Souls Unitarian Church in Washington, D.C., and later published in the *New Leader*, September 19, 1960.

'What the South is now facing is of great moral and political significance, and it involves not only students but all of us'

The South and its people are facing a spiritual crisis. We have been in ordeal a long time and have had outbursts of violence and localized crises again and again: in Little Rock, in Montgomery, Clinton, Nashville, Tallahassee and in other spots in the South.

But what we are now facing is not localized and cannot be. It is something different, something that has not happened in this country before; it has a new quality of hope in it and is, I believe, of tremendous moral and political significance. Somehow it involves not only students but all of us, and there is a growing sense that what we say or fail to say, do or fail to do, will surely shape the events that lie ahead.

This hour of decision—and certainly it is that for the South—was precipitated on February 1 by an 18-year-old Negro student, a freshman in a college in Greensboro. He had seen a documentary film on the life of Gandhi; he had heard about Montgomery and the non-violent protests made there; he had probably listened to Martin Luther King—certainly he knew about him; he had his memories of childhood and its racial hurts; and he had his hopes for the future. But millions of Southerners, young and old, of both races, have had similar experiences. What else was there in this young student that caused him to be capable of his moment of truth? Courage, of course, imagination and intelligence—and enough love to respond to Gandhi's love of mankind, and enough truth-seeking in his mind to realize the meaning of Gandhi's teaching of non-violence and compassion as well as their redemptive, transforming power.

Was this all the young man had? No, there was more: an indefinable, unpredictable potential for creating something new and lasting and doing it at the right time. Every leader and every hero, and many artists and scientists, possess this talent for fusing their lives with the future. And yet, I doubt that the young man knew he possessed this special quality, or knows it even now.

In some strange way, however, his thoughts, memories and hopes came together and he talked about what was on his mind with three young friends. And a short time afterward, the four of them went on their historic journey to a Greensboro 10 cent store.

From this small, almost absurd, beginning, so incredibly simple and unpretentious that we Americans—accustomed to the power of big names and money and crowds and Madison Avenue and Gallup polls—can scarcely believe in it, there started the students' non-violent protests which have caught the imagination of millions of us.

Why are we stirred so deeply? What is it we feel? What are we hoping for? I cannot answer for you. For me, it is as if the *No Exit* sign is about to come down from our age; it is almost as if a door is opening in a wall where there was no door. The older generations, to which I belong, have found decisions hard to make, they have wobbled this way and that in their beliefs, they have postponed the right action until the right time for it has passed. And suddenly, completely unexpectedly, the students' sit-in protests began, spreading from college to college, school to school. It is exciting to watch them discover a freedom and purpose within themselves that they have not experienced in the outside world, to see them acting out, actually living, their beliefs in human dignity, democracy and the redemptive power of love and non-violence, and going to jail for their beliefs.

What has impressed me most has been the way they have done this, and their attitude toward the white race. By their acts they are saying something like this: "Look, I may be Negro and you may be white; but all of us are human beings; and because we are human, we have moral and intellectual potentialities. We can create our future, we don't have to be prisoners of our grandfathers' past. We who are young can free ourselves—you and me, white and Negro. Freedom is not an object: Freedom is a relationship that each man creates with his world; freedom is a dialogue between man and his God; freedom is the sacred ground on which the human spirit lives. It can't be divided up; it is ours, together, or it is nobody's."

Thoughts like these are forming in the students' minds as they live out their new purpose. Groping, slow words, maybe; faltering sentences, perhaps, for the language of the human spirit is complex and subtle, though its grammar is structurally simple and strong.

Wait now, you say: You are giving these students quite a build-up. Do you actually think they are so extraordinary? No, I don't. I think they are probably quite ordinary young people in most ways. They are extraordinary only in their awareness that the hour we live in is an hour calling for courage and commitment, and they are making their commitment, and in doing so they are finding their courage. Actually, I suspect they were pretty shaky, those first ones who walked in to the stores with their books and their Bibles to make their protest. They probably didn't have one grand, noble thought in their heads; they had made their decision in all earnestness and they were going through with it, and they were probably praying that they'd find the strength just to sit there—just sit there, that's all. But afterward, they must have felt an exaltation, a sudden rush of both pride and humility.

We who have accused the young of hungering for security, of not really caring about the big important things of the spirit, who have called the intellectual ones "beatniks" and the livelier ones "rock-'n'-rollers," may have been right four years ago, or even last year. But we are not right today. For what these students are doing in the South is awakening students in the North and the Midwest to action, and something is happening.

But even as I say this, I know that this spiritual renascence can be snuffed out by us—by our apathy and stupidity and lack of imagination. I know police measures can become so cruel and massive and overwhelming that the students may not be able to take it. I am aware that a terrific effort will be made by certain powerful groups in the South who have close economic ties with the North to smother the movement by hushing the national press and the TV networks. I know that a few men in strategic places, by saying irresponsible things, can throw pretty big obstacles in the students' path. There will be accusations of the most vicious kind, idiotic and dangerous misinterpretations and persistent persecution.

But I believe the movement *can succeed* if enough of us have the imagination to see its significance and its creative possibilities and to interpret these to others who do not see; and if we give the students the moral support and the money they are going to need. There is a tremendous power in the non-violent protest that the sensitive Southern conscience and heart will find hard to resist. But even so, the students may have to struggle a long time. They will need friends during their ordeal. Americans in other sections can help them and should, for this concerns not only the South, it concerns the entire nation and the nation's relationships with the rest of the world. It also concerns each person's relationship with himself and his beliefs.

But there are some things that only good, responsible, decent Southerners can accomplish. Only they can create a new climate of opinion in which mob violence and the hoodlums and the police and the White Citizens Councils can be controlled; and they can do this only by speaking out. To speak out for law and order is not enough today; there is a higher law which we Southerners must take a stand on that concerns justice, mercy, compassion and freedom of the spirit and mind. Thousands of us must also speak out against segregation as a way of life; not simply racial segregation but every form of estrangement that splits man and his world into fragments. But will Southerners do it? I don't know. I hope so but I don't know. They let Little Rock happen when they could have kept that debacle out of the history books simply by taking a stand for the right things at the right time.

Our responsible people are silent not because they are in the minority: They outnumber the demagogues and Klans and hoodlums and crackpots 20-to-1. In their hands are the communications media, the power and the money, the education and the techniques to create an atmosphere of vigorous, healthy-minded concern where good words can be heard and good acts carried through, an atmosphere where people can plan, think clearly and find ways to do what is right.

Why, then, are they silent? Why do they evade their responsibility at this time of crisis?

Is it fear? I don't think so. I think it is anxiety. There is a vast difference between the two.

It is difficult to analyze briefly a complex state of mind, but let me try: We white people of the South think of ourselves as free, but we are chained to taboos and superstitions, tied to a mythic past that never existed, weakened by memories and beliefs that are in passionate conflict with each other. The tragedy of the South lies just here: Segregation has made psychic and moral slaves of so many of us. And we are torn apart inside by a conflict that never lets up: How can a man believe simultaneously in brotherhood and racial discrimination? In human freedom and forced segregation? How can he fight Communist dictatorship and surrender himself to the dictatorship of an idea like White Supremacy? How can he do and think these things and fail to see the moral inconsistency, the intellectual absurdity of his position?

But many Southerners can. And some of them are educated men who think of themselves as the community's moral and civic leaders. But the psychic result has been that a deep anxiety possesses them and they feel that any change would be only for the worse. When they are asked why they fear the crumbling of segregation they cannot tell you that what they really fear is the crumbling of the walls inside them. Instead, they talk about intermarriage. It makes poor sense but they think it explains their acute anxiety.

But there are other Southerners who have changed, who don't like discrimination, who don't believe in segregation. And I am often asked: Why don't they say so? Some are speaking out, of course, hundreds of them; others want to but are afraid they will do "more harm than good." Here, once again, we have the result of a rigid, inflexible training in early childhood, given to us during a time of panic and dread. I was born at the turn of the century when the first segregation statutes were being put on the law books of the Southern states. During my first 10 years there were a thousand lynchings in the South. It was in this atmosphere of terror and brutality, of internal and external disorder, that we were taught our lessons in segregation. No wonder so many Southerners of my age cling to it. We were told as children never to question it, never to talk about it. This silence which is today so puzzling to others is a built-in silence; its foundations go down to babyhood, to our mother's hushed whispering; there is a hypnotic quality about such learning and only the rebellious mind, the critical intelligence or the loving heart can hope to defy it.

The truth is that our parents and grandparents paid a terrible price for a security which they believed segregation could give them. When they permitted the system to be set up, they did not foresee that emergency measures would be frozen permanently into state laws. They did not dream that segregation would become a ritual so sacred that it would be given priority over the teachings of Christ in our churches. They did not know a time was ahead when the politician would exert more moral force than the preacher. But the price they paid for security was exorbitant and their children are still paying today. For they have been as surely injured in mind and spirit by segregation as have Negro children: Both have been warped; both have been kept from a free, creative life; both find it difficult to be courageous, strong individuals who can defy conformity and find their own responses to the world.

But some white Southerners are speaking out; and more would if they could hear others do so. There is a serious lack of communication between liberal Southerners. We can't hear each other speak because there are so few places where the person who opposes segregation can speak in the South. The local radio and TV forums have not as yet been opened up to many white Southerners who oppose segregation, nor have the national forums been opened to them. Again and again, on TV, the nation sees Senator Herman Talmadge or Senator James Eastland or other racial demagogues and hears them say the same old things they've said for 10 years about mongrelization. Why can't we have a change? There are eloquent and courageous young ministers in the South who oppose segregation and have something fresh to tell the country. This would give encouragement to those in the South who have never heard any Southerner state in a public speech that he is opposed to segregation. This is one way to help break the taboo of silence.

Once the silence is broken the South will change quickly, more quickly than we think. There are so many ready for change: thousands of ministers who have taken a good stand; hundreds who preach strong eloquent sermons against segregation; there are close to 100,000 women in Georgia willing to give up segregation in all public places including the schools; and there are hundreds of them working hard every day to rid our state of a system that has hurt everybody. These women are informed; many of them have thought and studied and examined their own souls and have given their children better training in human relations than my generation had.

It is important for us to break the word "South" into a thousand pieces: not only geographically, culturally, sexually, vocationally and psychologically, but also into generations. There are gradations of opinions in all of these groups, and gradations of moral strength. What is terrifying to the older generation doesn't bother the young students; the Southerner over 40 is likely to suffer from taboos the 18-year-old does not feel. The poor and ignorant often feel a psychic and social hunger to belong "to the white race" as if it were a club, while the more sophisticated, the more economically and culturally secure, do not have this need; their sense of "belonging" has come to them in other ways.

And too, differences go beyond the groups; the South is full of individuals each with his own ideas—this, despite our somewhat totalitarian training and our one-party system. People may act the same under pressures and not feel the same or believe the same or have the same values. The lumping of all Southerners together by those who speak and write of us is a false thing and makes for identifications which we don't feel.

These differences I have been speaking of are potentially good; this actual lack of conformity in feelings and beliefs keeps the door open. All that our Southern people need is something that will fire their imagination and stir their good feelings, until leaders can rise up and open the way. That is why I have such hopes for the students' non-violent protests. If white students join with Negro students, their mutual experiences, self-discipline and philosophical training will create a fine reservoir of new leadership for the South. We cannot change the South until we change our leadership and ourselves. As a region, we can have our moment of truth only when we begin to think of ourselves as persons, when, by taking the walls down within us, we open up our imaginations and our hearts. Then it will come. And it will be a healing time for us and perhaps for the whole world, for we are so sensitized one to another, so closely related, with the common purpose of creating a future, that whatever brings wholeness to us as persons will bring wholeness to others across the world.

Perhaps, even now, our moment of truth is near; let's pray that it does not turn into a time of sin and error.

Are We Still Buying a New World with Old Confederate Bills?

Lillian Smith gave the following speech at Mount Moriah Baptist Church in Atlanta, Georgia, at the open meeting of the Regional Students Nonviolent Movement (later known as SNNC), October 16, 1960. It was reprinted in the Fall 2012 issue of the *Georgia Review*.

I am glad to see old friends again; and proud to speak to this group of students. Why am I proud? Because it is good to see courage showing itself in our South: good to see the young running risks for important things; good to see thousands of students choosing the hard way for that is the only way our South can be freed from its ancient fears and tyrannies. I regret that there are so few southern white students, as yet, working side by side with you; I am sorry they have not yet realized that segregation is their enemy also; that it harms their minds and souls as much as it does yours; that it blocks their freedom and their future as severely as it does yours. When they do see they will not be afraid to do their share; they too have courage; it is vision they do not, as yet, possess.

It is this future, yours and theirs, this new world in the making that I want to talk about. What is it? Where is it coming from? Who is creating it? Who is paying for it? What kind of currency are we using in this great transaction?

Let's begin to answer these questions by taking a look, first, at our South, and ourselves:

Ever since I remember, southern politicians have been trying to put over a Big Deal: They have been trying to buy a new life for the people, a new world, with old Confederate bills. And they don't seem to know why it can't be done. They do not, even now, understand why the old Confederate bills they flash around are not real currency. They have not learned a bitter lesson I learned, when I was six years old.

Let me tell you that story: We children found an old trunk in the attic; we opened it and to our delighted astonishment saw it was chock-full of money; paper money, piles of it. We felt rich; richer than the Rockefeller children or any children. We knew we could now buy anything we wanted. So we stuffed a basket full of the bills and raced down to the drugstore. We marched in, my brother and I—aged 8 and 6—and asked for five pounds of candy. "We have lots of money," we said. "We're coming every day and buy five pounds of candy." Then we showed the man our basket of bills. There they were: hundreds of Confederate bills. He looked at the basket, picked up a bill, dropped it, shook his head. Then he said a devastating thing: "That money," he said, "is not worth a penny."

My brother did not give in. He said, "We have a whole trunk full at home. How about that? I can run bring you another basket full." It is hard for an eight year old—and some grown people—to realize that a lot of nothing is worth no more than a little of nothing.

But the man in the drugstore knew. He said, "Son, if you had a roomful it wouldn't be worth a cent. That money won't buy anything." I was easy with tears in those days and I let them come. The sound of my heartbreak filled the drugstore. It was too much for the manager. He scooped up some candy and filled our hands and then told us to go home and burn that money. He said, "Don't keep it around; it will mix you up; get you all mixed up about everything."

I let out a new howl. "I thought money was *always* money," I said.

"Money is not money, sister, unless it is based on something real. This is old Confederate money and there is no Confederacy. See? It has no value because there's *nothing back of it*."

That was the day my education began. But our southern politicians? Well, they weren't there that day and they have not yet learned this basic lesson. They are still trying to buy a future for the South, and for our country, with currency that is worthless: with ideas that have no validity, opinions that are not based on facts, values that are not human and Earth-size. They keep flashing the old bills around and they still believe they'll get their bargain.

But how can they believe this? How can intelligent men, in this tumultuous, changing decade of the Sixties, tell our people that we must hold on to segregation, we must cling to old spurious fears, we must cling to archaic defenses! How can they solemnly declare, in this age of nuclear weapons, that the greatest danger facing the South and this Nation is the danger that a few white people and a few Negroes may possibly marry each other!

How can any man in his senses say these things—when he can turn on TV and see for himself how Khrushchev works. How can he believe this is a white man's world when all he has to do to learn the score is count the Afro-Asian votes in this United Nations. Surely he knows, surely every American knows, today, that these votes can be and will be the deciding factor in any world issue. How then can our politicians say that intermarriage is our #1 concern! Is it our great hazard? Or is our #1 hazard the fact that the Communist powers may win the admiration and allegiance of these new nations while we are still clinging to a past gone forever, still using moral and intellectual currency that has no value in this present world?

Is it segregation that we want or is it national security? Is it segregation or a new moral purpose? Is it segregation or is it a desire to keep the earth safe from nuclear war?

Ask the southern politician and he does not answer. He keeps on doggedly, stubbornly trying to buy a seat in the legislature or a seat in Congress by telling the voters he will pay for it by seeing that they have plenty of segregation; plenty of Confederate money.

And people listen to this nonsense. Presidents of banks listen; heads of industry, ministers, storekeepers and ordinary people. They listen because, like my little brother and me, they want something for nothing.

It is an old human trait and few of us are free from it. You read in the paper, did you not, about the slick operator who came to Georgia this past month offering to businessmen and farmers a Machine that makes money by duplication. It worked like this: He made up a mysterious fluid, took out a ten dollar bill, swished it around in the fluid and pulled out two ten dollar bills. He put those in, stirred things up, and pulled out four ten dollar bills. And some well-to-do farmers and businessmen fell for this old trick. One gentleman who had just cleared $18,000 from his peanut crop put the whole sum into these machines that can "make money by duplication."

We say, How can people be so stupid? But all we have to do is look around us. We know the South has fallen for such trickery year in and year out; and watching Mr. Nixon work, it seems to me the Republicans and quite a few Democrats are falling for the same old sleight-of-hand tricks: the juggling of spurious fears with spurious hopes and spurious accusations and calling the mixture "a new life for our people."

Let's come closer home: Let's look at the Baptists and Methodists and other denominations, who are spreading bigoted talk against the Catholics. Once more, clutching at a spurious danger to keep from looking at the real dangers confronting us. Here are preachers arousing hate and fear against Catholics when they should be leading their congregations to the asking of important questions such as: How can we make brotherhood work? How can we create warm, Christian understanding relations between people? How can we lift away the barriers that are smothering the human spirit? Here are preachers, appealing not to the conscience of their congregations but to their irrational dreads! Seducing them into play-acting: for it is play-acting to pretend to fight a battle that was won by Martin Luther three hundred years ago. It is silly, childish and dangerous play-acting to pretend that the Pope, who doesn't even own a pop-gun, is our great national enemy! It must delight Mr. Khrushchev to see how easy it is to confuse some of the American people. While he is here, he who is so adept at creating confusion, he may learn a few new tricks from us.

My father was an astute man who liked to use old-fashioned phrases. Were he alive today he would say all this is the work of the Devil. And I think I rather agree. The Devil did not die at the end of Medievalism. He appears in every age; he gives himself a fresh new image, but he always appears. We speak of evil today; it is intellectually fashionable and philosophically wise to do so; we often use Dr. Paul Tillich's phrases, and Martin Buber's, and Karl Jaspers', but the word *Devil* is hard to match: it has so much life and energy in it and is, I think, a better symbol of what we are talking about.

The Devil always appears when something important is going on. He comes to get his share as that great theologian Denis de Rougemont reminds us. He appears at critical moments to confuse our minds; he delights in persuading us to fear false dangers and fight false battles. He must be hilarious over the ease with which he has persuaded many Protestant preachers and their congregations to fight the already-won battles of the Reformation instead of concentrating on the real conflicts of the 1960's. He must delight in the fog of hate and fear that is whirling through minds, driving even some good Democrats to vote for Mr. Nixon because they think he is more "Christian" than is Mr. Kennedy, and will protect us, also, from the Pope. It is funny but it is a matter of tears, not laughter.

The Devil knows that if you want to destroy a man, all you need do is fill him with false hopes and false fears. These will blind him to his true direction and he will inevitably turn away from the future and destroy himself and those close to him.

It is as true of a nation: fill its people with false hopes and false fears, and they will do the rest; they will go straight to their appointment with Death; and they will drag all nations friendly to them down into the maelstrom of their moral and mental confusion.

The false fear of "the Catholic menace"; the false fear of "inter-marriage of the races," the false fear that compassionate concern for people's needs is a giant step toward socialism: these fears are looming up like monstrous ghosts, today, blinding us to the magnificent opportunities we Americans have to help bring the whole world to a higher plateau of free, creative human endeavor; blinding us to our role as the world's Good Neighbor, a good neighbor not a fellow-conspirator; a neighbor concerned for all children in the world, concerned for the human being's right to grow and learn and create.

The evil within the human heart is a chilling thing to contemplate. And it is in every one of us. Dormant hates, dormant greed, dormant lust for power, restless foolish fears, the desire to get Something for Nothing, the willingness to cheat, to betray great causes for small ambitions; the irresponsible temptation to arouse men's anxiety so as to profit from their panic.

These things we see in politicians; these things you, as members of the Negro race, see in white folks. Do you also see how the Devil gets his share of your life? Do you see how he stirs your false fears and false hopes and exploits your hurts and humiliations, making you choose the wrong leaders, vote for the wrong party, sometimes, to take your revenge?

Do you think the leaders of the young African nations are listening to the Devil's whispers as he tempts them to use their color, their black skins, to build for themselves political power—just as the white man did in the 18th and 19th and early 20th centuries? Just as our southern demagogues still try to do? Are some of them turning to Khrushchev because of their deep hurts? Are they even now making wrong choices as to the friends who will really help them? Is the Devil telling them: "The white race sinned in a big way; why don't you now sin in an equally big way? It's equality you want, isn't it? OK. If you want equality then you have an equal right to sin, don't you? to discriminate, to exploit and build power and take revenge?" I don't doubt for a moment that the leaders of the new nations are being whispered to by the Devil and his earthly henchmen, even in their sleep and dreams. Why not? Are they different from the rest of us? I doubt it. Are they different from Christ, who was also tempted?

But let's come closer home. Let's look at this truly important nonviolent movement of the students: this historic movement. A movement that has as its immediate goal a small, vivid, heart-clutching aim: to open lunch counters in stores so that Negro women and their children—and others, too, of course—while shopping can have a place to sit down and eat. But the sit-in movement is much more: it has great moral goals and uses moral methods. Its vocabulary lifts the heart: nonviolence . . . love . . . truth . . . compassion . . . reconciliation. Words that the young and the brave take seriously enough to go to jail for.

It is, and I say this reverently, God's movement: It is a flowering of the Judaic-Christian ethic; it is built on the sanctity of the person, on the dignity of man, on the spiritual power of love, on the light of reason; it is grounded on a certitude that there is a Divine Center in each one of us; it is based on faith in the redemptive power of sacrifice.

What better place than this for the Devil's hang-out? The plain bad people do the Devil's work for him. But when there's work to do among good folks the Devil does it himself. This is where he exhibits his stupendous versatility and talent.

How is he working or about to work in the nonviolent movement? In his usual way: by whispering it is possible to get Something for Nothing. He has already done rather a good job on some of the college presidents. The Devil was ready for them. He whispered, "Remember the money; take care of those funds for the college and let the students take care of civil rights. You'd better fire a few of them, you know; don't be caught collaborating with them; if you're caught, you may not get that money. And money is money," says the Devil. He's been working on the businessmen too. "Too much of this will hurt you financially," he whispers. "You get along fine with white folks but these kids—they're too young to know how to lick 'em up. Oh sure, put up bond for the boys and girls, get 'em out of jail, it's not respectable to stay in jail; but tell 'em enough's enough. Tell 'em to take it easy now."

But this isn't enough for the Devil. He is jealous of goodness and decency, jealous of a young clean conscience, jealous of any man or woman, girl or boy, who holds his integrity sacred. So he impudently walks around the campuses where the movement was born. What doing? I think you know. Whispering things like this: "You've done a fine job but it's time now you got something out of it for yourself. Get your name in the paper; build yourself into a leader; make a big deal out of all this publicity."

And then he shrewdly goes to the heart of the matter: to the ones who are working to coordinate the movement and who are doing it at great personal sacrifice. He may not have whispered to them yet, but if he hasn't already, he will. Make no mistake about it. He'll tell them, "You folks need money. Can't grow without money. So take it when it is offered you, even though it has a few dirty strings tied to it. After all, money is money, you know."

How will you students answer these whispers? Will you say, "Is money always money, or is it sometimes Confederate bills? or other currency of no value to us? Is this a big deal for the organization or is it a betrayal of a great cause for Thirty Pieces of Silver? Am I helping to win civil rights for the people, or am I losing my own soul?"

How those questions are answered will determine the future of the Nonviolent Sit-in Movement. It is up to you. You alone, each one of you, in the quietness of your heart, must answer. What happens in the South during the next decade depends on how our people respond to the diabolical temptations to sell out big causes for little ones. What happens to our country depends on our skill in separating false fears from rational ones, false dangers from the real ones confronting the whole world. What happens will depend on whether we choose to live in a past full of ghosts or in a future full of hard jobs and great opportunities.

I say these hard things to you because I respect and admire you. I have a feeling of awe as I consider the bravery and spirit of self-sacrifice that many of you have shown the whole world this past year. I want your movement to succeed: I want it to reach high and attain that quality of spiritual excellence which is necessary if it is to transform our region into a better place for Negro and white to live and if it is to do its part in transforming the whole world. I believe it has magnificent possibilities: I want only to suggest some of the dangers that may betray you, and beg you to take care: Do this: Try to recognize the Devil when he comes around you; don't be betrayed by his new image.

You have an important work ahead of you and it is yours to do: only yours. We who are older cannot do it.

For the river Jordan is a chilly place. Full of whirlpools and quicksand. Only the young and the brave can cross it and still have strength for their new jobs. But you must do it if you are to bring not only your race but all our people to the Promised Land, the new world the youth of the entire earth must make together.

We of the older generation cannot go on that great journey with you. We cannot help build the new frontier. But here is something we can do: We can make of our lives, our knowledge, our experiences, our wisdom and our hopes and faith and insight a *bridge*, a strong sure bridge, over which you can cross into the new unmade world. Perhaps in this way we who are older can help keep you out of the quicksands and the worst whirlpools. Perhaps by our firm support, our unwavering belief in you we can give you that extra lift you are going to need. I hope so. And now let me say, God bless you.

Letter to Gerda Lerner

Gerda Lerner wrote Smith after reading Smith's *Saturday Review* essay, "Novelists Need a Commitment," published on December 24, 1960. While expressing her appreciation for Smith's writing, Lerner wrote that her personal experience as a writer indicated that more than just a commitment was necessary to get her work published. She described a novel she had written (which she had been told was out of tune with the literary market) as being in keeping with Smith's concepts of dehumanization and fragmentation in human relationships. Feeling blocked as a writer and in need of affirmation, Lerner asked Smith if she would read the manuscript.

Smith's response not only documents one of the many instances of her willingness to help younger writers but also serves as an excellent example of the way her correspondence became more autobiographical and philosophical, especially in her later years, as she reiterated or reinterpreted her life and thought to those she felt would be a receptive audience. Significantly, just as Smith's support of political activists included challenging their understanding of the process of working for social change, so her support for other writers included both networking efforts and theoretical discussions about writing and the creative process. Such correspondence demonstrates the consistent interrelatedness of theory and practice in her life.

Sunday [January] 22, 1961

Dear Gerda Lerner:

I was deeply moved by your letter. Warmed by your appreciation; hurt by the sudden glimpse you gave me of your own frustration; troubled and brightened, shocked and encouraged by vistas your words opened up. I am going to answer now, for fear that things, THINGS THINGS will keep me from doing so, later.

This sharp edged, cutting, upthrusting age we are living in makes inhuman demands on human beings. I think this about my own life. I am by nature shy, quiet, withdrawn; every move I have made in my life toward people, toward relating myself to my external world has hurt behind it; something pushes; sometimes, my conscience, my awareness of the hurt of others; sometimes, my own blazing rebellion against the false, the hypocritical; sometimes, my simple, almost childlike curiosity about people, things, customs, defenses—I want to read, to brood, to study, to think. I want simply to look. Just look. At mountains. At a face. At a painting. I want to listen to the music that was the only real joy I had for the first twenty-two years of my life. I was absorbed in it, covered by it, hidden by it, exalted by it, excited—All my life was involved in music, except my two sharp eyes that kept staring at people. Then, in my own life, things happened; parents crumpled with psychic burdens and financial ones; I had to come out of myself and help them, take over. This call on me from them gradually spread and became a call[,] a silent call from the South on me for my help. Only the poor South did not know it needed me. *I* felt it did. Not southern people. And so, a conflict began which has never for one year let up: the conflict between my deep desires, my instinctual needs, my hunger to create something, to make a thing—and this crying, pleading but even now silent cry of my people, Come over to Macedonia and help us. The tragic knowledge that they have not known they were crying for help and resented the help I have tried to give is one of the wounds of human life.

What I mean when I say an artist, a writer must have a sense of commitment (by the way that title was not mine, but the *Saturday Review*'s: my title was more accurate: *Out of Creative Tension Comes Peace*. They subtly altered my real meaning by that title which they used without my permission.) is that the artist must have a sense of vocation, a sense of being "called" to his work; it is something he must do; he must listen when he is told to "make a new thing." This is what I meant, truly. This is my belief. But since this artist lives in a world of people, a world of surging life, ambivalent life, aching, passionately hurting life, he must make his "thing" his "new thing" out of this life, out of his own personal experience of life. Because my experience of life has to do with chasms and walls, with "a trembling earth" which literally was true since the earth near the Great Swamp of my childhood does actually tremble when one walks on it—because my experience was in the actual living a kind of metaphor of the white race, of all its grandeurs and all its errors; because I also lived with Negroes, close to them, not as problems but as people, because I saw the cruelties, felt them abrade me as well as my Negro friends, I could write of nothing else. How could I! I had to explore the meanings of the trembling earth beneath my feet: the philosophical and ethical meanings, the psychological meanings, yes—the esthetic meanings too. I have always looked at racial segregation as something that has spelled out a doom for white people that black people may escape. I have always seen our human dilemmas from the point of view of the corroding effect of arrogance and hate, of moral blindness and intellectual obscurantism rather than from the point of view, "Let's help the poor Negro." The Negro has had a hellish time: he has been bound outwardly by many bonds, but the white man has bound his soul and mind and heart until they are abject slaves to this sick worship called White Supremacy. Always, I have looked at things this way.

As for problems: There is neither a white nor Negro problem. There is no racial problem; no "problem" of racial relations. These matters are not simple, sharpedged problems which can be solved. The only thing that can happen is for us to "make a new thing," to do, as does God the artist, "create the new." We abandon human dilemmas, we never solve them. And that is why I say even the young writer (although I did not say this in the *Sat. Review* article) must have a commitment: a commitment to make something new of the life around him. But does he see this life? I don't think Faulkner, for instance, really sees the life around him or even inside him. He has made something new, something interesting; but nothing great, nothing that can find its place in the future of mankind. As I said of him, twenty-five years ago, he is truly a great finger painter. That was the term I used then; today, I'd say, Faulkner has tried to do with words (but has not succeeded because words have set meanings) what Pollock and de Kooning have tried to do with the drip method. With him, not quite abstraction for words are symbols not abstractions and he cannot make pure abstraction out of them. But he has used a method something like theirs. But there is a fallacy here: The writer and the painter are not in the same creative category; they can never be equated with each other. Not even the poet can be equated with the painter. The painter is much closer to music and when he tries to achieve pure abstraction as music does often achieve, then he is on solid ground. But the writer can never do this. He cannot take a word and drain all its old meaning from it, mash it into pulp and make "something new out of it." He can try as Joyce tried but he cannot do it. The word is there. In the beginning was the Word. It has meaning; it has ten thousand layers of meaning, maybe; but meaning which human beings know is there; and so you cannot begin as if you were God and make the material, too, with which you work. Your subject matter can be personally yours, and should be. If it also happens to affect the whole world as my material does, then that is both good and bad. Good because it is important. Your treatment of it may not be; but the subject matter is important. It is "bad" for the writer because readers are always reading into your words and your subject matter what they want to see there; or what they fear to see there. You cannot get esthetic distance from subject matter that involves "race" for instance. When Melville wrote *Moby Dick*, no one read him; reviewers sneered at the book. Why? Because whale hunting was an actual business at that time; they couldn't get esthetic distance. They felt he was dealing with a "problem" although actually he was not, as every reader today knows. But then, it seemed so; and only Hawthorne grasped his real intent. But never said so publicly. Only privately to Melville.

As a citizen, I have sometimes used my writing talent, my talent for finding a simple way to say something that is hideously twisted and complex, to help view a fragment of "race relations" more clearly. I have even suggested, as a housewife might during a thunderstorm, that there are ways to shut windows, and doors, and put pans under the bad leaks; and call the children in out of reach of lightening, etc. But as a serious writer, as I think of myself in *Strange Fruit* (yes, even that first book) and *Journey* and *Killers of the Dream* and *One Hour*, I have always tried to make something new out of what was before hackneyed, trite, and false; I have always tried to show invisible things (in this sense, I am a realist. I do like to dredge up what even my own eyes have never seen before). I have tried. I do not think I have quite succeeded in making a new, wondrous, shining thing out of the big Nightmare. And I want to do this. I want to do as Auden and poets before him have said, "teach my terrors to sing." When I do this maybe I can take a nasty, obscene, hating, panting monstrosity and show it in a way that even it, even it, takes on some of the luminous quality of first creation.

I am sorry that your books have been lost in the awful, crazy shuffle of our times. Yes, I'd like to read your book. Our reviewers and critics are to blame. They are men lost in the present; talking of nihilism as if they had discovered it. It would make us laugh, except it is no laughing matter for serious writers. They now talk of "total rejection"—and one moans, Oh God. Dostoevski did all this 80 years ago and did it so well, always setting the nihilism cleanly against the great shadowy Affirmation. But they have nothing to affirm. Why? Because these critics and reviewers do not see the actual life we are living. They see what the 19th century saw; they see even what was seen up to 1940; but they don't really see the invisible things. This kind of realism is the realm of the creative writer: to show the invisible things actually present in contemporary life. This is one duty; one that we can commit ourselves to. Then we have another duty, another commitment to make. And that is to show it reflected against the future; and the past. Then we have a third commitment: to show these visible and invisible things as they look to each of us, in the dim depths of our own heart and mind, as they link on to what they find there. This is art as the writer deals with it. Art as the composer deals with it is something different; art as the painter and sculptor deals with it is different, too. And the painter's art is clearly different from that of the sculptor. Actually, writer and sculptor are closer together in their needs, their materials, their actual results.

Thank you for writing me. And thank you for letting me write you.

(*HH* 266–70)

From *Killers of the Dream*, Revised Edition, 1961

In February 1961 Smith wrote her sister Bertha Barnett: "It has been a most active fall and winter for me: the South is in turmoil, the young people are turning to me for help all down the line; they've never known who I was before; most have never read my books but somehow they've heard I'll help; I do." If most of the young activists had not heard of her books when the sit-ins began, their actions helped create a receptive climate and a new audience for her work. In the fall of 1961 Smith wrote the preface for James Peck's *Freedom Riders,* and Norton published a revised edition of *Killers of the Dream,* which became a classic among the movement volunteers who traveled to Mississippi in the summer of 1964 to conduct "freedom schools" and voter registration drives (*HH* 239–40).

Given the opportunity to update the 1949 edition of *Killers,* Smith added a new foreword and revised two concluding chapters. In content and style, the following chapter exemplifies the ideal "commitments" for a writer, which she named in her letter to Gerda Lerner: "to show the invisible things actually present in contemporary life" ... "to show it reflected against the future and the past" ... "to show these visible and invisible things as they look to each of us, in the dim depths of our own heart and mind, as they link on to what they find there" (*HH* 270).

The Chasm and the Bridge

The years go by. We are still fighting false battles or dead ones. We are still defending old worn-out systems, pitting them against each other. We know, our minds know, that the Twentieth Century dialogue has to do with relationships not systems; but we have not confessed it. Nor are we basing plans for the future on this knowledge. It is as if we cannot bridge the chasm between the past and what lies ahead. Perhaps we feel too insecure about the status of the human being. Man's spirit is certainly not held in high esteem, today: color is put above it by millions, and economic systems and nationalism and science and institutions by more millions, and gadgetry and profits by more and more millions.

And yet, we know the time is drawing near when we shall be compelled to take sides either for or against the continuing growth of the spirit of man. But most do not want to make a decision. It is this failure to make a fundamental choice that is driving us to take on more and more spurious conflicts while we cling to the old dead causes. How else can we explain the unreasonable way in which the European powers have clung to colonialism even though they know it is a corpse and know the consequences of this stubborn refusal to give up what is dead? How can they fail to measure the bitterness not only against them but against the entire West because they have failed to accept with wisdom and grace what is inevitable?

How else than by attributing it to a basic indecision can we explain the unloosening grip of "Marxism" and capitalism on each other, even though both have quietly died in the midst of the sound and fury? In Russia and the United States, private and public sectors of the economy are becoming more and more mixed as they bend to the exigencies of world conditions and their own country's internal needs—and this process is likely to continue. What, actually, are Russia and the United States fighting about? Do we know? Is it that we are promoting human freedom and they are promoting human welfare? I doubt that we should be willing to settle for that. We think, and rightly so, that we are deeply concerned for the people's welfare. But—and here things tangle—though we declare to the world our unshakeable belief in freedom our defense of it at home has been faltering and our failure, even now, to give the Negro group its full rights has shaken the world's faith in our words. But Russia, too, has failed in lamentable ways: not only by its refusal to let its citizens speak freely and choose their leaders freely, but in its loudly advertised plan for the common people's welfare; it certainly has not made good its promises. So where are we? What is it all about? Can it be true, as some neutrals say, that Russia looks toward the future and we look toward the past? Is the fight about what age we are living in? Or is it as others say, that Russia is for the peasants of the world and we are for the middle classes? Would we settle for that? Or is it as cynics say, that the whole mess is a raw struggle for power? Whatever the answer, the issues are insanely confused.

The same confusion hovers over the question of racism here at home: we know White Supremacy is indefensible in today's world, we know that as an idea it is dead, but the bitter struggle goes on, South and North:

wasting minds and time and hearts and economic resources, tying us to a past where ghost battles ghost. And while this happens the human spirit sits on the rim of things, waiting.

Why does this have to be?

I do not know the full answer, of course. I think it is, partly, because we have lost a vision of man. We are not sure how different he actually is from animal or vegetable or rock or machine. It is partly, I think, because we have ceased trying to relate ourselves to God: we no longer even cry that God is dead; instead, we have named him an hypothesis, a dream, and turned him over to the laboratory to "prove." And since we have stopped searching for God we have stopped searching for ultimate meaning, saying there is no purpose in human existence. Hence all is absurdity, all is nothing. The more honest among those who want God "proved" tend to seek uneasy solace in neo-nihilism; or, putting heart above logic, in humanism,—while the less honest settle for their own brand of idol worship, sacrificing all to success or skin color or capitalism or communism or their work or their pleasure, whispering, *Let's don't think about it.*

But whether we think or don't think, the soul is left free-floating and becomes lost and we grow more and more lonely, and are filled with *angst.* We begin to deny our essence; we do not see that the human situation is conditioned on uncertainty and based on fragmentation, that its inner laws force upon it splits and fissures and uncounted separations which we must bridge in order to find wholeness. But we cannot admit this, and turn away: trying not to believe the bridging is a necessity, and that sometimes, faith is the only bridge available. We still want to believe man is, by nature, solid and proof-sure.

We forget Eden. We forget that it was man's tearing himself in two that made him human; that the Primal Moment for him was when he stepped back and looked at himself. Awareness—call it Eve, if you like—came between him and his Self. And out of this awareness came the symbol and the word, and love, and wonder and curiosity and hope and hate and greed and the dream and the painful, hurting knowledge that he is a torn thing always in need of being tied to something else.

But modern man is embarrassed about this need to be related; he keeps wishing he were solid and self-sufficient and tries to behave as if he is. And holding on to this false confidence, and refusing faith, he cuts himself off from what he need not do without—almost as if to convince himself that he can do so. Being armored in arrogance he finds it hard to genuflect to an unproved God, and impossible to relate to Him. How strange! For we all cling to meanings we cannot prove just as we cling to love and hope, and to art whose importance to the human being in us, though unproved, we are somehow sure of.

Every intelligent person knows, today, that proof is a valid requirement on some levels of experience and totally irrelevant on others. But there is a difference between knowing and accepting of what one knows. Around this theme of "proof" we have piled confusions which have intensified anxiety until some of us are unable to relate to anything. Instead, we try to find a system to fuse ourselves with, or we spin out ideologies and chain ourselves to them.

There are many other causes of anxiety, of course: beginning with what happens in our hearts when we are young and extending into the world in every direction. But perhaps the most obvious is our dread of annihilation from bombs which are increasing in power and number. This strange whizzing business of nuclear armaments, the rockets and the missiles and the rest of it, shakes us to our depths. And added to this, is the bleak certainty that too much power rests in too few hands and some of these hands belong to underlings who may—it is possible—in a sudden dark moment, push the wrong button.

These matters press hard on us. Where do we turn for the strength simply to endure?

But there is another way to look at the human situation; a way that may give us new purpose and hope. The crisis in human affairs which we feel occurring on many levels and which seems, often, to be intensifying as it spreads is basically caused by the slow-growing realization that from here on out we have our destiny in our own hands; and this destiny is not so much concerned with where we are going as with what we are becoming.

It is as if God has brought the Earth people through a long, labored journey of slow growth and evolvement beginning four billion years ago and now has put everything into their hands—even their relationship with Him. How it started, we don't know. Some say a little cloud of neutrons may have appeared in the emptiness, and in three or four minutes things as we think of them today—neutrons and protons and electrons—may have begun the fabulous and unending binding and dispersal out of which the universe has come. Now, after a billion years of life's natural evolution—during which living forms succeeded and replaced living forms again and again until finally a creature was made who could stand off and look at himself and speak—God, in effect, is saying to Man:

> From now on, you do it; use your own culture, the knowledge you have accumulated, your own ideas and dreams, your skills and technics and inventiveness—and become what you like. As a human being, you are only partially evolved; if you want to, you can continue changing yourself. But it is up to you. There are laws you

cannot break, even though you try: you cannot return to a one-cell existence; you cannot become any of the forms of life I created before you—jellyfish, or animal or even neolithic man; you cannot reverse the irreversible. You have your natural inheritance and it is within you but from now on you are man, cultured by man; not nature's doing. Call yourself modern, if you like, but you cannot stand still because you are not nearly completed. You are now in a dangerous state of flux: you could with ease become a monster or destroy yourself and your earth, but you cannot move backward. You are only a broken piece of life, remember, and cannot live without The Others. To live as a man you must somehow find ways to relate to Me, to yourself, to other men, to knowledge and to uncertainty, to past and future, all you have made: your art, your science, your things, your understanding; and you must somehow learn to bridge your mythic to your rational mind, you must somehow learn the difference in merging and relating. This is a big part of your trouble, your forgetting this elementary lesson. In all your history you have not really learned it. But when you do, your addiction to proofs will lessen and you will realize that you are a strange, versatile and fascinating creature who can live on many levels simultaneously and in many communities of thought whose laws are different—such as science and art and religion; in only one of these is proof needed, in the others, it is irrelevant; your trouble comes, it always has, when you try to merge them into one instead of relating them to each other and to yourself, permitting each to abide by its inner laws which I, God, have made and which you, Man, cannot break. You can never become one with what you love or hate or fear or long for: only related; therefore your loneliness will always, like your shadow, be with you.

There must be millions of people across the earth listening to an inner voice which is whispering words similar to these. At least, I like to think so.

When we consider man's evolution which is now in his own hands, when we ponder the awesome possibilities for good and evil that he controls, we see the task before him as prodigious. But it is also magnificent adventure. Yet it could come to a quick and terrible end. Imaginations cringe as they peer into this dark uncertainty. But one cannot think about it long without feeling new purpose stir the heart; a thin edge of meaning touches the mind—and suddenly one believes, again. Believes what? Let me say it this way: I believe every creative act, every poem, every painting, every honest question or honest dissent, every gesture of courage and faith and mercy and concern will count; every new awareness will count; every time we defend the human spirit it will count; every time we turn away from arrogance and lies, this, too, will count in the project called *Human Being Evolving*. And as we think of what could happen to the human race, if we want it to happen—when we think of the billions of dormant seeds in our nature and culture awaiting warmth and cultivation, we find ourselves ready to pick up our little watering pot and sacks of rich soil and start out on the million-year plan for the growing of a New Man. We may in our thinking need to stretch the old-fashioned minute into a year; and the year into a thousand years, as we map our way. No matter: time can be nothing or something, long or short, here or not here; human beings learned, long ago, a few tricks in dealing with it. We shall soon be able to cup a thousand years in the mind quite comfortably.

Against the sounding board of this gigantic purpose to which we can commit ourselves if we want to, the sniveling we have heard in recent years makes an unendurable sound. We grow angry at those who deliberately try to shrivel the person into something mean and weak. They become the earth's enemy—not to be killed but to be deaf to. Set against this plan of evolution we see the battles now being fought, cold and hot—and the armaments that make them possible—as something crazy and useless and wasteful. Who cares, we begin to say, about either capitalism or communism! They are mere epicycles that have had their day. Who cares about skin color when he discovers a human being inside himself or his neighbor! Who cares about national power when power belongs in this century to all or to none! What we need to do is get on with the job; on with the art and the science and the philosophy and the technology of evolution which will be slow—we are not forgetting this—but not as slow as in the past. We have found ways to compress time; and we have so much access to energy that some, in their panic, want to reject all of it because it seems to be without limit. But we also have the inner strength to match the new powers; and I hope we have the wisdom to protect us from the men who would exploit them in their mad confusion.

It is possible that the Devil is luring us into outer space to divert us from this project of evolving a new being. But perhaps we are capable of both giant tasks. To try either of them without tapping our moral and psychic resources, and without safeguarding the soul in us would be an irreversible mistake.

So we stand: as in every crisis since life began, confronting both good and evil in our nature and in our world. The only difference is that the good and the evil now have unlimited potentialities and the size of our world is expanding every day. But so is the size of our imagination and our love. Geography is no longer a deterrent to relating our concern and hope or hate or fears to others, however distant they may be.

Our home is the whole earth but home is also the place we were born. Let us return for another look at the South:

So little, in comparison with the vast changes sweeping the world, has happened in our region during the past decade. We have grown more prosperous, we have more things and we produce more things; we have better communication with the rest of our country and with each other; our population has shifted from rural to urban centers, great migrations of blacks and whites to the North are still in progress and hence the center of racial conflict is shifting, or rather breaking into a number of small centers from which trouble radiates. But we are still fixed on old fears; our demagogues at home and in Congress are still wailing about mixing and mongrelizing and "our way of life" and the "outsiders" and the "agitators"; and are still giving communism credit for every brave, intelligent, decent act done by a southerner.

But events are loosening our grip on the past: Supreme Court decisions and new implementation of Civil Rights bills have crumbled segregation in the Armed Services and are in process of doing so in employment in governmental agencies and industries which hold government contracts; public schools are slowly, reluctantly, obeying these decisions; other decisions affecting interstate travel and bus and railroad stations and airports are opening these, without segregation, to all our citizens, although here, too, the local opposition is fierce and irrational; numerous secondary court decisions and Presidential directives are pushing us forward even though the people still struggle wildly and bitterly.

Added to these firm pressures are the "incidents" which release a horde of ghosts who wander inside and outside us, terrorizing our best and worst citizens, each in a different way. For these happenings, these communal acts, are loaded with symbolism and behave like explosives: throwing the stuff within our minds into the open where all can see. We dread this sharp, savage exposure, the spill-out of hate and obscenity and stupidity. And perhaps, most of all, we dread to confront the emptiness that is revealed at the center of our peoples' lives.

The mob has become, for us, not only an ugly reality where people may get hurt, it has also become a new symbol of our spiritual deprivation and moral chaos. There are worse things than mobs: segregation is worse, and the continuous drip drip of shame and indignity that goes along with it is worse, and the refusal to come clean and confess our wrong-doing, and the reluctance to commit ourselves to the future. All this is worse and far more threatening to our survival than is a mob. But to many white southerners, today, a mob has become our most feared ghost, possessing a numinous power that shakes us to our depths. All the good elements of a community—and some of the evil—can be counted on to take their stand against the mob on the streets; certainly, after experiencing one. Only the lunatic fringe and the criminal element seem not to feel its symbolic significance. But their leaders do. These men know the community's fear of a mob and deliberately use the threat of stirring up one to keep the good people silent and passive. "You see what happens?" they say; and the good people sometimes agree that all would have been fine had only the "agitators" and the "outsiders" and the "communist elements" stayed away, and left it to them, although most of them had, up to that moment, done exactly nothing to change the racial *status quo*.

The dread comes, of course, from the naked exposure that occurs. Actually, the community often improves after this Return of the Repressed takes place. Good things begin to happen, not immediately, but soon; public opinion becomes more informed; the people's apathy lessens, their complacency shows a few fissures; and reason, at least to a limited degree, prevails. Little Rock greatly harmed American prestige and our foreign relations are still suffering from its effect on world opinion. But Little Rock, itself, is better off than it was before its debacle. A perverted kind of catharsis, yes; but catharsis seems to have occurred. New Orleans harmed American prestige and worsened the injury to our foreign relations which Little Rock inflicted, but New Orleans, too, will "come to its senses," and the process of change will be quickened.

The Emmitt Till case . . . Clinton . . . Birmingham . . . Montgomery . . . Anniston . . . Americus . . . the riot on the campus of the University of Georgia . . . Jackson, Mississippi—and more and more and still more incidents have shaken the heart and mind of American people. They have lessened apathy and complacency, and have stirred consciences wherever consciences can be stirred by acts of cruelty and arrogance. But this business of burning down the village in order to roast the pig is expensive in its waste of the human spirit, in its muddling of minds, in its loss to the community of new industry, and civic order and that tranquility which is necessary for creativity. But it will go on until we change our leaders to those who know and can use the magic of the good word; who understand the difference in facts and symbols and who can keep from merging their mythic with their rational mind. Heart is needed, too; concern, compassion, a sense of what it is going to take to survive in an uncreated future. But even though people have these good feelings and desires, if they cannot handle their symbols, if they cannot keep the mythic mind out of the rational mind's business, there is inevitable trouble.

Here is the place where we in the South are having difficulty. (Is it necessary to add that others throughout the world are having the same kind of trouble?) For our people mingle symbols and facts as if they were molasses and feathers. When we were children, our nurse, to keep us quiet, often poured molasses in our hands and then gave us a wad of feathers—which resulted in our being preoccupied for hours. Any child, having had this experience, knows there is no such thing as picking the feathers from either hand: the only device that works is soap and water. But in racial affairs, and others, too, we have not learned this: and the old molasses-and-feathers game goes on and on and on and on, supervised by politicians who always have more of the same if the constituents grow restless.

We cannot get along without symbols, it would be unthinkable. But they are full of strange power and can destroy us quickly when used improperly—as the Germans' experience with them demonstrated. They need to be handled as carefully as nuclear energy and the rules for doing so should be learned by all. Symbols should be kept in their place; they should not be mixed with facts and then treated as though they are facts; nor should facts be mixed with symbols and treated as though they are symbols, for facts have their place, too. It is the merging and mixing that causes most of the trouble. The trouble is worsened when "ordinary acting" is suddenly, without warning, transformed into symbolic acting. We feel turned upside down when this happens; much as we should feel were we to see a painting walk down Main Street arm in arm with the village banker. In such a situation we are likely to decide that we are no longer in a reasonable, factual world but have been transported to the mythic world where art and fairy tales and poetry live—or else that we might as well face the dreary fact that things are out of order in our own heads.

But this mixing of the levels of thinking, this confusion of the qualities of reality has been accepted by many in Dixie as a normal way to behave. This is revealed in our attitude toward the word, *relationships*. On the rational level of the mind we understand that a relationship is a kind of bridge, a dialogue, a question and answer. When we use the word, we see in our mind one person relating or responding to another, etc. But the mythic mind sees nothing of the kind: it sees mongrelization, fusing, merging, melting. Why? Because the mythic mind is not capable of relating: its *modus operandi* is one of spreading: it is not restrained by barriers of time and space, or cause and effect, or facts that contradict, or logical categories. It licks like a flame at everything that comes near it, making its own kind of Phoenix out of the ashes. It likes to create something big out of the small: it can take one quality, such as whiteness and cover a neighborhood or a quarter of the earth with it, declaring that all beneath this great white sheet are the "same."

Once tangled in the stuff of the mythic mind, it is difficult to escape, unless you are an artist. Thousands of fairly intelligent people get permanently stuck in such feathers and molasses as "The Outsiders did it," . . . "Leave us alone and we'll take care of things" . . . "We white folks and black folks were getting along just fine until the agitators came" . . . "It is the extremists on both sides who cause the trouble." The rational mind would be embarrassed by this business; it would keep trying to fit the statements to facts: the facts of a changing world, the facts of local conditions, the facts of African nationalism, the facts of the American Constitution. But the mythic mind couldn't care less. Why should its statements fit facts? There is no law in the mythic region to make them do so.

It is, however, as dangerous to overvalue facts and undervalue symbols as it is to mix them.

We have brought much trouble upon ourselves in Asia and Africa because we have turned away when we thought what we heard was not sensible or not based on "realistic facts." The colonies have been demanding for a long time that they be given their freedom; and finally, reluctantly, the powers are now turning the countries back to their rightful owners. Listening to their demands for freedom, we Americans have tended to think that the new nations, after experiencing political domination, now want a form of government that will be democratic, that will give the citizens full voice and control over their political affairs, and that will safeguard their civil liberties. Actually, nothing is further from the truth. What they want, these Asians and Africans, is to be free of the old symbols of contempt that they were burdened with by their colonial masters. They have not forgotten, they cannot forget, that as the symbols of contempt were being laid on them their old symbols, which had given them a sense of dignity and value, were being stripped away. These new nations are, in a sense, without symbols, today, and men cannot live that way. To them, democracy is merely a fine idea. Whatever symbolic meaning it may have for Americans, for the former colonial people it has little—and this little (tied to the fact that the colonial powers also called themselves 'democracies') carries with it some bad memories. *Democracy*, certainly at present, cannot meet their need for symbols. But *equality* does. And they will trample the earth to get it. They may cry freedom as they trample but in their hearts they are singing of equality.

All men are equal is a phrase heavy with meaning, powerful in its emotional effect upon those who have been long oppressed by the white man. But what are the facts about this statement? Are men equal? No. They are not equal, will never be, have never been. Indeed, the end of the human race would have come long ago, had they been equal, or the same. We are different in ten thousand ways from each other and we know it. We know, too, that out of these differences, these infinite variations, big and small, comes mankind's chance of evolving into a new being. We also know that "equal" while relevant when we speak of refrigerators is senseless when we speak of people. And the Asian and African leaders know it, too. But they also know that underneath the surface facts of men's differences, the symbolic truth is that we *are equal as human beings*: equal before God; equal in that we are born and will die; equal in that we get sick, get well, grow, and learn and become aware and are hurt and can be reasoned with; equal in that we can burn with anger and light up with hope and can work and create and destroy and sleep and dream and make love and kill and use words and symbols, and ask questions; equal in that we long to reach out toward the great Unknown; equal, too, in our need of each other, for the weak need the strong and the strong cannot long survive without the weak.

All this is true. But there are "realistic" facts in the Asian-African situation that we Americans keep feeling sensible men should put first: food, for instance, when people are starving; medicines when half the population is ill; housing when so many are without shelter; and schooling and hospitals and roads and better farming and electric power, and so on. We may be right. It might be more sensible to nourish the body before bothering much about the soul and the heart, but it would be difficult to persuade people that this is so. Symbol-hunger is importunate, it pushes sensible needs and facts away from it. We southerners should remember this from our own experience. Whether we understand or not, the African and Asian leaders do; and though they are working to meet their people's physical necessities, what they long for, dream about and connive to get is "equality"—equality as persons, equality in terms of human rights, equality in the United Nations—and let's say it, "racial equality." They want a black face to count as much as a white face does in every situation in the world. And what they hate and fear more than hunger and more than death are those symbols: segregation, apartheid, colonialism—and the actions that are tied fast to them. Of course they know the facts of the communist threat to their newly found political freedom; but remember, these are *facts*: they do not enter the part of the mind where the old symbols crouch breathing out poison.

When African leaders tell us they are not interested in communism or capitalism, we should listen. If we don't, once more the white man's blindness, his own confusion about facts and symbols may drive these leaders to pick out of the historic mud a symbol on which they *can* nourish their hurt dignity: Black Supremacy. It has happened before, in our own South. After the Civil War, when things were in chaos and misery was everywhere and people were without food and learning and shelter and medicine, our politicians picked up the symbol of White Supremacy and made it a flag and a doctrine and a passion by which to "unify" poor white and rich white (who felt they had little in common) in a mutual hostility against the Negro. It was one easy way to build power. In Africa, there are tribal hostilities hard to deal with, prickly and mind-consuming which pull against national loyalties and aims. Why not siphon off the tribal fury and turn it into hatred of whites who continue so stubbornly to think of themselves as superior? A black leader would be stupid not to be tempted—and a tragic fool, were he to succumb to the temptation.

For the South, for Africa, for the whole world, the road to the future is piled high with such psychological and political impediments. Some of it is junk and waste; some of it is pulsating with energy. And in addition to these blocks, there are the floods of emotion which blind men to their direction—brought on by frustration and physical exhaustion and verbal confusion as well as by sheer poverty.

But not all people are blind: more and more see what it is all about. In every country this is so. In the South—and once more, let's turn back to it—our big hope lies in the fact that ten years ago, only a few saw things clearly; now, thousands see. Not only the lonely individuals and the Cassandras, but groups—and these groups are growing larger and more energetic. We have the churchwomen who have patiently been untangling the racial confusion for years; the Southern Regional Council; the Human Relations Councils; civic clubs, the League of Women Voters, the Ministerial Councils, and more and more newspaper reporters and editors; some still see as if through a glass darkly, but they, at least, keep peering. And there are a few writers and artists who understand the ambivalent hungers beneath these seething tensions. But the hopeful sign is that just plain people, men and women, rich and poor, are searching for the right questions. In addition, there are the groups of parents who intuitively avoid mythic matters, edging away from the radioactive symbols, holding tight to reason, as they stress "keeping our schools open so children may become educated." This simple statement is so sane, so sensible that defenses have fallen before it as though Joshua had once more picked up his trumpet.

And the Negro? For so long, the Negro in the South was silent. There were many exceptions, but there appeared to be some validity in the old demagogues' statements that "the niggers like it this way." Of course, they never liked it but they acquiesced in the condition imposed upon them because they felt it had to be. Like peasants the world over, the southern Negro was too impoverished and illiterate for a long time to find a way out of his dilemma. So he settled for another life in heaven; and planned for it—and his hope and faith kept him sane and shrewd as he whittled out defenses against the hard and the hateful of this earth. That the Negro has been a worthy antagonist, any white man who has lived near him will admit; for there is no white man who has not at one time or another been worsted in a deal with a Negro. He learned to outcheat the cheaters and sometimes delighted in his amoral bargaining. Nevertheless, he had lost his human birthright and he knew it. And it has always showed: in his laughing talk and his weeping song—or as he danced off his rage. He has, through the years, repelled anxiety by the sheer power of his endurance and by a persisting vitality. However the white man may have enslaved the Negro's body he did not enslave his soma—his inner stamina, his functions were kept free; and this audacious fact is one of the causes of some white men's envy and fury.

Now things have changed. The change has been abrupt and dramatic and has pierced the depths of the southern situation. There is, today, a revolution going on within the Negro's mind. He is discovering his powers: moral, economic, psychological, political.

It startled him when he realized that big department stores are dependent upon his dollars; he was slow to learn that his own group spends billions and can shake the southern economy; that often his trade is the difference between profit and loss; that his vote counts; that his voice has moral weight in the world's councils; that his talents are cherished by everybody; and that the winds of change are blowing him in the right direction.

Realizing his strength, he has begun to resist the old segregated way of life. Resistance did not spring out of nothing; for decades, a few Negroes and whites had been preparing the way, and events in Asia and Africa had stirred imaginations. Let us say, it seemed to begin suddenly a few years ago: when the young Martin Luther King led the Montgomery Negroes in their passive resistance to segregated local buses. Their famous walking to work stirred the world as nothing had since Gandhi's walk to the sea to make salt in protest against the British salt tax. The walking continued for more than a year and during that time Negroes opened their eyes and ears and began to listen to their own cries for help.

Once begun, it could not stop. More and more protests—and more. But the voices were quiet, conciliating, firm; and there was no violence on the part of leaders and almost none among their followers. Their self-discipline, their compassion, their knowledge of the redemptive power of suffering amazed the entire world.

In February of 1960, came the first of the young Negro students with their dramatic and nonviolent sit-ins at segregated lunch counters—in protest against the old system. And then, in May, 1961, Freedom Rides started. Their aim was to test the treatment given Negroes in interstate travel in the South. The white mobs gathered and a bus was burned and wholesale jailings of "the agitators"—the nonviolent group—took place in Alabama and Mississippi, even though Robert Kennedy, the U.S. Attorney General, did all in his power to protect the "Riders." And through it all, the Freedom Riders retained their calm and used no violence to counter the violence; and the Negroes' determination throughout the South—and the nation—hardened. They will not stop now until they arrive at their destination, which is the achievement of full civil rights as American citizens.

The philosophy of these students is a mixture of Thoreau, Jefferson, Gandhi, Martin Buber, the teachings of Jesus and something uniquely theirs: humor, and a natural sense of historical direction.

They are greatly influenced, and frequently advised, by Martin Luther King—a personable, intelligent, and deeply religious young man with nerves of iron and emotions that lie down like lambs within him. He holds stubbornly to his values, is not easily tempted, and will, I think, never succumb to rage against the white man; he is for the human being and has taken his stand.

The nation-wide enemies of the group of nonviolent resisters were too startled at first to organize against them. But a virulent campaign is now on, worthy of Joseph McCarthy, to throw heavy suspicion on their loyalty and motives and affiliations. Even so, the majority of Americans are sympathetic and the leaders in our government are, although many find it difficult to accept the philosophy of nonviolence which these students sustain themselves on.

So it goes: violence and nonviolence; factual arguments and gobbledygook; quiet protest and noisy mob. Terrorism flares up in one town while the neighboring town is developing a courageous concern; sudden insights light up public opinion, foul words blur the situation, one act of heroism stirs the heart, one cruel incident pierces the conscience—then apathy creeps back, until another incident occurs.

If only we could afford this zigzagging walk into the future! But each day the slowness becomes more dangerous. What will quicken us? What will illumine our minds? What can be said or done that will compel us to slough off inertia and complacency and take our stand for the human being against his unnumbered enemies? If only we could see the brokenness in each of us and the necessity for relationships; if we could realize our talent for bridging chasms that have always been and always will be. If only we could rise up against the killers of man's dream. But, sometimes, that killer of dreams is in us and we do not know how to rid ourselves of it.

Once, long ago, a little crazy hypothesis was thrown across a dark sky and left there. And people could never forget it. Religions were built by its light, poets' minds shone in its brightness, political systems used its warmth to draw men closer together, and science examined it cautiously and "proved" it to be the essence of sanity, the seed of human growth. It may be only a bedtime story that men told themselves in their loneliness; it may be a lie: this sanctity of the human being, this importance of man the individual, this right of the child to grow, but when it is proved so, there will no longer be an earth to witness the lie's triumph and no men here to mourn the loss of their dream.

So we stand: tied to the past and clutching at the stars! Only by an agonizing pull of our dream can we wrench ourselves from such fixating stuff and climb into the unknown. But we have always done it and we can do it again. We have the means, the technics, we have the knowledge and insight and courage. All have synchronized for the first time in history. Do we have the desire? That is a question that each of us must answer for himself.

And now, I must break off this story that has not ended; a story that is, after all, only one small fragment, hardly more than a page in a big book where is being recorded what happened to men and women and children of the earth during the Great Ordeal when finally they separated themselves a little way from nature and assumed the burden of their own evolution.

From *Our Faces, Our Words*

Our Faces, Our Words, a collection of nine dramatic monologues and a final essay, was written by Lillian Smith in 1964 and recorded by Arthur Klein for *Spoken Arts*. In a letter to Phyllis L. Meras, correspondent for the *Providence Journal* (Rhode Island), Smith described her intent for the book:

> I decided I wanted to do some dramatic monologues which might reveal some of the complexity, conflict, ambivalence, courage, suffering, and satisfaction these young civil rights workers are experiencing. So many of them have come to see me; we have had such intimate talks far into the night; I feel I have a deep sense of what they have gone through this summer in Mississippi. So I did nine monologues. Some are the thoughts of young Negroes, northern and southern. I tried by using *not* the method of the journalist or that of the case worker *but that of the artist* to probe deep into the heart of the young of our times at this troubling moment of our history. I ended the little book by doing an epilogue in which I spoke my own thoughts on the civil rights movement. This epilogue will appear in *McCall's* Magazine . . . in the November issue. The little book will have photographs, too. That is why I called it *Our Faces, Our Words*. But it is, remember, a creative thing [. . .] shaped by imagination and intuition. Recordings are to be made of most of these monologues; I did some of them and the Negro actor Ossie Davis did others. (*HH* 309–10)

Following are two of the monologues, "The Search for Excellence Takes Us to Strange Places," and "What Do We Want?" Smith's essay, "The Day It Happens," also concludes this collection of her work. As you listen to the recorded monologues (www.piedmont.edu/lilliansmith-resources), remember Smith's report to her editor George Brockway: "Well—the first reaction to the *McCall's* piece was an anonymous phone call threatening to dynamite my house" (*HH* 313).

The Search for Excellence Takes Us to Strange Places

I was twelve when the Supreme Court decided segregated schools wouldn't do. I took it for granted that before long things would be different at our school. But nothing happened. And nothing much happened anywhere. In our school, some of the kids told more rough jokes than usual, repeated more words that would hurt Negroes if they heard, some said they'd fight back if desegregation came, they'd show those colored kids what was what. A lot of us didn't like this talk but we didn't do anything. Most of us wouldn't have minded integration. But we didn't do anything. We didn't tell our principal how we felt, or the teachers, or the school boards, or those white kids who were muttering the nasty jokes. We were scared. Not scared of the integration experiment but scared to act freely according to how we really felt; scared of those mobs folks talk about, scared that Negroes, if they came to our school, would get hurt, scared of the unknown, I suppose. So, we made ourselves indifferent. We tried to tell ourselves we felt all right but after all, why was it our business to speak out!

People away from here asked why? Why didn't you do something! Remember how the commentators asked it over and over? And nobody could say. I was dumb, I couldn't say. But now I know that is what segregation has done to us whites: it has paralyzed us; we don't dare act out what we know is right. We don't dare say what we know should be said. We let the demagogues say anything but we are mute. Oh I know: we are scared of the goons and the ghosts and the monsters segregation has bred. For a hundred years, the nice people sat here and let politicians and the power structure that supported them chain our minds with their lies until we couldn't think straight. Listen to intelligent white people talk on this subject! Most of them lie and they don't care; they don't want to find the truth, they just repeat sleazy excuses they've heard before. People, even with Ph.D.'s, can't think critically; half of them end up talking about mongrelizing or states' rights. And when you say the states don't have any rights, read your Constitution, they stare as if you're crazy.

Oh well—I was as bad as the rest. I wanted to do the right thing, I wanted to be decent, I wanted to become something you might call a human being but I was scared. Later, at college (I went North to school) I heard Martin Luther King speak; then I heard Bayard Rustin; I went down to New York to hear them; then I had an interview with Anna Arnold Hedgman. I began to read. I was watching what was happening in Africa, I kept up with the sit-ins. After last summer—it hit me hard, everything hit me—I thought, Join the movement; get out and help break down the segregation system; do it quick before you get scared; picket, sit-in—you've got to, to save your own soul. And I did it.

And it wasn't long before I was in jail. The cops are rough on white girls, rougher than on Negro girls, and they're rougher with Negro girls than with Negro men. Well, there I was and they had put me by myself. I'm not very brave. I was more scared than a white girl from the North who was jailed at the same time. She went in laughing. I admired her but I knew she didn't know what was ahead.

Or maybe I was scared from a lifetime of being warned, Don't do that, don't speak out, don't take a stand, you can't, something awful will happen. I don't know. I had heard the stories of how a matron in one jail had made some of the girls in the movement strip naked, then she let other inmates hit them, make foul jokes, etc.

I held as steady as I could; walked back and forth in my cell; there was a small window, I stood there looking out. And to keep from sliding into panic I sang the songs of the movement, *We Shall Overcome, Freedom*, and the rest of them.

I am from a Methodist family. Pretty soon I was singing old Sunday School songs. Funny, how deep-down they go in you. I was humming *Wash Me and I Shall be Whiter than Snow*, thinking of those old days—sin sin sin—everything, nearly, was a sin except segregation. Whiter than snow, that means we are pure; dark, that means they are impure—how asinine can the human mind get! Segregation, a holy ritual, more meaningful than the Lord's Supper. You couldn't question it. You bowed down and worshiped the Whiteness it ritualized. It scared me to think this. I had read it before; now in that jail I believed it. We've lost God. We've surrounded ourselves with godlets; our white skin is the #1 god we worship. When you've got white skin you don't even need a soul. I tried to laugh; I cried a little.

Mississippi . . . that is where I was. Bleak and beautiful and terrible, that state. Beyond tragedy. What holocaust will they bring on themselves? Will they push things as far as did the Nazis? Can they and still remain a part of our nation? Is there no way—

Someone was at the door. The cop. I had on my shirt and jeans, just as I was when he arrested me. He arrested me for breaking a traffic rule, he said. He knew I was working with "the niggers" so he took me to jail. No accident, no one hurt, nothing had happened, I hadn't even broken a minor traffic law. But things are not real, here; truth is an irrelevance; I have never met a truthful cop; there may be some somewhere, I'm sure there are a few in Atlanta, or Richmond, maybe in North Carolina or Tennessee; but I have never come near one in the movement. He began to talk. I tried not to hear; the words were mostly words I can't say aloud. He wanted to know what nigger I had slept with the night before. Was it fun? Did he screw me better than white men can? "You must have some excuse, a damned good one, for going out and sittin-in with these niggers! They pay you for it, do they, at nights?"

I stood there, humming. I didn't dare stop. My heart was skipping, I was scared, outraged. There was nobody to call to for help. This is the worst part of segregation, this foul obscenity that rots white people's minds away. You feel minds are crawling with lice that have crept out of the rotten dirty places in our lives. And cops seem to have more than their share. Why? Why do we have these people for policemen? Is it true the world over that the dregs are the police? I don't know. They should be the very best, men we believe in and admire for their good judgment, their moral cleanness, their self discipline. But in the South, it doesn't turn out that way. Down here, most of them seem obsessed about "mixed children." Millions of mixed children: sex and sin wrapped up in a dirty cloth called segregation. But it is all right just so the kids are "illegal." A "legitimate" mixed-race child—ah, there's the horror, the taboo! A child born from a holy marriage? Oh no, that's terrible!

I couldn't sleep after he walked away. It was so still. All the big sounds deathly still. But a thousand thin noises ran along my nerve endings. I was cold, shaking cold. I clung to the window, I clung to outer space, hung on desperately, trying to forget everything behind me: the South I love and fear, its sweet stench, its gentle terrors, its sudden naked horrors—and its desire "to be good." And its apathy—aching to be good and yet unable to move.

Why can't the warmhearted, intelligent southerners change? Why can't they move? Why can't they speak out? Daddy, why haven't you spoken out? You have nice feelings, you didn't join a White Citizens' Council, you wouldn't lynch or dynamite anyone, you wouldn't push and scrouge (or would you?), you don't say "nigger," but you're against the Public Accommodations measure, you think a city has a holy right to close itself up against a part of the citizenry because of color; you think property rights are more important than human rights, don't you? You're really against the entire Civil Rights bill, aren't you? "They're taking away our rights," you say, "they're tearing up the Constitution!" You say this, my father whom I adore, and yet you read Plato; you're supposed to be a kind of local authority on the old Greeks, all time quoting Aeschylus. How can you? How can you . . . how can you . . . I'm crying, I'm a little girl crying because she wants a brave, honest father who seeks the truth of *his time* not the Greeks' time, who can look beyond this awful mess we're in. You went to Harvard—and yet you fall for the lies Mr. Rich White told Mr.

Poor White long ago, to keep him satisfied with poverty and sharecropping, and all the rest of it. How can you? Don't you know why all that was said? Don't you know it was to keep the poor whites from demanding *their* rights as Americans? Do you need me to tell you that is why Mr. Rich White handed them a drug instead of bread? A tranquilizer for their hungry souls to feed on—and now it has driven some of them mad.

I love you. That is what hurts. I admire so much of you; when you're off this subject of race you are sane and erudite and charming. And Mother—she does more about the problem than you do, Dad, but she does it secretly; she's afraid of what you'll say. That isn't fair to her, there's an edge of you that troubles her, too; she worships you but there is a little edge she keeps the bright light off of.

Last summer, when the trouble happened in Birmingham, in our hometown, you didn't do anything. Even after the bombings, even after those four little girls were killed, you didn't do anything. Not a damned thing! You're respected, you're prominent, you're popular, you're a member of the best clubs, you're on the Board of Stewards of our church and you didn't do a thing to help, to say This is Wrong. Oh I know, you said at home, That's pretty bad—but you didn't say it where anyone else could hear. What could you have done? You and Mother could have got in your car and called on the heartbroken parents, you could have said, "We're sorry." That one little thing might have unbound you. Freed you.

Mother says you think I sat-in just to embarrass you, to shame you. She says you think I deliberately got myself put in jail. Maybe I did! Maybe I did just that! If I did, I was wrong; that's a poor reason for fighting for any good cause. But whatever my motive, I had to do *something!* Maybe I screamed to drown out your silence. And so I ended up in a Mississippi jail, listening to a dirty lowdown cop talking about "niggers screwing" me—me, your Vassar-educated, summer-camp-trained daughter who loves poetry and philosophy and art and human beings and the excellence her father told her always to search for. But the search for excellence can be dangerous—it takes us to strange places, sometimes, doesn't it, Dad?

What Do We Want?

You ask me what we want. And I say, Who are *we?* Some of us are Negro, some are white; many are students, young, yeah—but we're not the same: our minds fill with different thoughts, we love different things, want different futures, hate different people—maybe I don't mean that—yes, I guess I do—some of us hate like hell; oh we try not to but we hate. We fight it, some of us, we lie about it to ourselves, make like we're compassionate, make like we're willing to suffer to redeem our fellow Americans from evil, but—listen: when a dog is nipping your tail—hell, not even Gandhi could feel compassion. Dogs . . . ever think what that means? White men using animals as allies against their fellow human beings. Man—you get that? Get the significance? You better than a nigger, white man says to dog, go after him, go after that little kid! Tear her to pieces! She's just a hunk of black flesh who's forgot to stay where she belongs; you're superior, you're a fine animal, you're our friend, we don't segregate you, it's the nigger we segregate.

There's something terrible about that. You feel it? It ought to hurt, ought to scare you if you really see what those cops and their bosses are doing. Human beings, all human beings, are different from animals—there's a profound and irreversible difference between animal and man. Talk about mongrelization . . . all human beings can breed with each other—they can because it is God's will that they do so if they want to; but a man can't lay with his dog and bring forth a living creature; yet dogs are used against *us*, the whites' fellowmen. This hurts. There's an irreversible difference. This hurts. See! I sound like I can't get out of the groove.—And I keep saying "irreversible" because I mean it: all human beings have a million things in common that no animal shares with them: speech, the power to make new things, the power to question, to search for meaning, to explore, discover—and the knowledge that we all must die; maybe that is the biggest difference of all, it's your shadow, you never shake it; and the power to think of historical time, that in itself makes you need something to steady you, if you think about it long enough: think how we go back and dig, not for a bone to gnaw as do the dogs but for a bone to study and maybe write a poem about, or use as a clue as we are putting a billion years of the past together; all this, our power to plan for the future, to paint, to write music. Wonder what'd happen if we'd get quiet all over the earth and think about this, what makes us human, for five minutes. Maybe we'd see each other different. But those cops—maybe I'll ask the next one who sticks an electric prod to my tail, maybe I'll just stop and say, "Socrates, what is a human being?" You reckon he does actually think a white skin makes a human being? It's all so crazy—

Oh, I know: plenty of Negroes don't know either. And some are in the movement: there because it gives them a chance to let out their resentment, a chance to defy that awful ghost, "white power." But deep in them, they know the real reasons, too; only they don't know words to say it right; they want what we all want, freedom to breathe, feel, think, move. White ghetto—black ghetto: both are mean places to grow a kid, as mean as the Mississippi delta, in a different way.

And, making things worse are the cops turning against their own kind and using animals to beat down their unarmed fellowmen. I used to go to church; well, I still go, my body goes, I'm not sure my heart goes anymore, I am messed up inside. But I have a feeling about blasphemy; and I say it is blasphemy for one human being to use dogs against another human being.

What's ruining the nonviolent movement, what's bringing out the hate that a little compassion and hope had sort of diluted, is the cruelty of these cops; the vicious extremes to which the powerful whites will go to maintain a system even they no longer profit from. But you can't help but think they are deliberately provoking us to violence. I said we were sort of naïve. Well, we were. But you go out on the streets, unarmed mind you, having had a session with yourself in which you've prayed for self control, for the power to forgive, and then—here come those dogs. Whatever you are afterward, you're not naïve.

Can't you laugh? somebody said. Jesus . . . laugh! Oh sure, once you're back home—if you don't land in jail as most of us do—you laugh to your family. Try to. Then that night you dream about those dogs—I reckon it went deep with me—you dream you're on the street, in front of a restaurant, say; and first, you see a lot of white faces staring at you, then the faces begin to twist with rage, terrible rage that's beyond words and then, face after face, they turn to snarling dogs, ears droop, mouths open, and now there's a hundred dogs after you and you're running running round the earth, round the earth and the dogs are at your tail and you run and choke and pant—And then, you wake up. And your heart is racing, and you're sweating wet but you're still and you feel your soul is bleeding to death—your po' little ole soul, as your grandma might say, is bleeding to death.

And you're supposed to keep loving white folks, keep being patient and courteous and wait another hundred years for their convenience. And then, if some fool idiot who's black makes a crazy-wild suggestion like turning on all the water taps, white folks say, "Ain't you shamed? Don't you know this is America and Americans don't do things like turning on water taps?"

This is the moment folks go raving crazy; some laugh for days and can't stop; raving, yeah, raving mad. And folks says, Why can't the leaders control "their people"? We are not the leaders' people—we're America's people and America is letting us down down down down.

Oh I know—not all white people would turn the dogs on us. Not one in a thousand would do it. And I know it is not just the white southerners, they're using the dogs up North, too. And they used them in the war—and Hitler used them in concentration camps. But the millions who say they wouldn't do it let the hundreds have their way—and these hundreds are not white goons, they're the official police who are under the control of the mayor of the city and the chief of police.

Why don't decent people say something? Why the silence? Why the passivity? They're not under Hitler, they're under President Johnson, and he is for us having our civil rights; I honestly believe he is. What are these people scared of? What their neighbors will say? What are they so loyal to? Is it loyalty? Is it a taboo they're too primitive to break? or are their souls already dead—and they don't know it. You can go to church with a dead soul inside you; you can give a lot of money to the church and still be what the Bible calls a "whited sepulchre."

What is really wrong with our people! *Our people.* No, I didn't slip up. I meant that. That's the way I feel. Americans, black and white, are my people. Deep in my heart I feel this way. Maybe I should feel glad I feel this way—thankful that I don't automatically hate people because they're white. But I *don't* feel good; all this tears me to pieces—it's hell to love and hate white folks, but that's what I do: my conscience, my reason say, You love them, you pity, you understand they, too, were born into this mess; but my heart says No! you hate them—not for the few who dynamite and kill but for the many who let these terrible things happen and don't move to stop them.

I struggle with this. I guess if you think, if you feel ambiguities, if you see evil and good braided together, you shouldn't get involved in life, much less involved in a revolution. You ought to go to Paris, and sit on the Left Bank and make like you're living in Proust's and Gide's time. That's just great—and you wouldn't have to go through the hell we're going through here in this so-called revolution.

Is it a revolution? I don't know. Certainly not a political one. Maybe it is a spiritual one: maybe; we started out hoping it would be something that would go deep into the soul of all our people, white and black, and change us so that our future could be different, richer, more open. But now—here we are hating; here we are talking about black this and black that—worse than the Mississippians with their whiteness. Is everything falling into a heap of ruins? It makes me want to cry when I remember how we colored kids started in the Movement, some of us naïve, yes; but we were pure-hearted; some of us had mothers who had given us a deepdown security that pushed hate away. We were sort of beautiful black Galahads going forth in search of the twentieth century's Holy Grail—the lost Grail which we must find in order for us to live as human beings should. Well—here we are, now, and some of us are not doing so well, are we.

Oh, yes—your question. What do we want? *Dignity.* Oh sure. As if dignity can be given! You grow it from deep inside you, or you don't have it. Our civil rights? Yes. But I want more. I'm beginning to see, I want more.

I want a life where the human being is known for what he can be, where he can dream big and not feel like a fool. Pompous? Vague? Forget it. All I'd better say is this Movement has got my soul to aching. And it hurts. God . . . how it hurts.

The Day It Happens

For some it happened yesterday. For some it is beginning today. For a few it happened years ago. Eyes turn, and are looking in a new direction. Ears pick up a sentence never understood before. A child moves across one's imagination, a crash startles one's soul, a whisper shakes the memory.

In such small ways comes the big change.

The movement of whites and Negroes toward a new future has its beginning for each of us without help of calendar. "Except for the still point, there would be no dance." There is a waiting; a long waiting for some; a waiting without end for those who cannot meet the new life. For those who can, there comes their moment in time—and a new beginning.

For Joseph A. McNeil, David Richmond, Ezell A. Blair, Jr., and Franklin E. McClain it began when they sat-in at a white restaurant in Greensboro, N.C., in 1960, and somehow startled the whole world by their act. For Martin Luther King it began in Montgomery, Alabama, one night in 1955. For Mrs. Rosa Parks, the moment came a few days earlier in the same city, as she sat in a bus, tired from a day's work: she was asked to move back, and suddenly her entire life came together, fused in one terrific moment of decision, and she said "No." That word "No," which she had not planned to say, did not know she was about to say, changed the tempo of racial change for our entire nation.

For others, the new movement began in their childhood, building itself out of minute hurts, insights, dreams, hopes, until somehow a new design was created and a new way of living began. It must have started in the first decade of this century for Walter White, who saw the act of lynching as a metaphor of dehumanization for his entire race and committed his life to finding a new way for his people. For that doughty old warrior, Philip Randolph, his moment came when he first entered the labor movement, for always he saw the shadow of race haunting its struggles; for Jim Farmer, for Roy Wilkins, for Anna Hedgman, for Bayard Rustin, for Constance Baker Motley, for numerous other Negroes and whites, one turns back to the late '30's and '40's for the moment they said No to the old way.

Perhaps it does not matter when and how the Movement started: perhaps it began too long ago to find a certainty of date, too long to know just who spoke out when, and how. But as Negroes, one by one, and ten by ten and finally hundreds by thousands stood up and cried, No! to the old pressures of white supremacy, a few hundred white southerners also said No! And a few hundred white northerners also said No! And then, more and more. Many a struggle, many a shrewd act, many a quiet talk with "the Powers" had taken place, many new patterns of non-violent protests had been formed long before the Montgomery protest, long before Little Rock, long before the famous Supreme Court decision of 1954. Books that shook the world had been written long before; there had even been one sudden, large-sized grass-roots protest in the South made against segregation by both Negroes and whites, in 1938, in 1940, in 1942; earlier, southern churchwomen had protested lynching in persistent and dramatic ways.

Teilhard de Chardin has said so rightly that the beginnings of all change on this earth are lost in a creative dimness; there is surely no need here to do more than remind those who wonder why it began to happen in 1960 that it actually did not begin to happen then. Never, since the Civil War, has protest ceased entirely; it was almost crushed, almost smothered, again and again, but never completely so: always it took another breath, kept breathing—and through the decades because of two World Wars, because of at least five mind-shaking books, because of many test cases carried to the Supreme Court by the NAACP, because of individuals (Negro and white) who spoke out bravely and beautifully, because of studies made on all aspects of this thing we call "race," insights spread, illuminations touched minds, and we as a people acquired a new sensitiveness to our failures and inadequacies. Perhaps more than all else, was the effect television had on us in our homes and on the news gatherers; where once newspapers had played down incidents, smothered stories that should have been told, television met the challenge with startling directness and forced newspapers to tell things as they are. (Not that all newspapers even now do, but there has been, during the past ten years, a tremendous change.) The awakening of Africa and Asia to the political potentials had its effect, also.

Perhaps we should say this: by 1960 the flood of protests, the powerful words spoken or written by a few poets and novelists, the decisions of the courts, the world political currents, and the acts of protest, added up to a kind of awesome Orphic truth which once heard transforms the hearer into something better—or worse.

The mind of America shuddered, trembled—and changed. How could any but morons and mad men be the same after the dynamiting of those four little girls at Sunday School in Birmingham? How could complacency remain uncracked after seeing on TV the courage of the nine students in the Little Rock high school? How could any heart bear the weight of the cowardly killing of Medgar Evers? Of the killing of growth in children everywhere? Even domestic animals feel shame: surely most Americans must have felt shame at watching the Oxford affair, and before that, the wanton behavior of women in front of schools in New Orleans. There are images that can never be forgotten, sounds that echo through a lifetime: bind these with the searching truth of a few who have written and spoken and acted—and the past becomes a catalyst which the future cannot escape the effect of.

The future is, to a large extent, already shaping up. The greedy politician will not admit it; the morons cannot change their minds; the mad men have expressed their madness so long in terms of racial hate that it will take time for them to find another way of living out their frustrations and rage. And always the ones who profit in money are stubbornly, stupidly slow. Profiteers rarely know why they profit; because they don't know, they try to hold on to the entire *status quo*, since they have little idea which part of it has actually profited them.

Crises are two-edged; they always create possibilities for both evil and good. While those which have piled on us during the past few years have shaken many white people awake, they have done something different to Negroes. Twenty million Negroes have been wounded by each crisis, often stripped of hope, often humiliated. The dynamite that killed children and blew up churches and homes has also blown open repressions in minds and hearts: each blast has freed hate and resentment in hundreds of thousands; every stubborn form of resistance of governors and officials, every police brutality has aroused an equal stubbornness in the protesters.

There were many Negroes who had found a way of forgiving their white enemies; they had clung to the way of nonviolence believing it to be not only the Christian way but the only sane way of living; but every nasty speech of a politician, every police dog, every fire hose and cattle prod used on black human beings, has lessened their love, their faith—and their prayers have grown shorter. How long, O Lord, how long can they endure such pressures!

Their leaders are beginning to ask themselves: can nonviolence work in our American society? Can it work unless it is understood? Can it be understood if white people harden their hearts and turn away? The leaders are also asking, How can we convince the young Negroes that this is the right way, the only creative way to work? How can we persuade them of the need of dialogue when fire hose and cattle prods are turned on them? The students' calmness, their patience, their self-control under the vicious circumstances they confront has been amazing. But how long can it last? How long can they endure the pompous scolding of white editorials when U.S. senators say what they say, and the "big mules" do what they do, and are only mildly rebuked by a few editors and often not rebuked at all.

It is more than access to public accommodations that the Negroes and their white friends want but this access must be won first so the people can be as free as are other citizens. It may well be that voting is more important, in that voting brings power; but to move freely in public places brings grace to one's life. It may be more sensible to go after better jobs and better job training, but being human, one still longs more for freedom to be at ease in one's hometown.

But there is something beyond rights, something not more important but more desperately urgent: bodily need. There are millions of Negroes in such desperate need in town and country and city that talk of "rights" leaves them dull and dazed. The young protesters who come, in large part, from middle-class families have stumbled on this: to their stunned amazement they have found a primitive misery which pushes the phrase "civil rights" out of their vocabulary.

They have found in Mississippi, Alabama, Louisiana, other states, too, and in cities, North and South, pockets of raw deprivation where all a human craves is a piece of bread, a coat, a shelter. The economic problem in these places is often not "low wages" but no money at all. Many cannot read or write even their name. This is zero land. In the Delta, it acquires a nightmare edge of absurdity for soil is rich, rainfall favorable, climate pleasant: nature has been good to people—all that is wrong is the White Supremacy system and those who run it. The Federal government is willing to give aid to these sufferers in the usual way of surplus foods and aid to children under state welfare departments but the white powers of certain Delta counties often will not let Negroes accept this aid.

In the city ghettos, as in New York, it is almost worse: a wolf-like misery has gnawed at an entire family until the little children act as though their tongues were bitten off. Some of them have lost or never acquired the ability to speak. They look at you mutely, they cannot make a sentence. They need not their "rights" but love—a human necessity some have not experienced; and without a little love, without a little care, the human child sometimes cannot learn even to say words.

Realizing this, many in the Student Nonviolent Coordinating Committee, in CORE, in the NAACP are now turning their energies in new directions. "Civil rights" is the name of one destination that must be arrived at quickly, for the sake of the nation's spiritual equilibrium; but hidden away, in the rural places, in alleys, on back streets in open and closed cities and towns there are these giant needs that will not be put off.

To meet them, to help people want to learn, want to work, want to live, one must work out a very real relationship with them; it is not enough to give them hand-outs of food, things, books; one must give concern, understanding—this is the only bridge these tremulous, quietly raging people can walk across. The students in the Movement are learning this.

Here is the point of change: where systems are abandoned and human relationships are begun. Thank God, there are some places in the North but also in the South, where bridges can even now be built, where walls are low enough to climb over. One exciting expression of this new realization of the need to relate is that of the college students' tutorial committees. Many students are giving hours of their time to tutoring the Negro pupils who need help; some work with the drop-outs to help them gain the confidence to go back and try again.

How did this start? No one quite knows. One day, an imagination stirred, energies awakened, a problem was confronted, a mind saw a way to help; others, hearing about it, responded. Each student has his day when it happens to him: *here is something I can do that is worth doing.*

The Movement is by no means limited to sit-ins, picket lines, parades of protest. The March to Washington was an important gesture of spiritual depth and one participated in by most of the serious groups of nonviolent protesters. Hundreds of smaller symbolic protests have been made. But the Movement is much more than what happens in public places. There have been (and are) the legal battles in courtrooms that moved things but oh, so slowly until the sit-ins, acting as enzymes, began to accelerate the consequences. There is the organized search for jobs and training to prepare for jobs. There is the housing problem and its syndrome of social ills and much is being done about it by the Urban League. There are the quiet tutorial personal relationships now being developed by the thousands; there are the voter registration campaign and the programs of adult education.

Above all else, the Movement is in no sense a revolution against our political system. It opposes the extra-legal, subversive system of White Supremacy with its mobs and its ghosts and its rituals and its Witches' Sabbath murders and its web of spies and censorship, and police pressures. It opposes all this, yes; but it has no rival system to set up in its place. The Movement thinks of itself as a valid expression of the democratic way; and its leaders remember that democracy is not a system, that it has no ideology; it is a way of life, a *Tao*, a continuous series of specific attempts to protect every individual's freedom to grow, to ask questions, to work, to explore inner and outer space, to create the New Thing and the New Relationship.

We are on trembling earth now: ground that is sensitive to the slightest pressure; a place where the weight of authority and force does not belong. For we are trying to substitute relationships, each with its inner dynamics, its specific pulls and strains, and its easements, for a rigid system. No wonder both Negroes and whites are confused!

To be half animal, half automaton and live under a regime that makes the decisions is so much easier than accepting one's own responsibilities. Many Negroes, today, are only too willing to slip out of one slave system straight into another, as the popularity of Black Nationalism suggests. Black Nationalism offers no follower his freedom; it offers him a flight from freedom, a new form of slavery—this time, slavery to hatred of whites and to black arrogance.

Perhaps one can explain the Sahara-minds of many white segregationists as another consequence of the System. There are the U.S. Senators from the South who seem to know only one crude human relationship called "sex." The struggle for human rights, complex and deeprooted, brings only one question to their minds: *Would you want your sister to marry, etc.?* How tiresome and empty! How hideously absurd! But this is the way the System works: by tearing out nuances, differences, all the varieties and subtleties of the human experience, life is reduced to one sliver. Segregation has so dessicated [*sic*] minds that it is impossible for its adherents to conceive of a Negro's and white's ability to respond, to relate each to the other—or both to a Bartok Quartet, or to a William Golding novel, or to a painting or a poem or a winsome song, or to an errand of mercy; or to the reading and discussion, perhaps, of Teilhard de Chardin's *Phenomenon of Man*; or to watching a film of Bergman's, or enjoying a James Bond escapade, or talking politics, or maybe hoeing together a row of cabbage, or cooking hot dogs, or watching a fog come over East River. No; the tight old segregationists apparently cannot conceive of minds and souls responding one to another on various levels, and to the world around them; no, always and always and always, they snicker and ask, *Do you want your sister etc.*

Knowing this, how can we fail to acknowledge the awesome injuries which segregation has inflicted on every one of us! I cannot believe one American has escaped its effect. We only have to observe how crookedly, awkwardly our minds work in the entire field of human and personal relationships. Segregation is a potent idea for evil: it almost forces one to shun the truth; the word itself holds a witch doctor's holiness, a form of "holiness" which that interesting writer, Rudolph Otto,* speaks of as that "overplus" beyond the good, that portion of the numinous which is the antonym of God. Man is a broken creature who can never be solid: he is

*The Idea of the Holy, Rudolph Otto. [Original note]

made whole only by his relationships: segregation is, therefore, his mortal enemy for it tears his relationships to pieces. No one ever segregated man or idea or dream without segregating his own life on many of its levels. For Malcolm X and his hate-filled followers to talk now of a new kind of segregation reveals the cruel stupidity that hate imposes on minds; their minds are now functioning on the same splintered level as Klansmen and white racial fanatics.

Feelings, thoughts, intuitive flashes such as these are running as a quiet current beneath the sounds and acts of the Movement. Will hate win by setting up new systems of bondage? Will love lose in its search for the real relationship that can grow? Do we yet realize that the quality of every person depends on how many real relationships he can create or respond to?

And now, these questions are exacerbated by the intruders in the Movement. Perhaps it could not have been otherwise in this world of good and evil. There was a purity of vision the Evil One was compelled to contaminate. The leaders and their early followers went into their non-violent activities with a deep sense of commitment, with a cleanness of purpose, a longing to absorb through their suffering the wrongs of all our people. *Redemption* became for them a numinous word—for the more naïve, almost a magic word—certainly one they all hungered to understand. And there was a surge of joy, of adventure, yes; of courage—almost reckless courage, full of laughter. It was beautiful to see. Perhaps never in American history has there been a movement of such gayety and intellectual richness—the poetry some of the students chant (and write), the philosophy the leaders read, the theology young and old struggle through—Buber, Tillich, Bultman, Kierkegaard—all this done in their search for the good life which they hunger to substitute for the hollow thing-obsessed life too many of us have lived. And all of it streaked with a fine sense of humor and a humility they express in prayer—and an increasing closeness to "the people."

Then, slowly and more and more swiftly, came the Intruders: exploiting the amazing success many of the projects had had. For the sit-ins opened hundreds of restaurants, hundreds of hotels and motels, many parks; the picketing opened all the services of one big department store after another to Negroes; many stores began to hire Negroes even in the deep South; buses were integrated. These things were miracles. They happened and happened swiftly. Sympathetic city officials, editors, chambers of commerce often begged for a let-up; they even suggested that the Negroes would do better by getting off the streets and back into the courts. But Negroes and their white friends smiled at this: for it was only after public sit-ins and picketing and other forms of public protest that results were obtained. What the thoughtful whites had in mind, however, was not unreasonable: they wanted rest periods to give the next level of whites time to adjust to the new conditions; all whites are not equally intelligent, all are not equally informed; all are not equally balanced, emotionally; time is needed for many to bend physical and mental muscles in new ways. And perhaps we should remember that it takes time to recover from drug addiction; and many whites are addicted to White Supremacy: it has affected minds, emotions, values. The whole country is suffering from withdrawal pains.

Just at this sensitive moment, came the Intruders: North and South they began to make a dangerous caricature of the Nonviolent Movement: with diabolical cleverness they assumed the outer ways without making the inner sacrifices and spiritual decisions. There is nothing on earth more dangerous than a violent man pretending to be nonviolent—nothing more dangerous except ten or a hundred of them.

The work of the Intruders is the activity of hate disguised. This is what Denis de Rougemont calls, "the Devil's shrewd trick." Always the Devil appears in each age in the costumes of the Good and using their vocabulary. Here he is, with his hating, half-mad followers dressed up as nonviolent protesters, wreaking ruin as he goes, stirring the wrath even of the Negro group's most loyal friends, irritating every fair-minded Negro and white. Added to this serious situation is the not well controlled ambition of a few, a very few (let's remember) young leaders who are listening to the neo-nihilism of our times (a curious mixture of Genet, Sartre, Spengler and American Beats), and somehow blending this foamy stuff with their own personal ambition—with results that arouse even their friends' grave concern.

But let me say this plainly: these Intruders, and the few young leaders who have been seduced by quick success and their own lack of intellectual maturity, are no more dangerous, no more blind and not nearly so ruthless as the group of whites who cling to their Whiteness, who listen to their secret hate feelings and are quick to criticize every protest of Negroes, although they never seem to see the cruelties and greed of whites who control real estate and industry and certain unions, and who put the stealthy, unbearable pressures on urban Negroes.

We must take care that we see the picture whole: that we measure, also, what the never-ending apathy of the "good people" has done to the Negroes' minds; there are limits to what can be endured and the good respectable people of our country have pushed these limits dangerously. Going along with Denis de Rougemont, perhaps we might say the Devil is doing his most efficient work in the local churches and in pleasant, well-bred homes.

Here is the big danger. Here is the place where we must take care that we do not criticize the whole movement because of a few half-mad, foolish people who have lost their inner control and good judgment. We cannot let ourselves underestimate the heavy pressure on hearts of the wanton murder of children, of the dynamitings, the crude, obscene use of violence by the police force in cities, South and North; the never-ending insults and humiliations broadcast by politicians and other vested interests. "We take and take and take and take . . . day comes we can't take any more." Dr. Sam's words[**] are haunting us now.

To criticize today without taking the entire situation into honest account, without measuring the little that most white people do to alleviate the suffering and the stress, is an irresponsible act. One prays for reason, one appeals to the conscience—and sometimes, the answer is so small and sometimes, there is no answer. The Negro Movement (with its thousands of white helpers) would like to speak softly; it wants to be reasonable but the noise of white goons, white politicians, white Citizens' Councils, Birch Societies have forced its followers to raise their voices; the dynamitings, the dogs, the electric cattle prods, the fire hose, the long imprisonments for a few minutes of picketing, the vicious treatment given in some of the jails, the exorbitant bonds, the fantastic waits in prison without even preliminary trials, the obscene needling of girl students by policemen, the sadistic judges—this intransigence of whites is now forcing a few desperate Negroes who are intruders in the nonviolent movement to try to take it over, to try by their insane, half-idiot tricks to get the nation-wide attention of whites. Small, sick children do the same; but the Movement is no place for the sick or the stupid or the immature, or the sleazy-minded.

What can be done?

An old Negro preacher, evicted with thousands of other sharecroppers in the Delta, long ago in that bleak winter of 1940, met in a little church in Arkansas with a group of whites and Negroes to see what could be done. There were complaints, accusations; there was also a power struggle going on among those who had come "to help." Finally, after a song, the old man was asked to pray. Standing still and silent until the little church was still and silent, he pressed his old hands against the chair he leaned on and said, "Break their hearts, O God; give them tears."

Give us tears. . . . Ah, that is it: how to break our hearts without breaking the unity of this country, the inner conciliation that must never be weakened. How to appeal? How to level walls without the consent that comes from good personal relationships? How to have good relation-

[**] *Strange Fruit*, 1944. [Original note]

ships while walls stand? How to turn on lights in imaginations so that we can see the little things building into the big ones. These are the unanswered questions.

I have not ended the story for there is no end. This Movement is alive, it is growing, it has already become a part of our life as Americans; it is joyous, still a singing movement, still one full of compassion and love; and being so, it is flexible, amenable to the best our minds and hearts can offer it. Amenable also to the worst we offer it. A brave vigorous movement that is here to stay: rich with infinite creative possibilities, potent—and dangerous, for the potential good can be distorted and lost by the despairing restlessness of those from the ghettos who have no hope, and who are too uninformed historically, too unsure emotionally to analyze current conditions or foresee the consequences of their acts. We, as a people, could be confronted soon by a series of catastrophes. Whether this happens depends on the wisdom of responsible Negroes but more, much more on what every responsible white American does next. One thing is certain in a plexus of uncertainties and that is, our encounter with the future cannot be evaded, it must be met by both the artist and the scientist in us, by our deep intuitions and our rigorously proved knowledge—and by the human being in us, too, that creature who knows the power of compassion, the potency of a strange love that keeps reaching out to bind one man to another.

AFTERWORD

I have known the name Lillian Smith for most of my life. I knew her as a white southerner opposed to segregation with whom my family felt aligned. In graduate school I studied her as an early supporter of equal rights. Then, one warm September day not long after I became a faculty member at a liberal arts college in the northeast Georgia mountains, I stepped out of the sunshine into the cool, dark stacks of the library to browse Piedmont College's literature collection before classes began. As I ambled down the American literature aisle, I spotted the title *Strange Fruit* in the Southern American literature section. Ah, my old friend. I took down the stained volume from the shelf and opened the front cover where I found the following:

> To my friends at Piedmont College in honor of the time I spent there.
>
> LILLIAN SMITH 1915–16

So she had been here before me.

I had always considered her an admirable woman whose works should be read within the context of her time—mid-twentieth-century American literature and culture. But when I reread Lillian Smith for this project, I was shocked by how relevant her writings are to our time; listening to or reading the news, I often thought, "Lillian Smith says that . . ." "Lillian Smith addresses that kind of demagoguery in . . ." And thus I realized that Lillian Smith is as relevant today as she was in the 1940s, 1950s, and 1960s.

We are aware of that relevance because Smith shared with us her stories: from the magical moments of childhood in her Eden, Jasper, Florida, a land of "swamps and cypress and sand and great oaks where we were born and where our memories still live," to her exile in the hill country of north Georgia with its beauty as well as extreme poverty, a landscape she came to love and call home.

From her camp, looking up to the summit of Old Screamer Mountain, Smith wrote most of the works we know today: novels, plays, collections of essays, speeches, book reviews, and a successful cultural magazine. She told us her stories of travels not only around the world but also deep into her psyche, those inner places most of us dare not go, fearing the imperfections of parents, the contradictions inherent in culture, community, religion, and nationalism. She was willing to do the difficult work of knowing herself and her world, and she knew *that* work never ends.

During her lifetime, many people, such as Dr. Martin Luther King Jr. and Eleanor Roosevelt, admired and respected her. Dr. King wrote near the end of his 1963 "Letter from a Birmingham Jail":

> I believe that voices like those of... Miss Lillian E. Smith of Georgia... represent the true and basic sentiments of millions of southerners, whose voices are yet unheard, whose course is yet unclear and whose courageous acts are yet unseen." (King 298)

Others hated her—enough to send her death threats and to set fires in the woods near her home. But she met ordeals with resilience, as her father had taught her. She rejected either/or thinking, advocating that we use both head *and* heart, dispassionate science *and* compassionate spirituality, poetry *and* technology in facing our ordeals and healing the wounds of our culture. She asks her readers repeatedly to question, explore, remain open, and imagine that an individual can overcome fear and hatred and that our children can be free from those chains.

Although in retrospect it may seem to us that her causes were clear, her enemies clearer, her side in the fight the "right side," possessing that knowledge is almost impossible in the midst of the struggle. Perhaps we should ask ourselves what our children's grandchildren will be able to see so clearly about "right" and "wrong" in our time that is opaque to us now.

What Lillian Smith offers the twenty-first century is a much-needed alternative to the sound bite, to the "meme," to the "Tweet," to the instantaneous "news" story. What she offers is an antidote to our lack of understanding: her willingness to explore, to probe our inner depths, to look deeply at issues that affect us all. In our age of nanoseconds and quantum universes, time management, utilitarianism, and worship of the free market, Smith's remedies for our problems seem almost impossible: we must take the time to discover inner and outer truths, past and present.

Yes, it can be frightening enough to look deeper at our own motivations, our unexplored emotions and experiences, and the fragments of our own lives, not to mention the challenges of understanding our neighborhoods, communities, towns, states, nation, and world. It is easier to rely on hearsay and half-learned civics lessons and what our parents believe. Changing ourselves and our world is not only hard work but also involves losing our illusions and delusions, as well as facing our terrors and walking through, not around, our ordeals. It is seeing the world for what it is while keeping to our ideal notions of what we think it should be.

Not only did Lillian Smith suggest to us what we should do as a nation to heal the wounds dividing us, she modeled a way forward. She pointed in the direction of hope and wholeness, and in her books she invites us to walk with her. Smith's epitaph reminds us that our stories do not end. For, as this book reminds us, even when we are dead our stories are not finished.

Like Socrates and other great teachers, Lillian Smith compels her listeners to question.

1. What is social justice? How can we undo injustice in our society? What can one person do to make a difference in an unjust society?
2. What forces splinter us? Fragment us? Segregate us by race, gender, body, class? What do those terms mean and encompass?
3. What are our ethical values? Where do they come from? Have our homes, communities, churches, families given us our hatreds as well as our loves? Can we challenge those values, examine them, give them up, commit to them?
4. What sources do we use to define "democracy," "equality," "freedom," "individual," "tradition," "heritage," "history," "change," and "community"? What sources will we use to redefine those terms if necessary?
5. What does it mean to be "African American," "Southern," "white," "European American," "Hispanic/Latin American," "Asian American," or "Native American," in the United States today? Who determines the meaning and use of those terms?
6. What is the role of violence/nonviolence in a democratic society?
7. What is "honesty" in studying history? Our region's history? Our country's history? Our own personal history? What is the cost of holding on to old mythologies, whether our family's, our community's, our region's, or our country's?
8. Whom can we trust? Why? What media sources are reliable? How do we know? Who are today's demagogues?
9. Resistance: What happens when we become cynical or give up on our world? What effect does cynicism have on our society and on ourselves? Should we try to avoid cynicism? How? What will the world become if we give up?
10. If children have the right to grow up free, whose children? What does "free" mean? How do we educate them to become free? Whose "lives matter"?

11. According to Lillian Smith (and many others) creativity is a basic human trait. Why do we need creativity? What is the role of the arts in our lives and in politics? What is the role of the arts in our culture?
12. How do we face ordeals? How can we use both the scientist and the artist in us to face those ordeals? Do we have the courage to answer these questions honestly? Are we brave enough to face all the truths?

BIBLIOGRAPHY

PRIMARY WORKS CITED

Smith, Lillian. "Along Their Way." *North Georgia Review* 2.1 (1937): 3–4, 20–22. Rpt. in *FTM* 31–37.

———. "And the Waters Flow On." *North Georgia Review* 3.2 (1938): 7–12. Rpt.in *FTM* 55–65.

———. "Are We Still Buying a New World with Old Confederate Bills?" Regional Students Nonviolent Movement Open Meeting. Mount Moriah Baptist Church, Atlanta, Georgia, 16 Oct. 1960. Speech. Rpt. in special issue of *Georgia Review* (Fall 2012): 480–87.

———. "Behind the Drums." *North Georgia Review* 4.2–3 (1939): 12–21. Rpt. in *FTM* 69–83.

———. "The Chasm and the Bridge." *KD*. 1961 ed. 233–53.

———. "Children Talking." *Progressive Education* 23 (October 1945): 6–9, 39–40.

———. "The Crisis in the South." *New Leader* 19 Sept. 1960: 12–14.

———. "The Day It Happens." *OFOW* 105–28.

———. From "Dope with Lime." "On Lanterns on the Levee." *North Georgia Review* 6.1–4 (1941): 5–6.

———. From "Dope with Lime." "Visit with Margaret Mitchell." *Pseudopodia* 1.2 (1936): 11–12.

———. "Growing into Freedom." *Common Ground* 4 (Autumn 1943): 47–52.

———. "Growing Plays: *The Girl*." *South Today* 8.1 (1944): 32–49. Rpt. in *Educational Leadership* May 1945: 349–60.

———. "The Harris Children's Town—Maxwell, Georgia." *Pseudopodia* 1.1 (1936): 3–4, 9–12. Rpt. in *FTM* 19–27.

———. "He That Is without Sin." *North Georgia Review* 2.4 (1937–38): 16–19, 31–32. Rpt. in *FTM* 47–55.

———. *How Am I to Be Heard? Letters of Lillian Smith*. Ed. Margaret Rose Gladney. Chapel Hill: University of North Carolina Press, 1993.

———. *The Journey*. Cleveland: World Publishing, 1954.

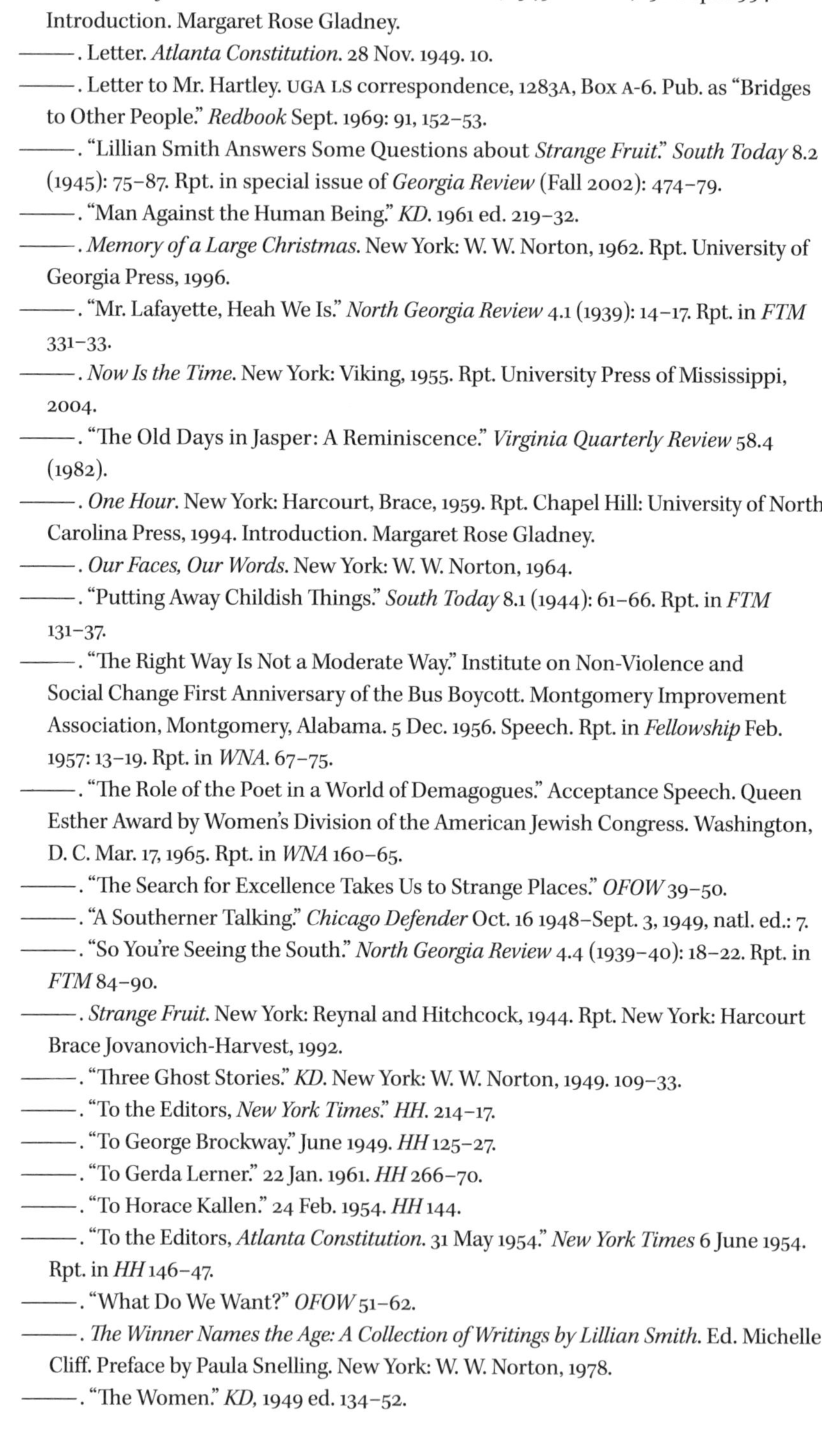

———. *Killers of the Dream*. New York: W. W. Norton, 1949. Rev. ed., 1961. Rpt. 1994. Introduction. Margaret Rose Gladney.

———. Letter. *Atlanta Constitution*. 28 Nov. 1949. 10.

———. Letter to Mr. Hartley. UGA LS correspondence, 1283A, Box A-6. Pub. as "Bridges to Other People." *Redbook* Sept. 1969: 91, 152–53.

———. "Lillian Smith Answers Some Questions about *Strange Fruit*." *South Today* 8.2 (1945): 75–87. Rpt. in special issue of *Georgia Review* (Fall 2002): 474–79.

———. "Man Against the Human Being." *KD*. 1961 ed. 219–32.

———. *Memory of a Large Christmas*. New York: W. W. Norton, 1962. Rpt. University of Georgia Press, 1996.

———. "Mr. Lafayette, Heah We Is." *North Georgia Review* 4.1 (1939): 14–17. Rpt. in *FTM* 331–33.

———. *Now Is the Time*. New York: Viking, 1955. Rpt. University Press of Mississippi, 2004.

———. "The Old Days in Jasper: A Reminiscence." *Virginia Quarterly Review* 58.4 (1982).

———. *One Hour*. New York: Harcourt, Brace, 1959. Rpt. Chapel Hill: University of North Carolina Press, 1994. Introduction. Margaret Rose Gladney.

———. *Our Faces, Our Words*. New York: W. W. Norton, 1964.

———. "Putting Away Childish Things." *South Today* 8.1 (1944): 61–66. Rpt. in *FTM* 131–37.

———. "The Right Way Is Not a Moderate Way." Institute on Non-Violence and Social Change First Anniversary of the Bus Boycott. Montgomery Improvement Association, Montgomery, Alabama. 5 Dec. 1956. Speech. Rpt. in *Fellowship* Feb. 1957: 13–19. Rpt. in *WNA*. 67–75.

———. "The Role of the Poet in a World of Demagogues." Acceptance Speech. Queen Esther Award by Women's Division of the American Jewish Congress. Washington, D. C. Mar. 17, 1965. Rpt. in *WNA* 160–65.

———. "The Search for Excellence Takes Us to Strange Places." *OFOW* 39–50.

———. "A Southerner Talking." *Chicago Defender* Oct. 16 1948–Sept. 3, 1949, natl. ed.: 7.

———. "So You're Seeing the South." *North Georgia Review* 4.4 (1939–40): 18–22. Rpt. in *FTM* 84–90.

———. *Strange Fruit*. New York: Reynal and Hitchcock, 1944. Rpt. New York: Harcourt Brace Jovanovich-Harvest, 1992.

———. "Three Ghost Stories." *KD*. New York: W. W. Norton, 1949. 109–33.

———. "To the Editors, *New York Times*." *HH*. 214–17.

———. "To George Brockway." June 1949. *HH* 125–27.

———. "To Gerda Lerner." 22 Jan. 1961. *HH* 266–70.

———. "To Horace Kallen." 24 Feb. 1954. *HH* 144.

———. "To the Editors, *Atlanta Constitution*. 31 May 1954." *New York Times* 6 June 1954. Rpt. in *HH* 146–47.

———. "What Do We Want?" *OFOW* 51–62.

———. *The Winner Names the Age: A Collection of Writings by Lillian Smith*. Ed. Michelle Cliff. Preface by Paula Snelling. New York: W. W. Norton, 1978.

———. "The Women." *KD*, 1949 ed. 134–52.

SECONDARY WORKS CITED

Gladney, Margaret Rose. "A Chain Reaction of Dreams: Lillian Smith and Laurel Falls Camp." *Journal of American Culture* 5 (Fall 1982): 50–55.

———. Introduction. *Killers of the Dream*. By Lillian Smith. New York: W.W. Norton, Rpt. 1994.

———. Introduction. *One Hour*. By Lillian Smith. Rpt. Chapel Hill: University of North Carolina Press, 1994. vii–xiii.

———. "Lillian Smith's Hope for Southern Women." *Southern Studies* 22.3 (1983): 274–84.

King, Martin Luther, Jr. "Letter from Birmingham Jail." *A Testament of Hope*. New York: Harper and Row, 1964. Rpt. New York: HarperOne, 2003. 298.

Loveland, Anne C. *Lillian Smith: A Southerner Confronting the South*. Baton Rouge: Louisiana State University Press, 1986.

Peck, James. *Freedom Ride*. New York: Simon & Schuster, 1962.

Perry, Imani. *More Beautiful and More Terrible: The Embrace and Transcendence of Racial Inequality in the United States*. New York: New York University Press, 2011.

Schmich, Mary. "In Racist Time, Camp Planted Seeds of Reason." *Chicago Tribune* 10 February 2002.

Snelling, Paula. Preface. *WNA*, 11–16.

———. Foreward. "A Bibliography of Lillian Smith & Paula Snelling." By Margaret Sullivan. *Bulletin of the Mississippi Valley Collection* 4 (Spring 1971): 5–7.

White, Helen, and Redding S. Sugg. Eds. Introduction. *From the Mountain: An Anthology of the Magazine Successively Titled* Pseudopodia, the North Georgia Review, *and* South Today. Memphis: Memphis State University Press, 1972. xi–xxvi.

WORKS CONSULTED

Blackwell, Louise, and Frances Clay. *Lillian Smith*. Twayne's United States Authors Series 187. New York: Twayne, 1971.

Brantley, Will. Afterword. Smith, *NT*. 2004. 121–45.

Dominy, Jordan J. "Reviewing the South: Lillian Smith, *South Today*, and the Origins of Literary Canons." *Mississippi Quarterly: The Journal of Southern Cultures* 66.1 (2013): 29–50.

Egerton, John. *Speak Now Against the Day: The Generation Before the Civil Rights Movement in the South*. New York: Knopf, 1994.

Garcia, Jay. "Race, Empire, and Humanism in the Work of Lillian Smith." *Radical History Review* 101 (2008): 59–80.

Gladney, Margaret Rose. "Biographical Research on Lesbigay Subjects: Reflections on Editing the Letters of Lillian Smith." *Daring to Find Our Names*. Ed. James V. Carmichael Jr. Westport: Greenwood Press, 1998. 47–54.

———. "Paula Snelling: A Significant Other." *Modern American Queer History*, Allida Black, Ed. Philadelphia: Temple University Press, 2001. 69–78.

Haddox, Thomas F. "Lillian Smith, Cold War Intellectual." *Southern Literary Journal* 44.2 (2012): 51–68.

Hobson, Fred. "The Sins of the Fathers: Lillian Smith and Katharine Du Pre Lumpkin." *Southern Review* 34.4 (1998): 755–79.

Leonard, George B. "Not Black Power, But Human Power." *Look* 6 Sept. 1966: 40–43.

O'Dell, Darlene. *Sites of Southern Memory: The Autobiographies of Katharine Du Pre Lumpkin, Lillian Smith, and Pauli Murray*. Charlottesville: University of Virginia Press, 2001.

Patton, Randall. "Lillian Smith and the Transformation of American Liberalism: 1945–1950." *Georgia Historical Quarterly* 76.2 (Summer 1992). 373–92.

Poister, Robert C. "At Home on the Mountain: Appalachia in Lillian Smith's Life and Work." *Appalachian Journal: A Regional Studies Review* 37.3–4 (2010): 268–85.

Robinson, Jo Ann. "Lillian Smith: Reflections on Race and Sex." *Southern Exposure* 4.4 (1977): 43–48.

Sullivan, Margaret. "A Bibliography of Lillian Smith & Paula Snelling." *Bulletin of the Mississippi Valley Collection* 4 (Spring 1971): 1–82.

Watson, Jay. "Uncovering the Body, Discovering Ideology: Segregation and Sexual Anxiety in Lillian Smith's *Killers of the Dream*." *American Quarterly* 49.3 (1997): 470–503.

Wolfe, Andrea Powell. "The Subversive Potential of the Abjected Black Maternal Body in Lillian Smith's *Strange Fruit*." *Flannery O'Connor Review* 8 (2010): 130–44.

CREDITS

Most of the selections appear courtesy of Piedmont College, which houses the Lillian E. Smith Center and controls the rights to Smith's literary estate. The editors thank the permissions holders for use of material not under the aegis of the Smith estate and Piedmont College as listed below:

"Trembling Earth" from *VQR* (August 1982), as "Old Days in Jasper." Permission courtesy of Joan Titus.

Excerpts from *Strange Fruit*. Copyright 1944 by Lillian Smith. Copyright © renewed 1971 by Paula Snelling. Reprinted by permission of Houghton Mifflin Harcourt Publishing Company. All rights reserved.

Excerpts from *Killers of the Dream*. Copyright 1949, © 1961, by Lillian Smith. Used by permission of W. W. Norton & Company, Inc.

"The Right Way Is Not a Moderate Way" speech from *The Winner Names the Age: A Collection of Writings by Lillian Smith*, edited by Michelle Cliff. Copyright © 1978 by W. W. Norton & Company, Inc. Used by permission courtesy of Piedmon College and W. W. Norton & Company, Inc.

Excerpts from *Our Faces, Our Words*. Copyright 1964 by Lillian Smith. Used by permission of W. W. Norton & Company, Inc., and McIntosh & Otis.

INDEX